COBOL for Small and Medium-sized Computers

COBOL

for Small and Medium-sized Computers

Asad S. O. Khailany
Eastern Michigan University

Claude V. Duplissey
University of Arkansas at Little Rock

HOUGHTON MIFFLIN COMPANY   *Boston*
Atlanta Dallas Geneva, Illinois Hopewell, New Jersey Palo Alto London

Library of Congress Catalog Card Number: 75–23647

ISBN: 0-395-18921-7

Contents

CHAPTER 10   The PERFORM Statement   160

CHAPTER 11   Table Handling   183

CHAPTER 12   Sorting and Subroutines   211

CHAPTER 13   Programmer Goals and Some Sample Programs   242

Preface

Cobol for Small and Medium-sized Computers has been designed to teach a novice the essentials of writing programs in the COBOL programming language for the digital computer. The text provides students with the essentials of COBOL (COmmon Business Oriented Language) through numerous example programs and programming assignments.

The text emphasizes COBOL as implemented on the IBM-1130, which is a subset of the full ANSI COBOL. COBOL is somewhat easier to learn this way because many statements included in the language are not necessary to program the IBM-1130. At the same time, the coverage is sufficiently complete to learn all the essentials of COBOL programming. We feel that average students can learn COBOL more thoroughly by concentrating on these essentials. We have also included information about COBOL on the IBM System 3, the Burroughs 1700, and the DECSYSTEM-10 because these computers are similar to the IBM-1130.

The text can be studied thoroughly and in its entirety during a semester or quarter of study. In that time most students should understand programming logic and the correlation between COBOL programming statements and their effect on a program.

In conjunction with their study of Chapter 1, students should be given a tour of the computer center and shown how to operate a keypunch. Students should understand what the major components of a digital computer are and how they function. Chapter 2 explains the organization of a COBOL program; division, section, and paragraph names; basic punctuation principles; and reserved and unreserved words. Chapter 3 should clarify the concepts introduced in Chapter 2, and students should understand the paragraphs in the IDENTIFICATION DIVISION.

The use of files for input, output, and I-O and how the organization and access of a file determine how a COBOL program will process the file are discussed in Chapter 4. Chapter 5 covers the organization of the ENVIRONMENT DIVISION and, in addition, explains how to name files and assign them to card, printer, and disk devices and why opening and closing files is important.

Chapter 6 explains the organization of the DATA DIVISION and how to edit printed data properly—for example, how to suppress leading zeros and insert decimal points and currency symbols. Chapter 7 explains how to control vertical spacing on the line printer and discusses program logic and flowcharting. Writing efficient programs that contain simple arithmetic calculations is explained in Chapter 8; and the GO TO and the IF statements are discussed in Chapter 9.

Chapter 10 discusses the simpler forms of the PERFORM statements. Chapter 11 explains how to work with simple tables, especially for sorting, merging, and locating records. Chapter 12 shows how to combine a main program and a subroutine; and Chapter 13 contains sample programs for students to examine.

We wish to thank the Burroughs Corporation, the IBM Corporation, and the Digital Equipment Corporation for their technical assistance in preparing this book. We are also grateful to Jack D. Cundiff, Muskingum College, Ohio, Seymour V. Pollack, Washington University, and Laurence J. Mazlack, University of Guelph, Ontario, for their careful readings of the original manuscript.

Our special thanks for assistance in preparing this book is extended in particular to Dr. John Hodges, Chairman of the Department of Mathematics and Computer Science at the University of Arkansas at Little Rock, for his friendship, patience, and support throughout our work on this text. We wish to thank Laura Khailany for her advice and suggestions, many of which were incorporated into the text.

Acknowledgment

The following acknowledgment is reproduced from *American National Standard COBOL* (1969), published by the American National Standards Institute, New York.

Any organization interested in using the COBOL specifications as the basis for an instruction manual or for any other purpose is free to do so. However, all such organizations are requested to reproduce this section as part of the introduction to the document. Those using a short passage, as in a book review, are requested to mention 'COBOL' in acknowledgment of the source, but need not quote this entire section.

"COBOL is an industry language and is not the property of any company or group of companies, or of any organization or group of organizations.

"No warranty, expressed or implied, is made by any contributor or by the COBOL Committee as to the accuracy and functioning of the programming system and language. Moreover, no responsibility is assumed by any contributor, or by the committee, in connection therewith.

"Procedures have been established for the maintenance of COBOL. Inquiries concerning the procedure for proposing changes should be directed to the Executive Committee of the Conference on Data Systems Languages.

"The authors and copyright holders of the copyrighted material used herein

FLOW-MATIC (Trademark of Sperry Rand Corporation), Programming for the UNIVAC® I and II, Data Automation Systems copyrighted 1958, 1959, by Sperry Rand Corporation; IBM Commercial Translator Form No. F28–8013, copyrighted 1959 by IBM; FACT, DSI 27A5260–2760, copyrighted 1960 by Minneapolis-Honeywell

have specifically authorized the use of this material in whole, or in part, in the COBOL specifications. Such authorization extends to the reproduction and use of COBOL specifications in programming manuals or similar publications.

"This complete American National Standard edition of COBOL may not be reproduced without permission of the American National Standards Institute.

CHAPTER 1

Digital Computers

Basic Computer Systems

The digital computer is used widely in business and science. Indeed, the ability of the computer to process large amounts of data quickly and accurately makes it a natural choice for processing customer billing, inventories, and payrolls. The computer accomplishes such tasks by following a collection of instructions called a *program* written by a *programmer*.

The major activities of the computer system fall into three categories: input, processing, and output. The machinery that performs these functions is the *computer hardware* (see figure 1.1).

Processing is performed in the *Central Processing Unit (CPU)* of the computer system. The CPU is composed of the *main storage* (or *main memory*), the *control section,* and the *arithmetic-logical unit.*

Main storage is used to store programs and data. Any time the computer runs, it follows the instructions of a program located in main storage. Although the computer can store information in other types of storage devices, it must transfer the information to main storage if it is to be able to work with the information.

The control section enables the computer to follow the instructions of a program stored in main memory. The control section determines the meaning of the instructions stored in main memory and causes the arithmetic-logical unit to perform the specified operations.

Under the direction of the control section, the arithmetic-logical unit can perform certain operations (see figure 1.2):

1. move data from one part of main storage to another part of main storage,
2. perform arithmetic on numbers stored in main storage,
3. compare data in main storage and take alternate actions on the basis of the comparisons, and
4. request an input unit to move data into main storage (an *input operation*) or request an output unit to move data out of main storage (an *output operation*).

Figure 1.1 Major activities of the computer system.

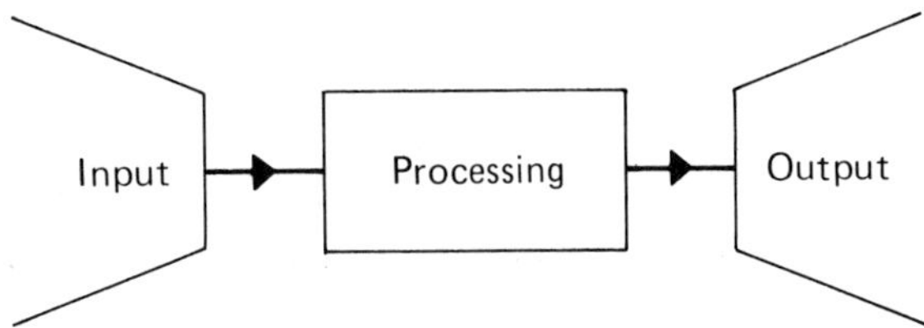

Figure 1.2 Major hardware components of a computer system.

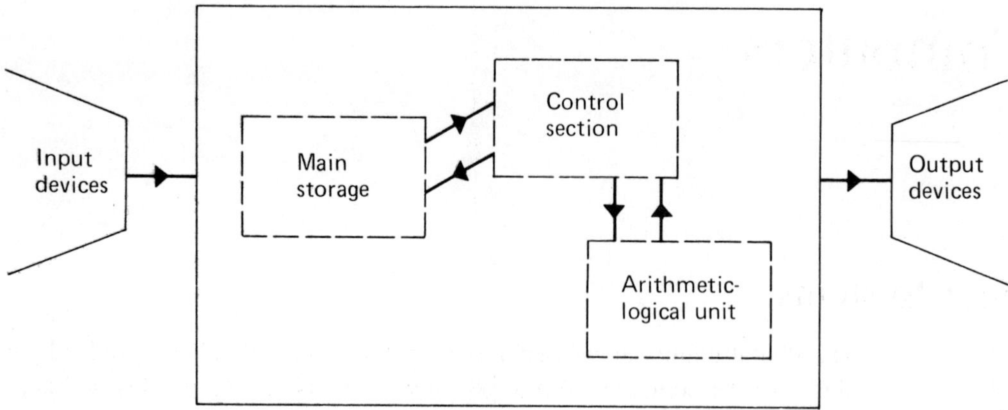

Many devices are used as input devices, such as card readers, paper tape readers, disk units, and magnetic tape units. Thus the programmer can type data or instructions into main storage, move information on punched cards or punched paper tape into main storage, or move information on magnetic disks or magnetic tapes into main storage. Similarly, output devices—such as card-punching units, line printers, paper-tape-punching units, console typewriters, disk units, and magnetic tape units—can be used to record information moved from main storage. These hardware devices are usually called *peripheral components.*

Programs provided by the manufacturer of the computer are called *computer software;* and the *monitor* (also called *executive* or *supervisor*), is a collection of programs. The computer system operates under the direction of the programs contained in the monitor. When a program is to be executed, the monitor initiates the instructions to store the program in main storage and to perform the instructions given in the program. To *execute a program* is to perform the instructions of the program. When the computer finishes executing the program or terminates execution because of an error, the monitor resumes control of the computer system.

The main storage of the computer is divided into many parts. On an IBM-1130, each part is called a *word.* On many other computers, each part is called a *byte.* As we use the term, byte is equivalent to half a word on an IBM-1130 in the sense that a byte can store only half as much information as a word. A good way to think of words or bytes is to think of them as mailboxes. Data or instructions can be stored in the mailboxes and retrieved later. The mailbox is identified by a number, called its *address.* The address can specify the location of a piece of data or a computer instruction.

Flowcharts

An *algorithm* is a set of directions or instructions for performing operations designed to lead to the accomplishment of a task or to the solution of a problem. Examples of algorithms include a recipe for cooking, the formula for computing compound interest when the principal is known, or the formula for finding the area of a right triangle when the base and height are known.

Figure 1.3 IBM-1130 computer system.

*In the foreground is the IBM-1130 Computing Systems Console that contains a
console typewriter and control buttons on its surface. The right side of the lower part
of the console contains a disk unit and 8,192 words of main storage to which another
24,576 words of main storage can be added. The disk unit provides about 1,500,000
words of auxiliary storage. To the right of the console is an IBM-1132 Printer and to
the left is an IBM-1442 Card Reader/Puncher.*

(Photo courtesy of the IBM Corporation.)

The Flowcharting language is a graphic language for depicting and summarizing algorithms. Programmers use geometric shapes to represent the discrete operations of a computer. The programmer expresses his program in a series of geometric diagrams connected by arrows that indicate the order of the operations. Figures 1.4 and 1.5 show some symbols that are used in the flowcharting language. A complete list of flowcharting symbols and their meanings can be found in the appendices.

Example 1.1   Suppose you have the data for several loans on punched cards. Each card has the principal amount and the rate of interest for a loan. You wish to write a program to compute and print the interest for each loan.

You must first write a flowchart for the algorithm. The formula for computing simple interest is $I = PR$, where P is the principal amount and R is the rate of simple interest. The steps of the algorithm are

1. Start.
2. Read a card.
3. If this card marks the end of the data cards, go to step 7; otherwise, go to step 4.
4. $I = P*R$. (In COBOL formats, an asterisk * means multiply.)
5. Print the interest.
6. Go back to step 2.
7. Stop the program.

Figure 1.4 Flowcharting symbols and their meanings.

Flowcharting symbols

Operation

Start, exit, or stop

Input or output

Arithmetic operation or data manipulation

Logical test with two branches for two possible outcomes

Preparation

Label connections

Direction of flow

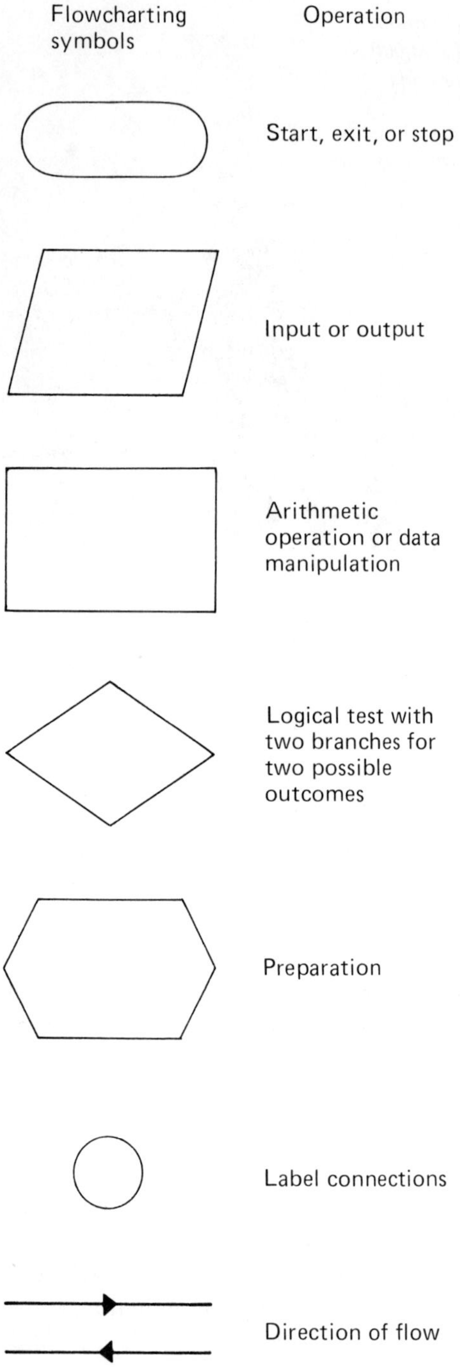

Figure 1.5 System flowcharting symbols and their meanings.

Punched card

Document

Magnetic tape

Disk storage

Display

Sort

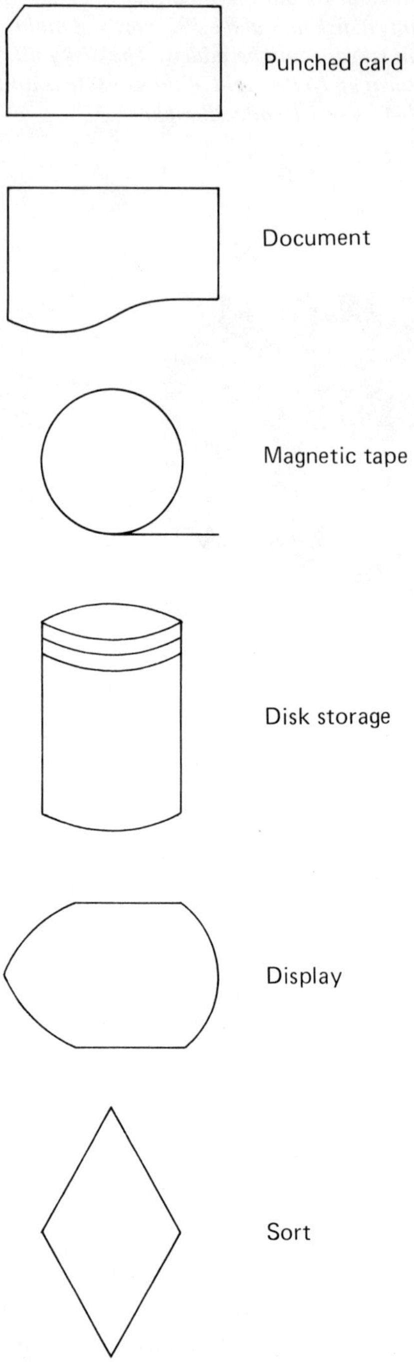

The computer will always go to the next step unless told explicitly to go to a different step. For example, the computer will go from step 3 to step 4 unless it reads the last card. The repetition of steps 2 through 6 is an example of a *loop*. Figure 1.6 is the flowchart for example 1.1.

Note that a flowcharting diagram depicts an algorithm to solve a problem. Once you have made a flowcharting diagram, all that remains to do is to write a program in the computer language you are using. All flowcharts in this text will be converted to COBOL programs.

Figure 1.6 Flowchart for example 1.1.

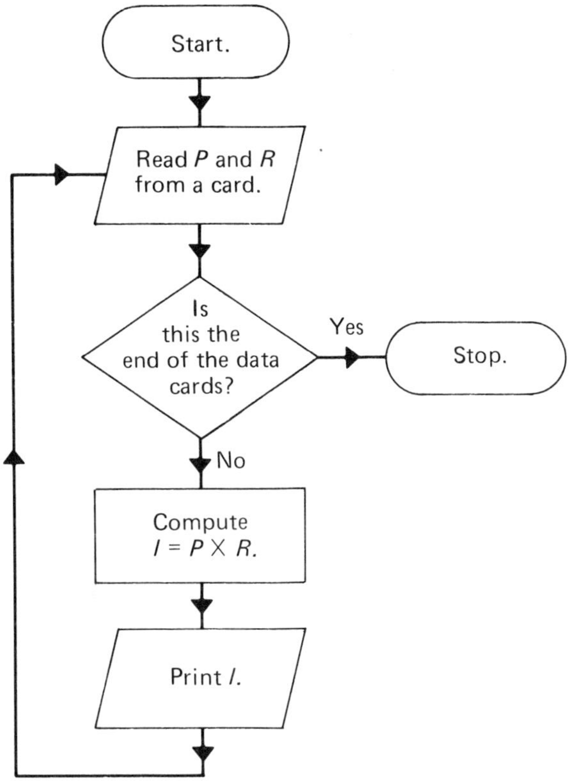

Start.

Read P and R from a card.

Is this the end of the data cards?

Yes — Stop.

No

Compute I = P X R.

Print I.

Flowcharts are used to represent algorithms graphically. Any computer-based algorithm should have three characteristics: (1) generality, (2) finiteness, and (3) unambiguity. An iterative algorithm—such as the loop in example 1.1—must terminate after a finite number of steps and should give a desired result. The algorithm must have the necessary internal control to achieve the two goals. In example 1.1 the internal control is the test for the end of the card file that determines when the algorithm is finished. The goal of the algorithm is achieved by printing the result of the computation, $I = PR$.

The four computers that we will discuss in this text are the IBM-1130, the IBM System 3 (IBM-S3), the Burroughs 1700 (B1700), and the decsystem-10 (DECSYSTEM-10). COBOL programs written for one of these computers, say the IBM-1130, can be run with minor modifications on any of the other three computers. For the sake of simplicity, we will use the IBM-1130 for our discussions, and wherever feasible we will point out adaptations that must be made in the programs to run them on the B1700, the IBM-S3, or the DECSYSTEM-10. If you have difficulty adapting your programs for the B1700, the IBM-S3, or the DECSYSTEM-10, refer to the appendices of this book or the manuals published by the manufacturers of the computers, or ask someone familiar with your computer installation for assistance. Note that the DECSYSTEM-10 was formerly called the PDP-10. The two names refer to the same computer system, and the computer will recognize either form of address. For the remainder of this text, we will use the current name, DECSYSTEM-10.

Summary   The major activities of a computer system are *input, processing,* and *output.* The computer has input devices, a *Central Processing Unit,* and output devices for carrying out these activities. The CPU is composed of the *main storage,* the *control section,* and the *arithmetic-logical unit.* Each location in main memory is identified by a number called its *address.* A *monitor* system is a collection of programs provided by the manufacturer of the computer that controls the general activities of the computer system.

An *algorithm* is a stepwise procedure for solving a problem. Flowcharts are used to represent algorithms. Any useful algorithm must have (1) generality, (2) finiteness, and (3) unambiguity. An algorithm must provide for accomplishing the goal in a finite number of steps.

Review Questions

1. The major activities of the computer system are divided into three categories: ____________, ____________, and ____________.
2. The part of the computer system that determines the meaning of instructions and controls the CPU is the ____________.
3. The main storage is the computer ____________.
4. A subdivision of the main storage is called a ____________.
5. The location of a word is known by its ____________.
6. The monitor system is a collection of programs, such as the monitor. This collection of programs is stored on a disk. To use the programs, it may be necessary to move them to ____________.
7. The three characteristics for any computer-based algorithm are (1) ____________, (2) ____________, and (3) ____________.
8. Arithmetic calculations are performed by the ____________.
9. Comparison of data is carried out by the ____________.
10. The meaning of instructions stored in the computer memory is determined by the ____________.
11. Peripheral components include devices such as ____________ ____________.

Suggested Projects

1. Write a stepwise algorithm and draw a flowchart for instructing the computer to read a card file of employee records and to accomplish the following tasks as each card is read. (*Note:* Each card contains NAME, NUMBER-OF-PRIME-HOURS and NUMBER-OF-OVERTIME-HOURS. Additionally, the card contains RATE-PER-PRIME-HOUR and RATE-PER-OVERTIME-HOUR.)

   a. Calculate gross pay according to the formula

      GROSS-PAY = NUMBER-OF-PRIME-HOURS * RATE-PER-PRIME-HOUR + NUMBER-OF-OVERTIME-HOURS * RATE-PER-OVERTIME-HOUR.

   b. Calculate FEDERAL-TAX = GROSS-PAY * 0.18
   c. Calculate STATE-TAX = (GROSS-PAY − FEDERAL-TAX) * 0.05

   d. Calculate NET-PAY = GROSS-PAY − FEDERAL-TAX −
      STATE-TAX

   e. Print the employee name, gross pay, and net pay on the line printer.

2. Write an algorithm describing the steps necessary to place a phone call. Include the steps for (a) finding the number in the phone directory, (b) acquiring a dial tone, and (c) hanging up the phone at the end of the conversation. Keep in mind such possibilities as that (a) you reach a wrong number; (b) the phone is defective and you get no dial tone; (c) you get a busy signal; or (d) the number that you reach is no longer the number of the party you desire to reach.

3. The arithmetic mean of a collection of numbers is the *sum of the numbers divided by the number of items in the collection.* Write an algorithm and draw a flowchart for instructing the computer to read the grades for 20 students from cards and compute the arithmetic mean (average) of the grades. Assume that there is one grade per card.

4. The registrar's office of a large university has decided to keep information on students in a file of punched cards. Each card contains the student's name, address, and the word YES or NO to indicate whether the student has paid the tuition for the current semester. Write an algorithm and draw a flowchart for instructing the computer to read the card file of student records and print a message to each student who owes money for this semester's tuition.

5. To rent a car from the Second Best Car Rental Agency, you must pay a fee of $8.00 per day as well as $0.10 per mile that you drive. Write an algorithm and draw a flowchart for instructing the computer to read a card file of customer records and compute the amount each customer owes. Each card contains the customer's name, and address, and the number of days and number of miles the car was driven.

CHAPTER 2

Basic Concepts of COBOL

COBOL is a *high-level language,* which means that a special program, the *COBOL compiler,* must translate COBOL instructions into machine language. The COBOL program is the *source program,* and the machine language translation is the *object program.* It is the object program that the computer executes because the computer can follow only instructions written in its particular machine language. The computer that compiles the source program is the *source computer,* and the computer that executes the object program is the *object computer* (see figure 2.1). In most programs the source computer and the object computer are the same machine.

Organization of COBOL Programs

Any COBOL program is constructed from precisely four divisions (see figure 2.2). Each division has a name usually called the *division header.* The division headers must be written in the following order and spelled (including the period) exactly as shown.

```
IDENTIFICATION DIVISION.
ENVIRONMENT DIVISION.
DATA DIVISION.
PROCEDURE DIVISION.
```

That is, the first division must always be the IDENTIFICATION DIVISION and the last division must always be the PROCEDURE DIVISION.

Both the ENVIRONMENT DIVISION and DATA DIVISION are subdivided into sections. The PROCEDURE DIVISION sometimes, though rarely, contains sections, and there are no sections in the IDENTIFICATION DIVISION. Sections are usually subdivided into *paragraphs;* although, in the PROCEDURE DIVISION there can be paragraphs without

Figure 2.1 The compilation process.

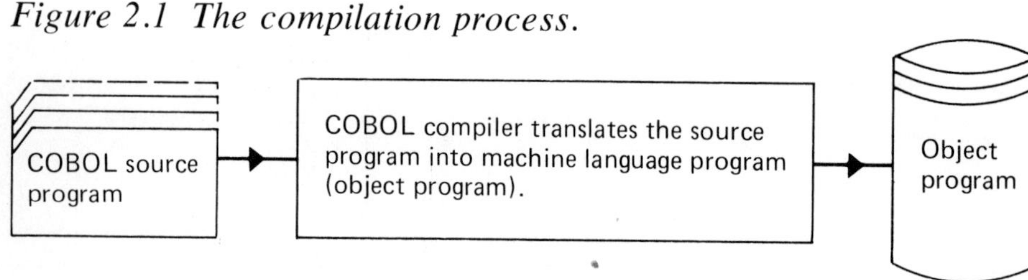

Figure 2.2 The divisions of COBOL programs.

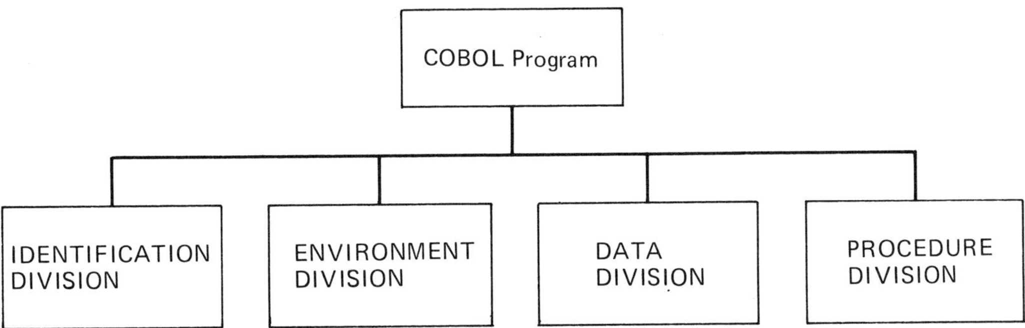

sections. Paragraphs are constructed from *sentences* and sentences are constructed from *statements*. Some statements may be formed from *clauses*.

The words and symbols of the COBOL source program must be formed from the COBOL *character set*. Note carefully the listing of the complete COBOL character set for the IBM-1130 computer on the inside covers. The word character set includes

> A through Z the *alphabetic* characters,
> 0 through 9   the *numeric* characters,
>   the *hyphen* or minus sign.

In COBOL, words are formed from the word character set. Words must be formed according to three rules.

1. A word can have from 1 through 30 characters from the word character set.
2. Hyphens cannot be used as the first or last character in a word.
3. A word should contain at least one alphabetic character except in the PROCEDURE DIVISION, where paragraph names and section names can be formed with only numeric characters.

In COBOL there are *reserved words* and *unreserved words*. Reserved words have preassigned meanings and must be used according to certain rules that we will discuss later. A list of reserved words is on the inside cover. Examine them. The COBOL compiler will not recognize the reserved words unless they are spelled exactly as shown in the list. Unreserved words are chosen by the programmer and do not appear in the list of reserved words. When these words are formed correctly, they meet the criteria established in the preceding three rules.

Since the programmer chooses the words to name and describe items in a program, unreserved words are also called *programmer-supplied names* or *programmer-chosen names*. Thus programmer-supplied words must be formed according to the three rules for forming COBOL words and they cannot be chosen from the list of reserved words. For example, a programmer cannot use WRITE, READ, OPEN, CLOSE, DIVISION, or PROGRAM-ID as programmer-supplied words because they are reserved words. Similarly, a programmer cannot use any of the following words as programmer-supplied names for the reason indicated.

Invalid programmer-supplied words	Reason
LAST-ITEM-	The word ends in a hyphen.
AMOUNT$	The $ is not from the word character set.
STUDENT NAME	The space is not a character from the word character set.
IDENTIFICATION	This is a reserved word.

On the other hand, SALARY, STUDENT-ID, FACULTY-DATA-LIST, and OLD-BALANCE are valid programmer-supplied words since they are formed correctly and are not in the list of reserved words.

Now that we have the preliminaries out of the way, let's see some COBOL. When you have finished studying this chapter, you will be able to run your first COBOL program.

Example 2.1 Write a COBOL program to instruct the computer to read a file of student records and print the file. Assume that each student's record contains three items of information: the student's number, name, and major.

Before you learn how to write the program, you should know that a student record (or any other *record*) is a collection of related data and a *file* is simply a collection of records. Figure 2.3 is the program for example 2.1.

Note that the first division in the program is the IDENTIFICATION DIVISION. In this division we used the following reserved words: IDEN-TIFICATION, DIVISION, PROGRAM-ID, AUTHOR, INSTALLA-TION, and REMARKS. The other words in the IDENTIFICATION DIVISION are *programmer-supplied names*. Remember that the programmer-supplied names (words) can be spelled in any way the programmer wishes, as long as the programmer constructs them according to the rules for the construction of words. (Did you check to see that they indeed conform to the rules for forming words?)

Notice that in our program (as in any COBOL program), line 1, the first division, is the IDENTIFICATION DIVISION; line 6, the second division, is the ENVIRONMENT DIVISION; line 14, the third division, is the DATA DIVISION; and line 30, the fourth and last division is the PROCE-DURE DIVISION.

IDENTIFICATION DIVISION

The IDENTIFICATION DIVISION is constructed from several paragraphs. The first paragraph is line 2. The word PROGRAM-ID is the *paragraph header* (name), and the word SAMPLE-1 is a programmer-supplied name. The second paragraph is

```
    AUTHOR.   KHAILANY-DUPLISSEY.
```

paragraph header   programmer-supplied name
reserved word   unreserved word

In our program we have four paragraphs in the IDENTIFICATION DIVI-SION, and the header of the last one is REMARKS. (Remember that there are no sections in this division.)

Figure 2.3 Control cards, program cards, and data cards to run example 2.1 on an IBM-1130. (Statement numbers added for reference.)

```
   // JOB T
   // COBOL
   *LIST
   *S TNO
 1         IDENTIFICATION DIVISION.
 2         PROGRAM-ID. SAMPLE-1.
 3         AUTHOR. KHAILANY-DUPLISSEY.
 4         INSTALLATION. UALR.
 5         REMARKS. THIS PROGRAM IS WRITTEN IN AMERICAN NATIONAL
               STANDARD COBOL TO READ AND PRINT A FILE OF
               STUDENT RECORDS, EACH RECORD IS COMPOSED
               OF A STUDENT-NUMBER, NAME, AND MAJOR.
 6         ENVIRONMENT DIVISION.
 7         CONFIGURATION SECTION.
 8         SOURCE-COMPUTER. IBM-1130.
 9         OBJECT-COMPUTER. IBM-1130.
10         INPUT-OUTPUT SECTION.
11         FILE-CONTROL.
12             SELECT CARD-FILE, ASSIGN TO RD-2501.
13             SELECT PRINT-FILE, ASSIGN TO PR-1403.
14         DATA DIVISION.
15         FILE SECTION.
16         FD  CARD-FILE,
               LABEL RECORDS ARE OMITTED,
               DATA RECORD IS CARD-IN.
17         01  CARD-IN.
18             02 STUDENT-NUMBER          PICTURE 99999.
19             02 STUDENT-NAME            PICTURE X(20).
20             02 STUDENT-MAJOR           PICTURE X(10).
21         FD  PRINT-FILE,
               LABEL RECORDS ARE OMITTED,
               DATA RECORD IS PRINT-RECORD.
22         01  PRINT-RECORD.
23             02 FILLER                              PICTURE X(20).
24             02 PRINT-NUMBER                         PICTURE 9(5).
25             02 FILLER                              PICTURE X(10).
26             02 PRINT-NAME                          PICTURE X(20).
27             02 FILLER                              PICTURE X(15).
28             02 PRINT-MAJOR                         PICTURE X(10).
29             02 FILLER                              PICTURE X(40).
30         PROCEDURE DIVISION.
31         BEGIN.
32             OPEN INPUT CARD-FILE, OUTPUT PRINT-FILE.
33         READ-A-CARD.
34             MOVE SPACES TO PRINT-RECORD.
35             READ CARD-FILE, AT END GO TO END-OF-JOB.
36             MOVE STUDENT-NUMBER TO PRINT-NUMBER.
37             MOVE STUDENT-NAME TO PRINT-NAME.
38             MOVE STUDENT-MAJOR TO PRINT-MAJOR.
39             WRITE PRINT-RECORD.
40             GO TO READ-A-CARD.
41         END-OF-JOB.
42             CLOSE CARD-FILE, PRINT-FILE.
43             STOP RUN.
   /*
   // XEQ
   12345SMITH S. ROSE       MATH
   12346JOHN J. SMITH       COMPUTER
   12347WATTS L. ROBEN      HISTORY
   /*
```

ENVIRONMENT DIVISION

In contrast, the ENVIRONMENT DIVISION in the program is divided into sections: the CONFIGURATION SECTION and the INPUT-OUTPUT SECTION. The CONFIGURATION SECTION in our program has two paragraphs.

(1)

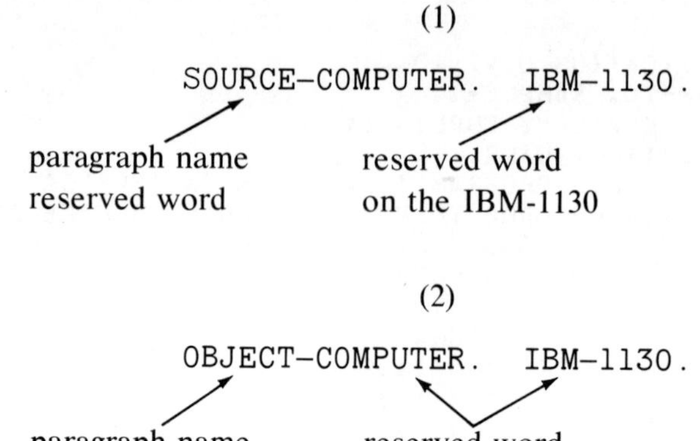

(2)

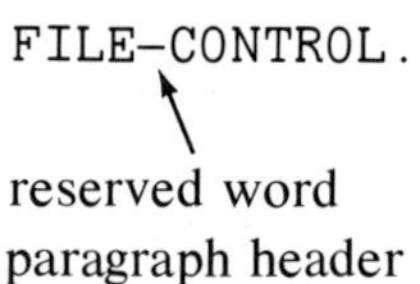

The INPUT-OUTPUT SECTION has only one paragraph.

FILE-CONTROL.

reserved word
paragraph header

In general, it is not necessary that the name of sections or paragraphs be reserved words. However, in the IDENTIFICATION DIVISION the paragraph names and in the ENVIRONMENT DIVISION the paragraph names *and* section names are always reserved words.

The FILE-CONTROL paragraph has two sentences.

(1)

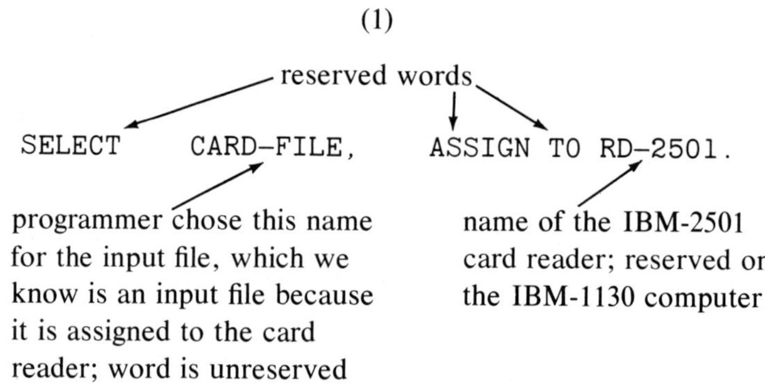

(2)

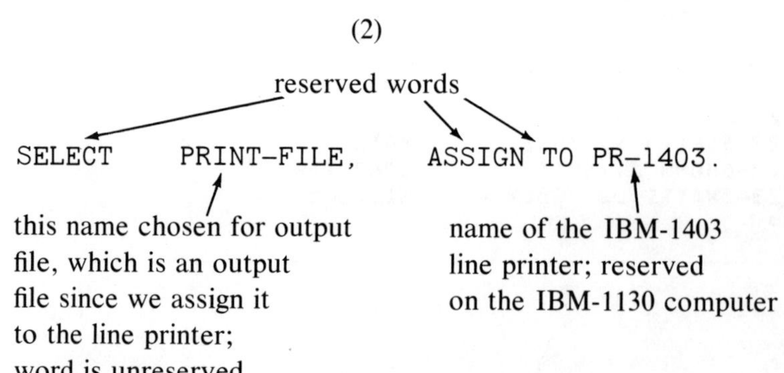

Thus in the ENVIRONMENT DIVISION we told the computer what computer compiles our source program and what computer will run the object program. We also told the computer what input-output files we use and assigned them to the appropriate physical devices.

DATA DIVISION

In example 2.1, the DATA DIVISION contains only one section, the name of which is a reserved word, FILE SECTION. This section is divided into *file description* (FD) *entries,* and there is one FD entry for each file selected in the FILE-CONTROL paragraph that is contained in the INPUT-OUTPUT SECTION of the ENVIRONMENT DIVISON. An FD entry is a detailed description of the file. Note that CARD-FILE, LABEL RE-CORDS ARE OMITTED, DATA RECORD IS CARD-IN. is one sentence, although it is written differently in the program for clarity. Note that the commas are used only for (optional) punctuation and that the period terminates the sentence. The *level numbers* 01 and 02 in lines 17, 18, 19, 20, 22, 23, 24, 25, 26, 27, 28, and 29 indicate the organization of the file. For example, the first level number following the FD entry of CARD-FILE is the 01 level number of CARD-IN, which indicates that CARD-IN is the record of CARD-FILE. When the level number of an item is higher than the preceding level number, the new item is part of the preceding item. Thus 02 indicates that STUDENT-NAME is a part of CARD-IN. Since no higher level numbers follow the 02 entries, the 02 entries are the *elementary items* (*fields*) of our record. Elementary items are always described by the reserved word PICTURE. Observe that CARD-FILE has one *group item* (any item that is subdivided into smaller items) and PRINT-FILE also has one group item. Let us look more closely at the record CARD-IN of CARD-FILE. Note that CARD-IN has three items of information. Two of these are composed of characters, and the third is composed of only numeric characters. An X indicates a character, and a 9 indicates a numeric character.

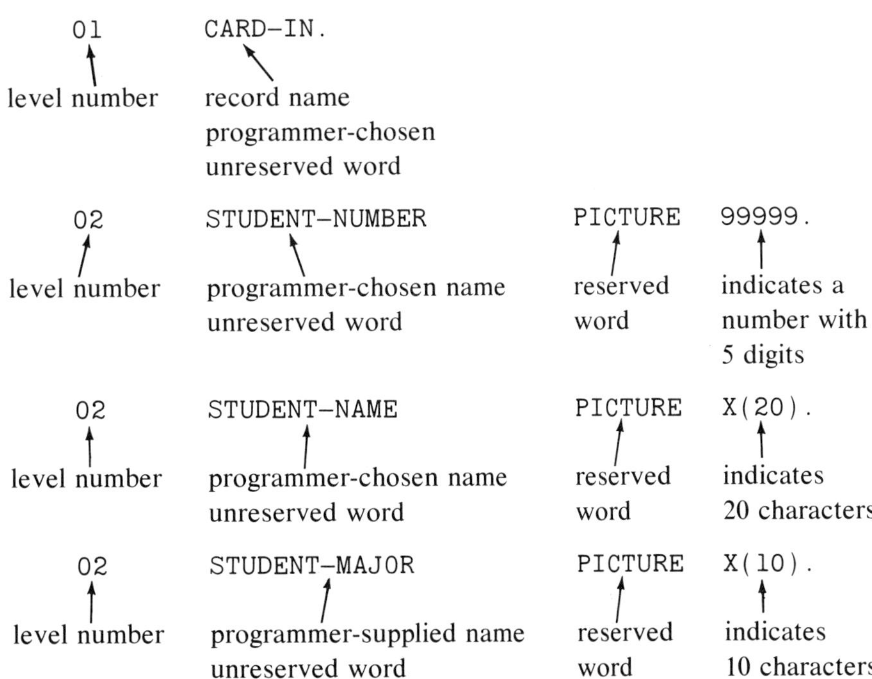

The preceding description tells us that the input record of CARD-FILE is CARD-IN because it is an immediate 01 level entry after the FD entry of CARD-FILE. CARD-IN has three *fields*. Examine lines 21 through 29 to see if you understand them.

PROCEDURE DIVISION

The last division is the PROCEDURE DIVISION. As always, this is a division header formed of reserved words. The first paragraph in this division is

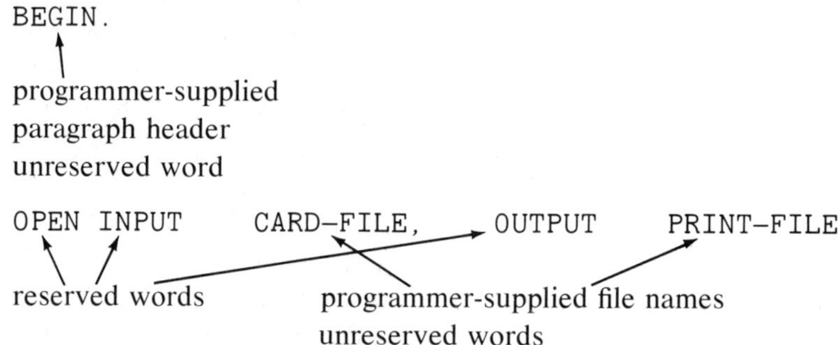

A paragraph ends when another one starts. Thus the preceding paragraph is ended because the second paragraph immediately follows it:

```
READ-A-CARD.
      MOVE SPACES TO PRINT-RECORD.
      READ CARD-FILE, AT END GO TO END-OF-JOB.
      MOVE STUDENT-NUMBER TO PRINT-NUMBER.
      MOVE STUDENT-NAME TO PRINT-NAME.
      MOVE STUDENT-MAJOR TO PRINT-MAJOR.
      WRITE PRINT-RECORD. GO TO READ-A-CARD.
```

In this paragraph the statement MOVE SPACES TO PRINT-RECORD fills PRINT-RECORD with spaces. READ CARD-FILE, AT END GO TO END-OF-JOB, causes one record to be read. If that record indicates the end of data, then control transfers to paragraph END-OF-JOB; otherwise the computer goes to the next statement. The statement MOVE STUDENT-NUMBER TO PRINT-NUMBER places the content of STUDENT-NUMBER in PRINT-NUMBER. In the same manner, the other two MOVE statements place the contents of STUDENT-NAME and STUDENT-MAJOR in PRINT-NAME and PRINT-MAJOR, respectively. The statement WRITE PRINT-RECORD writes the content of PRINT-RECORD into the file PRINT-FILE. The last statement GO TO READ-A-CARD sends the control back to the beginning of the paragraph.

The computer stops reading cards when it detects the end of the card file and immediately goes to paragraph END-OF-JOB. This paragraph contains the statements: CLOSE CARD-FILE, PRINT-FILE. STOP RUN. in which the underlined words are reserved. These statements close the opened files and stop the execution of the program. These steps are always necessary.

Running the Program

Now it is time to run your project. Examine the COBOL coding form in figure 2.4. There are 80 columns on a line just as there are 80 columns on a card, and each line is punched on one card.

You must first key punch a card deck for the program. If necessary, check with your supervisor to make changes in the program that may be necessary to run it on your computer. You may need to ask your supervisor how to use the key punch. When you are finished, your deck of punched cards should look much like the one in figure 2.5, except for the changes you might have made to adapt the program for your computer. All division, section, FD, 01 level number, 77 level number, and paragraph headers must begin in columns 8, 9, 10, or 11. These columns constitute *area A,* also called *margin A.* Columns 12 through 72 constitute *area B,* also called *margin B.* Although a paragraph name begins in area A, the remainder of the paragraph must be in area B. Similarly, although FD is in area A, the associated file name and descriptive information must be in area B.

Remember that blanks may never immediately precede a comma or period and that at least one blank must always follow a comma or period.

In addition to the cards for the program, you will also need some *control cards* for your particular computer installation. Since we ran this program on an IBM-1130 computer, we showed the control cards for the IBM-1130. In the Appendices of this book, you will find illustrations showing the cards that would be used to run the program on a variety of other computers. If you cannot find the information you need to run the program on your computer, then ask the personnel at your computer installation for help.

Figure 2.6 is the program flowchart for your program, and figure 2.7 is the system flowchart.

We wish you the best of luck in preparing and running your first COBOL program. Take care in punching the cards for your program. If the program will not run and does not print the information that you expect, it may be because you made an error in preparing your deck of program cards. In most cases, the computer will print a list of error messages telling you the line in which you have made the error; this should help you to correct your mistake quickly.

Figure 2.4 COBOL coding form for example 2.1.

```
IDENTIFICATION DIVISION.
PROGRAM-ID. SAMPLE-1.
AUTHOR. KHAILANY-DUPLISSEY.
INSTALLATION. UALR.
REMARKS. THIS PROGRAM IS WRITTEN IN AMERICAN NATIONAL
         STANDARD COBOL TO READ AND PRINT A FILE OF
         STUDENT RECORDS. EACH RECORD IS COMPOSED
         OF A STUDENT-NUMBER, NAME, AND MAJOR.
ENVIRONMENT DIVISION.
CONFIGURATION SECTION.
SOURCE-COMPUTER. IBM-1130.
OBJECT-COMPUTER. IBM-1130.
INPUT-OUTPUT SECTION.
FILE-CONTROL.
    SELECT CARD-FILE, ASSIGN TO RD-2501.
    SELECT PRINT-FILE, ASSIGN TO PR-1403.
DATA DIVISION.
FILE SECTION.
FD  CARD-FILE,
    LABEL RECORDS ARE OMITTED,
    DATA RECORD IS CARD-IN.
01  CARD-IN.
    02 STUDENT-NUMBER  PICTURE 99999.
    02 STUDENT-NAME PICTURE X(20).
    02 STUDENT-MAJOR PICTURE X(10).
FD  PRINT-FILE,
    LABEL RECORDS ARE OMITTED,
    DATA RECORD IS PRINT-RECORD.
01  PRINT-RECORD.
    02 FILLER            PICTURE X(20).
    02 PRINT-NUMBER      PICTURE 9(5).
    02 FILLER            PICTURE X(10).
    02 PRINT-NAME        PICTURE X(20).
    02 FILLER            PICTURE X(15).
    02 PRINT-MAJOR       PICTURE X(10).
    02 FILLER            PICTURE X(40)
```

```
17   PROCEDURE DIVISION.
18   BEGIN.
19       OPEN INPUT CARD-FILE, OUTPUT PRINT-FILE.
20   READ-A-CARD.
01       READ CARD-FILE, AT END GO TO END-OF-JOB.
02       MOVE SPACES TO PRINT-RECORD.
03       MOVE STUDENT-NUMBER TO PRINT-NUMBER.
04       MOVE STUDENT-NAME TO PRINT-NAME.
05       MOVE STUDENT-MAJOR TO PRINT-MAJOR.
06       WRITE PRINT-RECORD.
07       GO TO READ-A-CARD.
08   END-OF-JOB.
09       CLOSE CARD-FILE, PRINT-FILE.
10       STOP RUN.
```

} THE PROGRAM ENDS HERE. BELOW ARE SOME SAMPLE CONTROL CARDS NEEDED FOR THE PROGRAM (SEE FIGURE 2.5).

```
//  JOB T 4000
//  COBOL
*LIST
*STNO
```

} THESE FOUR CONTROL CARDS MUST PRECEDE YOUR PROGRAM IN THIS ORDER. (THE NUMBER 4000 MAY BE DIFFERENT AT YOUR INSTALLATION.)

(YOUR PROGRAM CARDS HERE.)

```
/*
//  XEQ
```

} THESE TWO CONTROL CARDS SHOULD FOLLOW YOUR PROGRAM IN THIS ORDER.

```
12345SMITH S. ROSE        MATH
12346JOHN J. SMITH        COMPUTER
12347WATTS L. ROBEN       HISTORY
```

} THESE ARE THE DATA CARDS. THEY SHOULD FOLLOW THE CONTROL CARD, //XEQ.

```
/*
```

} THIS IS A CONTROL CARD INDICATING THE END OF DATA.

Figure 2.5 Deck of punched cards for example 2.1.

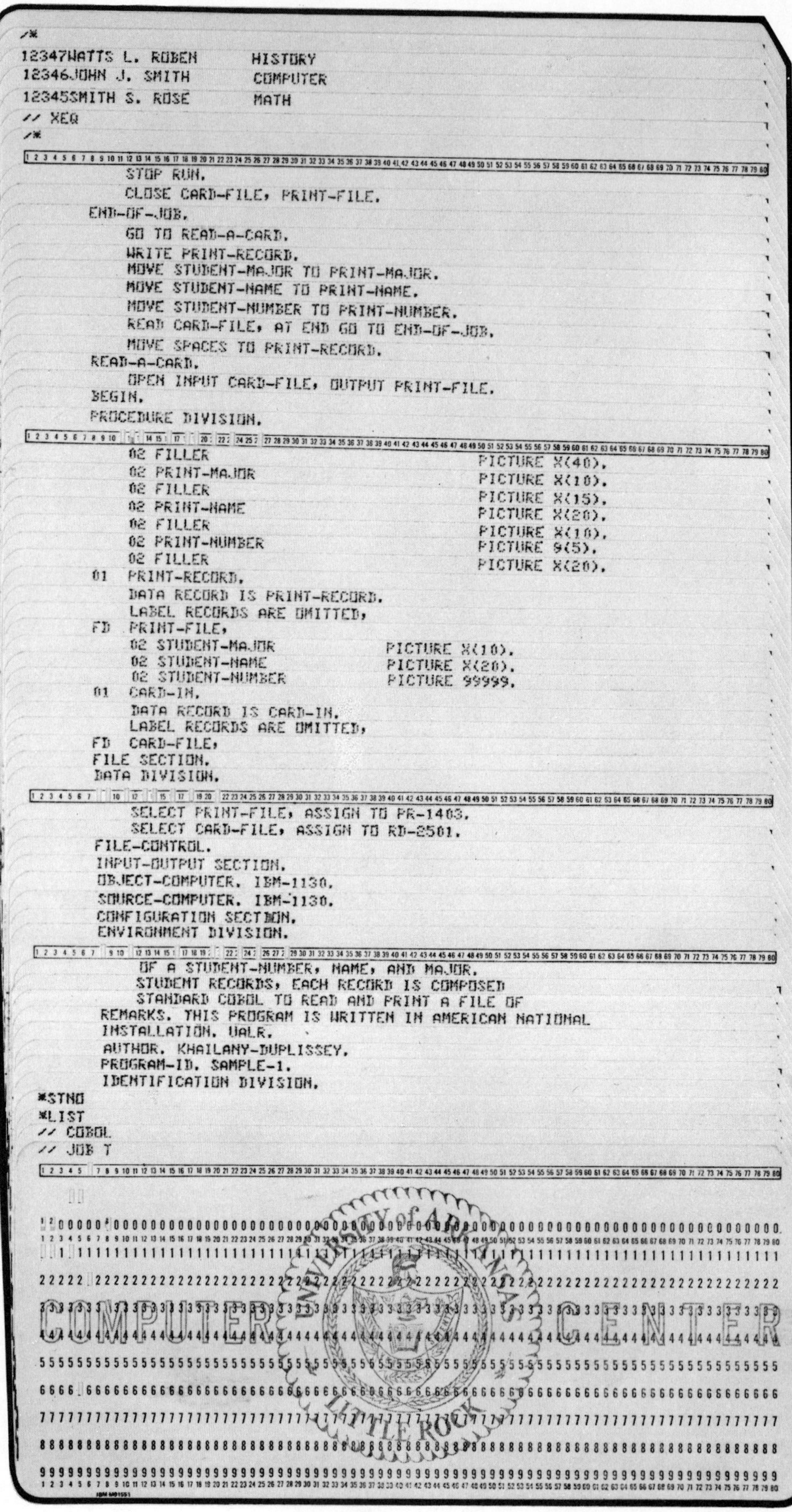

```
/*
12347WATTS L. RUBEN       HISTORY
12346JOHN J. SMITH        COMPUTER
12345SMITH S. ROSE        MATH
// XEQ
/*
            STOP RUN.
            CLOSE CARD-FILE, PRINT-FILE.
        END-OF-JOB.
            GO TO READ-A-CARD.
            WRITE PRINT-RECORD.
            MOVE STUDENT-MAJOR TO PRINT-MAJOR.
            MOVE STUDENT-NAME TO PRINT-NAME.
            MOVE STUDENT-NUMBER TO PRINT-NUMBER.
            READ CARD-FILE, AT END GO TO END-OF-JOB.
            MOVE SPACES TO PRINT-RECORD.
        READ-A-CARD.
            OPEN INPUT CARD-FILE, OUTPUT PRINT-FILE.
        BEGIN.
        PROCEDURE DIVISION.
            02 FILLER                          PICTURE X(40).
            02 PRINT-MAJOR                     PICTURE X(10).
            02 FILLER                          PICTURE X(15).
            02 PRINT-NAME                      PICTURE X(20).
            02 FILLER                          PICTURE X(10).
            02 PRINT-NUMBER                    PICTURE 9(5).
            02 FILLER                          PICTURE X(20).
        01  PRINT-RECORD.
            DATA RECORD IS PRINT-RECORD.
            LABEL RECORDS ARE OMITTED.
        FD  PRINT-FILE.
            02 STUDENT-MAJOR    PICTURE X(10).
            02 STUDENT-NAME     PICTURE X(20).
            02 STUDENT-NUMBER   PICTURE 99999.
        01  CARD-IN.
            DATA RECORD IS CARD-IN.
            LABEL RECORDS ARE OMITTED.
        FD  CARD-FILE.
        FILE SECTION.
        DATA DIVISION.
            SELECT PRINT-FILE, ASSIGN TO PR-1403.
            SELECT CARD-FILE, ASSIGN TO RD-2501.
        FILE-CONTROL.
        INPUT-OUTPUT SECTION.
        OBJECT-COMPUTER. IBM-1130.
        SOURCE-COMPUTER. IBM-1130.
        CONFIGURATION SECTION.
        ENVIRONMENT DIVISION.
            OF A STUDENT-NUMBER, NAME, AND MAJOR.
            STUDENT RECORDS, EACH RECORD IS COMPOSED
            STANDARD COBOL TO READ AND PRINT A FILE OF
        REMARKS. THIS PROGRAM IS WRITTEN IN AMERICAN NATIONAL
        INSTALLATION. UALR.
        AUTHOR. KHAILANY-DUPLISSEY.
        PROGRAM-ID. SAMPLE-1.
        IDENTIFICATION DIVISION.
*STNO
*LIST
// COBOL
// JOB T
```

Figure 2.6 Flowchart for the program for example 2.1.

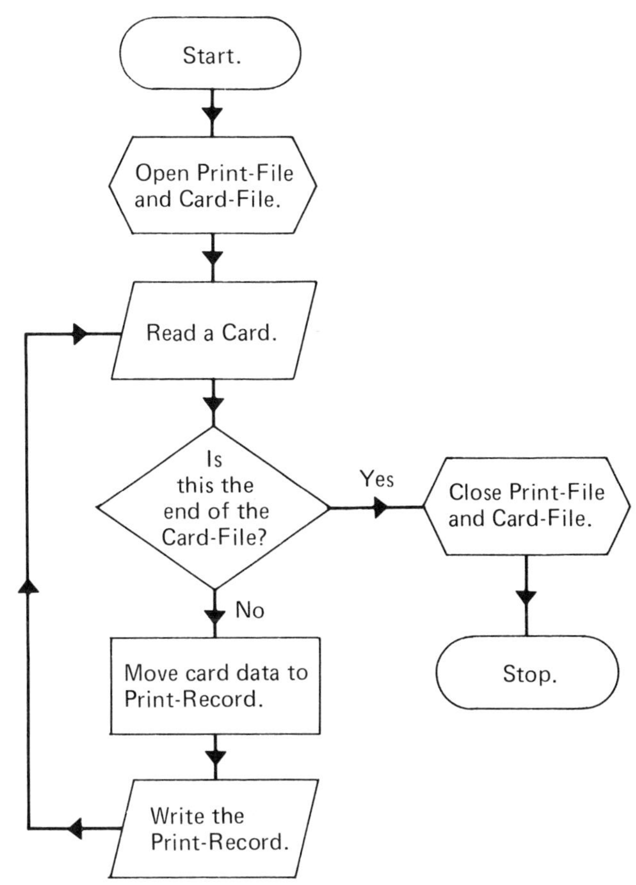

Figure 2.7 System flowchart for example 2.1.

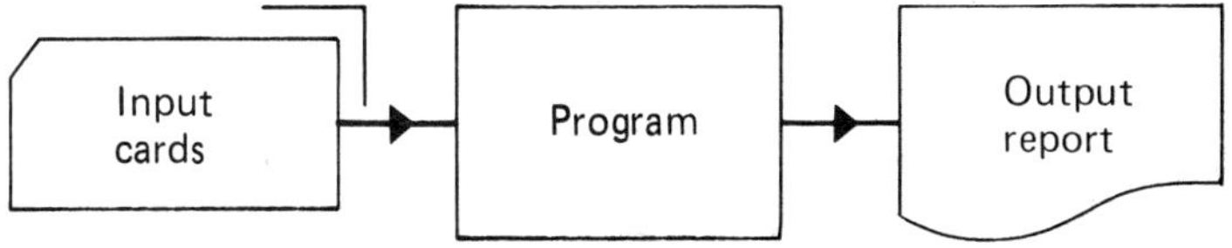

Summary   The *COBOL compiler* translates a *source program* written in the COBOL programming language into an *object program* written in the machine language.

Every COBOL program has four divisions: IDENTIFICATION DIVISION, ENVIRONMENT DIVISION, DATA DIVISION, and PROCEDURE DIVISION. The divisions are usually subdivided into *sections;* sections are subdivided into *paragraphs;* paragraphs are subdivided into *sentences;* sentences are subdivided into *statements;* and statements are subdivided into *clauses.* Sentences and statements are formed from words. Words can be *reserved,* that is, have a special meaning in COBOL programs, or they can be *unreserved,* that is, be selected by the programmer for a particular use.

A *file* is a collection of *records*. A record comprises data items that are usually related in some way. Data items are classified according to their structural complexity. A *group item* is a data item that is subdivided into smaller items. An elementary item is a data item that cannot be subdivided into smaller items. If elementary items are associated with information on cards or printed lines, then they are also called the *fields* of the cards or *printed line*. Every elementary item is described by a PICTURE clause. The PICTURE clause indicates the size of the item and the type of data it can contain, that is, whether it can contain only numbers or only alphabetic characters or special characters such as $ + . , .

Records appear in COBOL programs with *level number* 01. Files always have records, and their record entries always follow the *file description entry* (*FD*) in the COBOL source program. If the record is a group item, then its subdivisions may have level numbers from 02 through 49.

Area A (or *margin A*) is the area comprising columns 8 through 11 on a card or COBOL coding form. *Area B* (or *margin B*) comprises columns 12 through 72. All division names, section names, paragraph names, FD entries, level number 01, and level number 77 must begin in area A. All COBOL statements must be contained entirely in area B.

Review Questions

1. COBOL programs are translated by the _________________.

2. A collection of related data is a _____________.

3. The number of divisions in a COBOL program is always _______.

4. The names of the divisions are _____________, _____________, _____________, and _____________.

5. Any collection of records is a _______.

6. The word character set contains the characters _____________, _____________, and _____________.

7. The number of characters in a word may be _____________.

8. Pick only the "legal" COBOL words from the list. DATA , INFO , 1 , 11 , PREASSIGN , PRE-ASSIGN , PRE ASSIGN , QUOTH-THE-RAVEN-NEVERMORE, SX .

9. Pick only the reserved words from the list: AT , TO , THE , AUTHOR , RUN , PROGRAM-ID .

10. In a COBOL picture specification, the symbol for a numeric digit is _______ and that for a character is _______.

11. Each line on a COBOL coding form corresponds on a one-line-to-one-card basis to how many punched cards? _______

12. There are group items and elementary items in COBOL. How can you recognize a group item? How can you recognize an elementary item?

13. How can you tell which data items are records of files?

Suggested Projects

1. Run example 2.1.

2. Run example 2.1 and include some of your own original data cards with those given in the chapter. Give particular attention to the description of

CARD-IN, and note the placement of the characters in the illustration of the data cards. You might like to see what happens if you place the data on the cards in a different way.

3. Write a COBOL program to instruct the computer to read a file of patient records at a hospital and print a list of the records. The records should be in the form of cards, and each card should contain

Card columns	Field
1–8	patient number
9–34	patient name
35–64	patient address

The records should be printed on the line printer. Prepare a flowchart for your program. Prepare data cards for your program and run the program. (*Hint:* You can use the ideas shown in example 2.1. However, change STUDENT-NUMBER, STUDENT-NAME, and STUDENT-MAJOR to reasonable choices for this project. Make similar changes in PRINT-RECORD.)

4. Prepare a flowchart, write a program, and run a program to read a card file of inventory records and print a list on the line printer. Each card contains

Card columns	Field
1–20	item name
21–50	item description
51–60	item number

Note that the order of the fields is different from the order of the fields in example 2.1

5. The record of each player on the Kuramatsu Dragons baseball team is kept on cards. Each record (a card) contains the following information.

Card columns	Description
1–5	player's number
6–25	player's name
26–55	player's address
56–65	player's marital status
66–73	player's monthly salary

Write a COBOL program to read and print a list of the records of all players of the Kuramatsu Dragons. We suggest that you use PICTURE 9(6)V99 for the salary. This will tell the computer to assume that the two rightmost digits for the salary are the decimal digits for this number. Since the computer will assume the presence of the implied decimal point, you should not punch an actual decimal point in the number on the card. For example, to get the computer to read the salary $459.00 for a player, you must punch 00045900 in columns 66 through 73 of that player's card. To get the computer to print this salary correctly, you should use PICTURE 9(6).99 for the data item to be printed.

6. Run example 2.1 with the following changes and observe the effect upon the computer listing and compilation for your new program.

a. Misspell the word IDENTIFICATION.
b. Remove the period from the end of DATA DIVISION.
c. Rewrite a 0! entry so that 01 is in area B instead of area A.
d. Rewrite an FD entry so that FD is in area B.
e. Somewhere in the program leave the hyphen out of STUDENT-NAME.
f. Leave out one of the LABEL RECORDS ARE OMITTED clauses.
g. Remove the OPEN INPUT CARD-FILE. statement.
h. Remove the CLOSE CARD-FILE, PRINT-FILE. statement.
i. Write the statement MOVE STUDENT-NUMBER TO PRINT-NUMBER. so that it begins in area A.
j. Remove the FILE SECTION. header from the program.
k. Replace FILE-CONTROL by FILE CONTROL.

In each case the preceding changes should result in some type of error. Some of the errors will cause the machine to look for other errors besides the ones we have specified.

7. Rewrite example 2.1 so that the PICTURE clause for PRINT-NUMBER is Z(5) instead of 9(5). Be sure to include data cards whose student numbers are smaller than 10000—for example, 00567. Run the original version of example 2.1 with the data cards included, and run the new version of example 2.1 with the same data cards. Compare the results.

CHAPTER 3

Purposes of the Divisions and Some General Information

Primary Purposes of the Four Divisions

The purpose of the IDENTIFICATION DIVISION is the identification (or naming) and documentation of the program.

The purposes of the ENVIRONMENT DIVISION are to name the source and object computers (the computer hardware required for the program) and to assign input-output files to appropriate physical input-output devices.

The purpose of the DATA DIVISION is to describe all the information processed by the program. It provides detailed descriptions of the input-output files named in the ENVIRONMENT DIVISION and their records. It also describes WORKING-STORAGE items that are used in the program but are not records of files.

The purpose of the PROCEDURE DIVISION is to provide the instructions to be carried out by the computer during the execution of the program. These instructions can cause the computer to perform arithmetic operations, make logical decisions, move data in main storage, and request an input-output operation.

Structure of the IDENTIFICATION DIVISION

The IDENTIFICATION DIVISION is the simplest and the shortest of the four divisions. It is subdivided into paragraphs and its form is

```
IDENTIFICATION DIVISION.
PROGRAM-ID. program-name.
[AUTHOR. comment-entry.]
[INSTALLATION. comment-entry.]
[DATE-WRITTEN. comment-entry.]
[DATE-COMPILED. comment-entry.]
[SECURITY. comment-entry.]
[REMARKS. comment-entry.]
```

Only the PROGRAM-ID paragraph is required. The remaining paragraphs are optional, but if they are used, they must occur in the order indicated. The DATE-COMPILED paragraph is not permitted on the IBM-1130 or the IBM System 3. On computers where the DATE-COMPILED paragraph is permitted, the compiler will automatically insert the correct date in the place of comment-entry at the time the program is compiled. The remaining paragraphs are used for *documentation*—i.e., they are used to provide information to the reader about the program and its purposes. The comment-entries must appear in area B and may be formed from any valid string of words arranged according to the rules of COBOL. On the Burroughs 1700, the comment-entry may contain only one period, which must occur at the end of the entry to mark the physical end of the entry to the computer. However, on the IBM-1130, IBM System 3, and DECSYSTEM-10 there is no limitation on the use of periods for punctuation in a comment-entry.

A program-id entry in the PROGRAM-ID paragraph is required, because this entry provides a name for the COBOL program. It should begin with an alphabetic character and conform to the rules for forming COBOL words. See figure 3.1 for examples of IDENTIFICATION DIVISION entries on an IBM-1130.

Notation Method for Describing Format of Statements

The following notation system is used in this book for describing the format (form) of COBOL statements.

1. All words that are printed in capitals are reserved words.
2. All reserved words that are underlined are required unless the portion of the statement containing the underlined reserved word is itself optional.
3. All words that are printed in lowercase letters are programmer-supplied words (which are unreserved words).
4. Brackets, [ ], indicate that their content is optional.
5. Braces, { }, enclosing a vertical list of items indicate that one item chosen from the vertical list is required.
6. Ellipses, . . . , indicate that the type preceding them may be repeated as desired.

In our discussion of the IDENTIFICATION DIVISION we presented the complete format of that division. Note that according to our notation method, all the paragraph names and the division header are reserved words. The underlining indicates that only the division header and the PROGRAM-ID paragraph are required in this division. Program-id is in lowercase letters, and is hence a programmer-supplied, unreserved word. Similarly, the comment-entry must indicate unreserved words. The brackets around the comment-entries indicate that their content is optional. Of course, the underlining and the brackets are used only to indicate information about the form of the IDENTIFICATION DIVISION and do not actually appear in COBOL source programs.

Coding Forms

COBOL coding forms provide the programmer with a standard method for writing source programs. They are designed so that a program written on them can be punched easily on cards. In particular, the person punching the program on the cards need not know anything about the COBOL programming language.

Figure 3.1 Six examples of the IDENTIFICATION DIVISION.

```
            (1)

IDENTIFICATION DIVISION.
PROGRAM-ID. PROJECT-1.
AUTHOR. KHAILANY-DUPLISSEY.
INSTALLATION. UALR COMPUTER CENTER.
DATE-WRITTEN. THIS MODIFICATION OF SAMPLE-1 WAS
     WRITTEN AND COMPILED ON THE SAME DAY.
     IT WAS RUN THAT DAY.
```

Not permitted on some computers.

```
            (2)

IDENTIFICATION DIVISION.
PROGRAM-ID.   FIRSTRY.
AUTHOR. PSEUDONYM.
DATE-WRITTEN. 5/22/72.
```

```
            (3)

IDENTIFICATION DIVISION.
PROGRAM-ID.  GRADEPOINT.
INSTALLATION. UALR.
SECURITY.  FILE OF GRADES IS UNDER LOCK TO PREVENT
        ACCIDENTAL TAMPERING.
```

```
            (4)

IDENTIFICATION DIVISION.
PROGRAM-ID. NO1.
```

```
            (5)

IDENTIFICATION DIVISION.
INSTALLATION. UALR.
DATE-WRITTEN. 5/22/72.
```

Division is defective, since it lacks a PROGRAM-ID paragraph.

```
            (6)

IDENTIFICATION DIVISION.
PROGRAM-ID. GUMBA.
REMARKS.   THIS PROGRAM COMPUTES A STUDENT'S
        GRADE POINT AVERAGE.
```

Division is defective because the character ' is not allowed in these paragraphs.

Format of Coding Forms

Examine the coding form in figure 3.2. Each form has an area at the top where the programmer can write information not to be punched on cards. Beneath this top area is the portion of the form where the programmer writes the statements in the COBOL source program. This portion of the form allows for several lines of statements. Note the major subdivisions of the form: the sequencing area, the continuation column, area A, area B, and the identification columns. (The form shown in figure 3.2 is an IBM COBOL coding form. The coding forms provided by other computer manufacturers may be slightly different.) Each line on the coding form contains 80 columns, with one line on the form corresponding to one punched card. Some of the columns are numbered to help the programmer determine the location of the columns.

The first six columns of the coding form are used to indicate the proper order of the statements. The first three columns are used to indicate the page number. Writing 001 in the first three columns of a line would indicate that this is a line on page 1, and writing 012 would indicate a line on page 12. Columns 4 through 5 indicate the line number, and these numbers are preprinted on the form. Thus a line with 00305 in columns 1 through 5 indicates that it is the fifth line on page 3. At the bottom of the form are some unnumbered lines. The programmer can use these to indicate lines that were omitted accidentally from the numbered portion of the form. To do this, the programmer must use column 6. For example, suppose that after writing your program on the coding form, you discover that you have omitted a line that should have been between the statements in lines 2 and 3 of the form. To indicate the missing line, you must write a 0 in column 6 after 02 and also after 03 to get 020 and 030. This will allow you to add up to nine additional lines between lines 020 and 030. To do this, you must go to the bottom of the form (after line 20) and write in the missing lines. You should number the missing lines by placing 02 in columns 4 and 5 and putting a number from 1 through 9 in column 6. Thus you could number them with 021, 022, . . . , through 029.

If you use the sequencing numbers to indicate the order of the lines in your program, then the cards punched from the forms must be in the order indicated by the sequencing numbers. Otherwise, some compilers would indicate the sequencing error on the listing they print of your source program, and some compilers would not process your program. No sequence numbers are produced if columns 1 through 6 of the cards for a COBOL source program are left blank (unpunched).

Columns 73 through 80 are the identification columns of the form. Some programmers use columns 73 through 80 to identify and number the card deck. To use these columns to identify the deck by placing an abbreviated form of the program name in them is a good idea. However, the sequencing columns on COBOL cards should be used to number the cards rather than the columns 73 through 80. You can use these columns in anyway you desire. The content of the columns is ignored by the COBOL compiler and has no effect upon the source program.

Continuation of Lines on Coding Forms

When a programmer writes a source program on a coding form, there may sometimes not be a sufficient amount of space provided for what is to be included. There are several options available, and they are illustrated in figure 3.3.

Figure 3.2 A COBOL coding form.

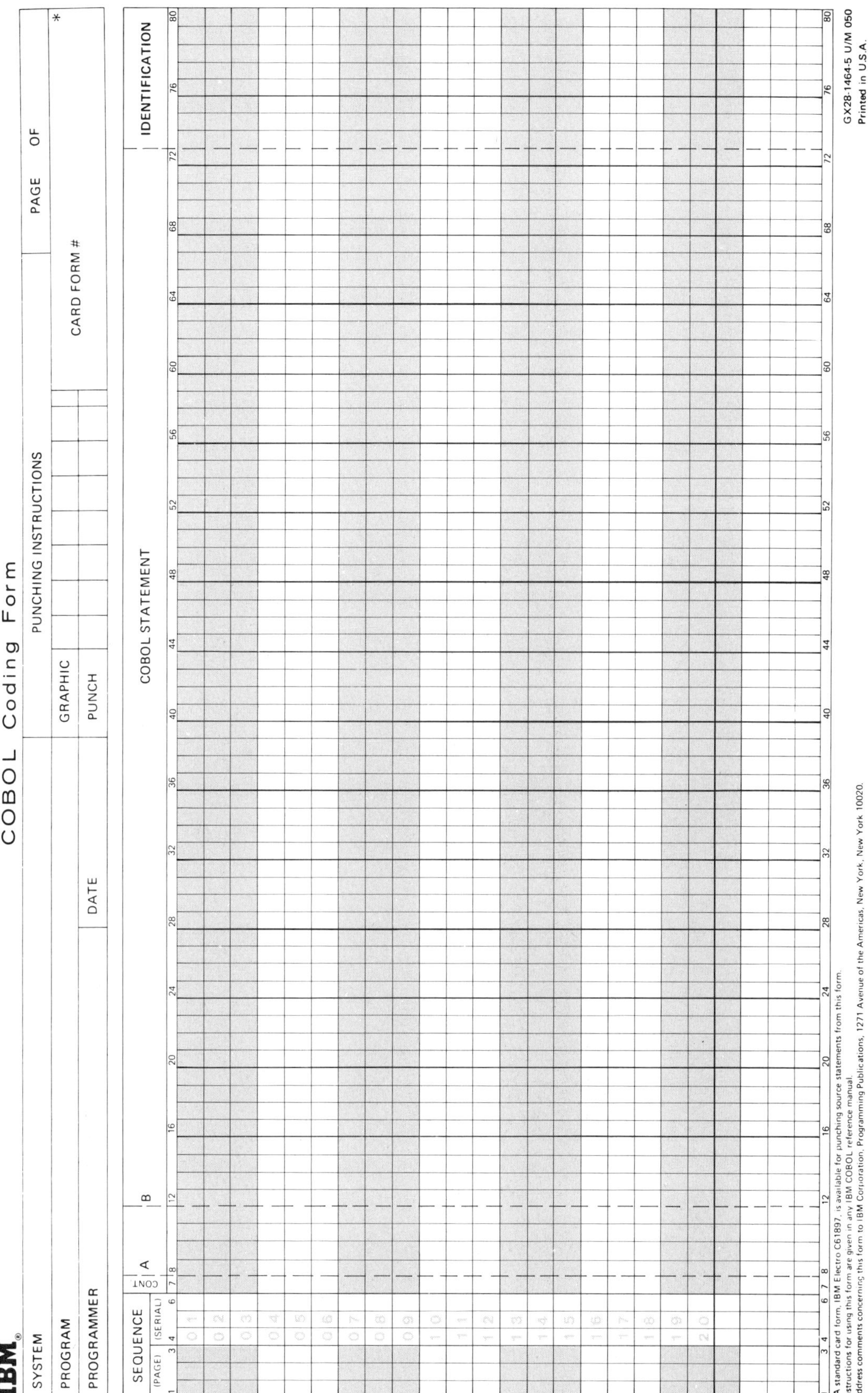

Figure 3.3 Examples of continuations of entries on a coding form.

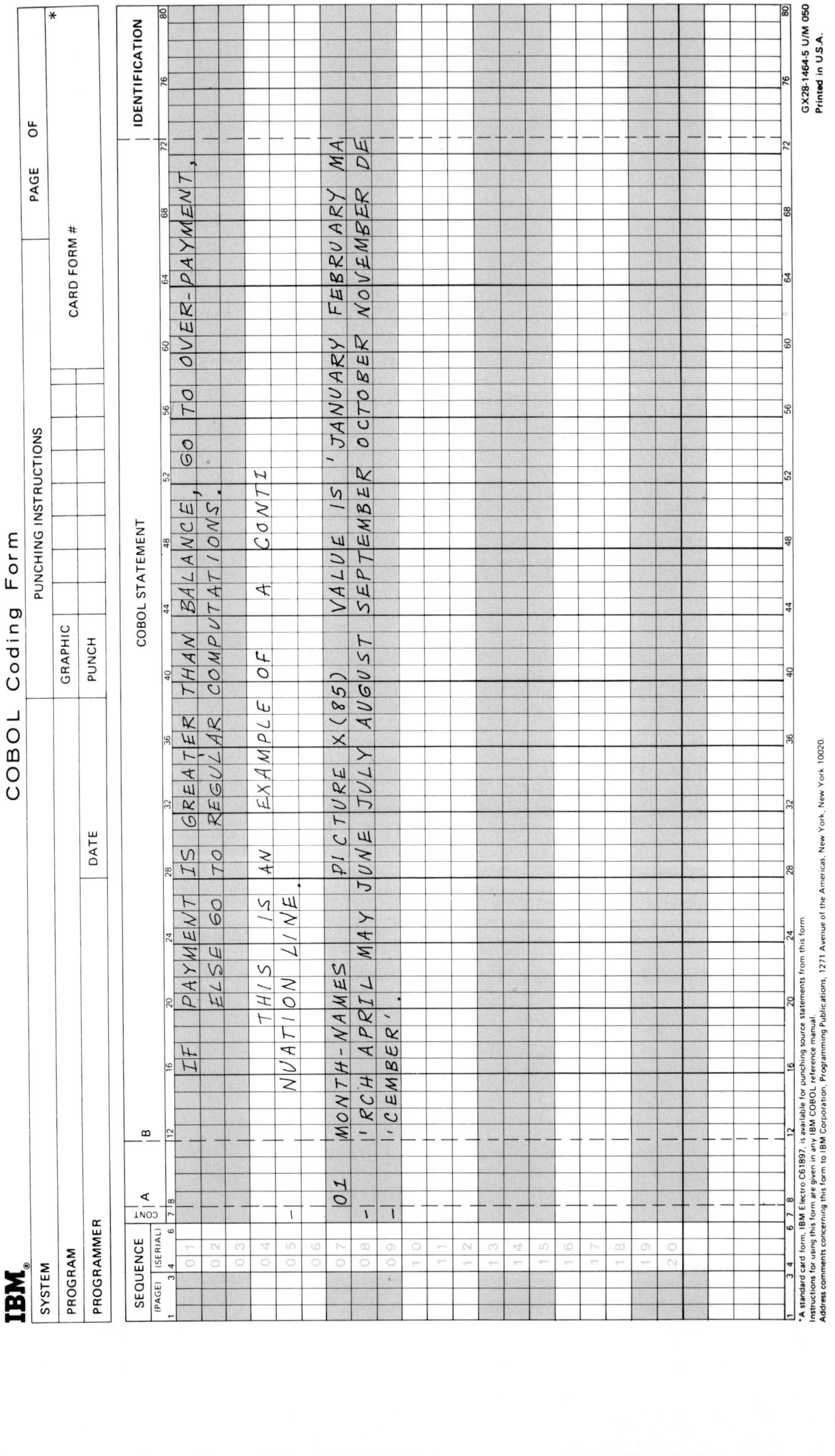

1. Examine item a in figure 3.3. COBOL statements or sentences are always placed in area B. If the space available in a single line in area B is insufficient, then the statement or sentence can continue on in area B to succeeding lines. However, the programmer should fit each word of the statement or sentence entirely in area B of a single line and not split a word between the first and second line. For example, suppose we wished to write IF PAYMENT IS GREATER THAN BALANCE, GO TO OVER-PAYMENT, ELSE GO TO REGULAR COMPUTATIONS. on the form. Examine item a in figure 3.3 to see one way of writing the statement on the form.

2. Suppose you wish to continue a line on a form so that part of a COBOL word or numeric literal (a *numeric literal* is an ordinary decimal number, such as 85, 117.28, or −298.47) is in area B of one line and the rest of the item is in area B of the next line. This is never necessary because you can use the method described in the first alternative. We encourage you not to continue COBOL words or numeric literals to successive lines in area B because the program will be difficult to read and to change, if necessary. Nevertheless, we will tell you how it can be done. When the programmer wishes to continue a word or numeric literal from one line to the next, a hyphen is placed in column 7 of the second line. This indicates that the first nonblank character in area B of the second line is to follow the last nonblank character of the first line, and all blanks between them are to be ignored. Item b in figure 3.3 is equivalent to THIS IS AN EXAMPLE OF A CON-TINUATION LINE.

3. Suppose you need to use a nonnumeric literal (a *nonnumeric literal* is a string of characters enclosed in two single quotation marks, such as 'March', '125', or 'Dec.') that is too large to place on one line. (This happens occasionally.) In item c of figure 3.3, the programmer wished to use the nonnumeric literal 'JANUARY FEBRUARY MARCH APRIL MAY JUNE JULY AUGUST SEPTEMBER OCTOBER NOVEMBER DECEMBER' in a sentence. Note that the hyphen is used to indicate a continuation line exactly as it is used to indicate the continuation of words and numeric literals. Each continuation line for a nonnumeric literal begins with an apostrophe in column 12. This enables the computer to distinguish between the two types of continuation. In this case, the computer does not ignore blanks as it did for the continuation of words or numeric literals. For item c the computer will consider the nonnumeric literal to comprise all the characters in line 7, which are in columns 54 through 72; all the characters in line 8, which are in columns 13 through 72; and all the characters in line 9, which are in columns 13 through 18. The apostrophes in the continuation lines tell the computer that the lines are continuations and are not to be considered part of the literal.

Some Rules for Writing COBOL Statements

1. In a division header, the name of the division must be followed by a blank, the word DIVISION, and a period. In a section header, the name of the section must be followed by a blank, the word SECTION, and a period. In a paragraph header, the name of the paragraph must be followed by a period. Division headers must not be followed by any other statements on

the same line. Section headers can be followed only by a COPY statement on the same line. (See Chapter 7 for more information on the COPY statement.) Paragraph headers are always terminated with a period and may be followed by statements on the same line.

2. All headers and FD entries must begin in area A. In an FD entry, only the letters FD are in area A, and the remainder of the entry must be located in area B. Level numbers 01 and 77 must begin in area A, and the remainder of the entries involving these level numbers must be located in area B. In all other entries beginning with a level number, the level number may begin in area A or area B, but the remainder of the entry must be located in area B. All COBOL statements in the PROCEDURE DIVISION must be located entirely in area B.

3. Sentences are always terminated by a period. Statements in sentences may be terminated by a comma or a blank (if this is not the last statement in the sentence) or by a period (if it is the last statement of a sentence). Some entries in the DATA DIVISION are formed from clauses. The clauses are listed one after another, and all except the last in the list are separated by commas or spaces. The last clause in the list is terminated by a period.

4. Generally speaking, COBOL is a freeform language. With few exceptions, the programmer can write any statement in area B. The spacing between words in statements is not important in most cases. Also, if a statement is too long to fit in one line, it may be continued to the next line in area B. The exceptions to this rule involve the headers, the FD, and some level numbers.

Figure 3.4 illustrates some of the concepts discussed in the rules for writing COBOL statements.

The GO TO, READ, WRITE, and STOP RUN Statements

A good time for you to learn about the branching statement *GO TO* and the input *READ* statement and the output *WRITE* statement would be when you study the PROCEDURE DIVISION, but since you will need to know about them to do the suggested projects at the end of this chapter, the simpler formats of the statements will be discussed here.

```
GO TO procedure-name.
```

The procedure name is the name of either a section or a paragraph in the PROCEDURE DIVISION. The GO TO statement is a transfer statement that causes the control to transfer unconditionally to the section or paragraph procedure name. For example, in the following segment of sentences,

```
GO TO LOOP-FIVE.
ADD 50 TO OLD-BALANCE.
    .
    .
    .
LOOP-FIVE. SUBTRACT 10 FROM OLD-BALANCE.
```

when the processor encounters GO TO, it will transfer to the paragraph LOOP-FIVE and subtract 10 from the OLD-BALANCE. Note that the sentence ADD 50 TO OLD-BALANCE is by-passed (not excluded).

Figure 3.4 Examples of the placement and spacing of COBOL entries on a coding form.

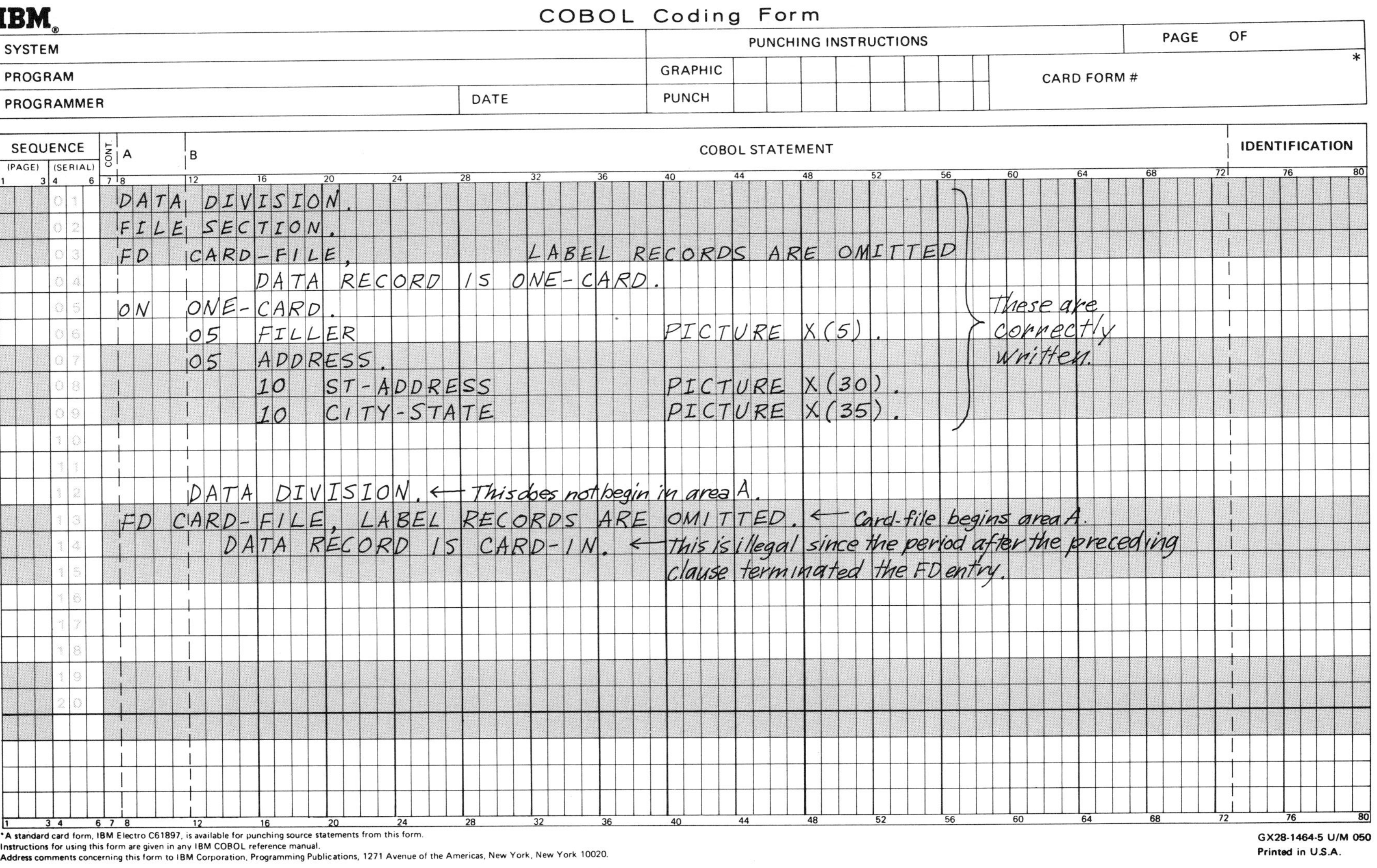

In addition to the GO TO statement, you will need the following statements.

```
OPEN OUTPUT file-name.
WRITE record-name.
OPEN INPUT file-name.
READ file-name AT END imperative-statement.
CLOSE file-name.
```

The preceding imperative statements specify unconditional actions to be taken by the computer. Note in the following example that after READ is a file name and after WRITE is a record name.

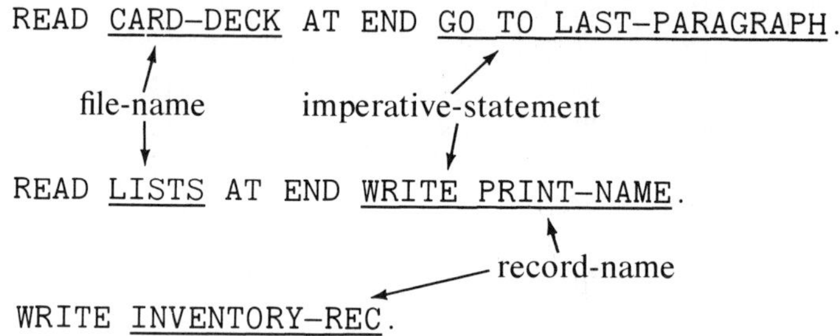

When working with files, the programmer must keep in mind the following information:

1. Before a file can be used, it must be opened. Thus if you wish to use CARD-FILE as an input file, you must write OPEN INPUT CARD-FILE. prior to the first instruction to read the file. Similarly, if you wish to use a file, say PRINT-FILE, as an output file, then OPEN OUTPUT PRINT-FILE. must precede the first instruction to write a record.

2. When the file is open, you can read or write with the file, depending on whether the file was opened for input or for output. If the file was opened for input, then you can read it; if it was opened for output, then you can write it.

3. When you have finished all READ or WRITE instructions with the file, you must close the file. To close EXAMPLE-FILE, you must write CLOSE EXAMPLE-FILE.

Finally, don't forget that when the computer finishes with all the instructions in your program, you must include one last instruction: STOP RUN. This statement informs the computer that your program has finished executing.

Summary   In this chapter we discussed the purposes of the four divisions of a COBOL program. The IDENTIFICATION DIVISION provides a name for the program and provides documentation for the program. The ENVIRONMENT DIVISION describes the hardware used in a program and assigns files to input-output devices. The DATA DIVISION defines and describes the information used in a program. The PROCEDURE DIVISION gives the instructions to be carried out by the computer during the execution of a program.

We discussed the notation system that will be used in this book for presenting the format of statements, and we listed some rules for writing COBOL statements. We also discussed the use of coding forms in writing a COBOL source program prior to punching it on cards.

We gave a preview of some basic statements so that you can begin writing simple programs.

Review Questions

1. The number of required paragraphs in the IDENTIFICATION DIVISION is ______.

2. The programmer provides detailed descriptions of all information that is to be processed in the ____________ DIVISION.

3. All COBOL operations are written in the ____________ DIVISION.

4. Headers begin somewhere in area ______.

5. Consider

```
[AUTHOR. [comment-entry] ... ]
```

Is this paragraph required in the IDENTIFICATION DIVISION?

______

If the paragraph is used, then it must always include the characters

____________.

Is comment-entry required if the paragraph is used? ______
Can comment-entry be repeated? ______

6. Outline the steps necessary to careful preparation and successful running of a computer program.

7. What is the general form of the comment-entries in the optional paragraphs of the IDENTIFICATION DIVISION?

8. Suppose that CARD-IN is the record of an input file called CARD-FILE. Which of the following statements are correct?

   a. READ CARD-IN AT END GO TO END-OF-JOB.
   b. READ CARD-FILE AT END GO TO END-OF-JOB.

9. Suppose that PRINT-RECORD is a record for the output file called PRINT-FILE. Which of the following statements are correct?

   a. WRITE PRINT-RECORD.
   b. WRITE PRINT-FILE.

10. We saw in Chapter 2 that paragraph names in the PROCEDURE DIVISION are programmer-supplied words. Can a paragraph name be constructed from only numeric characters? If so, is the following statement permissible in COBOL? "GO TO 18."

Suggested Projects

1. Rewrite the IDENTIFICATION DIVISION of project 1 in Chapter 2. Include your name and installation, the dates written and compiled, and some original remarks. Run the result.
2. Rewrite example 3.1 as follows: Instead of CARD-FILE and PRINT-FILE, use names of your own choosing. Run the result. Don't forget to change the names in every place they occur in the program.
3. Consider the records of the employees in a company as an input card file. Each input record (card) contains the following information.

Employee number	Name	Address	Marital status
10 digits	20 characters	20 characters	1 character

Write a program to instruct the computer to read a card file of employee records and print a list of the information. Provide your own choice of names for the input card file and the output line printer file. The records (lines) of the output file should appear as follows (the ⱷ indicates a blank):

```
9999999999ⱷⱷⱷⱷXXXXXXXXXXXXXXXXXXXXXXⱷⱷⱷⱷXXXXXXXXXXXXXXXXXXXXXXⱷⱷⱷⱷX
Employee                Name                        Addreʃs         Marital
 number                                                             status
```

A sample record could be

```
012346689    John Deere    5117 Kingsbury    S
```

4. Write a program to instruct the computer to read a card file of patient records in a hospital and print the patient records on the line printer. Each patient record contains

Card column	Field
1–5	patient number
6–20	patient name
21–50	name of person to notify in case of an emergency
51	one character code S satisfactory C critical G good
52–60	patient's physician
61–70	name of insurance company if patient has medical insurance; none if patient is uninsured

Prepare a flowchart for this program, and run it with at least 20 data cards of your own design.

5. Although you have not been introduced to arithmetic statements in COBOL, we feel that you will not have any difficulty in learning to use them to do simple computations. For example, if you write ADD 10 TO B. in COBOL, the computer will add 10 to the numeric data item B. If you write DIVIDE TOTAL BY NUMBER GIVING AVERAGE., the computer would take the value of TOTAL, divide it by the value of NUMBER, and store the result in AVERAGE. The value of TOTAL and the value of NUMBER will not be changed by this statement. Refer to

Chapter 8 on arithmetic statements in COBOL if you have difficulty with this concept.

Use the arithmetic statements in a COBOL program. Your program should instruct the computer to read a file of student records. Each record is punched on a card. Each card contains

Card column	Content
1–5	student identification number
6–8	student grade (a number)
9–28	student name
29–38	subject studied
39–68	student address

Calculate the average grade for all the students in the file. Print a list of all the students and their grades. At the end of the list, print the average grade for all the students.

6. Write a program to instruct the computer to read a card file of customer records in a bank. Each card contains

Card column	Content
1–5	account number
6–13	customer balance
14–20	amount of today's deposit

Print a list of the account numbers. For each account show the old balance, the amount of the deposits, and the new balance.

CHAPTER 4

Files: Organization and Access

Before we discuss the details of the ENVIRONMENT DIVISION, we need to know more about *files* and *records*. To review: A file is a collection of records; a record is a collection of group items (a group item can be subdivided into more group items); and group items can be formed from one or more elementary items also called fields. In example 2.1 we saw a design for a student record, which comprised three fields: STUDENT-NUMBER, STUDENT-NAME, and STUDENT-MAJOR. A typical example of a student record is

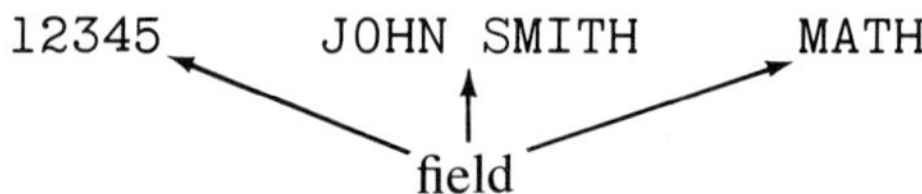

A collection of those student records could constitute a file of student records in a school.

As another example, suppose we want to create an inventory file for a bookstore. We must first decide what information is to be included in the inventory records. The following list indicates the kind of information you might want to be readily accessible for each book in inventory.

1. unit number (a catalog or serial number)
2. unit name (title)
3. unit price
4. number of units on hand
5. number of units requested
6. number of units on order
7. name of manufacturer (publisher)

Each of the seven pieces of information can be contained in a single field of an inventory record. Thus if the bookstore has 500 different books, the inventory file should contain 500 records, and each record should have 7 fields. For each book, there will be a corresponding record whose fields contain the information for that particular book.

Types of Files

Input operations feed the computer with information in that they take information from input devices—such as a card reader, a magnetic tape, or a disk—into the memory. Output operations move the information from the computer to the outside—i.e., from the memory to the line printer, magnetic tape, or disk. These processes require the use of three types of files.

Input Files

Input files are created externally, and their information is fed into the computer memory. A common example is a card deck in which each card is a record of the file. Input files can be on input devices such as disk, magnetic tape, or paper tape.

Output Files

Information in the computer memory can be routed to output devices to create output files. The output files can be stored on magnetic tape, disk, paper tape, or punched cards. The line printer and console typewriter, for example, use ordinary paper.

Input-Output Files

Suppose you have a file on disk or magnetic tape and you want to update it. You can read the file into the computer memory, update the contents, and write the result back on the storage area. To accomplish this task, you need an input-output file on disk. The input-output option for disk files is operational only if the file was created in a previous program. Note that there are no output-input files in standard COBOL (although the Burroughs 1700 does allow such files as an addition to COBOL).

File Organization

Files are classified according to their organizations, that is, their construction techniques. In general, files can be organized in the following ways:

1. sequential,
2. direct (random),
3. indexed sequential, and
4. relative.

ANSI COBOL (American National Standard Cobol) currently provides for only sequential and direct files. However, indexed sequential and relative files are permitted by many COBOL compilers as an extension to ANSI COBOL. Since there are no standards for the use of indexed sequential and relative files, we will not mention them further in this text.

File Accessing

File accessing means retrieving the information from previously created files. The accessing technique for a particular file is dependent on the organization method that was used to construct the file. The two techniques for retrieving information from a file are

1. sequential access and
2. random (direct) access.

Figure 4.1 Attributes of COBOL files.

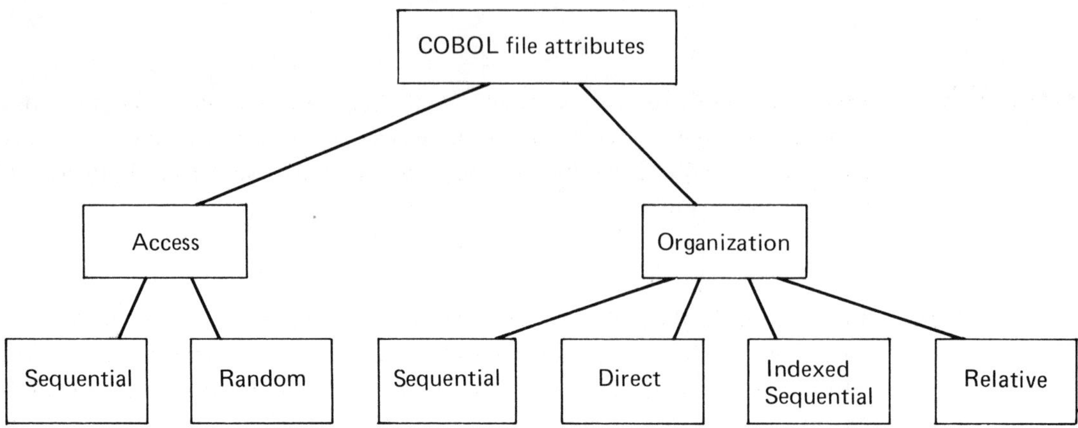

All files can be accessed sequentially, but a sequentially organized file cannot be accessed randomly (directly). Files organized directly, indexed sequentially, or relatively can be accessed randomly or sequentially. Figure 4.1 shows the attributes of COBOL files.

Sequential-access Files

The organization of a file is determined by the correspondence between the logical order of the records in the file and their physical order. A sequentially organized file is a file in which the logical order of the records in the file and their physical order are identical. Specifically, record number 1 of a sequential file is the first physical record of the file; record number 2 of the file is the second physical record of the file; record number 3 is the third physical record of the file; and so on. This concept is clear when we realize that the files on some input-output devices, such as a disk, do not have to be sequentially organized, that is, there need be no correspondence between the logical order of the records in the file and their physical order. In such files, the record we consider to be the fourth record of the file might not be the fourth physical record of the file, or the record we consider to be the last record of the file might not be the last physical record in the file.

Sequentially organized files are also characterized by the fact that the only permissible access method is sequential access. When using sequential access, you cannot specify the order in which records are processed. Under sequential access, the computer specifies the order of processing. When using sequential access, the computer will process the records in their physical order from first through last. Thus when using sequential processing, the computer will not process a record of the file until it has processed all its physical predecessors in the file.

Since the records in a card file can be processed only in their physical order, we must use sequential access for card files and therefore assume that the file is also sequentially organized. The same reasoning shows that files on a card puncher, line printer, paper tape device, or magnetic tape device should be sequentially organized. COBOL requires such files to be sequentially organized and assumes them to be so organized. Any attempt to give a different organization will be considered an error.

Direct (Random-access) Files

On many computer systems a file with direct organization is constructed differently from a file with sequential organization. The precise differences are not important to our work; what is important is that we realize that the principal difference permits us to process a direct file with either sequential access or random access. If sequential access is used to process a direct file, then the processing occurs exactly as that for a sequentially organized file. Thus the only new item of interest in our discussion is random processing of a direct file.

Random-access method   A direct file always has a key. This key is a data item whose values represent the location of records in the file. The computers we discuss in this text use keys whose values are always numbers. The value of the key specifies the record number we desire. To gain access to a particular record in a direct file, say the seventh record, you must set the key equal to 7 and request an input or output operation. The computer will then read or write the record specified in the key—in this case, the seventh record. To read the third record in the file, you must set the key equal to 3 and give a READ command for the file.

Direct files can be useful because random access for a direct file allows us to process the file in any order we want. For example, suppose we are responsible for maintaining the inventory of a bookstore. The bookstore has 500 books, each one of which has been assigned an inventory number that is an integer from 1 through 500. Each month we must update our inventory file for the bookstore. To do this, we maintain a card file; each card has the catalog number of a book, the number of copies of the book in stock, and the number of new copies ordered this month. To store this information, we decide to create a direct file on disk whose key is named INVENTORY-NUMBER. Each time we read a card from the card file, we set INVENTORY-NUMBER equal to the catalog number of that record and instruct the computer to write that record onto our disk file. Where does the computer place this record in the file? It places the record in the position in the file whose record number is the same as the value of INVENTORY-NUMBER. Thus if we read a card on which the catalog number is 239 and set INVENTORY-NUMBER equal to 239 and instruct the computer to write the record onto the file, it will place the record in the 239th record position of the file. When we finish writing onto the file, our records will be in ascending order according to the catalog number. If we later desire to read the information in the file about the book whose catalog number is 117, we need only set INVENTORY-NUMBER equal to 117 and instruct the computer to read the file, and it will read the record whose key is 117. Consequently, with a direct file whose access is random, we can gain access to any record at any time. Contrast this with a sequential file. To gain access to the record in position 117 of a sequential file, we would have to process the preceding 116 records.

Advantages of Sequential and Direct Organization

Is it better to give a file sequential or direct organization? The answer to this question depends on the nature of the job to be done, the hardware and software, the environment in which the file will be created, and the goals of the computer installation doing the job. The following list includes factors to be considered in making this decision.

1. A sequential file is generally more compact than a direct file and should therefore require less storage area. Most direct files will have record positions that are empty and unused. The records of a sequential file always occupy the physical front of the file, and wasted space can be minimized. However, it is not easy to expand a sequential file; in fact, if the programmer wishes to add new records to a sequential file, an entirely new file must be created to hold the old file records and the new additions.

2. A direct file is advantageous when the file is not very active in the sense that most work with the file requires accessing only a few records in the file at any given time. This type of file is also preferable when the programmer has to locate records in the file quickly. A file containing records of airline reservations is a good example of a situation in which a direct file is needed. The airline has to locate only a small number of reservation records at any given time, and needs these records quickly in order to minimize inconvenience to customers.

On the other hand, if a file is very active in the sense that someone would need to examine most of the records in the file on a frequent basis, then sequential organization is often the better of the two alternatives. The time required to access all the records in a sequential file is generally less than the time to access the same records in a direct file. (However, remember that *one* record in a direct file can be located more quickly than the same record can be located in a sequential file.) A file such as a payroll file in which all the records must be updated every payday would probably be better organized sequentially.

We will explain how to construct these files and work with them in succeeding chapters.

Mass Storage Devices

Mass storage devices are hardware items, supplied by the manufacturer of the computer, that are capable of storing large quantities of data.

There are two types of *mass storage devices:* (1) sequential-access storage devices, such as magnetic tape units and paper tape units; and (2) direct-access storage devices, such as magnetic disks. The sequential-access devices can access records only in sequential order. Direct-access devices can access records in random order or sequential order.

A magnetic tape reel is a continuous strip of plastic wound around a reel. A typical tape might be 2,400 feet long and ½ inch wide, although other sizes are available. Information is recorded on the surface of the tape in the form of physical records called *blocks*. Each block is separated from the next one by a blank space on the tape known as an *inter-block gap* (IBG). The length of an IBG is usually six-tenths or seven-tenths of an inch. Different magnetic tapes have different block sizes. More than one record can be written in a block. Also a record may occupy more than one block if the record size is bigger than the block size. The number of records within a block is called the *blocking factor*. A file organized so that each of its blocks contains the largest possible number (integral) of records is called a *blocked file*. If the file is unblocked, each record is stored in a single block by itself. The blocked file requires less storage than the unblocked file. Besides saving space by using blocking, a program which processes a blocked file becomes more efficient (from the point of view of speed) than that which processes an unblocked file. The reason for this lies in the input-output operations: the whole block is transferred between peripheral devices (such as a magnetic tape and disk) and main memory. See figure 4.2.

A reel of tape can be used to store several separate files, in which case, the reel is called a *multifile volume*. When a file is too large to record on one reel of tape, a programmer may continue the file to one or more additional reels. The file would then be called a *multivolume* file.

The unit that reads the information from a tape reel or writes information on a tape reel is called a *tape drive*.

Organization and Identification of Files on Magnetic Tape

In order to provide identification and correct processing of a file on magnetic tape, each tape file contains *labels*. In figure 4.3 you can see the way these labels would appear if they were visible. The reel of tape is identified by a *volume label* which supplies information about the name of the tape reel and the tape files it contains. Each file on the tape is identified by a file *header label* which supplies information about the name of the file and its records. The physical end of the file is marked by a file *trailer label* which also contains the name of the file. If there is a second file on the reel, then it will contain similar header and trailer labels.

Disks

The primary mass storage device of the IBM-1130 is the *disk cartridge*. Figure 4.4 illustrates a disk for the IBM-1130. Each disk cartridge contains a disk capable of recording information magnetically. The cartridge is placed on a *disk drive* that rotates the cartridge rapidly. The disk drive has a *head*

Figure 4.2 Organization of a blocked magnetic tape.

block	IBG	block	IBG	block	IBG	block

(One record per block)

block	IBG	block	IBG

(Several records per block)

Figure 4.3 Organization and identification of files on a magnetic tape.

VL	HL1	File 1	TL1	HL2	File 2	TL2

Figure 4.4 A typical disk and the read/write mechanism of the disk.

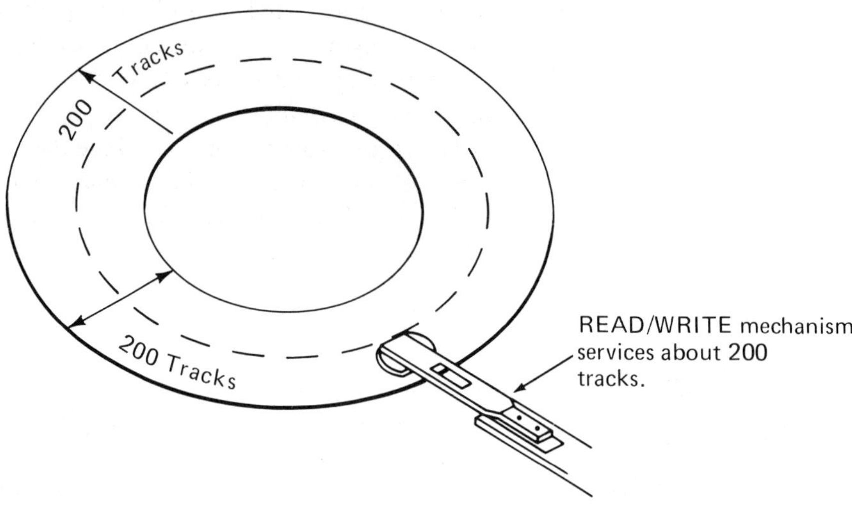

that moves to the appropriate position to read information from, or write information on, the disk. A disk drive is similar in concept to a phonograph except that information is stored magnetically.

Each disk has two sides. Each side of a disk has 200 concentric grooves or *tracks* on which data is stored. A track, together with its corresponding track on the opposite side of the disk, is known as a *cylinder*. Each track is divided into four *sectors,* and each sector can store 320 words of information—information that could include files and programs. Here is a summary of the physical features of the type of disk used on the IBM-1130.

> One *sector* is equivalent to 320 words.
> One *track* is equivalent to 4 sectors or 1,280 words.
> One *cylinder* is equivalent to 2 tracks or 2,560 words.
> One *disk* is equivalent to 200 cylinders or 512,000 words.

In addition, each sector contains one word not available for storage of data which is used by the computer to identify the sector.

Other computer models might require different models of disk units. The most common types used are similar to the IBM-2314 Direct-Access Storage Facility or the Burroughs B9372 Disk Drive.

The IBM-2314 Direct-Access Storage Facility can contain from one to nine independent disk drives. Each drive can hold one IBM-2316 *disk pack.* Here is a summary of the features of the IBM-2316 disk pack.

> One pack is equivalent to 11 disks or 20 recording surfaces. The top surface of the first disk and the bottom surface of the last disk are not used.
>
> One pack is equivalent to 200 cylinders.
>
> One cylinder is equivalent to 20 tracks.
>
> One track is equivalent to 7,294 bytes.

Thus one pack is equivalent to 29,176,000 bytes.

The Burroughs B9372 contains five disk drives. Each drive contains one nonremovable disk module. The Burroughs B9372 does not use the organizational concept of the cylinder. Here is a summary of the features of the B9372.

> One module is equivalent to 4 disks or 8 recording surfaces.
> One surface is equivalent to 12,500 segments.
> One segment is equivalent to 100 bytes.

Thus one module contains $8 \times 12{,}500 \times 100$ or 10 million bytes. Consequently, since a B9372 has 5 disk drives, it can contain 50 million bytes of information.

Summary

We discussed three types of files for COBOL—input, output, and input-output—and two types of organization—sequential and direct. Access to files can be sequential or random. A sequential file can be accessed only sequentially, but a direct file can be accessed sequentially or randomly. Files assigned to such devices as card readers, tape drives, paper tape readers, card-punching units, or line printer must have sequential organization and sequential access. Direct-access devices such as disk drives can be used for files with sequential *or* direct organization.

Review Questions

1. When files are classified by their function, the types of files are
   ______________, ______________, and ______________.

2. When files are classified by their mode of access, the types of files are
   ______________ and ______________.

3. When a file is on paper tape, its access mode should be ______________.

4. When a file is on cards, its access mode is ______________.

5. If a file is on disk and the file has *no* key, its access mode is
   ______________.

6. If a file is on disk and the file *has* a key, its access mode is
   ______________.

7. If a file is on magnetic tape, its access mode is ______________.

8. The number of computer words which can be stored on a disk on the IBM-1130 is ______.

9. If a file is to be stored on disk in the order in which it was read into the computer memory and then printed in that same order, then the natural choice for its access mode is ______________.

10. If the records in a file are to be ordered according to some associated number such as a catalog number, the natural choice for its access mode is ______________.

11. Which method do you think is generally faster: working with information in main memory or working with information on a disk?
    ____

12. How many computer words can be stored in a *sector* of a disk on the IBM-1130? ______

Suggested Projects

1. Prepare an input file of inventory records, using the following data, by punching the information for each item on a card.

Card column	Field	Type
1–5	unit number	number
6–26	unit name	character
27–29	unit price	number
30–34	number of units on hand	number
35–39	number of units requested	number
40–44	number of units on order	number
45–74	name of manufacturer	character

Figure 4.5 shows an example of a data card. Write a COBOL program to instruct the computer to read the card file and write the inventory file on the line printer.

2. Write a flowchart for project 1.

3. The multiplication instruction in COBOL is easy to use. (See Chapter 8 for thorough instruction.) If you have numeric data items named AMOUNT, RATE, and INTEREST, then writing MULTIPLY RATE BY AMOUNT GIVING INTEREST will cause the computer to multiply the value of RATE by the value of AMOUNT and store the result in the data item called INTEREST. The values of RATE and AMOUNT are left unchanged by this statement.

Write a COBOL program to instruct the computer to read a file of customer records. Each record is a card containing the following information.

Card column	Content
1–20	customer name
21–27	account number
28–35	balance in savings account
36–39	rate of interest
40–70	address of customer

The PICTURE for the balance should be 9(6)V99 and that for the rate, V9999. The PICTURE for the interest should allow for two decimal places (try 9(6).99). Your program should print the account number, name, balance, interest, and address.

4. Testing a condition in COBOL (see Chapter 9) is very easy. Suppose that you have data items named PAY, BALANCE, RATE, INTEREST, and UN-PAID-BALANCE. If you write

```
IF PAY IS LESS THAN BALANCE,
        SUBTRACT PAY FROM BALANCE GIVING UN-PAID-
        BALANCE
        MULTIPLY RATE BY UN-PAID-BALANCE GIVING
        INTEREST
        ADD INTEREST, UN-PAID-BALANCE GIVING
        BALANCE
ELSE NEXT SENTENCE.
```

the computer will determine whether or not PAY is less than UN-PAID-BALANCE. If this is the case, the computer will execute the three

Figure 4.5 Example of a data card.

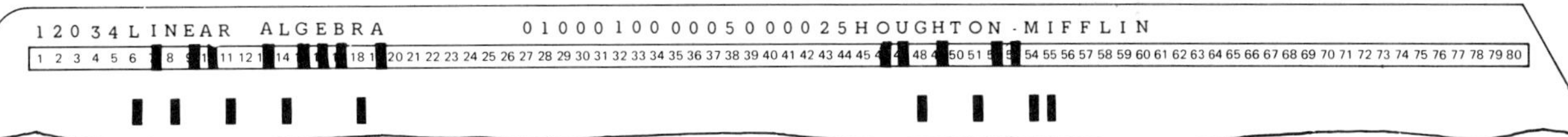

arithmetic statements following the IF statement. If PAY is not less than BALANCE, then the computer will not execute the three arithmetic statements and will simply go to the next sentence. Write a COBOL program to read a card file for accounts receivable of the Gigantic Super Discount Food Store and process these records. Each card contains

Card column	Content
1–7	account number
8–15	balance
16–23	payment
24–43	name
44–73	address

Calculate the interest due on the unpaid balance if the payment is less than the balance. Print out a listing containing the account number, name, new balance, interest, and address. You will need to make the amounts decimal items with two decimal places. See project 3 for suggestions about PICTURES for these items.

5. In project 1 of Chapter 1 you made a flowchart. Write a COBOL program to accomplish the tasks described in that project.

CHAPTER 5

ENVIRONMENT DIVISION

The COBOL language was devised to be *machine-independent*, which means that a COBOL program written to run on one computer can be run on another computer with only minor changes. Ideally, the changes are confined to the ENVIRONMENT DIVISION where the programmer describes the equipment to be used in running the program. This chapter explains the structure of the ENVIRONMENT DIVISION and gives examples of programs prepared for the IBM-1130. At the end of this text the appendices describe the information necessary for writing ENVIRON-MENT DIVISION entries on the Burroughs 1700, the IBM System 3, and the DECSYSTEM-10. If you are interested in writing programs for these computers, then read the appendices as you read the chapter.

Figure 5.1 Burroughs 1700 computer system.

On the left is a 96-column card data-recorder for card reading and punching. In the center is the central processor main memory and operator's console. The memory cycle time is from 2 million cycles per second up to 6 million cycles per second. The memory size can range from 24,000 to 262,000 bytes. The master control program supports virtual memory. The unit to the right is a disk cartridge drive. Each cartridge can hold 9.2 million bytes of information. On the far right is a Burroughs line printer that has a printing speed of 400 lines per minute.

(Photo courtesy of the Burroughs Corporation.)

Structure of the ENVIRONMENT DIVISION

The purposes of the ENVIRONMENT DIVISION are

1. to declare the types of computer equipment to be used in the program,
2. to assign files to the devices they utilize, and
3. to create special names that are used for certain input-output options and to exchange the roles of certain COBOL symbols, such as the comma and the period.

The general organization of the ENVIRONMENT DIVISION is

```
A    B
ENVIRONMENT DIVISION.
CONFIGURATION SECTION.
SOURCE-COMPUTER. computer-name.
OBJECT-COMPUTER. computer-name.
[SPECIAL-NAMES. special-names-entries.]
[INPUT-OUTPUT SECTION.
FILE-CONTROL.
[I-O-CONTROL.]]
```

The header of the ENVIRONMENT DIVISION is the following format. "A" indicates the beginning of area A, and "B" indicates the beginning of area B in our examples.

```
A
ENVIRONMENT DIVISION.
```

Note that the name of the division is followed by a blank, the reserved word DIVISION, and a period.

The ENVIRONMENT DIVISION has two sections:

```
A
CONFIGURATION SECTION.
INPUT-OUTPUT SECTION.
```

As with division headers, section headers begin in area A. The name of the section is followed by a blank, the reserved word SECTION, and a period.

CONFIGURATION SECTION

This section can contain three paragraphs:

```
A
SOURCE-COMPUTER. computer-name.
OBJECT-COMPUTER. computer-name.
SPECIAL-NAMES. special-names-entries.
```

The CONFIGURATION SECTION is optional on the IBM-1130, the IBM System 3, the DECSYSTEM-10 and the Burroughs 1700. If it is used, then the entry for the SOURCE-COMPUTER is

1. for the IBM 1130,

```
SOURCE-COMPUTER. IBM-1130.
```

2. For the IBM System 3,

```
    SOURCE-COMPUTER. IBM-S3.
```

3. For the DECSYSTEM-10,

```
    SOURCE-COMPUTER. DECSYSTEM-10.
```

4. For the Burroughs 1700,

```
    SOURCE-COMPUTER. B-1700.
```

The entry for OBJECT-COMPUTER is similar. Some additional clauses are permitted, but they are never required. The entries for the IBM-1130, IBM-S3, DECSYSTEM-10, and Burroughs 1700 are, respectively,

```
    OBJECT-COMPUTER. IBM-1130.
    OBJECT-COMPUTER. IBM-S3.
    OBJECT-COMPUTER. DECSYSTEM-10.
    OBJECT-COMPUTER. B-1700.
```

The SPECIAL-NAMES paragraph is optional in any COBOL program. This paragraph is used to assign mnemonic names (a name given to an item to help a person recall it easily and understand it), to hardware functions and devices and to allow the user to interchange the role of the decimal point and the comma in printing numeric values.

On the IBM-1130, IBM-S3, and the DECSYSTEM-10, the programmer can use this paragraph to assign names to console switches and to their ON and OFF status. On the IBM-1130, there are 16 console switches that are numbered from 01 through 15. The switches are named SW01, SW02, . . . , SW15. On the IBM-S3 there are 7 switches that are named UPSI-0, UPSI-1, . . . , UPSI-7. On the DECSYSTEM-10 there are 36 switches that are named SWITCH (0), SWITCH (1), . . . , SWITCH (35). There are no switches available on the Burroughs 1700.

On the IBM-1130, IBM-S3, and the DECSYSTEM-10, a programmer can assign a mnemonic name to any of the available switches by writing a clause of the form:

```
    switch-name IS mnemonic-name
```

The mnemonic name must be a programmer-supplied word. The programmer can also assign a name to the ON status of a switch or the OFF status of a switch by writing a clause in either of these two forms:

```
    1. switch-name ON STATUS IS mnemonic-name
    2. switch-name OFF STATUS IS mnemonic-name.
```

On the IBM-1130, IBM-S3, and DECSYSTEM-10, mnemonic names can be assigned to line printer channels. These channels are associated with physical positions on a printed page. On the IBM-1130, the channels are numbered from 01 through 12 and are named C01, C02, . . . , C12. On the IBM-S3, the only channel is C01. On the DECSYSTEM-10, the channels are named CHANNEL (1), CHANNEL (2), . . . , CHANNEL (8). On all three computers, channel number 1 is associated with the top line of a page on the line printer.

Figure 5.2 shows several ways of making SPECIAL-NAMES entries for channel 1 for the IBM-1130. In example 2 in figure 5.2 we see the SPECIAL-NAMES paragraph:

Figure 5.2 Examples of the CONFIGURATION SECTION

(a)

```
A    B
CONFIGURATION SECTION.
SOURCE-COMPUTER. IBM-1130.
OBJECT-COMPUTER. IBM-1130.
```

(b)

```
A    B
CONFIGURATION SECTION.
SOURCE-COMPUTER. IBM-1130.
OBJECT-COMPUTER. IBM-1130.
SPECIAL-NAMES.
     C01 IS TO-NEW-PAGE.
```

(c)

```
A    B
CONFIGURATION SECTION.
SOURCE-COMPUTER. IBM-1130.
OBJECT-COMPUTER. IBM-1130.
SPECIAL-NAMES.
     C01 IS TO-NEW-PAGE,
     CSP IS WITHOUT-SPACING, CURRENCY SIGN IS "L",
     DECIMAL-POINT IS COMMA,
     SW15 ON STATUS IS INITIALIZE-FILE.
```

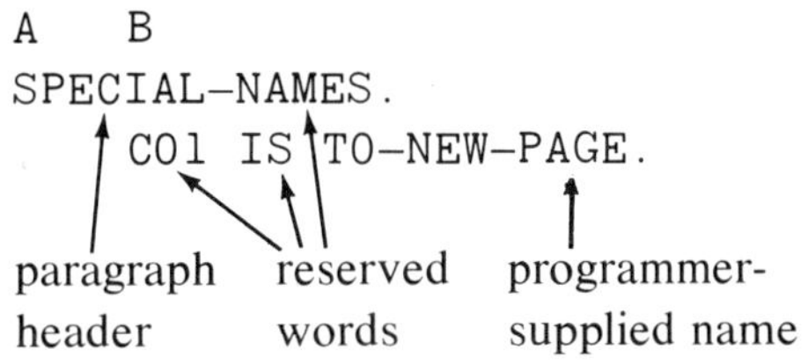

```
A    B
SPECIAL-NAMES.
     C01 IS TO-NEW-PAGE.

paragraph    reserved    programmer-
header       words       supplied name
```

In this case the programmer-supplied name TO-NEW-PAGE assumes the function of channel 1.

The statement

```
A  B
     WRITE PRINT-RECORD AFTER ADVANCING TO-NEW-PAGE.
```

will cause the computer to advance the paper on the line printer to the top of a new page and to print the content of PRINT-RECORD. Note that whereas WRITE, AFTER, and ADVANCING are reserved words, the choice of TO-NEW-PAGE was arbitrary. We could have chosen any unreserved word such as BOARDWALK for the name of C01, and then our statement would have read

```
A  B
     WRITE PRINT-RECORD AFTER ADVANCING BOARDWALK.
```

The choice of names is yours to make, but choosing data names and special names so that they indicate their role in the program is good *documentation*.

On the IBM-1130 and the IBM-S3, the programmer can also assign a mnemonic name to CSP, a device that suppresses vertical spacing on the line printer.

On the IBM-1130, the IBM-S3, and the B1700, the programmer can assign mnemonic names to various hardware devices. On the IBM-1130 and the IBM-S3, a special name can be assigned to the CONSOLE, which is the console typewriter on these computers. On the B1700, special names can be assigned to a wide variety of hardware devices. For example, the SPO is the name of the console typewriter on the B1700.

Here are some examples of CONFIGURATION SECTIONs on the B1700, the IBM-S3, and the DECSYSTEM-10, respectively,

(1)

```
CONFIGURATION SECTION.
SOURCE-COMPUTER. B-1700.
OBJECT-COMPUTER. B-1700.
SPECIAL-NAMES. SPO IS CONSOLE.
```

(2)

```
CONFIGURATION SECTION.
SOURCE-COMPUTER. IBM-S3.
OBJECT-COMPUTER. IBM-S3.
SPECIAL-NAMES. C01 IS TO-TOP, UPSI-7 IS FILE-
          STATUS, OFF STATUS IS UPDATE-FILE.
```

(3)

```
CONFIGURATION SECTION.
SOURCE-COMPUTER. DECSYSTEM-10.
OBJECT-COMPUTER. DECSYSTEM-10.
SPECIAL-NAMES. CHANNEL (1) IS TO-TOP, SWITCH (3) IS
          FILE-STATUS, ON STATUS IS INITIALIZE-FILE.
```

On the Burroughs 1700, IBM-1130, IBM System 3, or the DEC-SYSTEM-10, the following two optional clauses can be used:

```
1. CURRENCY SIGN IS literal
2. DECIMAL-POINT IS COMMA
```

The first clause allows the programmer to replace the currency symbol "$" by a nonnumeric literal such as "L". The second clause exchanges the roles of the decimal point and the comma in printing numbers. This option allows the printing of numbers as it is done in the British system of decimal notation.

INPUT-OUTPUT SECTION

The second section in the ENVIRONMENT DIVISION is the INPUT-OUTPUT SECTION. It is optional in a COBOL program and is used when the program uses files. It can have two paragraphs:

```
A    B
INPUT-OUTPUT SECTION.
FILE-CONTROL.
 ⋮
I-O-CONTROL.
 ⋮
```

Whenever the INPUT-OUTPUT SECTION is used, the FILE-CONTROL paragraph is required; but the I-O-CONTROL paragraph is optional.

FILE-CONTROL Paragraph

```
The general format of the FILE-CONTROL paragraph is
FILE-CONTROL.
```

$$\underline{\text{SELECT}} \text{ file-name } \underline{\text{ASSIGN}} \text{ TO system-name-1}$$
$$[\text{,system-name-2}] \ \ . \ \ . \ \ .$$

$$\left[\underline{\text{ACCESS}} \text{ MODE } \underline{\text{IS}} \ \left\{ \begin{array}{l} \underline{\text{SEQUENTIAL}} \\ \underline{\text{RANDOM}} \end{array} \right\} \right]$$

$$[\underline{\text{ACTUAL}} \text{ KEY } \underline{\text{IS}} \text{ data-name}]$$

$$\left[\underline{\text{RESERVE}} \ \left\{ \begin{array}{l} \underline{\text{NO}} \\ \text{integer} \end{array} \right\} \text{ ALTERNATE } \left[\begin{array}{l} \text{AREA} \\ \text{AREAS} \end{array} \right] \right]$$

$$\left[\left\{ \begin{array}{l} \underline{\text{FILE-LIMIT}} \text{ IS} \\ \underline{\text{FILE-LIMITS}} \text{ ARE} \end{array} \right\} \text{ integer-1 } \underline{\text{THRU}} \text{ integer-2} \right]$$

$$[\underline{\text{PROCESSING}} \text{ MODE } \underline{\text{IS}} \ \underline{\text{SEQUENTIAL}}]$$

Any file used in a COBOL program must be named and assigned to an appropriate physical input-output device. This is accomplished by use of the SELECT and ASSIGN clauses. The SELECT clause specifies the name of the file, and the ASSIGN clause specifies the physical device to which the file is assigned. These clauses are of the form

```
A    B
SELECT file-name, ASSIGN TO system-name
```

Every SELECT clause must be followed by an ASSIGN clause. The general *format* (form) of the SELECT clause is

```
SELECT file-name
```

where file-name is a programmer-supplied name for a file.

The format for the ASSIGN clause is very complicated and varies from one computer to another. The ASSIGN clause written in the following way is sufficient for most situations confronted by a programmer:

$$\underline{\text{ASSIGN}} \text{ TO system-name-1 [system-name-2] } \ . \ \ . \ \ .$$
$$\left[\text{FOR } \underline{\text{MULTIPLE}} \ \left\{ \begin{array}{l} \underline{\text{REEL}} \\ \underline{\text{UNIT}} \end{array} \right\} \right]$$

where each system name is a reserved word for an appropriate physical device. These system names are different for each type of computer. The system names for the DECSYSTEM-10, the B1700, and the IBM-S3 are discussed in the appendices. On an IBM-1130 only one system name is allowed for card and print files, but up to five system names can be used for disk files.

System names for disk files refer to physical storage areas on disk cartridges (or disk packs on some computers). It is possible to divide a file into two or more separate physical parts. If we list the names of these separate physical parts in the ASSIGN clause, our programs can treat two parts as though they were one disk file. Each part of a disk file on the IBM-1130 can contain no more than 32,767 records. A direct disk file can contain no more than a total of 65,535 records.

A special problem occurs in the following situation: Suppose that the physical parts of our file (on the IBM-1130 these parts are called *extents*) are located on several disk cartridges. Further, suppose that the number of disk drives available at our installation is less than the number of disk cartridges occupied by our file. In this case, we could not process the file in our installation if it were a direct file; but if it were a sequential file, then we could use the MULTIPLE UNIT clause to process it. When we process the records of a sequential file, we access them in their natural physical order. When our program processes the sequential file and reaches the end of the records available on the disk cartridges that are mounted on the disk drives, the computer will automatically ask the operator to remove one of the cartridges and replace it with the next cartridge of our sequential file. This occurs automatically only if we have specified the MULTIPLE UNIT clause and only if the file is too large for the number of available disk drives. You will probably not need to use this clause while you are learning to program.

The MULTIPLE REEL option is used for magnetic tape files that require more tape drives than are available. The effect of the clause is similar to that of the MULTIPLE UNIT option for disk files. Since tape files are not available on the IBM-1130, the MULTIPLE REEL option is not given on that computer.

System names for physical input-output devices vary from one computer system to the next. Here is a list of system names for the nondisk devices on the IBM-1130.

PR-1403	for the IBM-1403 line printer, used with optional control of vertical spacing (we will use this device in all examples in this text)
PR-1403-C	for the IBM-1403 line printer, used with required control of vertical spacing (if this option is used, the first character of each line to be printed is used by the computer to control vertical spacing and will not be printed; thus, if this option is used, the lines to be printed should be one character longer than the length on the printed page)
PR-1132	for the IBM-1132 line printer, used with optional control of vertical spacing
PR-1132-C	for the IBM-1132 line printer, used with required control of vertical spacing (see the remarks on the PR-1403-C)
RD-1442	for the IBM-1442-6/7 card reader and puncher, used as an input device only

PU-1442   for the IBM-1442-6/7 card reader and puncher, used as an output device only

PR-1442   for the IBM-1442-6/7, used for both an input and output device

PO-1442   for the IBM-1442 card puncher, used as an output device

RD-2501   for the IBM-2501 card reader, used as an input device

The list of system names for the IBM-S3, B1700, and DECSYSTEM-10 is as long as that for the IBM-1130. The appendices contain lists of all the possible system names for these devices. The names of the input-output devices for nondisk files follow.

1. For the B1700, the system name for input card files is READER and for line printer files (output), PRINTER.
2. For the IBM-S3, the system name for input card files is UR-1442-RD for the IBM-1442 used for input, and UR-5424P-RD for the 5424 MFCU used for input. For line printer files the system name is UR-1403-2-66 for the 1403 line printer with 120 columns per line and 66 lines per page, and UR-5203-2-100 for the 5203 line printer with 120 columns per line and 100 lines per page.
3. For the DECSYSTEM-10, CDR for input card files and LPT for line printer files.

On the IBM-1130, the form of the system name for a disk file is DF-filenumber-numberofrecords [-X] where filenumber is a positive integer in the range of 1 through 32,767, which is chosen by the programmer; and numberofrecords is the number of records to be allocated to this file and is also an integer in the range of 1 through 32,767. If the optional characters -X are used, this file will have an additional disk buffer. (A buffer is a space of main storage into which data is read or from which it is written. Usually the size of the buffer is equal to the size of one block. Data are transferred between peripheral devices, such as a disk, and the main storage on a block-by-block basis. A COBOL program reads or writes record-by-record from or into this block, or buffer, in the main storage.) This option should be used unless the computer does not have sufficient main memory for an additional buffer. This option will help to decrease the execution time of a program using disk files.

On the B1700, the form of the system name for disk files is DISK.

On the IBM-S3 the system name for disk files is complicated. The form is class-device-organization-name [-U]. The class must be UT or DA, and for our purposes we may as well use DA. The device must be 5444 or 5445. The organization must be S for sequential, R for direct, and I for indexed. The name is the external name of the disk file and is not necessarily the same as the name following the word SELECT in the file description. The name must be from one through eight characters in length. The characters -U are optional and are used precisely when the file is to be opened I-O in the program (to be discussed later).

On the DECSYSTEM-10, the system name for disk files is DSK.

Tape files are not permitted on the IBM-1130. On the B1700, the system name for tape files is TAPE. On the IBM-S3, the system name for tape files is complicated. For our purposes, the name will be UT-3400-name. The name is the external name of the file and is not necessarily the same as the name assigned to the file after the word SELECT. On the DECSYSTEM-10, the system name for tape files is MTA.

ACCESS MODE Clause

As you have seen, we can have only two basic modes of access to files, sequential and random. The format of the ACCESS MODE clause is

$$\underline{\text{ACCESS}} \text{ MODE } \underline{\text{IS}} \left\{ \begin{array}{l} \underline{\text{SEQUENTIAL}} \\ \underline{\text{RANDOM}} \end{array} \right\}$$

On the DECSYSTEM-10 the programmer can also make INDEXED the access of mass storage files. If you omit the ACCESS MODE clause, the computer will assume that the access is sequential. Random access will be used only for disk files in this text because random access cannot be specified for card files, tape files, or line printer files.

If random access is specified for a disk file, then you must specify an ACTUAL KEY clause for the file. The form of the clause is

$$\underline{\text{ACTUAL}} \text{ KEY } \underline{\text{IS}} \text{ data}-\text{name}$$

where data-name is the programmer-supplied name for the key. The presence of this clause always indicates that the organization of a file is direct. If the organization of the file is direct but the access is sequential, then this clause may be omitted.

RESERVE Clause

Recall that special buffers may be assigned for disk files on the IBM-1130 to increase the efficiency of the program. The RESERVE clause is an optional clause that can be used to assign additional buffers to files.

On the IBM-1130, the RESERVE clause cannot be used for disk files since the inclusion of the -X option already provided a method of assigning an additional buffer. The RESERVE clause can be used to provide one additional buffer for a card file or a line printer file.

On the IBM-S3, one additional buffer can be assigned for sequential disk and tape files by using the RESERVE clause.

On the B1700, the RESERVE clause can be used to assign additional buffers to any file. The number of additional buffers that can be assigned is limited only by the available main storage.

On the DECSYSTEM-10, the RESERVE clause can be used to assign additional buffers to any file. The number of additional buffers is limited only by the available main storage. If the clause is specified for a file whose access is random, it will be ignored.

The format of the RESERVE clause is

$$\underline{\text{RESERVE}} \left\{ \begin{array}{l} \text{integer} \\ \underline{\text{NO}} \end{array} \right\} \text{ ALTERNATE } \left\{ \begin{array}{l} \text{AREA} \\ \text{AREAS} \end{array} \right\}$$

where integer specifies the number of additional buffers to be assigned to the file.

FILE-LIMIT Clause

The format of the FILE-LIMIT clause is

$$\left\{ \begin{array}{l} \underline{\text{FILE-LIMIT}}\ \underline{\text{IS}} \\ \underline{\text{FILE-LIMITS}}\ \underline{\text{ARE}} \end{array} \right\} \text{integer-1}\ \underline{\text{THRU}}\ \text{integer-2}$$

where integer-1 specifies the location of the first record of the file, and integer-2 specifies the location of the last record of the file. This clause is optional on the IBM-1130, IBM-S3, and DECSYSTEM-10. On the DECSYSTEM-10 the clause is required for files with random access. It is used to calculate the number of records in the file. For instance, if integer-1 is 1 and integer-2 is 60, the DECSYSTEM-10 would determine that this file will have room for 60 records. On the DECSYSTEM-10 the programmer can also write the FILE-LIMIT clause in the form

```
FILE-LIMIT IS integer-1
```

PROCESSING MODE Clause

The PROCESSING MODE clause is optional and used only to provide information. It does not affect the program. Its format is

```
PROCESSING MODE IS SEQUENTIAL
```

I-O-CONTROL Paragraph

The I-O-CONTROL paragraph and all its clauses are optional. All our preceding examples have omitted this paragraph because you will probably not have much use for it while learning COBOL.

The first clause of this paragraph has the format

```
A    B
     RERUN ON system-name
     EVERY integer RECORDS OF file-name
```

The system name must have the form DF-integer where integer is between 1 and 32,767 on the IBM-1130. This must be the number of a previously created disk file. File-name can be the name of any file.

Every time integer number of records of file-name are processed, all content of the computer memory pertaining to the program is recorded in the disk file, system-name. Each time the status of the program is stored on system-name, the previous contents are destroyed. However, should the execution of a program be terminated because of an error, system-name will contain a record of the status of the program. You can correct the program error and start the execution of the program from the point where the status check was taken. See the references listed after the appendices for more information on how this clause works in the IBM-1130, IBM-S3, DECSYSTEM-10, and the B1700 systems.

The second clause of the I-O-CONTROL paragraph has the format

```
SAME AREA FOR file-name-1, file-name-2, . . .
```

The purpose of this clause is to minimize the storage area required for files. To be specific, if several files are to be used in a program and *no two will be open at the same time,* then it will save on storage space if they are used in this clause. The clause specifies that the files will use the same main storage area during processing.

Although there may be several SAME AREA clauses in a program, no file may appear in more than one.

Examples of File Manipulation in the ENVIRONMENT DIVISION

In the examples that follow, keep in mind that creating and working with files require the following steps.

1. In the FILE-CONTROL paragraph of the ENVIRONMENT DIVI-SION, a name must be selected for the file, and it must be assigned to an appropriate input-output device. If the file is not sequentially organized, then an ACTUAL KEY clause *must* be present. If the access is not sequential, the ACCESS IS RANDOM clause *must* be present.
2. In the DATA DIVISION there must be an FD entry describing the records in the file. If the file has a KEY, there must be a description of the KEY in the WORKING-STORAGE SECION of the DATA DIVI-SION.
3. In the PROCEDURE DIVISION the file must be opened before it can be used. This is accomplished by a statement of the form

$$\text{OPEN} \begin{Bmatrix} \underline{\text{INPUT}} \\ \underline{\text{OUTPUT}} \\ \underline{\text{I-O}} \end{Bmatrix} \text{file-name-1, file-name-2, . . .}$$

The abbreviation I-O is used for input-output.

Before the program stops, all files must be closed by using a statement of the form

```
CLOSE file-name-1, file-name-2, . . .
```

Example 5.1   Suppose we have a student file in the form of a deck of punched cards. We wish to write a program to instruct the computer to read the file. We will then punch the information on a new card file.

Figure 5.3 shows the form of a program to accomplish these tasks on an IBM-1130. Figure 5.4 shows the changes in the program to accomplish these tasks on the DECSYSTEM-10, the B1700, and the IBM-S3. The program assumes that the computer installation has a 2501 card reader and a 1442-5 card puncher. If the installation had a 1442-6/7 card reader and puncher, the

Figure 5.3 Outline of program for example 5.1 for the IBM-1130.

```
A    B
IDENTIFICATION DIVISION.
PROGRAM-ID. SAMPLE-2.
ENVIRONMENT DIVISION.
CONFIGURATION SECTION.
SOURCE-COMPUTER. IBM-1130.
OBJECT-COMPUTER. IBM-1130.
INPUT-OUTPUT SECTION.
FILE-CONTROL.
    SELECT STUDENT-FILE-IN, ASSIGN
    TO RD-2501.
    SELECT STUDENT-PRINT-LIST ASSIGN TO
    PO-1442.
DATA DIVISION.
FILE SECTION.
FD   STUDENT-FILE-IN,
  :
FD   STUDENT-PRINT-LIST,
  :
PROCEDURE DIVISION.
BEGIN.
    OPEN INPUT STUDENT-FILE-IN, OUTPUT STUDENT-PRINT-LIST.
    :
    CLOSE STUDENT-FILE-IN, STUDENT-PRINT-LIST.
      STOP RUN.
```


Figure 5.4 Outlines of the forms of the program for example 5.1 for the DECSYSTEM-10, the B1700, and the IBM-S3.

a. For the DECSYSTEM-10:

```
CONFIGURATION SECTION.
SOURCE-COMPUTER. DECSYSTEM-10.
OBJECT-COMPUTER. DECSYSTEM-10.
INPUT-OUTPUT SECTION.
FILE-CONTROL.
    SELECT STUDENT-FILE-IN, ASSIGN TO CDR.
    SELECT STUDENT-PRINT-LIST, ASSIGN TO CDP.
```

b. For the B1700:

```
CONFIGURATION SECTION.
SOURCE-COMPUTER. B-1700.
OBJECT-COMPUTER. B-1700.
INPUT-OUTPUT SECTION.
FILE-CONTROL.
    SELECT STUDENT-FILE-IN, ASSIGN TO READER.
    SELECT STUDENT-PRINT-LIST, ASSIGN TO PUNCH.
```

Figure 5.4 (Cont'd.)

c. For the IBM-S3:

```
CONFIGURATION SECTION.
SOURCE-COMPUTER. IBM-S3.
OBJECT-COMPUTER. IBM-S3.
INPUT-OUTPUT SECTION.
FILE-CONTROL.
     SELECT STUDENT-FILE-IN, ASSIGN TO UR-2501-RD.
     SELECT STUDENT-PRINT-LIST, ASSIGN TO UR-1442-PU.
```

same program would work provided we changed both ASSIGN clauses to read

```
ASSIGN to RP-1442
```

Note that since no ACCESS MODE clauses are included, the computer will assume that the mode is sequential. This is convenient, since card files can have only sequential access anyway.

Example 5.2   Assume the same situation as in example 5.1, but instead of writing the output file on cards, write it on the line printer.

Assuming that we wish to use the 1403 line printer without carriage control, we have to change only the second ASSIGN clause in figure 5.3 to

```
ASSIGN TO PR-1403
```

Example 5.3   Suppose a school has 500 students. Write an ENVIRONMENT DIVISION to create the following three files:

1. an input card file to be named CARDFILE,
2. an output line printer file to be named PRINT-FILE, and
3. an output disk file to be named DISK-FILE.

Figure 5.5 shows a possible program outline for the IBM-1130. Note that the installation has a 2501 card reader and a 1403 line printer. What is the ACCESS mode for these files? Figure 5.6 shows the changes necessary for running this program on the DECSYSTEM-10, B1700, and IBM-S3.

Example 5.4   Suppose that we have a bookstore with an inventory of 789 titles. Each title has a catalog number in the range of 1 through 789. We have a card file of inventory records. Each card has information on one title including its catalog number. We wish to read this file and store it on disk. The access to the disk file should be random because our card file will not be in any specific order.

Figure 5.5 Outline of program for the IBM-1130 for example 5.3.

```
A    B
IDENTIFICATION DIVISION.
PROGRAM-ID. SAMPLE-3.
ENVIRONMENT DIVISION.
CONFIGURATION SECTION.
SOURCE-COMPUTER. IBM-1130.
OBJECT-COMPUTER. IBM-1130.
INPUT-OUTPUT SECTION.
FILE-CONTROL.
     SELECT CARDFILE, ASSIGN TO RD-2501, ACCESS IS
     SEQUENTIAL,
     RESERVE 1 ALTERNATE AREA.
     SELECT PRINT-FILE ASSIGN TO PR-1403, RESERVE 1
     ALTERNATE AREA.
     SELECT DISK-FILE  ASSIGN TO DF-17-500-X  ACCESS IS
     SEQUENTIAL.
DATA DIVISION.
FILE SECTION.
FD   CARDFILE
        ⋮
FD   PRINT-FILE
        ⋮
FD   DISK-FILE
        ⋮
PROCEDURE DIVISION.
1ST.
     OPEN INPUT CARDFILE, OUTPUT DISK-FILE, PRINT-FILE.
        ⋮
     CLOSE CARDFILE, DISK-FILE, PRINT-FILE.
     STOP RUN.
```

Figure 5.7 shows the outline of a program to do this on the IBM-1130. (The monitor control card, *FILES, is necessary if our disk file is to be permanent.) Figure 5.8 shows the changes necessary for running this program on the DECSYSTEM-10, B1700, and IBM-S3.

Example 5.5   Figure 5.9 shows the outline of a program for the IBM-1130 with an unusual feature. The disk file, ACTIVE-FILE, which was created in a previous program as a direct file, is used in this program. Of course, we must use it as a direct file in this program since we cannot change the organization of a file. However, the access for this file is sequential in this program. This option was presumably used because we intend only to read or write the contents of the entire file in its natural order. We do not show the changes necessary for running on the DECSYSTEM-10, B1700, and IBM-S3 since the changes would be similar to those shown in figure 5.8 for example 5.4.

Figure 5.6 Outlines of the forms of the program for example 5.3 for the DECSYSTEM-10, the B1700, and the IBM-S3.

a. For the DECSYSTEM-10:

```
CONFIGURATION SECTION.
SOURCE-COMPUTER. DECSYSTEM-10.
OBJECT-COMPUTER. DECSYSTEM-10.
INPUT-OUTPUT SECTION.
FILE-CONTROL.
    SELECT CARDFILE, ASSIGN TO CDR, ACCESS IS SEQUENTIAL,
    RESERVE 1 ALTERNATE AREA.
    SELECT PRINT-FILE ASSIGN TO LPT.
    SELECT DISK-FILE ASSIGN TO DSK, ACCESS IS SEQUENTIAL,
    RESERVE 1 ALTERNATE AREA,
    FILE-LIMIT IS 1 THRU 500.
```

b. For the B1700:

```
CONFIGURATION SECTION.
SOURCE-COMPUTER. B-1700.
OBJECT-COMPUTER. B-1700.
INPUT-OUTPUT. SECTION.
FILE-CONTROL.
    SELECT CARDFILE, ASSIGN TO READER, ACCESS IS SEQUENTIAL,
    RESERVE 1 ALTERNATE AREA.
    SELECT PRINT-FILE ASSIGN TO PRINTER, RESERVE 1 ALTERNATE
    AREA.
    SELECT DISK-FILE. ASSIGN TO DISK, RESERVE 1 ALTERNATE
    AREA.
    ⋮
FD  DISK-FILE, FILE CONTAINS 500 RECORDS,
```

c. For the IBM-S3

```
CONFIGURATION SECTION.
SOURCE-COMPUTER. IBM-S3.
OBJECT-COMPUTER. IBM-S3.
INPUT-OUTPUT SECTION.
FILE-CONTROL.
    SELECT CARDFILE ASSIGN TO UR-2501-RD,
    RESERVE 1 ALTERNATE AREA.
    SELECT PRINT-FILE ASSIGN TO UR-1403-2-66.
    SELECT DISK-FILE  ASSIGN TO DA-5444-S-SCHOLFLE,
    RESERVE 1 ALTERNATE AREA, ACCESS IS SEQUENTIAL.
```

Figure 5.7 Outline of program for example 5.4 for the IBM-1130.

```
A    B
IDENTIFICATION DIVISION.
PROGRAM-ID. SMPL-3.
ENVIRONMENT DIVISION.
INPUT-OUTPUT SECTION.
FILE-CONTROL.
     SELECT CARDF ASSIGN TO RD-2501 RESERVE 1 ALTERNATE
          AREA.
     SELECT DISKF ASSIGN TO DF-18-789-X ACCESS IS RANDOM
          ACTUAL KEY IS LOCATER.
DATA DIVISION.
FILE SECTION.
FD   CARDF
     :
FD   DISKF
     :
WORKING-STORAGE SECTION.
77 LOCATER PICTURE S9(5) USAGE COMPUTATIONAL.
PROCEDURE DIVISION.
FIRSTPARAGRAPH.
     OPEN INPUT CARDF OUTPUT DISKF.
     :
     CLOSE CARDF, DISKF.
     STOP RUN.
     :
*FILES (18,DISKF)
```

Figure 5.8 Outlines of the forms of the program for example 5.4 for the DECSYSTEM-10, the B1700, and the IBM-S3.

a. For the DECSYSTEM-10:

```
CONFIGURATION SECTION.
SOURCE-COMPUTER. DECSYSTEM-10.
OBJECT-COMPUTER. DECSYSTEM-10.
INPUT-OUTPUT SECTION.
FILE-CONTROL.
     SELECT CARDFILE, ASSIGN TO CDR, RESERVE 1 ALTERNATE
          AREA.
     SELECT DISKF ASSIGN TO DSK, FILE-LIMITS ARE
          1 THRU 789,
          ACCESS IS RANDOM, ACTUAL KEY IS LOCATER.
```

Figure 5.8 (Cont'd.)

b. For the B1700:

```
CONFIGURATION SECTION.
SOURCE-COMPUTER. B-1700.
OBJECT-COMPUTER. B-1700.
INPUT-OUTPUT SECTION.
FILE-CONTROL.
    SELECT CARDFILE, ASSIGN TO READER, RESERVE 1
    ALTERNATE AREA.
    SELECT DISKF ASSIGN TO DISK, ACCESS IS RANDOM,
    ACTUAL KEY IS LOCATER.
  ⋮
FD  DISKF  FILE CONTAINS 789 RECORDS,
  ⋮
77 LOCATER  PICTURE 9(8) USAGE COMPUTATIONAL.
```

c. For the IBM-S3:

```
CONFIGURATION SECTION.
SOURCE-COMPUTER. IBM-S3.
OBJECT-COMPUTER. IBM-S3.
INPUT-OUTPUT SECTION.
FILE-CONTROL.
    SELECT CARDFILE, ASSIGN TO UR-2501-RD, RESERVE 1
        ALTERNATE AREA.
    SELECT DISKF ASSIGN TO DA-5444-R-BUKFLE, ACCESS
        IS RANDOM,
        ACTUAL KEY IS LOCATER.
  ⋮
77 LOCATER  PICTURE S9(7) USAGE COMPUTATIONAL.
```

Example 5.6.   The statement SELECT DISK-FILE ASSIGN TO DF-1-1000, DF-2-500, FOR MULTIPLE UNIT. together with the execution times FILES card *FILES (1,FILEA,4002),(2,FILEB,4001) specifies a multiple-unit sequential disk file of 1,500 records on the IBM-1130. Part of the file is on disk 4002 and the remainder is on disk 4001.

The use of this option requires special attention by the computer operator if the computer installation has only one disk drive. Consult appropriate manuals for the specific details for your computer.

Summary   In the CONFIGURATION SECTION of the ENVIRONMENT DIVISION, you must name the computer that compiles the program and the computer that will execute the program. In the FILE-CONTROL paragraph of the division, each file used in the program must be given a name and

Figure 5.9 Outline of program for example 5.5.

```
A   B
IDENTIFICATION DIVISION.
PROGRAM-ID. S4.
ENVIRONMENT DIVISION.
INPUT-OUTPUT SECTION.
FILE-CONTROL.
    SELECT ACTIVE-FILE ASSIGN TO DF-101-750 ACCESS
        IS SEQUENTIAL
        ACTUAL KEY IS FINDER.
DATA DIVISION.
FILE SECTION.
FD  ACTIVE-FILE
    :
WORKING-STORAGE SECTION
77 FINDER PICTURE S9(5) USAGE COMPUTATIONAL.
PROCEDURE DIVISION.
BEGIN.
    OPEN I-O ACTIVE-FILE.
    :
    CLOSE ACTIVE-FILE
    STOP RUN.
    :
*FILES (101,DISKF)
```

assigned to the device it will utilize. Each type of computer will have its own names for these input-output devices. The device names are reserved words on the particular type of computer for which they are used. At the same time that a file is named and assigned to a device, the ACCESS MODE for the file is specified; and if the access is random, an ACTUAL KEY is specified for the file. The I-O-CONTROL paragraph is used to specify the creation of checkpoint files to guard against unusual errors and to save on storage requirements for the record areas of files.

Review Questions

1. The sections of the ENVIRONMENT DIVISION are ________________ and ________________.
2. The paragraphs of the CONFIGURATION SECTION are ________________, ________________, and ________________.
3. The paragraphs of the INPUT-OUTPUT SECTION are ________________ and ________________.
4. Which paragraphs of the ENVIRONMENT DIVISION are optional?
5. The meanings of C01, C12, and CSP are ________________, ________________, and ________________.
6. Can a file that was created to be accessed randomly be accessed sequentially? ______

7. Can a file that was created to be accessed sequentially be accessed randomly? _______

8. An item is considered elementary if the name of the item is preceded by the level number 77 in the WORKING-STORAGE SECTION of the _____________ DIVISION.

9. The name following ACTUAL KEY in the FILE-CONTROL paragraph must be described as an elementary item with PICTURE S9(5) in the _____________ SECTION of the DATA DIVISION on an IBM-1130.

10. In COBOL for the IBM-1130, files may have _____________ or _____________ access.

11. In COBOL for the IBM-1130 files may have _____________ or _____________ organization.

12. Files are created in the FILE-CONTROL paragraph. How would the programmer determine the organization of a file from the FILE-CONTROL paragraph?

13. How can the programmer determine the access of a file from the information in the FILE-CONTROL paragraph?

14. What kind of access may a file have if it is assigned to RD-2501?

15. True or false: In a single program a file can be used for only one purpose, either input, output, or I-O. _______

16. In the WORKING-STORAGE SECTION, the description of a key always has the same picture. What is the picture? _______________

17. Clauses are used frequently in COBOL. They are used in the SPECIAL-NAMES paragraph and in the FILE-CONTROL paragraph, for example. Several clauses may be strung together to form a sentence. What type of punctuation is permitted between two clauses in the same sentence?

18. Write a FILE-CONTROL paragraph entry describing a disk file named HEADER-FILE that has direct organization, random access, and 10,000 records. It should also have its own unique disk buffer.

19. Write a FILE-CONTROL paragraph entry describing a card file named CARD-FILE assigned to a 1442 card reader and having an extra buffer.

Suggested Projects

1. In example 2.1 the access made for the files did not have to be specified. Since no access statement was given, the computer assumed the access was sequential. Rewrite the ENVIRONMENT DIVISION of example 2.1, and specify the access mode as sequential.

2. Add a SPECIAL-NAMES paragraph to the CONFIGURATION SECTION to the program for example 2.1. Provide mnemonic names for C01, C02, C03, C04, C05, C12, and CSP. Submit the new program to see if the COBOL compiler accepts your changes. Do not run the program.

3. Suppose you want to create an input card file named FILE-IN-1, an output file named FILE-PRINTOUT on the line printer, and an output disk file named FILE-DISKOUT. Write a complete IDENTIFICA-

TION DIVISION and a complete ENVIRONMENT DIVISION with all the paragraphs necessary to create these files. Choose appropriate system names.

4. Suppose that you wish to create a card file named FILE-IN-2 on the 2501 card reader as a sequential input file, a sequential output file named FILE-OUTPRINT on the 1403 line printer with carriage control, and a randomly organized output disk file named FILEOUTDISK that will have 900 records and a shared disk buffer. Write a complete IDENTIFI-CATION DIVISION and a complete ENVIRONMENT DIVISION to create these files.

5. Add a SPECIAL-NAMES paragraph to project 4. Exchange the roles of comma and period and assign a mnemonic name to C01.

6. Repeat project 3, but this time assume that FILE-DISKOUT is a pre-viously created file that will be used for both input and output.

CHAPTER 6

DATA DIVISION

The purpose of the DATA DIVISION is to provide a detailed description of all information processed by a COBOL program. In particular, the DATA DIVISION gives precise descriptions of the records of the files named in the ENVIRONMENT DIVISION and descriptions of other data items used during the execution of the program, which are described in the WORKING-STORAGE SECTION.

Data Items

Recall that a file is a collection of records. Each record comprises one or more items or fields. If an item includes two or more parts, it is a group item. If it does not have smaller parts, it is an elementary item. An item that is not a part of any larger structure is an independent item.

Data Names

In computer programs a *variable* is any data item whose value can change during the execution of a program. In COBOL the names of these data items, or variables, are called *data names*. A data name is a programmer-supplied word, containing at least one alphabetic character, that is used to identify a data item defined in the DATA DIVISION. The data names can be names of elementary or group items. Their values can be altered during the execution of a COBOL program through the use of a variety of COBOL statements.

In the PROCEDURE DIVISION qualified names must be used when the same name has been assigned for more than one item in the DATA DIVISION. The data name is qualified by the word OF or IN and the name of the data structure containing it. Suppose that both CARD-RECORD and PRINT-RECORD have the following structure in the DATA DIVISION.

```
DATA DIVISION.
    :
01   CARD-RECORD.
     02   CUSTOMER   PIC X(20).
     02   COMPANY   PIC X(30).
    :
01   PRINT-RECORD.
     02   CUSTOMER   PIC X(20).
     02   COMPANY   PIC X(30).
    :
```

Neither the name CUSTOMER nor the name COMPANY are unique because they are used as data names for the fields within both CARD-RECORD and PRINT-RECORD. Therefore, these names must be qualified when they are referenced in the PROCEDURE DIVISION. The statements

```
MOVE SPACES TO COMPANY IN CARD-RECORD,
MOVE SPACES TO CUSTOMER OF CARD-RECORD,
MOVE SPACES TO COMPANY OF PRINT-RECORD,
MOVE SPACES TO CUSTOMER IN PRINT-RECORD,
```

are valid; however, MOVE SPACES TO CUSTOMER is ambiguous because the computer cannot tell whether spaces should be moved to CUSTOMER of CARD-RECORD or to CUSTOMER of PRINT-RECORD. Thus every data name in a COBOL program must be either unique or qualified until it becomes unique.

A programmer can also qualify the names of paragraphs in the PROCEDURE DIVISION when the division is divided into sections. If the same paragraph name is used in two different sections, qualification of the paragraph name with the appropriate section name will identify the paragraph correctly for the COBOL compiler. However, if the name of the paragraph is not qualified, the COBOL compiler will assume automatically that the paragraph specified is the one in the section in which the reference is made to the paragraph.

Constants

In contrast to *data names* whose values can vary during the execution of a program, there are data items in COBOL whose values *cannot* be altered during the execution of a program. Thus these data items are *constants* in COBOL. Constants are never assigned data names; constants are also called *literals*. A literal is always a *nonvariable, elementary* item. There are three kinds of constants in COBOL.

1. A *nonnumeric literal* can be any string of characters from the character set for COBOL. The string of characters must be enclosed between quotation marks. However, on the IBM-1130, the IBM System 3, and the DECSYSTEM-10 the apostrophe is generally used in place of the quotation mark. *In our examples, we will use the apostrophe, ', instead of the quotation mark, ".* A nonnumeric literal cannot contain a quotation mark or an apostrophe within the string of characters and cannot contain more than 120 characters.

Example 6.1

Some examples of nonnumeric literals are

```
'B23K5'
'197.2'
'BOW-WOW'
'FAR OUT'
'DOLLAR'
'1A2BC. . .$( )-*M'
```

2. A *numeric literal* can be any string of COBOL characters that contains 1 through 18 numeric digits such that

a. It contains characters chosen only from 0, 1, 2, 3, 4, 5, 6, 7, 8, 9, +, ., and −.

b. + or − may be used only as the leftmost character of the string. (If the literal is unsigned, the + is assumed.)

c. No more than one decimal point may occur, and it is not the rightmost character of the string. (The literal is an integer when no decimal point is encountered.)

Thus a numeric literal is simply any number, signed or unsigned, with or without a decimal point, that includes from 1 to 18 digits.

Example 6.2   Some examples of numeric literals are:

```
       55
      835.052
      +59.1
          .01
      197.2
        0
       -1.1
```

Note that 197.2 is a numeric literal and ' 197.2' is a nonnumeric literal. Also in example 6.2, only the last entry is negative.

3. Figurative constants are reserved words that have predefined values recognized by the COBOL compiler. The following table summarizes the figurative constants and their usages.

Figurative Constants	*Use*
ZERO ZEROS ZEROES	Represent the value of 0 or one or more characters 0.
SPACE SPACES	Represent one or more spaces (blank).
HIGH-VALUE HIGH-VALUES	For numeric items, represents the largest value in the computer; for nonnumeric items, represents the highest value in the collating sequence.
LOW-VALUE LOW-VALUES	For numeric items, represents the smallest value in the computer; for nonnumeric items, represents the lowest value in the collating sequence.
QUOTE QUOTES	Represents one or more quotation marks.
ALL { figurative-constant literal }	Represents repetition of the string of characters. Comprises either a figurative constant or a literal.

Examples 6.3, 6.4, and 6.5 illustrate statements using data names and figurative constants.

Example 6.3

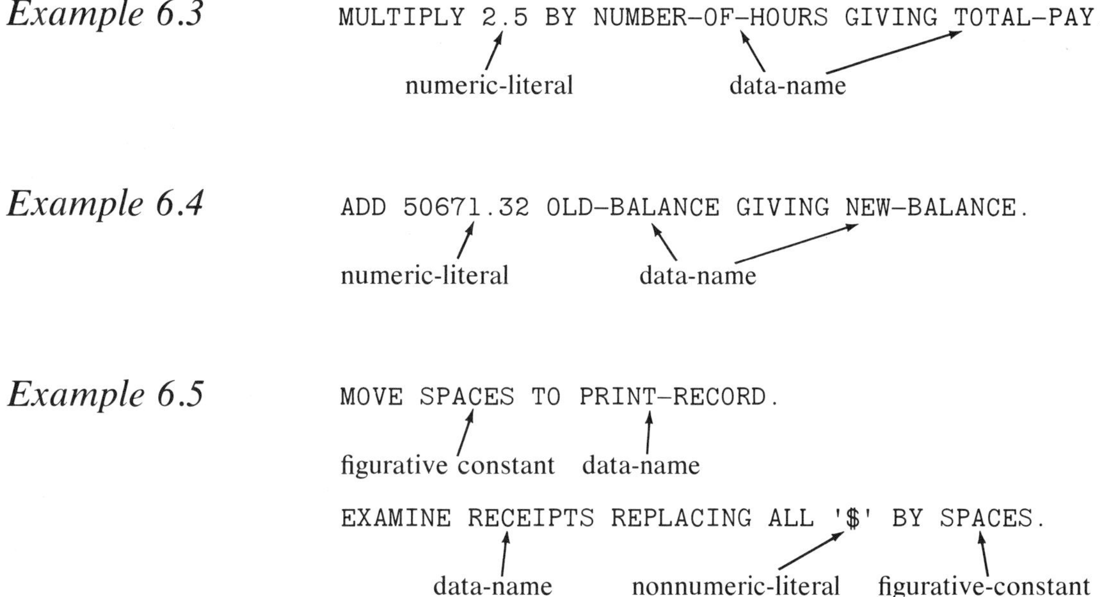

Example 6.4

Example 6.5

Structure of the DATA DIVISION

The DATA DIVISION has three sections on the IBM-1130. Each is optional and can be omitted. If the sections are used, they must appear in the following sequence:

```
FILE SECTION.
     ⋮
WORKING-STORAGE SECTION.
     ⋮
LINKAGE SECTION.
```

The general format of DATA DIVISION follows.

```
DATA DIVISION.
FILE SECTION.
FD      file name
        LABEL {RECORD IS   } {OMITTED }
              {RECORDS ARE }  {STANDARD}
        [BLOCK CONTAINS integer-1 {CHARACTERS}]
                                  {RECORDS   }
        [RECORD CONTAINS [integer-1 TO]
         integer-2 CHARACTERS]
        [DATA {RECORD IS   } data-name-1
              {RECORDS ARE }
        [, data-name-2] . . . . ]

        01-49 {data-name-1}
              {FILLER     }
```

```
                    [REDEFINES data-name-2]
                    [BLANK WHEN ZERO]
                    [[JUSTIFIED] RIGHT]
                     [JUST    ]
                    [[PIC     ] picture-string]
                     [PICTURE ]
                    [[SYNCHRONIZED] [LEFT ]]
                     [SYNC       ]  [RIGHT]
                                         (  [COMP         ]  )
                                         (  [COMPUTATIONAL]  )
                    USAGE IS             (  [COMP-n         ]  )
                                         (  [COMPUTATIONAL-n]  )
                                         (  DISPLAY          )
                                         (  INDEX            )
              88 condition-name  VALUE IS literal-1
              WORKING-STORAGE SECTION.
              77      data-name-1
                      VALUE IS literal
```

All clauses of the FILE SECTION starting from level number 01 through 49, up to and including level number 88, are allowed in this section.

LINKAGE SECTION.

The general format of this section is the same as WORKING-STORAGE SECTION; however, this section is used in subprograms only.

FILE SECTION

The first section is the FILE SECTION. In this section a file and record description entry must be made for each file selected in the ENVIRONMENT DIVISION.

Example 6.6

Suppose we want to process a card file of student records. Each record (a card) will contain a STUDENT-ID and a STUDENT-NAME. STUDENT-ID will contain a STUDENT-NUMBER and a SOCIAL-SECURITY-NUMBER. We shall name our file STUDENT-FILE, and the typical record in our file will be named STUDENT-INDEX.

The file and record description entries for example 6.6 could be as follows:

```
A    B
FILE SECTION.
FD STUDENT-FILE,
   LABEL RECORDS ARE OMITTED,
   DATA RECORD IS STUDENT-INDEX.
01 STUDENT-INDEX.
   06 STUDENT-ID.
      07 STUDENT-NUMBER  PICTURE 9(5).
      07 SOCIAL-SECURITY-NUMBER  PICTURE X(11).
   06 STUDENT-NAME  PICTURE X(30).
```

Note the following important characteristics of the file and record description entries for example 6.6.

1. A file description entry begins with FD located in area A. The name of the file follows FD and is located in area B. All the remaining clauses are located in area B. Only the LABEL RECORDS clause is required.

2. Following the file description entry is a record description entry. This entry is recognized easily because it always begins with level number 01 and immediately follows the FD entry. The record description entry has the level number in area A and the remainder of the entry is in area B. The rest of the entry begins with the record name. Our card record had two major items, indicated by the equal level numbers (06) assigned to both STUDENT-ID and STUDENT-NAME. The group item STUDENT-ID is divided into two parts that have equal level numbers (07) larger than the equal numbers (06) assigned to the two major items. Since elementary items are always those items with PICTUREs, we see that STUDENT-NUMBER, SOCIAL-SECURITY-NUMBER, and STUDENT-NAME are elementary items. Thus STUDENT-ID is a group item.

The file and record description entries for example 6.6 are typical entries in the FILE SECTION. The required LABEL RECORDS clause should be

```
LABEL RECORDS ARE STANDARD
```

for disk and tape files, and for all other files it should be

```
LABEL RECORDS ARE OMITTED
```

The DATA RECORDS clause is not required, but it can be used to document programs as shown in example 6.6.

Another clause may be included:

```
FILE CONTAINS integer RECORDS
```

This clause can be used to specify the number of records in a file. On the B1700, this clause *must* be used to specify the number of records in disk files; and on the IBM-1130, IBM-S3, and DECSYSTEM-10, it must *not* be used.

On the IBM-S3, a special clause must be used for files assigned to a line printer when you wish to control vertical spacing of the line printer file in your program. This clause cannot be used on the IBM-1130, B1700, or DECSYSTEM-10. Its format is

```
LINAGE IS integer-1 LINES
[WITH FOOTING AT integer-2]
```

The value of integer-1 specifies the number of lines that can be printed on one page. For standard forms this would normally be 66. The value of integer-2 specifies the beginning of the FOOTING AREA of the page. If the line printer spaces into this area (which extends from line integer-1 through line integer-2), then it is considered to be at the end of the area for printing. By using the END-OF-PAGE test, we can cause the printer to advance to the top of a new page when it reaches the FOOTING AREA.

The DATA RECORD clause is optional. Its format is

```
DATA {RECORD IS    } data-name-1 [data-name-2] . . .
     {RECORDS ARE  }
```

On the Burroughs 1700 and the DECSYSTEM-10, the programmer must occasionally use another clause in FD entries, the VALUE OF IDENTIFI-CATION clause. The format of this clause is

$$\underline{\text{VALUE}} \text{ OF } \underline{\text{IDENTIFICATION}} \text{ IS } \begin{Bmatrix} \text{literal} \\ \text{data-name} \end{Bmatrix}$$

On the B1700 and DECSYSTEM-10, IDENTIFICATION can be abbreviated to ID. Generally, the literal should be a nonnumeric literal of 10 characters or less. If the data name is used instead of the literal, then its value should be a nonnumeric literal of 10 characters or less. This clause is required with files whose LABEL RECORDS ARE STANDARD on the DECSYSTEM-10, and the literal should be exactly nine characters long. This clause is ignored for all other files on the DECSYSTEM-10. This clause is not required for files on the B1700; however, if it is *not* specified, the B1700 will use the first 10 characters of the name given the file in the COBOL program for its IDENTIFICATION.

On both the B1700 and the DECSYSTEM-10, the IDENTIFICATION is used to name the file externally. For example, on the B1700, several programs could be running at the same time, since this is a multiprogramming computer system. How does the computer know whether it is processing the correct files for a program? It knows which files to use for a program because of the file IDENTIFICATION. For example, if we need to read a card file whose IDENTIFICATION is STUDENTS, the computer will locate the card file to be read that has a card at the beginning of the deck with ?DATA STUDENTS.

Level Numbers

Level numbers are used to describe the organization of records and data items. There are three types of level numbers:

1. Level numbers 01 through 49

Level number 01 is used to indicate a record, and 02 through 49 are used to indicate the organization of the record.

Example 6.7

```
A   B
01 STUDENT-RECORD.
    02 STUDENT-NUMBER   PIC 9(5).
    02 STUDENT-NAME     PIC X(20).
    02 BIRTH-DATE.
        04  DAY         PIC 99.
        04  MONTH       PIC 99.
        04  YEAR        PIC 9999.
    02 MAJOR            PIC X(10).
```

The 01 indicates that STUDENT-RECORD is a record. The 02's indicate four major items in the record. The 04's following BIRTH-DATE indicate three items in BIRTH-DATE. The PICTURE clauses (where the permissible abbreviation PIC is used) indicates six elementary items, and thus BIRTH-DATE is a group item. Note that when an item is subdivided, the subdivisions have larger level numbers.

2. Level number 77 (and the WORKING-STORAGE SECTION)

The WORKING-STORAGE SECTION is used to describe data items or records that are not parts of files. The first entries in this section must always be all the independent, elementary items used in the program. These begin with level number 77 (in area A) followed by the data name and PICTURE clause in area B.

Example 6.8

```
A   B
DATA DIVISION.
FILE SECTION.
   ⋮
WORKING-STORAGE SECTION.
77    INCREMENT   PIC 9(5).
77    LAST-VAL    PIC 99.
77    TOTAL       PIC 9(3).
77    STORER      PIC X(10).

01    DUMMY.
      07 NAMER     PIC X(11).
      07 COUNTER   PIC 99.
01    MOVER.
      21  F    PIC X(6).
      21  G    PIC 9(4).
      21  H    PIC 9999.
```

In example 6.8, INCREMENT, LAST-VAL, TOTAL, and SORTER are independent elementary items.

Following all the level 77 entries are the entries for independent items that are *not* elementary. These group items are always assigned level number 01. DUMMY contains two elementary items, and MOVER contains three elementary items.

3. Level number 88.

Level number 88 is used to associate *condition names* with certain values that a data item can assume. The data item involved is called a *conditional variable*.

Example 6.9

Let us assume that we are processing records at a bank. Each card record is described by

```
A   B
01 CARD-RECORD.
   03 TRANSACTION    PIC 9.
      88 CHECKING    VALUE 0.
      88 SAVINGS     VALUE 1.
   03 AMOUNT         PIC S999999V99.
   03 AMOUNT-NUMBER  PIC X(10).
```

TRANSACTION is the name of a one-digit field. If TRANSACTION is 0, then we are processing a checking account transaction; if it is 1, then we are processing a savings account transaction. In the PROCEDURE DIVISION, writing IF TRANSACTION IS EQUAL TO 0 is equivalent to writing IF CHECKING. As you can see, the second statement has more meaning for the programmer and is preferable to the first statement. This is an example of testing the value of the conditional variable TRANSACTION. Chapter 9 contains more information about testing conditions.

FILLER Clause

If you need to reserve positions in main storage and you do not plan to refer to that area again, then you must create what is known as a FILLER area. For example, suppose that in an input record there are five blanks (columns 1 through 5). Our first entry would be

```
A   B
01  RECORD-IN.
    02   FILLER   PIC X(5).
```

Note that the PICTURE character is an X. If you want to use the PICTURE character 9 with the FILLER clause, you must have five digits in columns 1 through 5; otherwise, your program will not execute properly on some computers. Often, whenever the FILLER clause is used within a printing record, it is followed by the clause VALUE IS SPACES.

VALUE Clause

The format for the VALUE clause is

$$\underline{\text{VALUE}} \quad \text{IS} \quad \begin{Bmatrix} \texttt{literal} \\ \texttt{figurative-constant} \end{Bmatrix}$$

The VALUE clause must be used in condition-names entries (the data name preceded by level number 88), whether those condition names are entries in the FILE SECTION or LINKAGE SECTION or WORKING-STORAGE SECTION. In the WORKING-STORAGE SECTION only the VALUE clause may be used to assign initial values to a data name. See example 6.10 for the usage of the VALUE clause in the WORKING-STORAGE SECTION. In the FILE SECTION and LINKAGE SECTION, the VALUE clause may be used only for condition names.

WORKING-STORAGE SECTION

The WORKING-STORAGE SECTION is used to provide work areas, temporary storage areas, and storage of program constants. We will show how these are used in preparing headings and composing lines for printed ·output and in storing intermediate results.

Example 6.10

Suppose that the records for an inventory file are punched on cards in the following manner:

Card column	Field	Type
1–5	item number	number
12–32	item name	character
44–49	number on hand	number
50–54	number of demands	number

We wish to write a COBOL program to accomplish the following:

1. Print the heading THIS IS THE INVENTORY REPORT FOR THIS MONTH, starting from column 10 of the first line of a new page.
2. Skip five lines after THIS IS THE INVENTORY REPORT FOR THIS MONTH and print the heading (on one line):

```
___________CATALOGUE NUMBER___________
```
     10 spaces   10 spaces

```
ITEM-NAME____________________
```
            20 spaces

```
ON-HAND__________DEMAND
```
        10 spaces

3. Read and print out the inventory file.

The COBOL source program that accomplished the tasks called for in example 6.10 for the IBM-1130 follows. Figure 6.1 shows the input data cards for example 6.10; figure 6.2 shows the system flowchart for example 6.10; figure 6.3 shows the program flowchart for example 6.10; figure 6.4 shows the listing for example 6.10; and figure 6.5 shows the changes necessary to run the program for example 6.10 on the DECSYSTEM-10, the B1700, and the IBM-S3. Note that there are six control cards in the source program, four of those cards (// JOB T, // COBOL, *LIST, and *2501, 1403) are at the beginning; and the last two monitor cards (/* and // XEQ) are at the end of the source program. Note the following important facts about the program:

1. FILE-IN is the input file. CARD-IN is its record. Observe the data cards following the monitor control card // XEQ. You will see that these cards are described by the record CARD-IN. For example, when the first card is read, the data names in CARD-IN assume the following values:

```
Data  name          Value
ITEM-NUMBER         45210
ITEM-NAME           PRODUCT-ONEϕϕϕϕϕϕϕϕϕϕ
NUMBER-ON-HAND      01423
NUMBER-DEMANDED     04500
```

(The ϕ stands for a blank character.)

2. FILE-OUT is the output file for printing. Its record is PRINT-LINE. Statement 27 of the program is

```
01      PRINT-LINE      PIC X(120).
```

Figure 6.1 Input data cards for the program for example 6.10.

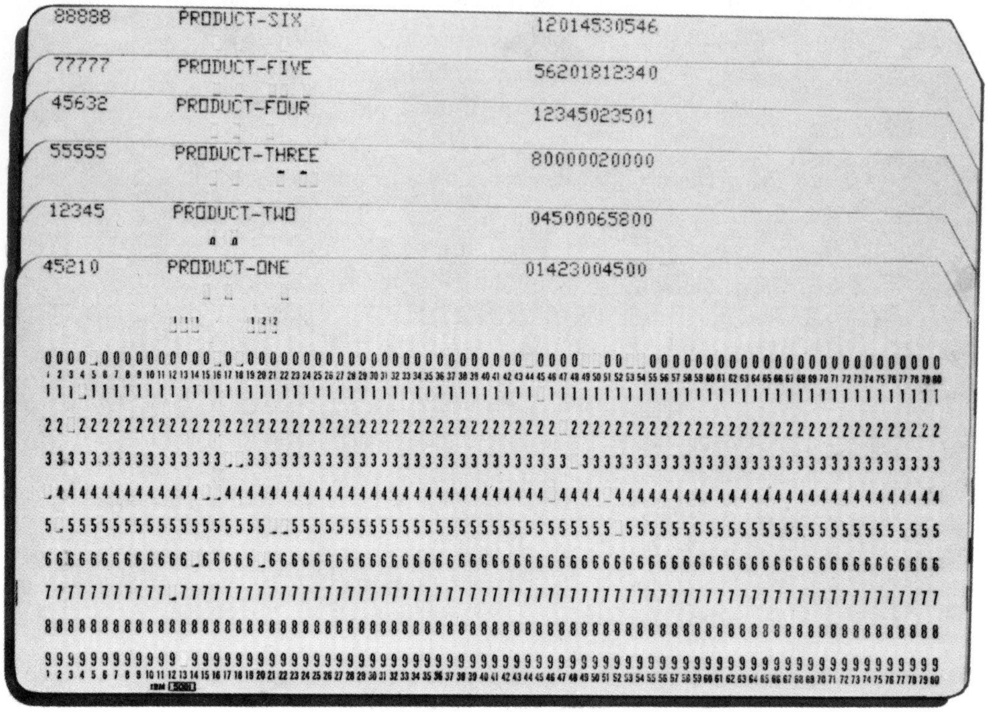

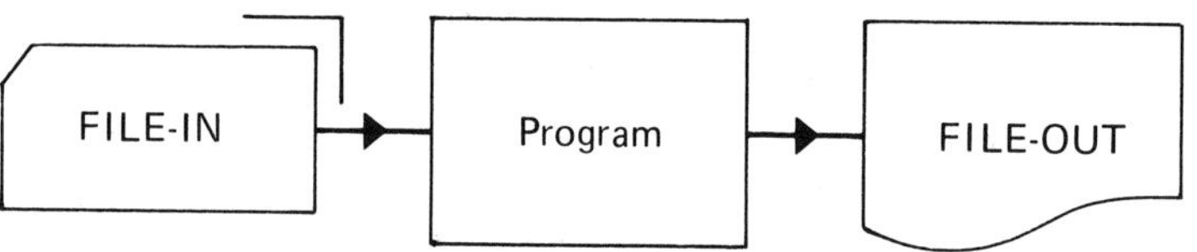

Figure 6.2 System flowchart for example 6.10.

Note that this file is assigned to the line printer and uses carriage control.

On some computers, the first character of each line is *not* printed. Instead, the computer uses the first character to give a code to the line printer that controls the vertical spacing. This used to be true of the IBM-1130, but it has been corrected to meet the requirements of standard COBOL. The maximum number of characters that can be printed on the 1403 line printer is 120. In the WORKING-STORAGE SECTION three temporary records, HEADING-ONE, HEADING-TWO, and DETAIL-PRINT, are created. The record PRINT-LINE will be copied from these temporary records and then printed. Since each of these temporary records begins with a FILLER, the loss of the first character from this item would be of no consequence if it were to occur. *When using the line printer it is always a good idea to begin each record with a FILLER even if it is only one character long.*

3. Note requirement 1 of example 6.10, and compare that with the structure of HEADING-ONE in the WORKING-STORAGE SECTION. Statements 29 through 31 indicate the structure of HEADING-ONE. Observe that statement 30 indicates that the first field of HEADING-ONE is composed of 9 characters that are filled with spaces, and the second field is 36

Figure 6.3 Program flowchart for example 6.10.

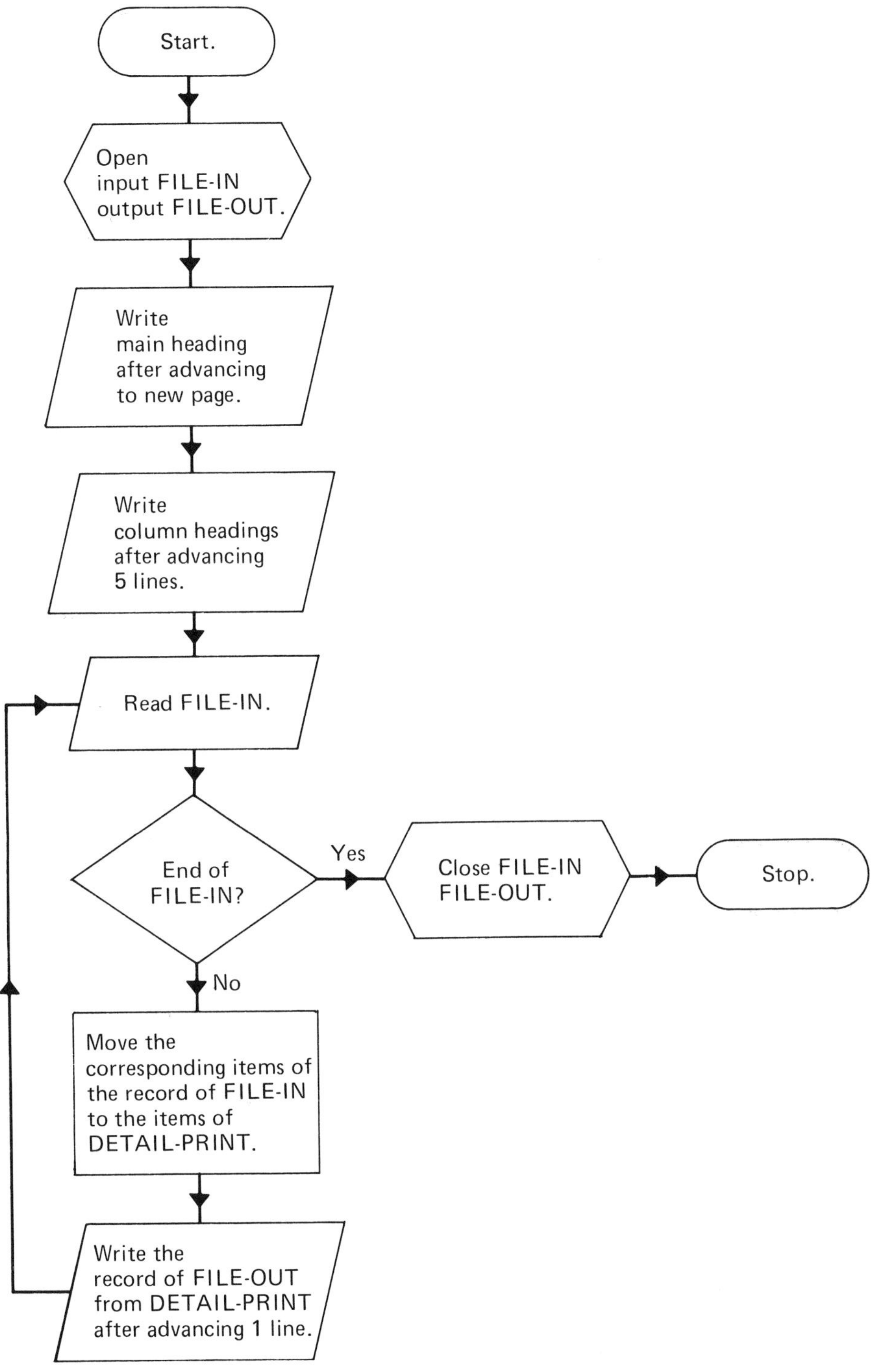

Figure 6.4 Listing of program run on the IBM-1130 for example 6.10.

```
// JOB T
// COBOL
*LIST
*2501,1403
      IDENTIFICATION DIVISION.
      PROGRAM-ID.  SAMPLE-7.
      AUTHOR. KHAILANY-DUPLISSEY.
      INSTALLATION.  UNIVERSITY OF ARKANSAS AT LITTLE ROCK.
      DATE-WRITTEN. JUNE, 1976.
      REMARKS.  THIS PROGRAM READS AND PRINTS AN INVENTORY FILE.
          THIS IS THE FIRST TIME THAT YOU SEE HEADINGS.
      ENVIRONMENT DIVISION.
      CONFIGURATION SECTION.
      SOURCE-COMPUTER. IBM-1130.
      OBJECT-COMPUTER. IBM-1130.
      SPECIAL-NAMES.
          C01 IS TO-NEW-PAGE.
      INPUT-OUTPUT SECTION.
      FILE-CONTROL.
          SELECT FILE-IN ASSIGN TO RD-2501.
          SELECT FILE-OUT ASSIGN TO PR-1403.
      DATA DIVISION.
      FILE SECTION.
      FD  FILE-IN,
          LABEL RECORDS ARE OMITTED, DATA RECORD IS CARD-IN.
      01  CARD-IN.
          02   ITEM-NUMBER        PICTURE     9(5).
          02   FILLER             PICTURE     X(6).
          02   ITEM-NAME          PICTURE     X(21).
          02   FILLER             PICTURE     X(11).
          02   NUMBER-ON-HAND     PICTURE     9(6).
          02   NUMBER-DEMANDED    PICTURE     9(5).
      FD  FILE-OUT,
          LABEL RECORDS ARE OMITTED,
          DATA RECORD IS PRINT-LINE.
      01  PRINT-LINE   PIC X(120).
      WORKING-STORAGE SECTION.
      01  HEADING-ONE.
      02 FILLER PIC X(9) VALUE SPACES.
      02 FILLER PIC X(36) VALUE 'THE INVENTORY REPORT FOR THIS MONT
      'H'.
      01  HEADING-TWO.
          02   FILLER PIC X(10) VALUE SPACES.
          02   FILLER PIC X(16) VALUE 'CATALOGUE NUMBER'.
          02   FILLER PIC X(10) VALUE SPACES.
          02   FILLER PIC X(9) VALUE 'ITEM-NAME'.
          02   FILLER PIC X(20) VALUE SPACES.
          02   FILLER PIC X(7) VALUE 'ON-HAND'.
          02   FILLER PIC X(10) VALUE SPACES.
          02   FILLER PIC X(6) VALUE 'DEMAND'.
      01  DETAIL-PRINT.
          02   FILLER PIC X(10) VALUE SPACES.
          02   PRINT-NUMBER PIC 9(5).
          02   FILLER PIC X(21) VALUE SPACES.
          02   PRINT-NAME PIC X(21).
          02   FILLER PIC X(9) VALUE SPACES.
          02   PRINT-NUMBER-ON-HAND PIC 9(6).
          02   FILLER PIC X(11) VALUE SPACES.
          02   PRINT-DEMAND PIC 9(5).
      PROCEDURE DIVISION.
      INITIALIZATION.
          OPEN INPUT FILE-IN, OUTPUT FILE-OUT.
          WRITE PRINT-LINE FROM HEADING-ONE
              AFTER ADVANCING TO-NEW-PAGE.
          WRITE PRINT-LINE FROM HEADING-TWO AFTER ADVANCING 5 LINES.
      PAR-1.
          READ FILE-IN AT END
```

```
        CLOSE FILE-IN, FILE-OUT, STOP RUN.
    MOVE ITEM-NUMBER TO PRINT-NUMBER.
    MOVE ITEM-NAME TO PRINT-NAME.
    MOVE NUMBER-ON-HAND TO PRINT-NUMBER-ON-HAND.
    MOVE NUMBER-DEMANDED TO PRINT-DEMAND.
    WRITE PRINT-LINE FROM DETAIL-PRINT AFTER ADVANCING 1 LINES.
    GO TO PAR-1.
/*
// XEQ
45210        PRODUCT-ONE                    01423004500
12345        PRODUCT-TWO                    04500065800
55555        PRODUCT-THREE                  80000020000
45632        PRODUCT-FOUR                   12345023501
77777        PRODUCT-FIVE                   56201812340
88888        PRODUCT-SIX                    12014530546
/*
```

Figure 6.5 Changes necessary to run the program for example 6.10 on the DECSYSTEM-10, the B1700, and the IBM-S3.

a. For the DECSYSTEM-10:

```
SOURCE-COMPUTER. DECSYSTEM-10
OBJECT-COMPUTER. DECSYSTEM-10
SPECIAL-NAMES. CHANNEL (1) IS TO-NEW-PAGE.
INPUT-OUTPUT SECTION.
FILE-CONTROL.
     SELECT FILE-IN ASSIGN TO CDR.
     SELECT FILE-OUT ASSIGN TO LPT.
```

b. For the B1700:

```
SOURCE-COMPUTER. B-1700.
OBJECT-COMPUTER. B-1700.
INPUT-OUTPUT SECTION.
FILE-CONTROL.
      SELECT FILE-IN ASSIGN TO READER.
      SELECT FILE-OUT ASSIGN TO PRINTER.
         ⋮
DATA DIVISION.
         ⋮
PROCEDURE DIVISION.
         ⋮
      WRITE PRINT-LINE FROM HEADING-ONE AFTER ADVANCING
            TO CHANNEL 01.
         ⋮
```

c. For the IBM-S3:

```
SOURCE-COMPUTER. IBM-S3.
OBJECT-COMPUTER. IBM-S3.
```

Figure 6.5 (Cont'd.)

```
SPECIAL-NAMES. C01 IS TO-NEW-PAGE.
INPUT-OUTPUT SECTION.
FILE-CONTROL.
     SELECT FILE-IN ASSIGN TO UR-2501-RD.
     SELECT FILE-OUT ASSIGN TO UR-1403-2-66.
```

---

characters long and is filled with the literal ' THE INVENTORY REPORT FOR THIS MONTH'. (The quotation marks are not included in the literal.) Recall that the hyphen between statements 31 and 32 is for the continuation of nonnumeric literals (discussed in Chapter 2). Now look at statement 53 in the PROCEDURE DIVISION, which is

```
WRITE PRINT-LINE FROM HEADING-ONE AFTER ADVANCING
TO-NEW-PAGE.
```

This sentence is equivalent to the following statements:

```
MOVE SPACES TO PRINT-LINE.
MOVE HEADING-ONE TO PRINT-LINE.
WRITE PRINT-LINE AFTER ADVANCING TO-NEW-PAGE.
```

Note that MOVE, SPACES, TO, WRITE, AFTER, and ADVANCING are reserved words.

4. The structure of HEADING-TWO (statements 32 through 40) fulfills requirement 2 in example 6.10. Statement 54, which is

```
WRITE PRINT-LINE FROM HEADING-TWO AFTER ADVANCING
5 LINES.
```

makes the content of PRINT-LINE all spaces and then moves the content of HEADING-TWO into PRINT-LINE and prints the record PRINT-LINE.

5. The arrangement of the printed output is presented in the structure DETAIL-PRINT (statements 41 through 49) in the WORKING-STORAGE SECTION. You can see that the temporary record DETAIL-PRINT is designed in such a way that when the record HEADING-TWO is followed by the record DETAIL-PRINT, the positions PRINT-NAME, PRINT-NUMBER-ON-HAND, and PRINT-DEMAND are directly beneath ITEM-NAME, ON-HAND, and DEMAND, respectively.

6. Statements 56 and 57 constitute a single sentence. Consequently, when the last input card is encountered, both files will be closed and the run is stopped.

PICTURE Clause

The PICTURE clause is used to specify detailed descriptions of elementary items. It indicates whether an elementary item is alphabetic, numeric, or alphanumeric. In a PICTURE clause, each occurrence of an A indicates a letter of the alphabet or a blank. Each occurrence of 9 indicates a numeric digit. Each occurrence of an X indicates an alphanumeric character—i.e., a number, letter, or special character.

Example 6.11

```
A  B
01 IN-RECORD.
   03 CARL     PIC AA.
   03 PHRED    PIC 999.
   03 SINTHIA  PIC XXXX.
```

CARL is an alphabetic data item. Its value is two alphabetic characters. (A blank is considered an alphabetic character.) PHRED is a numeric data item containing three digits. SINTHIA is an alphanumeric data item containing COBOL characters. Let us rewrite example 6.11 in a much more compact form by using the shorthand notation for the repetition of characters.

```
A  B
01 IN-RECORD.
   03 CARL     PIC A(2).
   03 PHRED    PIC 9(3).
   03 SINTHIA  PIC X(4).
```

Observe that the shorthand notation is indicated by an integer in the parentheses following the PICTURE character.

The PICTURE clause is also used for editing. (*Editing* means inserting or replacing one or more characters for printing purposes—for example, suppressing leading zeros, inserting a decimal point and/or comma, and using a currency symbol or *.) The full list of symbols used in PICTURE clauses includes A, X, 9, , , P, Z, *, B, 0, +, −, $; and S, V, . , CR, and DB. The first group of symbols may be repeated in a PICTURE clause, and the shorthand notation may be used.

The PICTURE clause for numeric items uses combinations of the symbols P, 9, S, and V. If the S is used as the leftmost symbol in the PICTURE clause, the computer will store the numeric item with a sign. If S is not used, the computer assumes the number is nonnegative. If a V is used in a PICTURE clause, the computer will store the numeric item as though it contains a decimal point in that position.

The character P is used to insert zeros and to specify an implied decimal point. For example, PIC 999PPPP instructs the computer to insert four zeros after the first three digits and to consider the number to have an implied decimal point to the right of the P's. The description PIC PP999 instructs the computer to insert two zeros before the last three digits and to consider the number to have an implied decimal point to the left of the P's. Thus we see that the P's used in a PICTURE clause must form an unbroken string inserted to the left or right of all the 9's in the PICTURE. Furthermore, the presence of the P's automatically specifies the location of an implied decimal point, so that the use of a V for this purpose is redundant. The P's in the PICTURE of the item do not require storage space in the computer memory, but they must be included when deciding whether the item has 18 or fewer digits specified in its PICTURE.

Example 6.12

If 3241 were read from a card using PIC 99V99 to describe it, the computer would store 3241 as though there were a decimal point between the 2 and the 4; and if the computer were to print the number, it would print 3241.

Example 6.12 illustrates what we mean when we say that the V indicates an assumed decimal point. The computer uses the assumed decimal point when it performs arithmetic but not when it prints. If 1 is added to the stored number, the computer will obtain 3341 with an assumed decimal point between the 3 and 4. If the computer reads 3241 from a card using PIC 9999PPP, then it will store the value 3241000. If the computer reads 3241 from a card using PIC PP9999, then it will store a value of .003241 (the decimal point will be an assumed decimal point).

Example 6.13

If −13.63 is moved from one storage location to another storage location described by PIC S99V99, it will be stored as though it were −1363 with an assumed decimal point between the leftmost 3 and the 6.

When numeric data items are to be used for *printed output,* the data items are always stored as DISPLAY items that are frequently *edited* for this purpose. The editing symbols most often used are B, Z, 0, , , *, +, −, CR, DB, and $.

The B, 0, and . may be used to insert blanks, zeros, or decimal points, and the , is used to insert commas.

Example 6.14

Type of Editing	Sending Item		Receiving Item	
	Picture	*Value*	*Picture*	*Result*
Insert 0	9(3)V9	123.9	ZZZ.90	123.90
Insert blank	S9(5)	−23456	Z(5)BCR	23456 CR
	S9(8)	01021973	99B99B9(4)	01 02 1973
	S9(8)	01021973	ZZBZZBZ(4)	1 02 1973
Insert decimal point	S9(4)V99	0139.28	9(4).99	0139.28
	S9(4)V99	0139.28	Z(4).99	139.28
	S9(4)V99	−0139.28	Z(4).990	139.280
	S9(4)V99	−0139.28	99V99	39.28

Note that when V is used, the computer keeps track of the assumed decimal point, whereas when . (the period) is used, the decimal point actually appears in the number and is printed during output.

As you can see, numbers are sometimes stored with leading zeros. The Z and * are used to suppress the printing of leading zeros. If Z is used in a digit position and a leading zero occupies that position in a number being printed, the computer will print a space in that position. If * is used in a digit position occupied by a leading zero in a number being printed, the computer will print an * in that position.

Example 6.15

If 0071.8 is printed from a storage location described by

a. PIC ZZZZ.9, it will be printed as 71.8 with two leading spaces;
b. PIC ****.9, it will be printed as **71.8;
c. PIC 99.99, it will be printed as 71.80;
d. PIC ZZZZ.99, it will be printed as 71.80 with two leading spaces;
e. PIC ***.**, it will be printed as *71.80.

The , or $ may be used to cause a comma or currency sign to be inserted for printing. For example, if 3697.81 is printed from a location described by $**,***.99, it will appear as $*3,697.81.

The $, +, and − may be used for what is called *floating insertion*. This causes the suppression of leading zeros and the insertion of the appropriate character to the left of the resulting number.

Example 6.16

If 0136.95 is printed from a location described by

a. PIC $$$$.99, it will appear as $136.95;
b. PIC $$.99, it will appear as $6.95;
c. PIC ++++.99, it will appear as +136.95;
d. PIC +++.99, it will appear as +36.95;
e. PIC −−−−.99, it will appear as 136.95 with one leading space. (If we had −0136.95, we would have gotten −136.95.)

If −27.369 is printed from a position described by

a. PIC $$$.99, it will appear as $27.36;
b. PIC ++++.999, it will appear as −27.369 with one leading space;
c. PIC −−−.99, it will appear as −27.36;
d. PIC −$$$.99, it will appear as −$27.36;
e. PIC +$$$.99, it will appear as −$27.36;
f. PIC $$$$9.99, it will appear as $27.36 with two leading spaces.

The CR and DB may be placed at the right end of the picture clause for insertion of these characters. As example 6.17 shows, the rules for insertion conform to standard accounting usage.

Example 6.17

Value	PIC	Result
13.56	$$$.99CR	$13.56
13.56	$$$.99DB	$13.56
−3.95	$$$.99CR	$3.95CR
−3.95	$$.99DB	$3.95DB

BLANK WHEN ZERO Clause

The BLANK WHEN ZERO clause is useful in processing numeric items or edited numeric items. Its format is

    BLANK WHEN ZERO

If the item ever has the value 0, it will be filled with blanks.

JUSTIFIED Clause

The clause

$$\left\{ \begin{matrix} \text{JUSTIFIED} \\ \text{JUST} \end{matrix} \right\} \text{RIGHT}$$

is used in positioning data in an alphabetic or alphanumeric field. Normally when data is moved to an alphanumeric or alphabetic field, the characters are placed into the field starting at the left. Excess characters are truncated, and unused positions are filled with spaces. When the JUSTIFIED clause is used, the characters are fed into the field starting at the right. Excess characters are truncated and unused positions are filled with spaces. This clause may be specified only for elementary items and cannot be used for level 88 data names.

To make the preceding concepts clear, suppose that the following structure is in the WORKING-STORAGE SECTION.

```
77 FILD-1 PIC X(6) VALUE 'ABCDEF'.
77 FILD-2 PIC X(2) VALUE 'AB'.
77 FILD-3 PIC X(4).
77 FILD-4 PIC X(4)  JUST RIGHT.
```

Then after the execution of the statement

```
MOVE FILD-1 TO FILD-3, FILD-4.
```

the content of FILD-3 becomes ABCD and the content of FILD-4 becomes CDEF. However, after the execution of the statement MOVE FILD-2 TO FILD-3, FILD-4, the content of FILD-3 becomes AB¢¢ (¢ means a blank character) and the content of FILD-4 becomes ¢¢AB.

USAGE Clause

The USAGE clause is used to specify the method by which data is stored in the internal memory of the computer. The format of this clause is

$$[\underline{\text{USAGE}} \text{ IS}] \left\{ \begin{array}{l} \underline{\text{DISPLAY}} \\ \underline{\text{COMPUTATIONAL}} \\ \underline{\text{COMP}} \end{array} \right\}$$

All data items except numeric items must have DISPLAY for their usage. If a numeric data item is used for input from cards or output to a line printer or cards, then it must have DISPLAY as its usage. If a numeric data item is *not* used for such purposes, then it may have COMPUTATIONAL as its usage; and if the numeric data item is used in many arithmetic computations, then it should have COMPUTATIONAL as its usage. Only numeric data items are used in arithmetic calculations. Before a calculation is performed, the computer makes sure that the usage of all data items involved in the arithmetic calculations are COMP. If the usage of any of these data items is DISPLAY, the computer converts their usage to the COMP each time prior to the performance of the calculation. Therefore, it is far more efficient to perform arithmetic operations on data items whose usages are COMP, because the time required for the conversion of the usages is spared. (COMP is an acceptable abbreviation for COMPUTATIONAL.)

On most computers there are other types of usages that the programmer can specify. For example, on the IBM-1130 one can specify COMP-4, which is equivalent to specifying COMP. For information on other usages for the B1700, IBM-S3, and the DECSYSTEM-10, consult the appropriate appendix in this book.

On the IBM-1130 numeric items with COMPUTATIONAL usages are stored in the internal memory of the computer in binary form. The amount of main memory required to store such an item is determined by the number of 9's in the PICTURE clause of the item. In particular, if the number of 9's is

1. 1 through 4, then this item requires one word of main storage;
2. 5 through 9, then this item requires two words of main storage; and
3. 10 through 18, then this item requires four words of main storage.

On the B1700 each 9 in the PICTURE clause of a COMP item requires one-half a byte of storage. On the DECSYSTEM-10 each item with 10 or fewer 9's in the PICTURE clause requires one DECSYSTEM-10 word. Each item with more than ten 9's in the PICTURE clause requires two DECSYSTEM-10 words. Note that a DECSYSTEM-10 word is not equivalent to a word on an IBM-1130. A DECSYSTEM-10 word contains 36 *bits,* whereas a word on an IBM-1130 contains 16 bits. On the IBM-S3, each 9 in the PICTURE clause requires one byte of main memory.

The storage requirements for a DISPLAY item on these machines is somewhat easier to describe. On the B1700 each character in the PICTURE clause other than a V, a P, or an S will require one byte of main storage. On the IBM-1130 each character in the PICTURE clause other than a V, a P, or an S requires one word of storage. On an IBM-S3 each character other than a V, a P, or an S requires one byte of storage. On the DECSYSTEM-10, each character other than a V, a P, or an S requires six bits of storage.

The USAGE clause may be written at the group item level. In this case it applies to each elementary item in the group. The usage of the elementary items in the group item cannot differ from the usage of the group item. However, on the IBM-1130 you can specify COMP usage for a group containing nonnumeric elementary items, and the compiler will automatically apply this usage only to the numeric elementary items involved.

Example 6.18

```
A  B
01 CARD-INFORMATION.
   02  TOTAL  PIC 9(6) USAGE IS DISPLAY.
```

In example 6.18, TOTAL requires six words of storage on the IBM-1130, six bytes of storage on the B1700, six bytes of storage on the IBM-S3, and thirty-six bits of storage on the DECSYSTEM-10. However, if we change example 6.18 to

```
A  B
01 CARD-INFORMATION.
   02  TOTAL  PIC 9(6) USAGE IS COMPUTATIONAL.
```

then TOTAL requires two words of storage on the IBM-1130, three bytes of storage on the B1700, six bytes of storage on the IBM-S3, and thirty-six bits of storage on the DECSYSTEM-10. Thus in some cases you can decrease the storage requirements of a program by specifying COMP usage. Also COMP usage is better for items used in arithmetic calculations.

The USAGE clause is optional on all computers. If it is omitted, USAGE IS DISPLAY is assumed by the COBOL compiler.

Example 6.19

```
A   B
    02 BIRTH-DATE USAGE IS COMP-4.
       03 DAY  PIC 99.
       03 MONTH  PIC 99.
       03 YEAR  PIC 99.
```

The usage for DAY, MONTH, and YEAR will be COMP-4. (Another form of USAGE is USAGE IS INDEX, which will be explained in Chapter 11 on Table Handling.)

REDEFINES Clause

The REDEFINES clause allows items with differing formats to occupy the same storage location. It gives another name and description to an item previously described to the computer. The format of this clause is

```
Level-number data-name-1 REDEFINES data-name-2
```

Level-number is that of data-name-1 and must not be level-number 88. The level number for data-name-1 must be the same as that for data-name-2.

Example 6.20

```
A   B
    03 D-ITEM  PIC X(50).
    03 E-ITEM REDEFINES D-ITEM.
       04 ITEM  PIC 9(5).
       04 ITEM-DESCRIPTION  PIC X(45).
    03 C-ITEM REDEFINES D-ITEM
       06 ITEM-NAME  PIC A(15).
       06 ITEM-NUMBER  PIC 9(5).
       06 ITEM-PRICE  PIC 999V99.
       06 ITEM-DESCRIPTION  PIC X(25).
```

Note the following in example 6.20:

1. data-name-2 is D-ITEM, and both E-ITEM and C-ITEM are data-name-1.

2. The number of characters in C-ITEM, D-ITEM, and E-ITEM is 50 in all three, but their groupings and descriptions are different. When this storage location is referred to by D-ITEM, it is expected to have 50 characters. However, when the same storage location is referred to by E-ITEM, it is expected to have 5 digits followed by 45 characters. And when it is referred to by C-ITEM, it is expected to have 15 alphabetic characters, followed by 5 digits, followed by another 5 digits, followed by 25 characters.

3. As you see in example 6.20, multiple redefinition of the same area is allowed. However, the reserved word REDEFINES must always be followed by data-name-2 (original data name). Thus it is incorrect to write

```
03 C-ITEM REDEFINES E-ITEM.
```

because E-ITEM is not the original data name.

The entries following data-name-1 must not contain the VALUE clause unless it applies to a condition name. However, they may contain the USAGE clause, and the USAGE of an area and its redefinition may be different as long as they occupy the same amount of main storage.

Example 6.21

```
A   B
   03 VAR-1 PIC X USAGE DISPLAY VALUE 6.
   03 VAR-2 REDEFINES VAR-1 PIC S99 USAGE COMP.
   03 VAR-3 REDEFINES VAR-1 PIC S9999 USAGE
         COMP-4.
```

The following should be noted:

1. VAR-1, which is followed by the VALUE clause, is data-name-2. The VALUE clause is not allowed to follow VAR-2 and VAR-3 because those are data-name-1.

2. On the IBM-1130 each of the data names VAR-1, VAR-2, and VAR-3 occupies one word of the computer storage location. The reason is that with DISPLAY, each character occupies one word; and with COMP or COMP-4, from one through five digits occupy one computer word. (See the description of the USAGE clause on page 84.) The value of VAR-1, VAR-2, and VAR-3 is 6 in our example.

A REDEFINES clause can be used to specify items subordinate to the items being redefined.

Example 6.22

```
   02 PATIENT-EXPENSE.
      03 MEDICINE-COST  PIC 9(4)V99.
      03 TREATMENT-COST  PIC 9(5)V99.
      03 PHYSICIAN  PIC X(12).
   02 PHYSICIAN-PAY REDEFINES PATIENT-EXPENSE.
      03 PHYSICIAN-NAME  PIC X(20).
      03 RATE-PER-HOUR  PIC 9(3)V99.
      03 NUMBER-OF-HOUR REDEFINES RATE PER HOUR
         PIC 99V999.
      03 AMOUNT-DUE REDEFINES RATE-PER-HOUR  PIC 9(5).
```

The REDEFINES clause must not be used with level-01 items in the FILE SECTION; however, it may be used with level-01 items in the other sections of the DATA DIVISION.

Files with Two or More Types of Records

Sometimes it will be necessary to have one file contain two or more types of records. There are two ways to accomplish this: The first one is to use the REDEFINES clause with a level-01 entry in the WORKING-STORAGE SECTION, as in the following example.

Example 6.23   Let us assume that we have a card file containing two types of records. One contains CARD-TYPE, ID, NAME, SOCIAL-SEC-NUM, and the other contains CARD-TYPE, ID, WAGES.

The record entry for CARDFILE is

```
FD CARDFILE.
   LABEL RECORDS ARE OMITTED,
   DATA RECORD IS CARD-IN.
01 CARD-IN.
   02 CARD-TYPE  PIC X.
   02 REST-OF-CARD  PIC X(79).
```

In the WORKING-STORAGE SECTION we would have the entries

```
01 FIRST-TYPE.
   02 CARD-TYPE  PIC X.
   02 ID  PIC 9(5).
   02 NAME  PIC X(20).
   02 SOCIAL-SEC-NUM  PIC X(14).
   02 FILLER  PIC X(40).

01 SECOND-TYPE REDEFINES FIRST-TYPE.
   04 CARD-TYPE  PIC X.
   04 ID  PIC 9(5).
   04 WAGES  PIC 999V99.
   04 FILLER  PIC X(69).
```

When we run the program, we can read CARDFILE and test CARD-TYPE OF CARD-IN to see if it is '1' or '2'. If it is '1', we can move CARD-TYPE to FIRST-TYPE to get the information in the desired form; and if it is '2', we can move CARD-TYPE to SECOND-TYPE.

A more common method of having one file contain more than one kind of record is to have more than one level-01 entry following the FD entry of the file as in the following example.

Example 6.24   Consider the following FD and record description entries.

```
FD CARDFILE.
   LABEL RECORDS ARE OMITTED,
   DATA RECORDS ARE TYPE-1, TYPE-2.
01 TYPE-1.
   02 NUM1  PIC S99V99 USAGE DISPLAY.
   02 NAMER  PIC X(10).
01 TYPE-2.
   02 NUM2  PIC S99V99 USAGE DISPLAY.
   02 COMPANY  PIC X(10).
```

Since TYPE-1 and TYPE-2 are 01 entries following the FD entry for CARDFILE, they are both records for CARDFILE. The computer will cause TYPE-1 and TYPE-2 to occupy the same part of main storage. Thus when a record of CARDFILE is read, the computer moves the information on the card to the area that is occupied in common by TYPE-1 and TYPE-2.

Other Clauses

There are two more *optional* clauses in an FD entry:

(1)

$$\underline{\text{BLOCK}}\text{ CONTAINS integer-1}\left\{\begin{array}{l}\underline{\text{RECORDS}}\\ \underline{\text{CHARACTERS}}\end{array}\right\}$$

(2)

$$\underline{\text{RECORD}}\text{ CONTAINS [integer-1 }\underline{\text{TO}}\text{]}$$
$$\text{integer-2 CHARACTERS}$$

The second clause is never required, and on the IBM-1130 the first clause has no effect. However, on other computers the BLOCK CONTAINS clause can be used to make a COBOL program more efficient. Remember from our discussion of tape files that the term BLOCK refers to the physical record size for our input-output device. In COBOL an input-output device always reads and writes a physical block of information. A block can contain many records of a file or it can contain one record of a file. Since the process of reading or writing information for a file assigned to a mass storage device is slow, it is generally desirable to make the number of file records in a physical block as large as possible.

There is another clause that may appear only at the elementary level

$$\left\{\begin{array}{l}\underline{\text{SYNCHRONIZED}}\\ \underline{\text{SYNC}}\end{array}\right\}\left[\begin{array}{l}\underline{\text{LEFT}}\\ \underline{\text{RIGHT}}\end{array}\right]$$

This clause can be used to increase the efficiency of performing arithmetic operations by minimizing the movement of data. However, in 1130 COBOL it is treated as a comment and has no effect.

Treatment of Numeric Data

The input of data from cards is done by using numeric items whose usage is DISPLAY. These items may have a sign and an implied decimal point in their picture. The data on the card does not have a sign or a decimal point. For example, if we read 5637 from a card using a DISPLAY item whose picture is 9V999, the value of the item would be 5637 with an implied decimal point between 5 and 6.

We can read negative numbers from cards by using DISPLAY items. The minus sign for the number must be overpunched in the rightmost column containing the number. For example, if we read 5637 (note the minus sign punched over the 7) from a card using a numeric DISPLAY item whose picture is S99V99, it will be stored as −5637 with an implied decimal point between 6 and 3. If we read 0345 from a card using a numeric DISPLAY item whose picture is S99V99, it will be stored as −345 with an implied decimal point between 3 and 4. Figure 6.6 illustrates a numeric data item on a punched card.

Figure 6.6 Example of a numeric data item on a punched card.
(If the first number is read from the card using a PICTURE of S99V99, then it will be
stored as though it had the value −12.35. If the second number is read using a
PICTURE of S99999, then it will be stored as though it had the value −50378. If the
third number is read using a PICTURE of 99999, then it will be stored as though it
had the value 63105.)

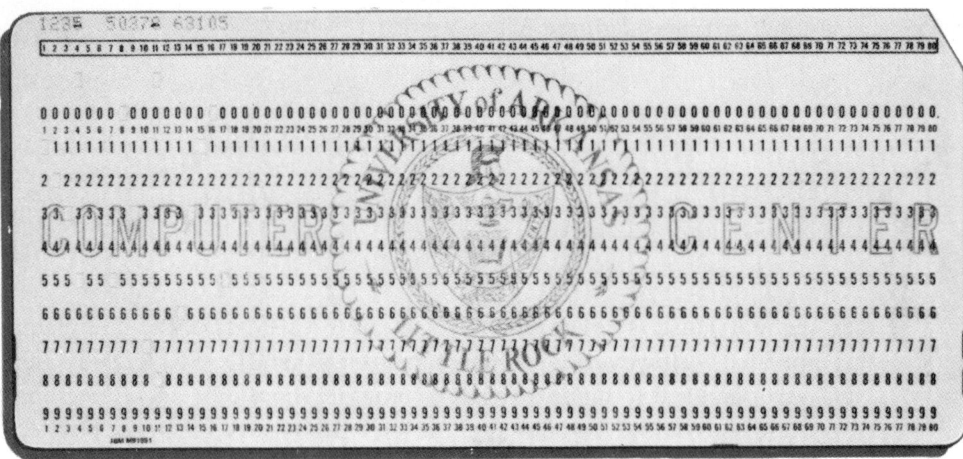

When you are working with numeric items in a computer program, it is important to remember that arithmetic computations are done most efficiently with COMPUTATIONAL items and that movement of data is most efficient for DISPLAY items.

Output of numeric items to a line printer or a card punch is done with only numeric or numeric-edited DISPLAY items. It is important to realize that a numeric-edited item cannot be moved to a numeric or numeric-edited item. Thus editing should be done only immediately prior to output. At all other times these items should be stored in unedited form.

Card File Input for Records of More than 80 Characters

On the IBM-1130 the physical size of a record (one card) for a card file is 80 characters. For a disk file the physical size of a record is 320 characters or less. On disk a record may be lengthened to as much as 4,096 words by using *spanned records*. There is no way to lengthen a record for card files, but there are several ways to overcome this limitation. Let us assume that we have a card file, and each record requires two cards. We could create two input files and read both files alternately, or we could piece the record together by use of a sufficiently large WORKING-STORAGE item. A third method would be to create one input file with two records, and a fourth would be to read the card file and piece the records together as in example 6.25.

Example 6.25

Write a COBOL program to instruct the computer to read customer records for an insurance company from a card file and create a permanent disk file of these records. Also, print a list of the records on the line printer. Each customer record contains

customer name	20 characters
customer age	3 digits
customer address	30 characters
illness	26 characters
physician	20 characters
premium factor	999V99
other insurance	15 characters

As you can see, the logical record size is 119 characters, which is too large for one card. Thus we shall make each logical record two cards long. The system flowchart in figure 6.7 and the program flowchart in figure 6.8 explain the procedures.

The program for example 6.25 for the IBM-1130 is given in figure 6.9. Adaptations in the control cards that the programmer must make to run the program for example 6.25 are shown in figure 6.10. In the PROCEDURE DIVISION of this program, several new statements are used. We will present a brief discussion here of these new statements; you can obtain further details about them in Chapters 7 and 8.

The IF statement is used to test a condition. If the condition specified is *true,* then the actions requested in the first part of the IF statement will be executed. If the condition specified is *false,* then the actions requested in the IF statement after the word ELSE will be executed. The format of this statement is

```
IF condition statement-1 [statement-2]...
    [ELSE [statement-3][statement-4]...]
```

The two formats for the READ and WRITE statements for a sequential disk file are

```
READ file-name AT END imperative-sentence.

WRITE record-name INVALID KEY imperative-sentence.
```

The DISPLAY and ACCEPT statements are used to read and write small amounts of data. The ACCEPT statement can be used to read the value of a data item from a card reader, a computer console typewriter, or a teletype terminal, depending on the computer you are using. The DISPLAY statement can be used to write data on a line printer, a computer console typewriter, or a teletype terminal. Which devices are permitted for use in these statements varies from computer to computer. However, all computers allow the use of the ACCEPT statement for the card reader and the DISPLAY statement for the line printer.

Example 6.25 also uses comment statements to document the program. Any line with an * in column 7 is a *comment line.* You may write anything you wish in columns 8 through 72 of a comment line. The COBOL compiler ignores the content of such lines. From now on, you should use comment lines in your program to explain what your program does. This is good documentation.

Figure 6.7 System flowchart for example 6.25.

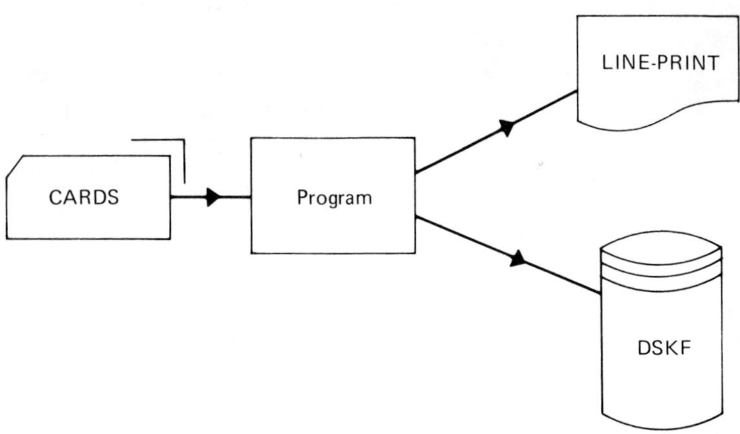

Summary The DATA DIVISION has three optional sections that are used in defining all the data used in a COBOL program. These sections are the FILE SECTION, the WORKING-STORAGE SECTION, and the LINKAGE SECTION.

Every file defined in a COBOL program must have an FD entry in the FILE SECTION. The format for this entry is

```
FD file-name,

    LABEL RECORDS ARE  {STANDARD}
                       {OMITTED }'

   [BLOCK CONTAINS integer-1  {RECORDS   }']
                              {CHARACTERS}

    [FILE CONTAINS integer-2 RECORDS, ]
    [RECORD CONTAINS integer-3 CHARACTERS, ]

   [DATA {RECORD IS   } record-name-1
         {RECORDS ARE }
         [record-name-2] . . . ]
```

Level numbers are used to indicate the organization of data items. Level number 01 indicates a record, and level numbers 02 through 49 indicate items within records. Level number 77 indicates an *elementary independent item.* Level number 88 indicates a *condition name.*

The following chart indicates the symbols used in PICTURE clauses.

Type of Item	*Symbols Used in PICTURE Clause*
numeric	S 9 V P
alphabetic	A
alphanumeric	X A 9
numeric-edited	9 B P V Z 0 . * + − CR DB $,
alphanumeric-edited	X and at least one 0, or X and at least B, or A and at least one 0

The USAGE clause is used to specify the internal form in which data is stored. The REDEFINES clause allows you to use different data names and data descriptions for the same locations in main memory.

Figure 6.8 Program flowchart for example 6.25.

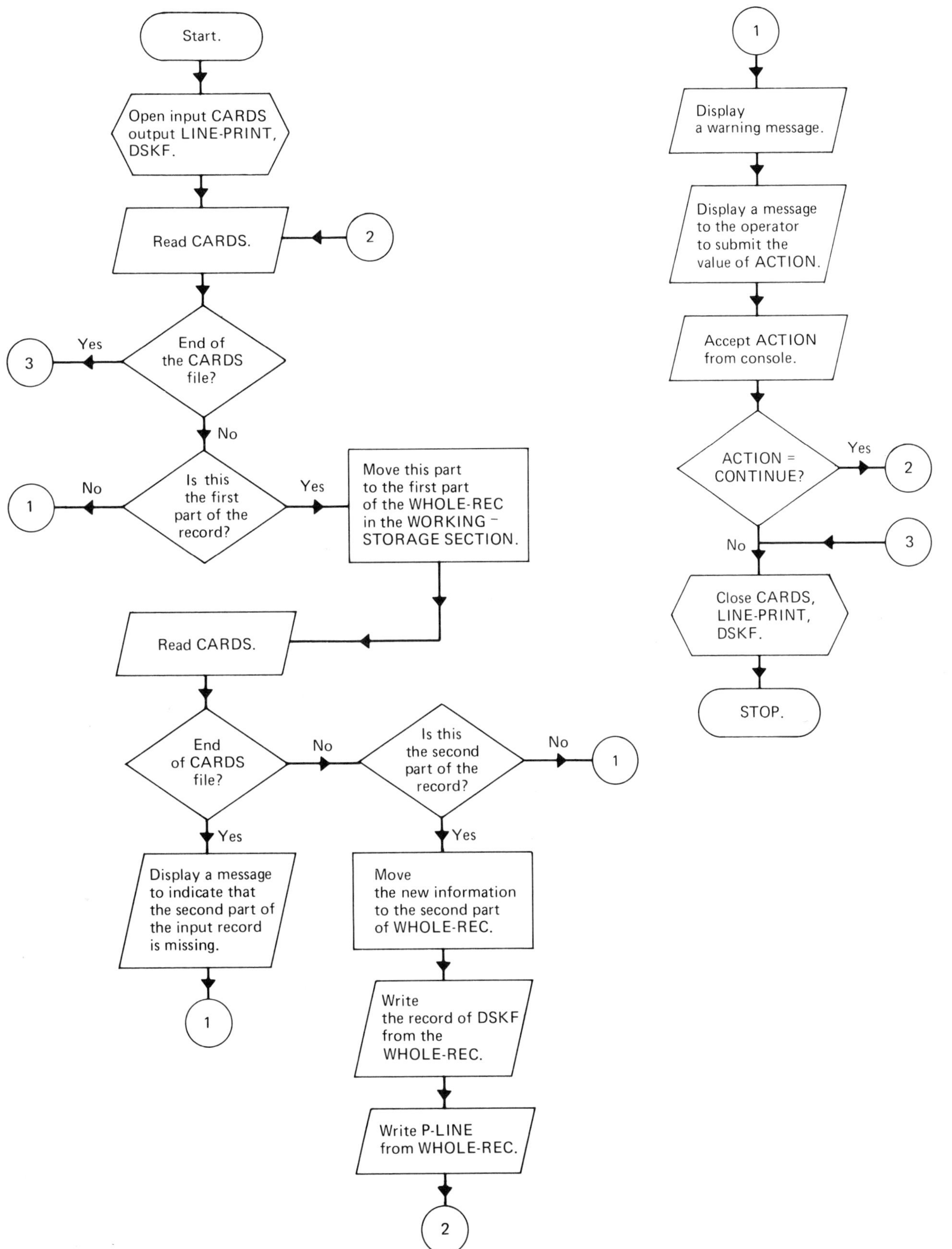

Figure 6.9 Computer printout of program run on the IBM-1130 for example 6.25.

```
// JOB
// COBOL
*LIST,2501,1403
      IDENTIFICATION DIVISION.
      PROGRAM-ID. INSURE.
      ENVIRONMENT DIVISION.
      CONFIGURATION SECTION.
      SOURCE-COMPUTER. IBM-1130.
      OBJECT-COMPUTER. IBM-1130.
      SPECIAL-NAMES.  C01 IS TO-NEW-PAGE.
      INPUT-OUTPUT SECTION.
      FILE-CONTROL.
          SELECT CARDS ASSIGN TO RD-2501.
          SELECT DSKF ASSIGN TO DF-100-50.
          SELECT LINE-PRINT ASSIGN TO PR-1403.
      DATA DIVISION.
      FILE SECTION.
      FD  CARDS,
          LABEL RECORDS ARE OMITTED, DATA RECORD IS CARD-IN.
      01  CARD-IN.
          02  PART-1  PIC X(79).
          02  PART-2  PIC 9.
            88  CARD1 VALUE IS 1.
            88  CARD2 VALUE IS 2.
      ************************************************************
      *****EACH LOGICAL RECORD IN OUR DISK FILE WILL CONTAIN THE INFOR-*
      *****MATION FROM TWO CARDS. COLUMN 80 OF EACH CARD CONTAINS A 1  *
      *****OR A 2 TO INDICATE WHICH CARD OF THE LOGICAL RECORD IS BEING*
      *****READ. THIS WILL BE USED TO MAKE SURE THE CARDS ARE IN THE   *
      *****PROPER ORDER.....                                          *
      ************************************************************
      FD  DSKF,
          LABEL RECORDS ARE STANDARD, DATA RECORD IS D-REC.
      01  D-REC  PIC X(119).
      FD  LINE-PRINT,
          LABEL RECORDS ARE OMITTED, DATA RECORD IS P-LINE.
      01  P-LINE  PIC X(121) JUSTIFIED RIGHT.
      WORKING-STORAGE SECTION.
      01  WHOLE-REC.
          02  PART-A  PIC X(79).
          02  PART-B  PIC X(40).
      01  ACTION  PIC X(8).
          88 CONTINUE  VALUE 'CONTINUE'.
          88 HALT  VALUE 'HALT'.
      PROCEDURE DIVISION.
      ST.
          OPEN INPUT CARDS,
              OUTPUT LINE-PRINT, DSKF.
          MOVE SPACES TO P-LINE.
          WRITE P-LINE AFTER ADVANCING TO-NEW-PAGE.
      READ-AND-PROCESS.
          READ CARDS AT END,
              CLOSE CARDS, DSKF, LINE-PRINT STOP RUN.
      ************************************************************
      *****THE CARDS MUST BE IN PROPER ORDER. THE NEXT STATEMENT TESTS *
      *****TO SEE IF THIS IS THE FIRST CARD OF THE LOGICAL RECORD BEING*
      *****PROCESSED......                                            *
      ************************************************************
          IF NOT CARD1 GO TO ERROR-ROUTINE,
              ELSE MOVE CARD-IN TO PART-A.
      ************************************************************
      *****NOW WE CAN READ THE SECOND CARD CONTAINING THE OTHER HALF OF*
      *****THE INFORMATION FOR THE DISK RECORD. NOTE THAT IF THE END OF*
      *****THE CARD FILE IS DETECTED, AN ERROR HAS OCCURED SINCE A CARD*
      *****IS MISSING FOR THIS RECORD BEING PROCESSED.....           *
      ************************************************************
          READ CARDS AT END GO TO ERROR-ROUTINE.
```

```
      ****************************************************************
      *****THE NEXT STATEMENT TESTS TO SEE IF THE CARD BEING READ IS  *
      *****THE SECOND HALF OF THE LOGICAL RECORD BEING PROCESSED.....  *
      ****************************************************************
          IF NOT CARD2 GO TO ERROR-ROUTINE,
              ELSE MOVE CARD-IN TO PART-B.
      ****************************************************************
      *****NOW BOTH PARTS OF WHOLE-REC ARE FILLED. WE MOVE THE CONTENT *
      *****TO D-REC AND P-LINE. WE THEN WRITE D-REC.........          *
      *****                                                          *
      *****ALL THREE STATEMENTS FOLLOWING AT END WILL BE EXECUTED IF  *
      *****WE ATTEMPT TO WRITE BEYOND THE PHYSICAL END OF OUR DISK    *
      *****FILE. PLEASE NOTE THAT THESE STATEMENTS ARE SEPARATED BY   *
      ****COMMAS.....                                                *
      ****************************************************************
          MOVE WHOLE-REC TO D-REC, P-LINE.
          WRITE D-REC AT END,
              DISPLAY 'DISK FILE IS FILLED, PROGRAM WILL STOP.',
              CLOSE CARDS, DSKF, LINE-PRINT,
              STOP RUN.
      ****************************************************************
      *****THE NEXT SENTENCE PRINTS P-LINE. IF THE END OF PAGE IS     *
      *****REACHED, THEN WE VERTICALLY SPACE TO THE THE TOP OF THE NEXT*
      *****PAGE......                                                *
      ****************************************************************
          WRITE P-LINE AFTER ADVANCING 2 LINES AT END-OF-PAGE
              MOVE SPACES TO P-LINE,
              WRITE P-LINE AFTER ADVANCING TO-NEW-PAGE.
          GO TO READ-AND-PROCESS.
       ERROR-ROUTINE.
      ****************************************************************
      *****THE VALUE OF ACTION WILL BE ENTERED FROM THE CONSOLE. THE  *
      *****VALUE OF ACTION MUST BE HALT OR CONTINUE. SEE THE ENTRY IN  *
      *****WORKING-STORAGE FOR THE CONDITIONAL VARIABLE, ACTION.....  *
      ****************************************************************
          DISPLAY 'CARDS FOR LAST RECORD OUT OF ORDER OR SECOND CARD MI
      -     'SSING'  UPON CONSOLE.
          DISPLAY 'IF YOU WISH TERMINATION, ENTER HALT AND PRESS EOF'
          UPON CONSOLE.
          DISPLAY 'IF NOT, CORRECT SITUATION SO NEXT RECORD READ IS
      -     'RECORD IN ERROR, ENTER CONTINUE, PRESS EOF'
          UPON CONSOLE.
          ACCEPT ACTION FROM CONSOLE.
          IF CONTINUE GO TO READ-AND-PROCESS,
              ELSE CLOSE CARDS DSKF LINE-PRINT,
                  STOP RUN.
/*
// XEQ
DATA CARDS GO HERE
/*
// DUP
*STOREDATA   WS   UA   INSFL 0025
```

Figure 6.10 Changes necessary to run the program for example 6.25 on the B1700, the IBM-S3, and the DECSYSTEM-10.

---

a. For the B1700:

```
SOURCE-COMPUTER. B-1700.
OBJECT-COMPUTER. B-1700.
SPECIAL-NAMES. SPO IS CONSOLE
INPUT-OUTPUT SECTION.
```

Figure 6.10 (Cont'd.)

```
FILE-CONTROL.
    SELECT CARDS ASSIGN TO READER.
    SELECT LINE-PRINT ASSIGN TO PRINTER.
    SELECT DSKF ASSIGN TO DISK.
DATA DIVISION.
   ⋮
FD  DSKF, FILE CONTAINS 50 RECORDS, LABEL RECORDS ARE OMITTED,
         DATA RECORD IS D-REC.
   ⋮
PROCEDURE DIVISION.
ST.
   ⋮
    WRITE P-LINE AFTER ADVANCING TO CHANNEL 01.
READ-AND-PROCESS.
    READ CARDS AT END,
        CLOSE CARDS LINE-PRINT,
        CLOSE DSKF WITH LOCK,
        STOP RUN.
*******************************************************************************
* CLOSING DSKF WITH LOCK MAKES THIS DISK FILE PERMANENT ON THE B-1700 *
*******************************************************************************
   ⋮
```

b. For the IBM-S3:

```
SOURCE-COMPUTER. IBM-S3.
OBJECT-COMPUTER. IBM-S3.
   ⋮
FILE-CONTROL.
    SELECT CARDS ASSIGN TO UR-2501-RD.
    SELECT LINE-PRINT ASSIGN TO UR-1403-2-66.
    SELECT DSKF ASSIGN TO UT-5444-S-INSFILE.
DATA DIVISION.
FILE SECTION.
FD  CARDS, LABEL RECORDS ARE OMITTED, DATA RECORD IS CARD-IN.
   ⋮
FD  LINE-PRINT, LABEL RECORDS ARE OMITTED,
         LINAGE  IS 66 LINES WITH FOOTING AT 61.
   ⋮
```

c. For the DECSYSTEM-10:

```
SOURCE-COMPUTER. DECSYSTEM-10.
OBJECT-COMPUTER. DECSYSTEM-10.
SPECIAL-NAMES. CHANNEL (1) IS TO-NEW-PAGE.
   ⋮
FILE-CONTROL.
    SELECT CARDS ASSIGN TO CDR.
    SELECT LINE-PRINT ASSIGN TO LPT.
    SELECT DSKF ASSIGN TO DSK, FILE-LIMIT IS 50.
   ⋮
DATA DIVISION.
```

```
FD  DSKF,
        VALUE OF IDENTIFICATION IS 'FIRST DTA',
        LABEL RECORDS ARE STANDARD.
  ⋮
WRITE DREC.
***********************************************************
* THE DEC-SYSTEM-10 DOES NOT USE THE INVALID OPTION *
* WHEN WRITING TO SEQUENTIAL DISK FILE.             *
***********************************************************
```

Review Questions

1. The sections of the DATA DIVISION are ________________,
   ________________, and ________________.
2. Level 01 entries may occur in the ________________ SECTION(s).
3. Level 77 entries may occur in the ____________ SECTION(s).
4. Level 88 entries may occur in the ________________ SECTION(s).
5. Independent elementary items have level number ______.
6. Nonelementary independent items have level number ______.
7. Condition names have level number ______.
8. On an IBM-1130 the number of words needed to store CARD-IN of project 1, Chapter 2 is ______.
9. The number of words needed to store TYPE-1 of example 6.24 is ______, and the number of words needed to store TYPE-2 of example 6.24 is ______.
10. DATA DIVISION

    ```
    FD  FILE-IN,
        LABEL RECORDS ARE STANDARD.
    01  CARD-IN.
        02  NUMBER  PIC 9999 VALUE 5678.
        02  REST    PIC X(74).
    ```

    Is the preceding VALUE clause correct? If not, why?
11. Can the VALUE clause be used with a nonconditional data name in the LINKAGE SECTION? See the material in the LINKAGE SECTION in Chapter 12. This question is related to preceding question 10.
12. Can the VALUE clause be used in a REDEFINES clause for a data name that is part of data-name-1?
13. WORKING-STORAGE SECTION.

    ```
    77 X  PIC 999 VALUE 987.
    77 Y  REDEFINES X  PIC 999.
    ```

    Is it true or false that when the program begins execution, the value of Y will be 987?
14. WORKING-STORAGE SECTION.

    ```
    77  XX  PIC X(20).
    01  A REDEFINES XX.
        02  B  PIC X(5).
        02  D  PIC 9(15).
    ```

    Is the preceding REDEFINES clause correct? If not, why?

15. What picture clause can be used to print a numeric item occupying eight positions on a line: if the item is to contain a decimal point, two decimal places, and a sign, and suppress leading zeros?

16. What picture can we use if we wish to print a numeric item suitable for check writing—i.e., two decimal places, a decimal point, and leading zeros suppressed by inserting asterisks?

Suggested Projects

1. Modify the card file used in project 1 of Chapter 2, so that STUDENT-NUMBER will have 3 digits, STUDENT-NAME will have 20 alphabetic characters, and STUDENT-MAJOR will have 15 alphabetic characters. Rewrite the DATA DIVISION to make these changes, create some new data cards to use, and run the new program. (*Hint:* Be careful in making up names for students for the data cards.)

2. Assume that the card file for the preceding project contains 57 records. How much storage is occupied by one record? By all 57 records?

3. Suppose that the record of the inventory file of example 6.10 now contains the following information.

Card column	Field	Type
1–5	item code	character
6–25	item name	alphabetic
26–45	item description	character
46–50	number on hand	number
51–55	number of demands	number
56–64	unit cost	number 999.99
65–70	suggested retail cost	number 9999.99
71–74	cost of handling	number 99.99

Write a COBOL program to do the following:

a. Print the heading THE UPDATE INVENTORY REPORT FOR THIS MONTH, starting from column 20 of the first line of the new page.

b. Skip three lines after THE UPDATE INVENTORY REPORT FOR THIS MONTH by printing three lines of spaces. Then print the following heading:

```
____ITEM CODE__NAME____________________DESCRIPTION
4 spaces     2 spaces     18 spaces
____________NUMBER ON HAND__DEMANDS__
12 spaces                    2 spaces     2 spaces
UNIT COST__SALE____DEL-COST
         2 spaces      4 spaces
```

c. Read and print the preceding inventory file under the appropriate heading. Your program should edit whenever it is required.

4. Create a card file of patients in a hospital so that each record contains the following information.

a. patient's name
b. patient's address
c. date admitted to the hospital
d. name of illness
e. patient's status (a code of one character: B for bad, G for good, and S for satisfactory)
f. the name of patient's insurance company
g. amount due

Try to fit all the preceding information on one card. You can use short names or codes if necessary. Punch the information in any order you want. Now write a COBOL program to instruct the computer to read and print the preceding file. Also, the computer should print the title of the file and a reasonable heading for the columns of the preceding information.

5. In project 4, the patient record contains seven fields; therefore, it is probable that a patient's record cannot be contained on one card, and that it will require two cards. Assume that the first card contains

Card column	Field
1–20	patient's name
21–50	patient's address
51–60	date patient was admitted to the hospital
61–80	patient's illness

and that the second card contains

Card column	Field
1	patient's status indicated by C for critical, S for satisfactory, and G for good
2–50	name and address of patient's insurance company
51–60	amount due.

Redo project 4 with these changes. (*Hint:* The examples in Chapter 6 should provide all the necessary ideas.)

6. In example 6.6, a description of STUDENT-FILE is given. Write a COBOL program to instruct the computer to read and print STUDENT-FILE. Choose appropriate headings for the printed output.

7. Redo project 6, this time using STUDENT-RECORD as described in example 6.7 as the typical record for STUDENT-FILE.

8. Suppose that we added the following field to the customer record in example 6.9.

```
03  ACTION  PIC X.
```

This field of one character contains D if the customer makes a deposit and W if the customer makes a withdrawal. Write a COBOL program to instruct the computer to read a card file, and

a. find the total and average amounts of deposits for a checking account;
b. find the total and average amounts of deposits to a savings account;
c. find the total and average amount of withdrawals from a savings account;
d. find the total and average amount of withdrawals from checking; and
e. print a list of customer names and the corresponding eight items mentioned in a through d.

(*Hint:* Specify each of the eight items as independent elementary items in the WORKING-STORAGE SECTION. When a card is read, test AC-TION with IF DEPOSIT and test TRANSACTION with IF CHECK-ING. Go to an appropriate paragraph in each case.)

9. Write a COBOL program to instruct the computer to process the sales records of the salespersons for the Own-A-Piece-of-Death-Valley Land Company. There are two or more cards containing personal information and sales information attributed to each salesperson. The first card contains

Card column	*Content*
1–10	employee number
11–30	name of salesperson
31–59	address of salesperson
60–62	age of salesperson
63–69	home phone number, including area code

The remaining cards for the salesperson contain

Card column	*Content*
1–5	number of lots sold in this tract
6–15	reference number of this tract of land
16–25	price of each lot
26–28	percent commission
29–58	district office address
59	continuation code

If column 59 of the second type of card contains a Y, it indicates that there are further cards to be read for this salesperson who sold lots in another tract.

a. Calculate the commission for each salesperson.
b. Calculate the total number of lots sold by each salesperson.
c. Print a list containing all the information about each salesperson that is on the first type of card and also include the results from parts a and b of this project.

CHAPTER 7

PROCEDURE DIVISION

The PROCEDURE DIVISION begins with the header

```
A
PROCEDURE DIVISION.
```

and is subdivided into sections or paragraphs. If no sections are present, then all the statements are grouped into paragraphs. Each paragraph begins with a programmer-supplied header in area A:

```
A
paragraph-header.
```

and the remaining parts of the paragraph are in area B. A paragraph begins with its header and ends where the next paragraph or section begins or at the end of the program. If sections are used, the first line of the division must begin with a programmer-supplied header:

```
A
section-header SECTION.
```

Sections are composed of one or more paragraphs and extend to the next section or to the end of the program.

The statements of this division are executed in sequential order unless a control statement deliberately directs otherwise.

We shall devote several chapters to explaining the statements of this division. This chapter is devoted to data-manipulation statements. Before we discuss the manipulation of data by using the MOVE statement, let's review the following classifications of data.

1. *binary:* a numeric data item whose PICTURE clause contains V, P, S, or 9 and whose USAGE IS COMPUTATIONAL (on some computers, binary items are known as numeric items),
2. *external decimal:* a numeric item whose PICTURE clause contains V, P, S, or 9 and whose USAGE IS DISPLAY,
3. *numeric-edited:* a data item whose PICTURE clause contains 9, B, P, V, Z, 0, . , *, +, −, CR, DB, $, or , and which is not external decimal (and whose USAGE must be DISPLAY),
4. *alphabetic:* an item whose PICTURE clause contains only A,
5. *alphanumeric:* an item whose PICTURE clause contains only X, and
6. *alphanumeric-edited:* an item whose PICTURE clause contains at least one X and at least one 0, or at least one X and at least one B, or at least one A and at least one 0.

When used as the sending operand of a MOVE statement, a numeric literal is treated as an external decimal, and a nonnumeric literal is treated as an alphanumeric item.

The MOVE Statement

$$\underline{MOVE} \left\{ \begin{matrix} \texttt{name-1} \\ \texttt{literal-1} \end{matrix} \right\} \underline{TO} \ \texttt{name-2 [name-3]} \ \ldots$$

The MOVE statement moves literal-1 or the content of name-1 to each data item following the word TO. The content of name-1 is not changed by this statement. The sending and receiving items can be any data item other than a file name or index name.

Difficulties may arise when the sending and receiving items involve different types of data. Figure 7.1 summarizes the permissible moves between data items.

The following rules should be observed when working with the MOVE statement.

1. No index item may appear in a MOVE statement. (Index items will be discussed in Chapter 11.)
2. Let us assume the sending and receiving items are elementary. *If the receiving item is numeric or numeric-edited;* then the items are aligned by decimal points; digits are stored in the appropriate positions; unused positions are filled with zeros; excess digits to the right or left of the decimal point are truncated. If the receiving item is not signed, any sign in the sending item will be lost. If the sending item is alphanumeric, it can contain only numeric digits and is considered to be an integer. A numeric-edited item can be moved only to an alphanumeric, alphanumeric-edited, or group item. A numeric-edited item cannot be moved to any elementary numeric or elementary numeric-edited item. In elementary moves, any necessary conversion of the internal representation of data or editing is done automatically.
3. If the receiving item is alphabetic, alphanumeric, or alphanumeric-edited, then the MOVE will cause justification and filling of unused character positions with blanks. If the sending item is too large, truncation will occur; and if the sending item is signed, the sign is eliminated.
4. A nonelementary MOVE—that is, when one or more group items is involved—is performed as an elementary alphanumeric move, except that no change in the internal representation of data is performed.

Figure 7.1 Table of permissible moves between data items.

Operand of MOVE \ Operand of TO	Group	Binary	External decimal	Numeric-edited	Alphabetic	Alpha-numeric	Alpha-numeric-edited
Group	✓	✓	✓	✓	✓	✓	✓
Binary	✓	✓	✓	✓	×	✓	✓
External decimal	✓	✓	✓	✓	×	✓	✓
Numeric-edited	✓	×	×	×	×	✓	✓
Alphabetic	✓	×	×	×	✓	✓	✓
Alphanumeric	✓	✓	✓	✓	✓	✓	✓
Alphanumeric-edited	✓	×	×	×	✓	✓	✓

✓ indicates a permissible MOVE   × indicates a nonpermissible MOVE

5. If the sending and receiving items share portions of their storage, the results of the MOVE are unpredictable.

Figure 7.2 gives several examples of the MOVE statement. See the COBOL language manual for your computer for a more detailed description of the MOVE statement.

EXAMINE Statement

```
EXAMINE name TALLYING  ⎰ UNTIL FIRST ⎱
                       ⎨ ALL         ⎬ literal-1
                       ⎱ LEADING     ⎰
          [REPLACING BY literal-2].


EXAMINE name REPLACING ⎰ ALL         ⎱
       BY literal-2.   ⎪ LEADING     ⎪ literal-1
                       ⎨ FIRST       ⎬
                       ⎱ UNTIL FIRST ⎰
```

The two forms of the EXAMINE statement are used to examine the characters of the display data item, name. Each literal must consist of one character or a figurative constant.

The first format causes the content of a special register, TALLY, to be set equal to the number of

1. characters before the first occurrence of literal-1 when the UNTIL FIRST option is used;
2. times literal-1 occurs in name when the ALL option is used;
3. times literal-1 occurs before the first character other than literal-1 is encountered, when the LEADING option is used.

If the REPLACING option is used, all the characters that are specified in the three cases are replaced by literal-2.

For example, if we have the following items in the WORKING-STORAGE SECTION,

```
77 ITEM-1  PIC X(14) VALUE 'GOODBBBMORNING'.
77 ITEM-2  PIC 9(8) VALUE 00001230.
77 ITEM-3  PIC X(14) VALUE 'D$BLINNLEDRMCK'.
```

Figure 7.2 Examples of the MOVE statement.

Value of sending item or literal	PIC	'USAGE'	PIC of receiving item	USAGE	Value after MOVE
− 002	S999	COMP	S999	DISPLAY	− 002
− 016	S999	COMP	+ 999.99	DISPLAY	− 016.00
9.68	____	literal	+ 99.9	DISPLAY	+ 09.6
SHOWBIZ	X(7)	DISPLAY	X(4)BX(3)	DISPLAY	SHOW BIZ
98.5	99.9	DISPLAY	999	COMP	illegal move
9.83	9V99	DISPLAY	$99.99	DISPLAY	$09.83
936	X(3)	DISPLAY	999V99	COMP	936.00

1. After the execution of EXAMINE ITEM-1 TALLYING ALL 'B' RE-PLACING BY SPACE. , the special register TALLY contains the value 3, and the content of ITEM-1 becomes GOOD   MORNING with three spaces between D and M.
2. After the execution of EXAMINE ITEM-2 TALLYING LEADING ZEROS REPLACING BY SPACE. , the content of TALLY is 4, and the content of ITEM-2 becomes 1230 with four leading spaces.
3. After the execution of the four sentences

```
EXAMINE ITEM-3 UNTIL FIRST 'L' REPLACING BY SPACE.
EXAMINE ITEM-3 REPLACING ALL 'N' BY 'T'.
EXAMINE ITEM-3 REPLACING FIRST 'D' BY SPACE.
EXAMINE ITEM-3 REPLACING FIRST 'M' by 'O'.
```

the content of ITEM-3 becomes LITTLE ROCK with three spaces before the first L.

The Input-Output Statements

For the input and output of small amounts of information, the ACCEPT and DISPLAY statements are often used. Their formats are

$$\underline{\text{DISPLAY}} \left\{ \begin{array}{l} \text{name-1} \\ \text{literal-1} \end{array} \right\} \quad \left[\begin{array}{l} \text{name-2} \\ \text{literal-2} \end{array} \right] \cdots$$

$$\left[\underline{\text{UPON}} \left\{ \begin{array}{l} \text{device-name} \\ \text{symbolic-name} \end{array} \right\} \right]$$

$$\underline{\text{ACCEPT}} \text{ data-name } \left[\underline{\text{FROM}} \left\{ \begin{array}{l} \text{device-name} \\ \text{symbolic-name} \end{array} \right\} \right]$$

The ACCEPT statement causes an input operation that places data in data-name. Data-name must be an item whose USAGE is DISPLAY. The input data is stored in data-name starting at the left, and if the input data exceeds the capacity of data-name, then the excess characters are truncated. If the input data will not fill data-name, then the unfilled positions in data-name are filled with blanks.

The DISPLAY statement causes an output operation that places the data in the listed items on an output device. Note that the list of items can contain both numeric and nonnumeric literals.

To use the ACCEPT and DISPLAY statements, the total length of the data items in these statements must not exceed the capacity of the input-output device they use. In general, for card readers, you should not exceed a total of 80 characters. For other devices, it is safer not to specify more than 120 characters.

The ACCEPT and DISPLAY statements are very useful when you are locating errors in a program. By using the DISPLAY statement, you can have the computer print the value of any data item at any time you desire the value of the item. The DISPLAY statement is not to be used on the B1700. On that computer you would use the MONITOR statement for this purpose. See Appendix I for information on the MONITOR statement on the B1700.

On the IBM-1130, the device name that can be specified in the ACCEPT statement is CONSOLE or a symbolic name for the CONSOLE that is assigned in the SPECIAL-NAMES paragraph. The same is true for the DISPLAY statement. If the symbolic name is DATE in the ACCEPT statement, the data that is accepted is a six-digit numeric data item whose value is the current date. The date is in the form of year, month, and day. If the ACCEPT statement is used without the FROM option, then the card reader is assumed to be the input device. The device that can be specified in the DISPLAY statement is CONSOLE or a symbolic name assigned to the console typewriter in the SPECIAL-NAMES paragraph. If the UPON option is omitted, then the output device is assumed to be the line printer.

On the IBM-S3, the devices that can be specified in the ACCEPT and DISPLAY statements are the same as those for the IBM-1130.

On the DECSYSTEM-10 the effect of the ACCEPT and DISPLAY statements depends on whether the program is being run from batch processing using cards or from manual entry at a teletypewriter console. If the program is being run from cards and no devices are specified, then the DISPLAY will be on the line printer, and the ACCEPT will be from the card reader. If the program is being run from a teletype console, then both the ACCEPT and DISPLAY statements will use the teletype console.

On the B1700 the ACCEPT statement must specify SPO (the console typewriter) or a symbolic name for SPO assigned in the SPECIAL-NAMES paragraph. The DISPLAY statement must also specify SPO or a symbolic name for SPO.

Examples 7.1 and 7.2 are not allowed on the Burroughs 1700. On the DECSYSTEM-10, CONSOLE refers to the operator's terminal.

Example 7.1

```
        :
OBJECT-COMPUTER. IBM-1130.
        :
SPECIAL-NAMES. CONSOLE IS TYPWTR.
        :
WORKING-STORAGE SECTION.
77 EMPLOYEE-NUMBER  PIC 9(5).
```

If you write

1. ACCEPT EMPLOYEE-NUMBER., the computer will read one card and move the contents of the first five columns to EMPLOYEE-NUMBER (*Note:* the usage of EMPLOYEE-NUMBER is DISPLAY); or
2. ACCEPT EMPLOYEE-NUMBER FROM CONSOLE., the computer will accept a message from the console typewriter. If the operator types 57321 and presses the EOF button (or RETURN if you are using a teletypewriter), the value of EMPLOYEE-NUMBER will be 57321. If you type 32, the value will be 32000; or
3. ACCEPT EMPLOYEE-NUMBER FROM TYPWTR., the result is the same as though we had written ACCEPT EMPLOYEE-NUMBER FROM CONSOLE. because of the SPECIAL-NAMES paragraph.

Example 7.2

```
        :
OBJECT-COMPUTER. IBM-1130.
        :
SPECIAL-NAMES. CONSOLE IS SLOWRTR.
        :
WORKING-STORAGE SECTION.
77 BALANCE   PIC 9(5)V9(5).
77 NUMBER    PIC 9(5).
```

If you write

1. DISPLAY BALANCE., the value of BALANCE will be printed on the line printer;
2. DISPLAY 'ERRORS ARE FOUND IN DATA'., the phrase ERRORS ARE FOUND IN DATA will be printed on the line printer;
3. DISPLAY 'ACCOUNT NUMBER', NUMBER, 'IS INCORRECT'., and the value of NUMBER is 34210, then ACCOUNT NUMBER 34210 IS INCORRECT will be printed on the line printer; or
4. DISPLAY 'ACCOUNT NUMBER ON CARD JUST READ IS IN-CORRECT, ENTER CORRECT VALUE.' UPON SLOWRTR. AC-CEPT NUMBER FROM CONSOLE., the message will be printed on the console typewriter, and the computer will wait for the operator to type the correct value and press the EOF button.

(*Note:* The compiler on the IBM-1130 assumes the 1442 reader-puncher and the 1132 line printer to be the devices for the ACCEPT and DISPLAY statements unless the QDFLT options were used when the compiler was loaded. If these devices are not available, make sure that the QDFLT options are in effect or specify the correct devices as compile-time options. The appendices tell how to specify the correct devices as compile-time options.)

The ACCEPT and DISPLAY statements have drawbacks: They cannot be used for disk input-output, and they cannot process large data files efficiently. For these reasons, we need the READ and WRITE statements for file input and output.

Before we can use a file, we must open it. All files should be closed before a program is terminated or before the files are opened a second time.

The OPEN and CLOSE Statements

The format of the OPEN statement is

```
OPEN  [INPUT    file-name-1 [file-name-2] ...]
      [OUTPUT   file-name-3 [file-name-4] ...]
      [I-O      file-name-5 [file-name-6] ...]
```

and the format of the CLOSE statement is

$$\text{CLOSE}\quad \text{file-name-1}\ \left[\begin{Bmatrix}\underline{\text{UNIT}}\\\underline{\text{REEL}}\end{Bmatrix}\right]\ [\text{WITH}\ \underline{\text{LOCK}}]$$

$$\text{[file-name-2}\ \left[\begin{Bmatrix}\underline{\text{UNIT}}\\\underline{\text{REEL}}\end{Bmatrix}\right]\ [\text{WITH}\ \underline{\text{LOCK}}]]\ ...$$

Example 7.3   The statement OPEN INPUT CUSTOMERS, SELLERS, I-O TRANS-
ACTIONS. opens for input the file CUSTOMERS and the file SELLERS
and opens for input-output the file TRANSACTIONS.

Example 7.4   The statement CLOSE CUSTOMERS, TRANSACTIONS. closes the files
CUSTOMERS and TRANSACTIONS. These files can be opened again
later in a program containing these statements.

The REEL option cannot be used on the IBM-1130. The UNIT and
REEL options are used with sequential-access files, in which case the
computer will treat the file as though it were composed of two or more
separate parts called *volumes*. When you close a unit of a file that is
composed of volumes, you close the current volume being processed. The
file is still open, but now it is open to the next volume of the file.

Closing a file with the LOCK option on the IBM-1130 and the IBM-S3
closes the file and also prevents the file from being opened again in the same
program. On the B1700 closing a file with LOCK closes the file, and if the file
is a newly created disk file, the use of the LOCK option makes it a permanent file, if it is a disk file. If the file is an old disk file and we close it with
LOCK on the B1700, then the file is simply closed. On the B1700 we can also
close a disk or tape file with PURGE. Any permanent file closed with
PURGE on the B1700 ceases to be permanent and is eliminated. If we close
a file on the B1700 with RELEASE, the file will be closed and will make
available the main storage areas that were used for processing the file.

If you close a file with the UNIT option and the file was not assigned to
several volumes, any attempt to READ or WRITE that file will cause the AT
END condition to be executed for the READ statement and the INVALID
KEY condition to be executed for the WRITE.

It is very important to close files when you finish using them. In particular,
a sequentially organized file should always be closed after you finish storing
records in it. When the file is closed, the computer automatically marks the
physical end of the records that were stored. When this file is read at a later
time, the computer uses this file *marker* to determine when it has read all the
records in the file. If the file is not closed when the records are stored, the
marker will not be present, and execution-time errors could result. On the
IBM-1130 the computer uses the hexadecimal number /8000 to mark the end
of a sequential disk file. On other computers the end-of-file marker would
probably be different. However, since the programmer never has to use this
marker, you need not be concerned about it. It is worth observing that your
programs have used end-of-file markers all along. You had end-of-file markers that marked the physical end of your COBOL source programs and also
the end of your card files. On the IBM-1130 a card with /* in the first two
columns is used for both types of markers. The same end-of-file markers are
used on the IBM-S3. On the B1700 the end of the COBOL source program is
marked with a card containing ?END in columns 1 through 4. The same type
of card is used to mark the end-of-data card files. On the DECSYSTEM-10
the end-of-file marker for card files is a card with $EOD in columns 1–4.

The READ Statement

The READ statement is used to bring the content of a file record into main
storage.

The format of the READ statement for a sequentially organized file is

```
READ file-name RECORD [INTO name]
    AT END imperative-sentence.
```

where file-name is the name of an open INPUT or I-O file, and imperative-sentence is the action the computer is to take when the end of the file is reached. If the INTO option is used, the content of the record is also moved to name, which must be a WORKING-STORAGE item, a LINKAGE SECTION item, or the output record of an opened file.

When the computer reads a sequential-access disk file, it assumes that the first READ statement for the file is to read the first record of the file; the second READ statement for the file is to read the second record; and so on.

The format of the READ statement for a random-access disk file is

```
READ file-name RECORD [INTO name]
    INVALID KEY imperative-sentence.
```

Recall that direct files can be created only on direct-access devices. The relative location of a record within the file is determined by the value of the ACTUAL KEY (file key) of the file. Thus to use the READ statement for a random-access file, the programmer must have assigned a value to the file key that specifies the record desired. When the READ statement is executed, the computer will locate the record specified by the file key and move the content to the file record area in main storage and also to name if the INTO name option is used. (The data is moved from the record area to name exactly as is done in a MOVE statement.) If the file key specifies a record that is not actually in the file, the computer executes the statements of the imperative sentence.

The SEEK Statement

When the computer is asked to READ a record of a random-access file, it can require a great amount of time because the disk unit must perform physical operations to locate the record. The SEEK statement can sometimes avoid these delays. The format of this statement is

```
SEEK file-name RECORD
```

where file-name is the name of the random-access file to be read. As soon as the key for the next record to be read is known, the computer can execute the SEEK statement. The computer causes the disk unit to search for the appropriate cylinder. If the key is invalid, the computer will use that fact if a READ is attempted. If the key is valid, the cylinder containing the record will be located before the READ statement is executed. *The advantage of the statement is that while the disk unit searches, the computer can execute other statements.* The statement is useful only if one can perform other tasks between the SEEK and the READ statements. Finally, the SEEK statement can be used also when writing on a random-access disk file.

Example 7.5

Suppose MASTER-FILE is an I-O random-access file with 5,000 records, and the name of its ACTUAL KEY is FINDER. FILE-IN is an input file from the card reader, and TEMP-LOCATION is a group item in the WORKING-STORAGE SECTION.

The following are examples of READ statements that could be used in the PROCEDURE DIVISION.

1. READ FILE-IN AT END <u>CLOSE FILE-IN, STOP RUN</u>.

imperative sentence

The execution of this statement causes the card reader to read one card, and if the end-of-file marker is read, FILE-IN is closed and the program run is stopped.

2. Suppose we want to read record 65 of MASTER-FILE. We could write

```
MOVE 65 TO FINDER.
READ MASTER-FILE, INVALID KEY,
DISPLAY 'THERE IS NO SUCH RECORD'.
```

Since 65 is between 1 and 5000, the content of record 65 will be moved into main storage, and the message will not be displayed.

3. We could also write

```
MOVE CUSTOMER-NUMBER TO FINDER.
SEEK MASTER-FILE RECORD.
READ MASTER-FILE RECORD, INVALID KEY DISPLAY
'THERE IS NO RECORD WITH NUMBER',
CUSTOMER-NUMBER, 'IN MASTER-FILE'.
```

If CUSTOMER-NUMBER is 6190, the computer will write THERE IS NO RECORD WITH NUMBER 6190 IN MASTER-FILE. Note that since there are no statements between the SEEK and READ statements, the SEEK statement is useless.

4. We could use the INTO option.

```
MOVE CUSTOMER-NUMBER TO FINDER.
SEEK MASTER-FILE RECORD.
    ⋮
READ MASTER-FILE INTO TEMP-LOCATION, INVALID KEY
DISPLAY 'INVALID KEY ENCOUNTERED'.
```

If the key is valid, the record will be moved to main storage and the content will also be moved to TEMP-LOCATION.

The WRITE Statement

The WRITE statement for disk files is similar to the READ statement for disk files. Its format is

```
WRITE record-name [FROM data-name]
      INVALID KEY imperative-sentence.
```

where record-name is the name of an OUTPUT or I-O disk file record, data-name is an item in WORKING-STORAGE SECTION, LINKAGE SECTION, or an FD entry, and imperative-sentence contains the actions to be taken if an attempt is made to write beyond the limits of the file. If random access is used, an invalid key causes the execution of imperative-sentence. If the file access is sequential, then each WRITE for the file causes a WRITE on the next record of the file, and, if an attempt is made to write beyond the physical end of the file, imperative-sentence is executed.

Example 7.6   For the IBM-1130:

```
                              ⋮
                    FILE-CONTROL.
                        SELECT DISK-FL-1, ASSIGN TO DF-1-5000,
                            ACCESS IS RANDOM, ACTUAL KEY IS LOCATER.
                        SELECT DISK-FL-2, ASSIGN TO DF-2-150.
                              ⋮
                    WORKING-STORAGE SECTION.
                    77 LOCATER  PIC S9(5) COMP.
```

For the IBM-S3:

```
                              ⋮
                    FILE-CONTROL.
                        SELECT DISK-FL-1, ASSIGN TO DA-5444-R-FILE1,
                            ACCESS IS RANDOM, ACTUAL KEY IS LOCATER.
                        SELECT DISK-FL-2, ASSIGN TO DA-5444-S-FILE2.
                              ⋮
                    WORKING-STORAGE SECTION.
                    77 LOCATER  PIC S9(7) COMP.
```

For the DECSYSTEM-10:

```
                              ⋮
                    FILE-CONTROL.
                        SELECT DISK-FL-1, ASSIGN TO DISK, FILE-LIMIT
                            IS 5000, ACCESS IS RANDOM, ACTUAL KEY IS
                            LOCATER.
                        SELECT DISK-FL-2, ASSIGN TO DISK, FILE LIMIT
                            IS 150.
                              ⋮
                    WORKING-STORAGE SECTION.
                    77 LOCATER  PIC S9(4) COMP.
```

For the B1700:

```
                              ⋮
                    FILE-CONTROL.
                        SELECT DISK-FL-1, ASSIGN TO DISK, ACCESS IS
                            RANDOM, ACTUAL KEY IS LOCATER.
                        SELECT DISK-FL-2, ASSIGN TO DISK.
                              ⋮
                    FILE SECTION.
                    FD DISK-FL-1 LABEL RECORDS ARE STANDARD, FILE
                            CONTAINS 5000 RECORDS.
                              ⋮
                    FD DISK-FL-2 LABEL RECORDS ARE STANDARD, FILE
                            CONTAINS 150 RECORDS.
                              ⋮
                    WORKING-STORAGE SECTION.
                    77 LOCATER  PIC 9(8) COMP.
                              ⋮
```

Suppose that RECORD-1 and RECORD-2 are the names for the typical records of DISK-FL-1 and DISK-FL-2, respectively, and that both files are now open as output files. Observe that DISK-FL-2 is sequentially organized and therefore a sequentially accessed file. DISK-FL-1 is a direct file with random access.

If we write

```
MOVE 65 TO LOCATER.
WRITE RECORD-1, INVALID KEY
DISPLAY 'INVALID KEY'.,
```

the content of RECORD-1 will be placed in record 65 of DISK-FL-1; or,

```
MOVE 6000 TO LOCATER.
WRITE RECORD-1, INVALID KEY
DISPLAY 'INVALID KEY'.,
```

the message, INVALID KEY, will be written or,

```
        MOVE 0 TO LOCATER.
LP-1.
        ADD 1 TO LOCATER.
        WRITE RECORD-2 INVALID KEY,
                        GO TO LP-2.
        IF LOCATER LESS THAN 151,
                        GO TO LP-1.
LP-2.
        CLOSE DISK-FL-1, DISK-FL-2. STOP RUN.
```

The content of RECORD-2 will be written on each record of DISK-FL-2, and when LOCATER is 151, the program run is stopped.

The WRITE statement for *nondisk files without carriage control* is as easy as the WRITE statement for disk files. The format is simply

```
WRITE record-name [FROM name]
```

where record-name is a record name assigned to an open output file. When the statement is executed, the content of record-name is written and creates one line of print on the line printer or one punched card on a card-punch unit or one tape record. If the output device is the line printer, vertical spacing is done automatically by the computer.

Example 7.7

```
        ⋮
ENVIRONMENT DIVISION.
        ⋮
FILE-CONTROL.
        SELECT PRINT-FILE ASSIGN TO PR-1403.
        SELECT PUNCH-FILE ASSIGN TO PO-1442.
DATA DIVISION.
FILE SECTION.
        ⋮
FD PRINT-FILE
        LABEL RECORDS ARE OMITTED.
```

```
01 LINE-OUT.
   03 CUSTOMER-NUMBER   PIC 9(5).
   03 CUSTOMER-NAME     PIC X(20).
   03 FILLER            PIC X(95).
FD PUNCH-FILE LABEL RECORDS ARE OMITTED.
01 CARD-OUT.
   02 CUSTOMER NUMBER   PIC 9(5).
   02 FILLER            PIC X(10).
   02 CUSTOMER-NAME     PIC X(20).
   02 FILLER            PIC X(45).
```

Assume the following MOVE statements.

```
MOVE SPACES TO LINE-OUT, CARD-OUT.
MOVE 55555 TO CUSTOMER-NUMBER OF LINE-OUT.
MOVE 'MR. GEORGE C. LAMB' TO CUSTOMER-NAME OF
   LINE-OUT
```

Then, if we write

```
WRITE LINE-OUT.
```

the output on the 1403 printer will be

```
55555MR. GEORGE C. LAMB
```

and, if we write

```
WRITE CARD-OUT FROM LINE-OUT.
```

we would have a *group move* yielding

```
55555MR. GEORGE C. LAMB
```

and, if we write

```
MOVE SPACES TO CARD-OUT.
MOVE 55555 TO CUSTOMER-NUMBER OF CARD-OUT.
MOVE 'MR. GEORGE C. LAMB' TO CUSTOMER-NAME OF
   CARD-OUT
```

we would get

```
55555     MR. GEORGE C. LAMB
```

In many cases it is desirable to skip lines or start on a new page when printing. To do this, we must work with files assigned to the line printer with carriage control. The format for the WRITE statement in this case can be

```
WRITE record-name [FROM data-name-1]
```

$$
\left\{ \begin{array}{l} \text{AFTER} \\ \text{BEFORE} \end{array} \right\} \underline{\text{ADVANCING}} \left\{ \begin{array}{l} \text{data-name-2} \\ \text{symbolic-name} \\ \text{integer LINES} \end{array} \right\}
$$

In this statement record-name is a record for the opened output file, and data-name-1 is a WORKING-STORAGE item, a LINKAGE SECTION item, or an item in an FD entry. If the AFTER option is used, the line printer spaces and then prints. If the BEFORE option is used, the line printer prints and then spaces. The amount of spacing is controlled by the item following ADVANCING. If data-name-2 is used, it must be an elementary numeric item whose value is an integer from 1 through 100. The printer uses the value of data-name-2 to determine the number of lines to space. Similarly, if one uses the option integer LINES where the integer is from 1 through 100, the printer will space the required number of lines. The symbolic-name or mnemonic-name option is somewhat complex. Vertical spacing on some line printers is controlled by a punched paper tape in the line printer. The first punch, which is called C01, is generally at the first line of the page, and the other punches correspond to other positions on the page. The exact correspondence depends upon the particular paper tape in use. One can also use the name of CSP to indicate no vertical spacing on some line printers. By assigning symbolic names for these items in the SPECIAL-NAMES paragraph, you can cause the printer to space to those positions corresponding to C01 and CSP. There is more information in the discussion of the SPECIAL-NAMES paragraph in Chapter 5 and in the appendices.

Example 7.8   Modify example 7.7 by adding

```
SPECIAL-NAMES.
     C01 is TO-TOP.
```

Then if we write

```
WRITE LINE-OUT AFTER ADVANCING TO-TOP.
```

symbolic-name

the printed line we showed in example 7.7 would be printed at the top of a new page.

Examples 7.7 and 7.8 were described for the IBM-1130. The same statements would work for an IBM-S3 if we change the devices to which the files are assigned.

Examples 7.7 and 7.8 would work on the DECSYSTEM-10 if we change the devices to which the files are assigned and if we change the SPECIAL-NAMES paragraph to

```
SPECIAL-NAMES. CHANNEL (1) IS TO-TOP.
```

The B1700 does not allow you to assign mnemonic names to line printer channels. To make examples 7.7 and 7.8 work on the B1700, you must change the devices to which the files are assigned, delete the SPECIAL-NAMES paragraph, and change the preceding WRITE statement to

```
WRITE LINE-OUT AFTER ADVANCING TO CHANNEL 01.
```

Suppose we do some additional processing and now wish to write the new contents of LINE-OUT leaving four blank lines between the printed results. This could be done by writing

```
WRITE LINE-OUT AFTER ADVANCING 5 LINES.
```

The printer will space five lines, print on the fifth line, and thus leave four of the lines blank.

The complete form of the WRITE statement for the line printer with carriage control is

```
WRITE record-name [FROM data-name-1]

{AFTER }            {data-name-2  }
{BEFORE} ADVANCING  {symbolic-name}
                    {integer LINES}

    [AT {EOP        } imperative-sentence].
        {END-OF-PAGE}
```

This final clause can be used to provide special instructions when the printer reaches the end of a page. When the printer reaches the end of the page, it writes and then executes imperative-sentence. A common use for this is to advance to the top of a new page and print a heading. This clause cannot be used on the DECSYSTEM-10 and the B1700.

Example 7.9   We can modify example 7.8 by using

```
WRITE LINE-OUT AFTER ADVANCING 1 AT EOP
   MOVE ' CUSTOMER INFORMATION ' TO LINE-OUT,
   WRITE LINE-OUT AFTER ADVANCING TO-TOP.
```

We have now presented the information on the READ, WRITE, AC-CEPT, DISPLAY, MOVE, and EXAMINE statements. To our discussion we would like to add the following warning: *Whenever a WRITE statement is executed for an I-O file in sequential-access mode, the preceding INPUT-OUTPUT statement for the file must have been a READ statement. Otherwise, an uncorrectable error results.*

Example 7.10   In the program in figure 7.4 we have the following files.

1. There is an I-O random file by the name MASTER-FILE that contains the information about the customers of a bank. The key to get information about a customer is the customer's number.
2. There is an input file that contains the records of the customers' withdrawals and deposits. This file is named FILE-IN.
3. There is an output file by the name PRINT-FILE to print the customers' number, withdrawals, deposits, and balance.

Figures 7.3, 7.4, and 7.5 are the flowchart and complete program to read the input file FILE-IN and accordingly to update the I-O random file MASTER-FILE and to print out the PRINT-FILE.

Compiler-directing Statements

The compiler-directing statements provide instructions for the COBOL compiler. They are the NOTE, ENTER, and COPY statements.

*Figure 7.3 System flowchart for the BANK-UPDATE-FILE
program for example 7.10.*

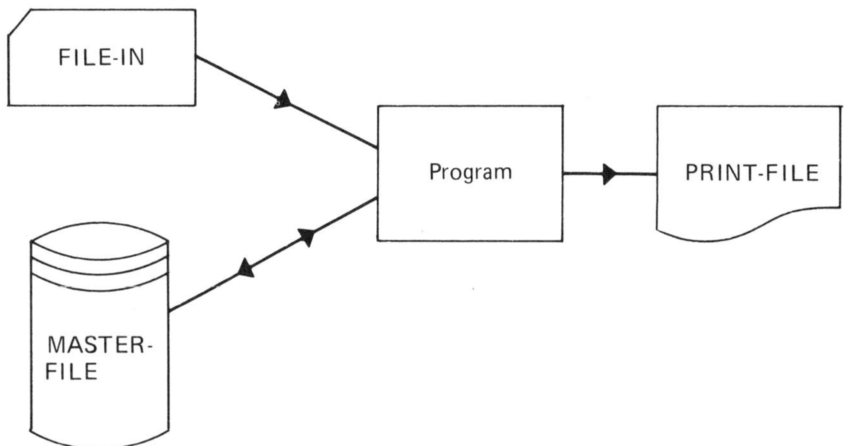

The NOTE Statement

The NOTE statement informs the COBOL compiler of the presence of programmer comments that are not to be used as a part of the compiled program. The format of this statement is

```
NOTE comment-entry.
```

If the NOTE statement is the first statement of a paragraph, the entire paragraph is considered to be a programmer comment. If a NOTE statement is not the first statement in a paragraph, then only the NOTE statement is considered a programmer comment—i.e., the comment starts with the word NOTE and ends with the first period after NOTE.

The ENTER Statement

The format of the second compiler-directing statement, the ENTER statement, is

```
ENTER language-name [routine-name].
```

In IBM-1130 COBOL this statement is used as a documentary comment. On other computers this statement allows a source language other than COBOL (such as assembler, FORTRAN, PL1, and so forth) to be used in a COBOL program.

The COPY Statement

The COPY statement is used to provide standardized information to a COBOL program. By using the COPY statement, you can use prewritten DATA DIVISION entries, ENVIRONMENT DIVISION clauses, and PROCEDURE DIVISION sections or paragraphs or set of instructions. The prewritten items are stored in the COBOL Source Program Library in your installation. The entries of the library are *modules* and each has a name. You can store a module in the library by using special routines. The routines differ from one computer to another. The text of the modules can be copied into a COBOL source program, and the effect is the same as if the

Figure 7.4 Program flowchart for the BANK-UPDATE-FILE program for example 7.10.

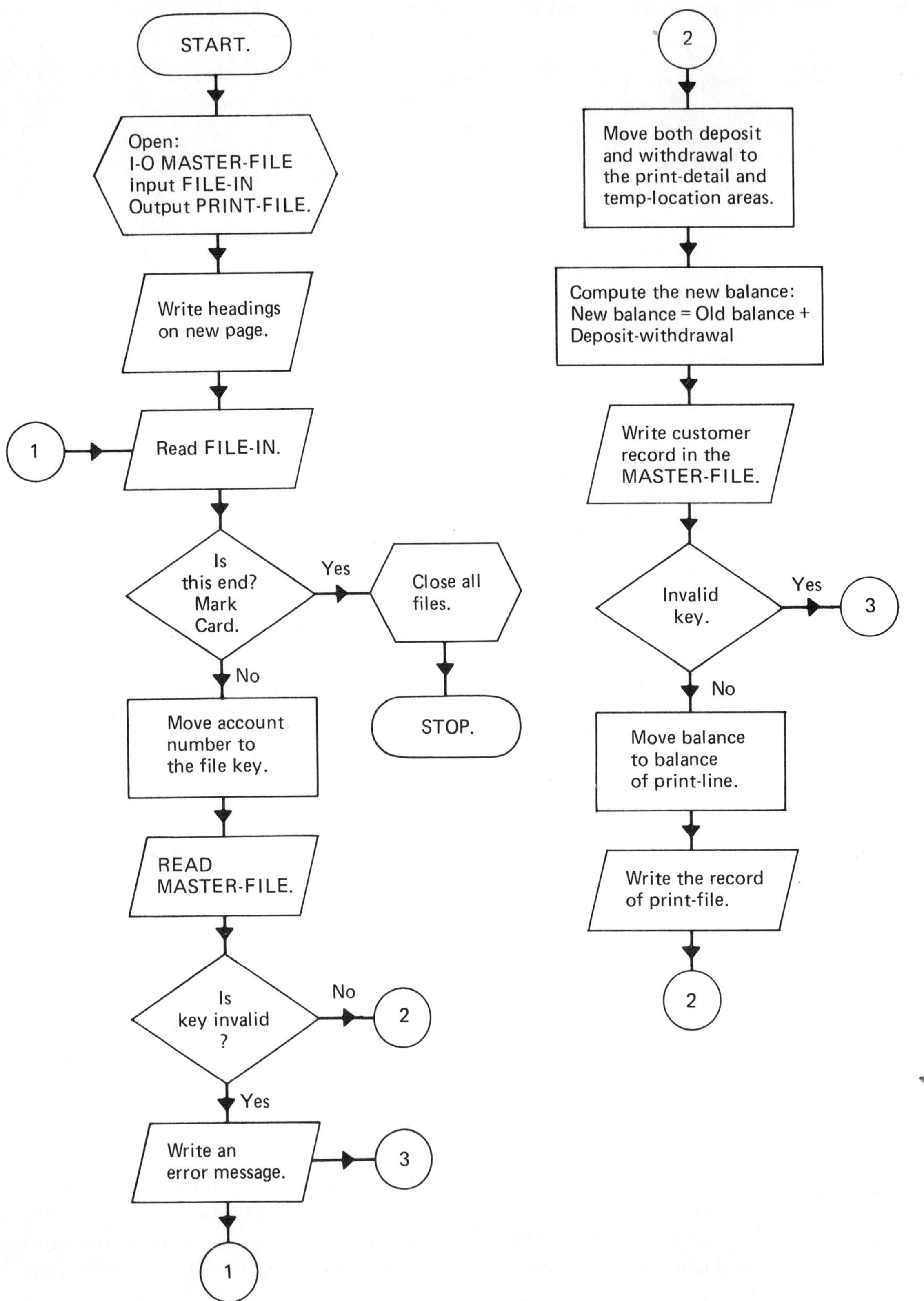

Figure 7.5 Program listing for example 7.10 as run on the IBM-1130.

```
// COBOL
*LIST,STNO,/01FE,XREF
       IDENTIFICATION DIVISION.
       PROGRAM-ID.  BANK-UPDATE-FILE.
       AUTHOR.  DUPLISSEY-KHAILANY.
       INSTALLATION.  UALR.
       SECURITY.  CUSTOMER'S RECORD CAN BE ACCESSED ONLY BY HIS
           ACCOUNT NUMBER AND THE ACCOUNT NUMBER IS CONFIDENTIAL.
       REMARKS.  IN THIS PROGRAM YOU WILL SEE MANY DIFFERENT I/O
           STATEMENTS.  THE ACTION OF SOME OF THOSE STATEMENTS IS
           EXPLAINED BY MEANS OF COMMENT STATEMENTS.  RECALL THAT
           IF THE FIRST STATEMENT OF A PARAGRAPH IS A NOTE STATE-
           MENT, THE PARAGRAPH IS CONSIDERED AS A COMMENT AND
           HAVING AN * IN COLUMN 7 CAUSES THE SENTENCE ON THE CARD
           TO BE CONSIDERED AS A COMMENT.
       ENVIRONMENT DIVISION.
       CONFIGURATION SECTION.
       SOURCE-COMPUTER.  IBM-1130.
       OBJECT-COMPUTER.  IBM-1130.
       SPECIAL-NAMES.  C01 IS TO-NEW-PAGE.
       INPUT-OUTPUT SECTION.
       FILE-CONTROL.
           SELECT MASTER-FILE ASSIGN TO DF-1-5000,
               ACCESS MODE IS RANDOM,
                   ACTUAL KEY IS FINDER.
           SELECT PRINT-FILE ASSIGN TO PR-1403.
           SELECT FILE-IN ASSIGN TO RD-2501.
       DATA DIVISION.
       FILE SECTION.
       FD  MASTER-FILE,
           LABEL RECORDS ARE STANDARD,
           DATA RECORD IS CUSTOMER-RECORD.
       **********************************************************************
       *****LABEL RECORDS CANNOT BE OMITTED FOR DISK FILES......         *
       **********************************************************************
       01   CUSTOMER-RECORD.
            02   CUSTOMER-ACCOUNT-NUMBER  PIC 9(4) COMP.
            02   CUSTOMER-NAME            PIC X(20).
            02   CUSTOMER-ADDRESS         PIC X(30).
            02   DEPOSIT                  PIC 9(6)V9(2) COMP.
            02   WITH-DRAWAL              PIC 9(6)V9(2) COMP.
            02   BALANCE                  PIC 9(8)V9(2) COMP.
       FD  FILE-IN,
           LABEL RECORDS ARE OMITTED
           DATA RECORD IS CARD-IN.
       01   CARD-IN.
            02   ACCOUNT-NUMBER           PIC 9(5).
            02   DEPOSIT                  PIC 9(6)V9(2).
            02   WITHDRAWAL               PIC 9(6)V9(2).
       FD  PRINT-FILE,
           LABEL RECORDS ARE OMITTED,
           DATA RECORD IS LINE-OUT.
       01  LINE-OUT                       PIC X(120).
       WORKING-STORAGE SECTION.
       77  FINDER                         PIC S9(5) COMP.
       **********************************************************************
       *****FINDER IS THE ACTUAL KEY FOR MASTER-FILE.  THE VALUE OF      *
       *****FINDER SPECIFIES THE POSITION OF THE RECORD IN MASTER-FILE   *
       *****TO BE READ OR WRITTEN. .....                                 *
       **********************************************************************
       01   TEMP-LOCATION.
            02   NUMBER                   PIC 9(4) COMP.
            02   NAME                     PIC X(20).
            02   ADDRESS                  PIC X(30).
            02   DEPOSIT                  PIC 9(6)V9(2) COMP.
            02   WITHDRAWAL               PIC 9(6)V9(2) COMP.
            02   BALANCE                  PIC 9(8)V9(2) COMP.
```

Figure 7.5 (Cont'd.)

```
    01  HEADING.
        02  FILLER          PIC X(10) VALUE SPACES.
        02  NUMB            PIC X(15) VALUE 'CUSTOMER NUMBER'.
        02  FILLER          PIC X(10) VALUE SPACES.
        02  W-DR            PIC X(10) VALUE 'WITHDRAWAL'.
        02  FILLER          PIC X(10) VALUE SPACES.
        02  DEPOSIT         PIC X(7) VALUE 'DEPOSIT'.
        02  FILLER          PIC X(10) VALUE SPACES.
        02  BAL             PIC X(7) VALUE 'BALANCE'.
    01  PRINT-DETAIL.
        02  FILLER          PIC X(10) VALUE SPACES.
        02  NUMBER          PIC 9(4).
        02  FILLER          PIC X(10) VALUE SPACES.
        02  W-DRAW          PIC $$$$$$9V99.
        02  FILLER          PIC X(10) VALUE SPACES.
        02  DEPOSIT         PIC $$$$$9.99.
        02  FILLER          PIC X(10) VALUE SPACES.
        02  BALANCE         PIC $$$$$$$9.99.
    PROCEDURE DIVISION.
    START.
        OPEN I-O MASTER-FILE,
             INPUT FILE-IN,
             OUTPUT PRINT-FILE.
    *****************************************************************
    *****SINCE WE PROCESS MASTER-FILE AS AN I-O FILE, EACH RECORD IS *
    *****READ AND THEN UPDATED AND WRITTEN BACK TO MASTER-FILE. THIS *
    *****TYPE OF PROCESSING ALWAYS ASSUMES THAT THE FILE INVOLVED    *
    *****WAS PREVIOUSLY CREATED.....                                 *
    *****************************************************************
        WRITE LINE-OUT FROM HEADING AFTER ADVANCING
        TO-NEW-PAGE.
    *****************************************************************
    *****THE HEADINGS ARE PRINTED ON A NEW PAGE.....                *
    *****************************************************************
     READ-A-CARD.
        READ FILE-IN AT END GO TO LAST.
        MOVE ACCOUNT-NUMBER OF CARD-IN TO FINDER.
    *****************************************************************
    *****NOW FINDER CONTAINS THE CUSTOMER NUMBER.....               *
    *****************************************************************
        READ MASTER-FILE INTO TEMP-LOCATION
            INVALID DISPLAY 'FILE KEY CONTAINS INVALID DATA.',
            GO TO READ-A-CARD.
        NOTE   IF THE FILE KEY CONTAINS A NUMBER BETWEEN 1 AND 5000
        THE INFORMATION WILL BE AVAILABLE IN BOTH TEMP-LOCATION AND
        THE RECORD OF THE MASTER-FILE.
     LP-1.
        MOVE DEPOSIT OF CARD-IN TO DEPOSIT OF PRINT-DETAIL,
            DEPOSIT OF TEMP-LOCATION.
        MOVE WITHDRAWAL OF CARD-IN TO W-DRAW OF PRINT-DETAIL,
            WITHDRAWAL OF TEMP-LOCATION.
        ADD DEPOSIT IN CARD-IN TO BALANCE OF TEMP-LOCATION.
        SUBTRACT WITHDRAWAL OF CARD-IN FROM BALANCE IN
            TEMP-LOCATION.
    *****YOU SHOULD REMEMBER THAT BOTH   IN   AND   OF   ARE EQUIVALENT *
    *****IN THE QUALIFYING OF DATA NAMES.....                          *
        WRITE CUSTOMER-RECORD FROM TEMP-LOCATION INVALID KEY
            DISPLAY 'KEY CONTAINS WRONG DATA.',
            GO TO READ-A-CARD.
    *****************************************************************
    ****THIS WAS A WRITE STATEMENT FOR A FILE WITH DIRECT ORGANIZA- *
    *****TION.....†                                                 *
    *****************************************************************
        MOVE BALANCE OF TEMP-LOCATION TO BALANCE OF PRINT-DETAIL.
        WRITE LINE-OUT FROM PRINT-DETAIL AFTER ADVANCING 2 LINES.
        GO TO READ-A-CARD.
```

---

† On the DECSYSTEM-10, INVALID with WRITE is not allowed.

```
**********************************************************************
*****THE CREATION OF TEMP-LOCATION WAS TO SHOW YOU HOW TO USE THE*
*****FRCM OPTION WITH A WRITE STATEMENT FOR A RANDOMLY ACCESSED  *
*****FILE.....                                                   *
**********************************************************************
  LAST.
      CLCSE PRINT-FILE, MASTER-FILE, FILE-IN.
      STCP RUN.
/*
```

text were actually present in the source program. The COPY statement can be used in a variety of places in a source program. The format for the COPY statement is

```
SOURCE-COMPUTER. COPY module-name.
OBJECT-COMPUTER. COPY module-name.
SPECIAL-NAMES. COPY module-name.
FILE-CONTROL. COPY module-name.
I-O CONTROL. COPY module-name.
FD file-name COPY module-name.
01 data-name COPY module-name.
```

or in the PROCEDURE DIVISION,

```
section-name SECTION COPY module-name.
paragraph-name. COPY module-name.
```

On the IBM-1130 and the IBM-S3, you can also use the formats

```
77 data-name COPY module-name.
SELECT file-name COPY module-name.
```

On the B1700 and the DECSYSTEM-10, you can use the COPY REPLAC-ING BY form of the COPY statement. The format of this statement is

$$
\text{COPY module-name } \underline{\text{REPLACING}}
$$

$$
\text{word-1 } \underline{\text{BY}} \begin{Bmatrix} \text{word-2} \\ \text{data-name-1} \\ \text{procedure-name-1} \end{Bmatrix}
$$

$$
\left[\text{word-3 } \underline{\text{BY}} \begin{Bmatrix} \text{word-4} \\ \text{data-name-2} \\ \text{procedure-name-2} \end{Bmatrix} \right] \ldots
$$

When a module is copied into a source program using the preceding form of the COPY statement, each occurrence of word-1 is replaced by the specified item, each occurrence of word-3 is replaced by the specified item, etc. The text of the module in the library is not affected.

Figure 7.6 is a typical program to set up the COBOL library on the IBM-1130. [See the appendix on the IBM-1130 for information on the Disk Utility Program (DUP) control cards.] The following discussion explains how the library is created and organized on IBM-1130.

Each library must have a directory, and the directory size must be computed on the basis of the following formula:

$$
\text{Directory size} = 4 + (4 \times \text{number of modules})
$$

In our example illustrated in figure 7.6, we are creating a library with 100 modules. The directory size is therefore 404 words. This will require two sectors of storage. The size of the directory was indicated by the card

    *INITIALIZE 002

The monitor cards / / DUP , and *STOREDATA WS UA QSLIB 202 cause the DUP to create 202 sectors of permanent storage in the User Area for the COBOL library under the name QSLIB. The latter name is always used for a COBOL library. The 202 sectors of storage provide storage for the directory as well as the library itself. How did we arrive at a figure of 200 sectors of storage for the library?

1. We decided that each module of our library could hold up to 20 cards of text. We estimated that each card would have about 50 nonblank characters. Each word of storage can hold 2 characters, and so we estimate that one card will require 25 words of storage. In addition, one word of storage is needed to indicate the end of one card and the beginning of another. Thus our 20 cards will require about 520 words of storage or 2 sectors of storage.

2. We assumed that we wanted 100 modules in our library, so the library will require 200 sectors of storage.

Figure 7.6 Example of a job on the IBM-1130 that creates a COBOL Library and stores a module in the Library.

```
  //JOB      4002
  LOG DRIVE    CART SPEC    CART AVAIL    PHY DRIVE
    0000          4002          4002          0000
  V2 M10    ACTUAL 16K    CONFIG 16K
  //DUP
  *STOREDATA    WS    UA    QSLIB    202
  CART ID 4002    DB ADDR    3BB0    DB CNT OCAO
// XEQ QLIBR

*INITIALIZE 002
ACTION COMPLETED
*ADD SPECNAMES
*** MODULE NAME CATALOGUED AS SPECN

SOURCE MODULE SPECN
PAGLIN - A...B... COBOL SOURCE STATEMENTS .......... IDENTFCN
          CONSOLE IS TYPWTR, CSP IS TO-SAME-LINE, C01 IS TO-TOP,
          C02 IS TO-CNL2, C03 IS TO-CNL3, C04 IS TO-CNL4, C05
          IS TO-CNL5, C06 IS TO-CNL6, C07 IS TO-CNL7, C08 IS
          TO-CNL8, C09 IS TO-CNL9, C10 IS TO-CNL10, C11 IS TO-CNL11,
          C12 IS TO-BOTTOM.
ACTION COMPLETED
LIBRARY RUN COMPLETED
```

The monitor card / / XEQ QLIBR causes the QLIBR program to be executed, and this program creates the COBOL library.

There are several functions necessary for the maintenance of the library. The format of the statements to perform these functions is

```
*function module-name option [,option] . . .
```

In our program the card *ADD SPECNAMES is an example of such a card. It adds a module called SPECNAMES to the COBOL library where it is stored under the name SPECN because SPECNAMES is longer than five characters. Other examples of functions are DELETE, COMPRESS, and LIST, etc.

To learn how to store modules in the libraries on the B1700, IBM-S3, and DECSYSTEM-10, consult the section on the COPY statement in the *B1700 COBOL Reference Manual;* the section on libraries in the *IBM-S3 COBOL Programmer's Guide;* and Chapter 9 in the *DECSYSTEM-10 COBOL Language Handbook.*

Example 7.11   Suppose the following statements are stored in the COBOL Source Library as a module with the name FDSCR.

```
LABEL RECORDS ARE STANDARD,
BLOCK CONTAINS 5 RECORDS,
DATA RECORD IS DS-REC.
```

If we write FD FILE-D COPY FDSCR. in the FILE SECTION, the effect will be as though our program contained

```
FILE-D
      LABEL RECORDS ARE STANDARD,
      BLOCK CONTAINS 5 RECORDS,
      DATA RECORD IS DS-REC.
```

Summary   In this chapter the following COBOL verbs were discussed.

Input-Output	Compiler-directing	Data manipulation
ACCEPT	COPY	MOVE
DISPLAY	ENTER	EXAMINE
OPEN	NOTE	
CLOSE		
SEEK		
READ		
WRITE		

The ACCEPT and DISPLAY statements are used to transfer small amounts of data to and from the main memory of the computer. The OPEN and CLOSE statements are used to begin the processing of a file and to terminate the processing of a file. The READ and WRITE statements are used for bringing information from an input file into main memory and placing information in main memory in an output file. The COPY statement allows the placement of text material into a source program that is stored in the COBOL Source Library. The ENTER statement can be used in some computers to allow appliance of other programming languages in a COBOL program. The NOTE statement can be used in documenting a program. The MOVE statement is used to move data stored in main memory and at the same time perform any changes in the format in which the data is stored that are required to carry out the move. The EXAMINE statement is used to determine or alter the content of data items.

Review Questions

1. The first line after the PROCEDURE DIVISION header must be

   ______________________.

2. All transfer of data from one storage location to another involves the

   ______________ statement.

3. Complete the following table.

Value of sending item	PICTURE of sending item	PICTURE of receiving item	"Value" of receiving item after MOVE
RALPH	A(5)	X(7)	
J JONES	A(7)	X(8)	
1946	———	99V99	
ALL '$'	———	X(6)	
SPACES	———	99	
$6.35	$$.99	$9.99	
−6.7	S99V9	+99.9	

4. If a card file contains 37 records, how many uses of the READ statement are needed to read the entire file? ______

5. The forms of the WRITE statement are ______________.

6. Why should you close all files before stopping a program run?

7. 77 AITEM   PIC X(11) VALUE 'GOODNNNLUCK'.
   77 BITEM   PIC X(8) VALUE '00278566'.
   77 KITEM   PIC X(19) VALUE '2$WDKWYKUWFEELWGKKD'.

   a. After the execution of EXAMINE AITEM TALLYING ALL 'N' REPLACING BY SPACE. , the special register TALLY contains the value ______ and the content of AITEM is ______________.

   b. After the execution of EXAMINE BITEM TALLYING LEADING ZERO REPLACING BY SPACE. , the special register TALLY contains the value ______ and the content of BITEM is ______________.

   c. Assuming that we have executed the statement in b, if we execute EXAMINE BITEM REPLACING ALL '6' BY '0'. , the content of the special register TALLY is ______, and the content of BITEM is ______________.

   d. Write the necessary EXAMINE statements so that the content of

KITEM becomes ɸɸɸDOɸYOUɸFEELɸGOOD where ɸ indicates a blank.

8. Match each of the following data types with a picture that is permissible for such a data type.

a. alphabetic	—— 77 A	PIC S99V9.
b. binary	—— 77 B	PIC 99V99 USAGE COMP.
c. external decimal	—— 77 C	PIC XXXBXX.
d. alphanumeric	—— 77 D	PIC X(18).
e. alphanumeric-edited	—— 77 E	PIC $$$99.99.
f. numeric-edited	—— 77 F	PIC AAA.

9. Assume the following data descriptions:

```
77 A      PIC 9(4)V99 VALUE 0083.42.
77 B      PIC $(5).99.
77 C      PIC −(5).99.
77 D      PIC 9(4).99.
77 E      PIC Z(4).99.
77 F      PIC $$.99.
77 G      PIC ++.09.
77 H      PIC +$$$.99.
```

The statement MOVE A to B C D E F G H. is executed, and the content of B, C, D, E, F, G, and H is printed. Show what will be printed in each case.

10. What is special register TALLY?

Suggested Projects

1. Rewrite the program for project 3 of Chapter 4. Each page of data output should have a header over the columns of output. The header should be

```
U−NO.  U−NAME.  U−PRICE.  NO−U.
   NO−REC.  NO−OR.  MANUFACTURER
```

and the columns should be separated by spaces. There should be 10 data items per page, and they should be double-spaced. Run the program using at least 23 data cards.

2. Write a COBOL program to check the result of the MOVE statements for the particular cases covered in examples 6.16 and 6.17. (*Hint:* All you need are some independent elementary items; Then MOVE the literals in the first column of examples 6.16 and 6.17 to these items, and use a DISPLAY to see the printout.)

3. At the beginning of Chapter 4 we described the records of a book file. Write a COBOL program to create a randomly organized disk file from an input card file of book records. The key for the records should be the book number. Once the file is created, close it and reopen it as an input file. Then print the file on the line printer and punch the file on cards. Use appropriate headers and spacing for the printed file.

4. Write a program to create a COBOL source library for 20 modules. Each module contains 15 cards, and the average card contains 40 nonblank characters. Do not attempt to run your program.

5. This project requires that one or more modules be stored for your use in your COBOL Program Library. A module similar to SPECNAMES would serve the purpose. Following the directions of your instructor, write a COBOL program that uses one or more modules in the COBOL Program Library in your installation.

6. A student information file is stored on a sequential disk file on the computer. The first field of each student record is a student number having two groups of three digits separated by a space—as in 123 987. The registrar's office has decided that the two groups of numbers should be separated by a hyphen—123-987. Write a COBOL program using the student information file as an I-O file to update the student numbers as requested. The numbers were stored in an area whose picture was X(7).

7. Do the preceding project (project 6) assuming that the numbers were stored in an area whose picture is 9(7) with DISPLAY usage.

CHAPTER 8

Arithmetic Calculations

In COBOL, the basic arithmetic operations can be performed and arithmetic expressions can be evaluated. First you must know the symbols for the arithmetic operators.

Symbol	Heirarchy	Operation
+	fourth	addition
−	fourth or first (negation)	subtraction or negation
*	third	multiplication
/	third	division
**	second	exponentiation

Arithmetic expressions may be formed in the following ways.

1. An arithmetic expression may be a numeric literal or a name of an elementary numeric item (the picture contains only 9, S, V, or P).
2. Two arithmetic expressions can be separated by +, −, *, or /; or two arithmetic expressions can be separated by ** where the value of the second expression is a positive integer (some compilers allow noninteger powers); or, an arithmetic expression may be preceded by −.
3. Any arithmetic expression enclosed in parentheses is also an arithmetic expression.

In any arithmetic expression, +, −, *, /, and ** must be preceded and followed by a space, except that a − after a left parenthesis must not be preceded by a space.

An arithmetic expression is evaluated by working from the innermost parenthesis outward. For items on the same level of organization, the order of performing calculations is determined by the hierarchy of operators: negation, exponentiation, multiplication and division, and addition and subtraction. If this still does not determine the value of the expression uniquely, then the operations are performed (in the order they occur within the expression) from left to right.

Example 8.1 Suppose BALANCE, PAY, TOTAL, DEPOSIT, and WITHDRAWAL are names of elementary numeric items. Then, the following are arithmetic expressions:

1. 534
2. −378.62

Figure 8.1 DECSYSTEM-10 computer system.

From the right in the back row are three movable disk drives, a fixed head disk, four magnetic tape drives, a channel controller, and the console board for the CPU. Above the console are two DEC tape drives. From the console to the end of the back row is the CPU that comprises the arithmetic and logical sections (the first two boxes) and the main memory (the last two boxes). In the front row are two teletype terminals, and between them and the magnetic tapedrives are two more movable disk drives that are followed by a line printer, a display unit, and a card reader. Both the display unit and the card reader are on the table in front of the line printer, and to the left of those are another display unit and a card puncher.

(*Photograph courtesy of the Digital Equipment Corporation.*)

3. DEPOSIT
4. TOTAL
5. 935.1
6. 534.29 + TOTAL
7. (5782 − PAY) + BALANCE + DEPOSIT
8. ((8 ∗∗ 3) / PAY) + WITHDRAWAL
9. ((−PAY ∗ 18) − WITHDRAWAL) / 12

The Arithmetic Statements

The arithmetic statements cause the evaluation of arithmetic expressions and the storing of the result in a specified data item.

The COMPUTE Statement

The COMPUTE statement is the easiest and the most efficient means of performing arithmetic in COBOL. The format of the COMPUTE statement is

```
COMPUTE name-1 [ROUNDED] = arithmetic-expression
        [ON SIZE ERROR imperative-sentence]
```

This statement causes the evaluation of arithmetic-expression and stores the result in name-1. While all data-names of arithmetic-expression are of elementary numeric items, name-1 may be an elementary numeric item or an elementary numeric-edited item. If the ROUNDED option is used, the result of the evaluation is rounded to the number of decimal places specified in the picture for name-1 and then stored in name-1. In some cases the result of the evaluation may contain too many digits to the left of the decimal to be stored in name-1. This is a SIZE ERROR, and unless the SIZE ERROR option is used, the results of the COMPUTE are unpredictable if one occurs. If the SIZE ERROR option is used, the result of the evaluation is not stored in name-1; imperative-sentence is executed instead. If ROUNDED and SIZE ERROR are used, then rounding is done before the check for a size error.

Example 8.2

Suppose the DATA DIVISION contains the following descriptions.

```
BALANCE      PIC      S9(4)V99      COMP.
PAY          PIC      9(4)V99       COMP.
A            PIC        99V99       COMP.
B            PIC      S99V99        COMP.
C            PIC        9V999       COMP.
PRINT-BAL  PIC     $$$$$9.99DB
```

a. COMPUTE PRINT-BAL = BALANCE - PAY.

This is a valid statement. Note that PRINT-BAL is to the left of the equality sign and is edited.

b. COMPUTE A = PRINT-BAL - PAY.

This is an invalid statement because the arithmetic expression contains PRINT-BAL which is a numeric-edited item.

c. COMPUTE A = B + C.

This replaces the value of A by the result of evaluating $B + C$.

d. COMPUTE A = 1.007.
COMPUTE C = 25.34.
COMPUTE B = 6 - 34.

The first two statements cause A to have the value 01.00 and C to have an unknown value due to the SIZE ERROR involved. The last statement causes B to have the value -28.00.

e. The arithmetic expression can be very complicated.

Give A the value of $\left[\dfrac{C + B}{2} + B^2 - \left(\dfrac{C}{3}\right)^2 \right]^{11}$

An equivalent COBOL statement would be

```
COMPUTE A =
    ((C + B) / 2 + B * B - (C / 3) ** 2) ** 11.
```

f.   Suppose *B* is 98.35 and *C* is 7.196. Thus the difference of *B* and *C* is 91.154, and the sum of *B* and *C* is 105.546. Then if we write

```
COMPUTE PAY = B + C.
```

PAY is 105.54; and if we write

```
COMPUTE PAY ROUNDED = B + C.
```

PAY is 105.55. (The rightmost digit retained is increased by 1 if the next digit is 5 or greater.)

g.   Suppose *B* is still 98.35 and *C* is still 7.196. The statement

```
COMPUTE A = B + C.
```

causes a SIZE ERROR. If we write

```
COMPUTE A = B + C, ON SIZE ERROR,
DISPLAY 'RESULT IS TOO LARGE', GO TO
READ-A-CARD.
```

the value of *A* will not be changed and the imperative sentence will be executed instead.

h.   Further examples are

```
COMPUTE A ROUNDED = (B ** 6 - 20.1) ** 2
   ON SIZE ERROR STOP RUN.

COMPUTE B ROUNDED = (A + 1934.8675) / C
   ON SIZE ERROR  GO TO NEW-CALCULATION.

COMPUTE B =
   (C + A) / 2 + ((C / 3) + 187.2) * 6
   ON SIZE ERROR GO TO END-OF-JOB.

COMPUTE C ROUNDED = A.
```

In addition to the COMPUTE statement, the four arithmetic operations ADD, SUBTRACT, MULTIPLY, and DIVIDE are also allowed.

In the following arithmetic statements, the meaning of the options ROUNDED and ON SIZE ERROR are the same as we explained in the COMPUTE statement and the data item, the operand of GIVING, is the only item that can be edited.

The ADD Statement

The two possible formats for the ADD statement are

(1)

$$\underline{\text{ADD}} \left\{ \begin{array}{l} \text{name-1} \\ \text{literal-1} \end{array} \right\} , \left[\begin{array}{l} \text{name-2} \\ \text{literal-2} \end{array} \right] \cdots \underline{\text{To}} \text{ name-m}$$

[ROUNDED] [ON SIZE ERROR imperative-sentence]

(2)

$$\underline{\text{ADD}} \left\{ \begin{array}{l} \text{name-1} \\ \text{literal-1} \end{array} \right\} , \left\{ \begin{array}{l} \text{name-2} \\ \text{literal-2} \end{array} \right\} , \left[\begin{array}{l} \text{name-3} \\ \text{literal-3} \end{array} \right] \cdots$$

GIVING name-m [ROUNDED]
[ON SIZE ERROR imperative-sentence]

If the first format is used, the values of the items following ADD are added to the value of name-m, and the result of the addition is stored in the item name-m. None of the items including item name-m can be edited.

Example 8.3   Suppose the values for *A, B, C, D* before addition are

A	*B*	*C*	*D*
5	6	7	8

After the instruction, ADD A, B, C TO D, the values of *A, B, C* are unchanged, but the value of *D* is now 26.

The instruction   ADD 1 TO A   increments the value of *A* by 1. Thus *A* would be 6. After the execution of the instruction   ADD 10   15.5   C   2 TO B,   the value of *C* is unchanged but the value of *B* is 40.5.

In the second format (with GIVING), the values of the items following ADD are added together, and the result is stored in the item name-m—that is, in the data name that follows the reserved word GIVING. Note: There must be at least two items after ADD and before GIVING, and item name-m is the only item that can be edited.

Example 8.4   Suppose in the DATA DIVISION we have the following.

```
TOTAL   PIC    $$$$9.99.
   A    PIC       99V999 COMP.
   B    PIC        99V99 COMP.
   C    PIC           99 COMP.
   D    PIC          S99 COMP.
```

Furthermore, suppose that the current values for *A, B, C,* and *D* are

A	*B*	*C*	*D*
8	5	4	3

Then after the execution of ADD A B C D GIVING TOTAL, TOTAL is $20.00. Remember that the variable TOTAL can be edited. However, if we use the TO option instead of GIVING, the item name-m cannot be edited.

The instruction ADD A B C D TO TOTAL is not valid because TOTAL is an edited data item. After the execution of   ADD   A   B   GIVING D, the value of *D* is 13.

Suppose the values are now

A	*B*	*C*	*D*
25.675	85.01	67	28

then after   ADD A   B   D   GIVING TOTAL ROUNDED, ON SIZE ERROR DISPLAY 'OVERFLOW' UPON CONSOLE, STOP RUN., the value of TOTAL is $138.69. Note that the third decimal place is rounded.

Suppose we write

```
ADD A B D GIVING C ROUNDED ON SIZE ERROR DISPLAY
     'TOO BAD', STOP RUN.
```

Since the rounded sum of A, B, and D is 138.69, which is too big for C, the size error condition occurs; the phrase TOO BAD will be printed on the line printer; and the program will stop.

The SUBTRACT Statement

The SUBTRACT statement also has two formats:

(1)

$$\text{SUBTRACT } \begin{Bmatrix} \text{name--1} \\ \text{literal--1} \end{Bmatrix} ,$$

$$\begin{bmatrix} \text{name--2} \\ \text{literal--2} \end{bmatrix} , \ \ldots \ \underline{\text{FROM}} \ \text{name--m}$$

$$[\underline{\text{ROUNDED}}] \ [\text{ON} \ \underline{\text{SIZE}} \ \underline{\text{ERROR}} \ \text{imperative--sentence}].$$

(2)

$$\text{SUBTRACT } \begin{Bmatrix} \text{name--1} \\ \text{literal--1} \end{Bmatrix} ,$$

$$\begin{bmatrix} \text{name--2} \\ \text{literal--2} \end{bmatrix} , \ \ldots \ \underline{\text{FROM}} \begin{Bmatrix} \text{name--m} \\ \text{literal--m} \end{Bmatrix}$$

$$\underline{\text{GIVING}} \ \text{name--n} \ [\underline{\text{ROUNDED}}] \ [\text{ON} \ \underline{\text{SIZE}} \ \underline{\text{ERROR}}$$

$$\text{imperative--sentence}].$$

If the first format is used, the values of the items following SUBTRACT are added together, and the sum is subtracted from the value of name-m. If the second format is used, a similar procedure is followed except that the final result is stored in name-n and the value of name-m is unchanged.

Example 8.5

Suppose the descriptions of TOTAL, A, B, C, and D are the same as in example 8.4 and the current values are

A	B	C	D
45	18	12	6

Then after the instruction

```
SUBTRACT B, C, D FROM A
```

the value of A is 9.

Note that the sum of B, C, and D is subtracted from A and the result is stored back in A. After

```
SUBTRACT −2.5, 3.8, D FROM B GIVING TOTAL
```

the value of TOTAL is $10.70 and the value of B is 18.

The MULTIPLY Statement

The two possible formats for the MULTIPLY statement are

(1)

$$\underline{\text{MULTIPLY}} \begin{Bmatrix} \text{name--1} \\ \text{literal--1} \end{Bmatrix} \underline{\text{BY}} \ \text{name--2} \ [\underline{\text{ROUNDED}}]$$

$$[\text{ON} \ \underline{\text{SIZE}} \ \underline{\text{ERROR}} \ \text{imperative--sentence}]$$

$$(2)$$

$$\underline{\text{MULTIPLY}} \begin{Bmatrix} \texttt{name-1} \\ \texttt{literal-1} \end{Bmatrix} \underline{\text{BY}} \begin{Bmatrix} \texttt{name-2} \\ \texttt{literal-2} \end{Bmatrix} \underline{\text{GIVING}} \ \texttt{name-3}$$

$$[\underline{\text{ROUNDED}}] \ [\text{ON} \ \underline{\text{SIZE}} \ \underline{\text{ERROR}} \ \text{imperative-sentence}] \ .$$

If the first format is used, the values of the two items (names) are multiplied together, and the result is stored in name-2. If the second format is used, the value of name-1 is multiplied by the value of name-2 and the result is stored in name-3.

Example 8.6   Suppose the current values are

A	B	C	D
10	6	20	11

where *A*, *B*, *C*, and *D* and TOTAL are those in example 8.4.
   Then after the instruction

```
MULTIPLY A BY B
```

the value of *B* is 60.

```
MULTIPLY A BY TOTAL
```

is invalid because TOTAL is an edited item. But, after the instruction

```
MULTIPLY A BY D GIVING TOTAL ROUNDED ON SIZE
ERROR DISPLAY 'RESULT OF MULTIPLICATION
IS TOO LARGE', STOP RUN.
```

the value of TOTAL is $110.00. After

```
MULTIPLY -3 BY D.
```

the value of *D* is −33. But

```
MULTIPLY D BY -3.
```

is not valid because the operand which follows BY in the first format cannot be a literal.

The DIVIDE Statement

The two formats for the DIVIDE statement are

$$(1)$$

$$\underline{\text{DIVIDE}} \begin{Bmatrix} \texttt{name-1} \\ \texttt{literal-1} \end{Bmatrix} \underline{\text{INTO}} \ \texttt{name-2} \ [\underline{\text{ROUNDED}}]$$

$$[\text{ON} \ \underline{\text{SIZE}} \ \underline{\text{ERROR}} \ \text{imperative-sentence}] \ .$$

$$(2)$$

$$\underline{\text{DIVIDE}} \begin{Bmatrix} \texttt{name-1} \\ \texttt{literal-1} \end{Bmatrix} \begin{Bmatrix} \underline{\text{BY}} \\ \underline{\text{INTO}} \end{Bmatrix} \begin{Bmatrix} \texttt{name-2} \\ \texttt{literal-2} \end{Bmatrix}$$

$$\underline{\text{GIVING}} \ \texttt{name-3} \ [\underline{\text{ROUNDED}}]$$

$$[\text{ON} \ \underline{\text{SIZE}} \ \underline{\text{ERROR}} \ \text{imperative-sentence}] \ .$$

If the first format is used, the value of name-2 is divided by the value of name-1 (or literal-1) and the result is stored in name-2.

If the second format is used, the value of name-1 (or literal-1) is divided INTO or BY the value of name-2 (or literal-2) and the result is stored in name-3.

Example 8.7   Suppose A, B, C, D, and TOTAL have been specified as in example 8.4, and their current values are

A	B	C	D
15	10	3	55

Then after execution of

```
DIVIDE 3 INTO A
```

the value of A is 5, and

```
DIVIDE B INTO D
```

makes 5 the value of D. (See the description of D in example 8.4.)

```
DIVIDE B INTO D GIVING A  or  DIVIDE D BY B
    GIVING A
```

makes 5.5 the value of A and

```
DIVIDE 5 INTO 25 GIVING TOTAL  or  DIVIDE 25 BY 5
    GIVING TOTAL
```

makes TOTAL $5.00. (See the description of TOTAL in example 8.4.) But,

```
DIVIDE 10 INTO C GIVING TOTAL
```

makes TOTAL equal to $0.30.

Example 8.8   Suppose A, B, C, D, and TOTAL are described as they are in example 8.4. Write COBOL statements that are needed for the evaluation of the following algebraic expression:

$$\text{Total} = \left[(A \times B) - \frac{3}{2}(D + C) \right]^2$$

We can write the necessary statement in two ways: The first way would be to use the COMPUTE statement, in which case the only COBOL statement necessary to find the value of TOTAL is

```
COMPUTE TOTAL  =
    ((A * B)  -  (3 / 2)  *  (D + C))  ** 2
```

The second way to find the value of TOTAL does not require the use of the COMPUTE statement. Since we would like to *keep* the values of A, B, C, and D—that is, not destroy their values—we need two temporary variables, say, TEMP1 and TEMP2. (Note that TEMP1 and TEMP2 will be described as independent elementary numeric variables in the WORKING-STORAGE SECTION.) The following statements are therefore needed to find TOTAL:

```
ADD D , C GIVING TEMP1.
MULTIPLY 1.5 BY TEMP1.
MULTIPLY A BY B GIVING TEMP2.
SUBTRACT TEMP1 FROM TEMP2.
MULTIPLY TEMP2 BY TEMP2 GIVING TOTAL.
```

Note that the execution was as follows:

1. $D + C$ is stored in TEMP1.
2. 1.5 is multiplied by TEMP1—that is, $D + C$—and the result is stored back in TEMP1. In other words, TEMP1 now contains the result of $3/2(D + C)$.
3. The result of $A \times B$ is stored in TEMP2.
4. The result of TEMP1 − TEMP2—that is, $A \times B - 3/2(D + C)$—is stored in TEMP2.
5. The result of TEMP2*TEMP2—that is, $\left[A \times B - 3/2(D + C)\right] \times \left[A \times B - 3/2(D + C)\right]$ or $\left[A \times B - 3/2(D + C)\right]^2$—is stored in TOTAL.

Example 8.9   Write a COBOL program to read the grades of 25 students and compute the average of these grades. Each grade is given as a 3-digit number, and all 25 grades are punched in the *first* 75 columns of one data card.

In order to work this example, we shall introduce the concept of an *array,* or *table*. A table is a data item composed of several smaller items. Thus a table is a group item. However, a table differs from the group items we have seen before in the way the items of the table are named. For example 8.9, we will make the input record of our card file a table named GRADE. GRADE is composed of 25 elementary items. In our sample program we refer to these items by the names STUDENT-GRADE (1), STUDENT-GRADE (2), STUDENT-GRADE (3), . . . , STUDENT-GRADE (25). Note how different these names are from the types of names we have used before. For one thing, there is a *space* in the middle of each name, something that has never been permitted in our past work. Note that each name is formed by writing STUDENT-GRADE, a space, a left parenthesis, an integer, and a right parenthesis. If this were the only way of naming these items, there would not be much reason for using them. However, suppose that J is a numeric data item whose value is 3. We can name STUDENT-GRADE (3) by writing STUDENT-GRADE (J). If we then change the value of J to 4, then STUDENT-GRADE (J) is a name for STUDENT-GRADE (4). A number or data name used as we used J is called a *subscript,* and STUDENT-GRADE is a *subscripted variable*.

To use a table or array in a COBOL program, we must make a special type of entry in the DATA DIVISION when we define the table. The simplest format for such an entry is

```
level-number OCCURS integer TIMES
```

For example,

```
01 GRADE.
    02 STUDENT-GRADE OCCURS 25 TIMES  PIC 9(3).
```

Figure 8.2 System flowchart for AVERAGE-GRADES program for example 8.9.

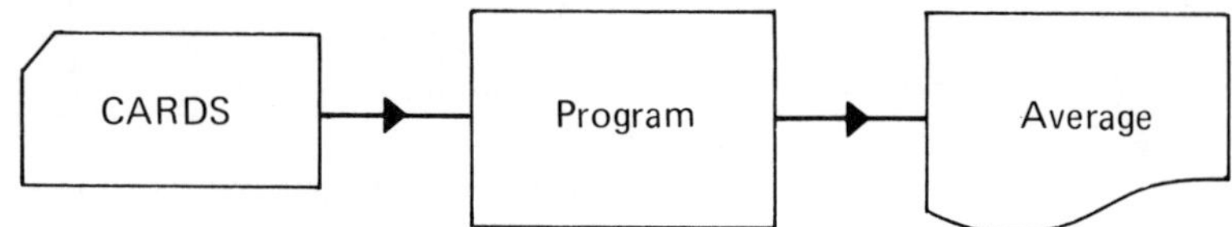

defines a table containing 25 elementary data items. Each elementary data item is a numeric item with three digits.

Figures 8.2 and 8.3 are the system and program flowcharts for example 8.9. Figure 8.4 is the printout of the program run on the B1700 for example 8.9. Figure 8.5 shows the modifications necessary to run the program on the IBM-1130, the IBM-S3, and the DECSYSTEM-10. For additional information about tables, read the first part of Chapter 11.

Summary   The arithmetic operators are $(-)$ (negation), $+$, $-$, $*$ (multiplication), $/$ (division), and $**$ (exponentiation to integer powers). The last four operators and the $=$ symbol must be preceded and followed by a space whenever used. These symbols are used in forming arithmetic expressions for use in the COMPUTE statement. The format for the COMPUTE statement is

```
COMPUTE name-1 [ROUNDED] = arithmetic-expression
        [ON SIZE ERROR imperative-sentence]
```

All data items used in this statement must be numeric items, except for name-1, which can also be numeric-edited. If the ROUNDED option is used, the result of the calculation is rounded to the number of decimal places specified in the PICTURE of name-1. If the SIZE ERROR option is used and the result of the calculation is too large to store in name-1, then the actions specified in the imperative sentence will be carried out.

The four basic arithmetic statements can also be used in COBOL. These statements begin with one of the four verbs, ADD, SUBTRACT, MULTIPLY, and DIVIDE. These statements can be used to perform the arithmetic operation specified and can be used also with the ROUNDED and SIZE ERROR options. The results of the calculations done with these statements can be stored in numeric-edited items when the GIVING option is used. These statements can only be used to perform arithmetic calculations on numeric data items.

Review Questions

1. COMPUTE A = 2 $**$ (-1) will cause *A* to be 1/2. True or false?
2. For efficiency, all numeric data items should have COMPUTATIONAL usage if they are used in arithmetic computations. True or false?
3. The 'ON SIZE ERROR' option, when used, will automatically stop the machine for a possible recovery procedure. True or false?
4. The ROUNDED option in an arithmetic procedure will adjust the result and is required in all arithmetic operations. True or false?

Figure 8.3 Program flowchart for AVERAGE-GRADES program for example 8.9.

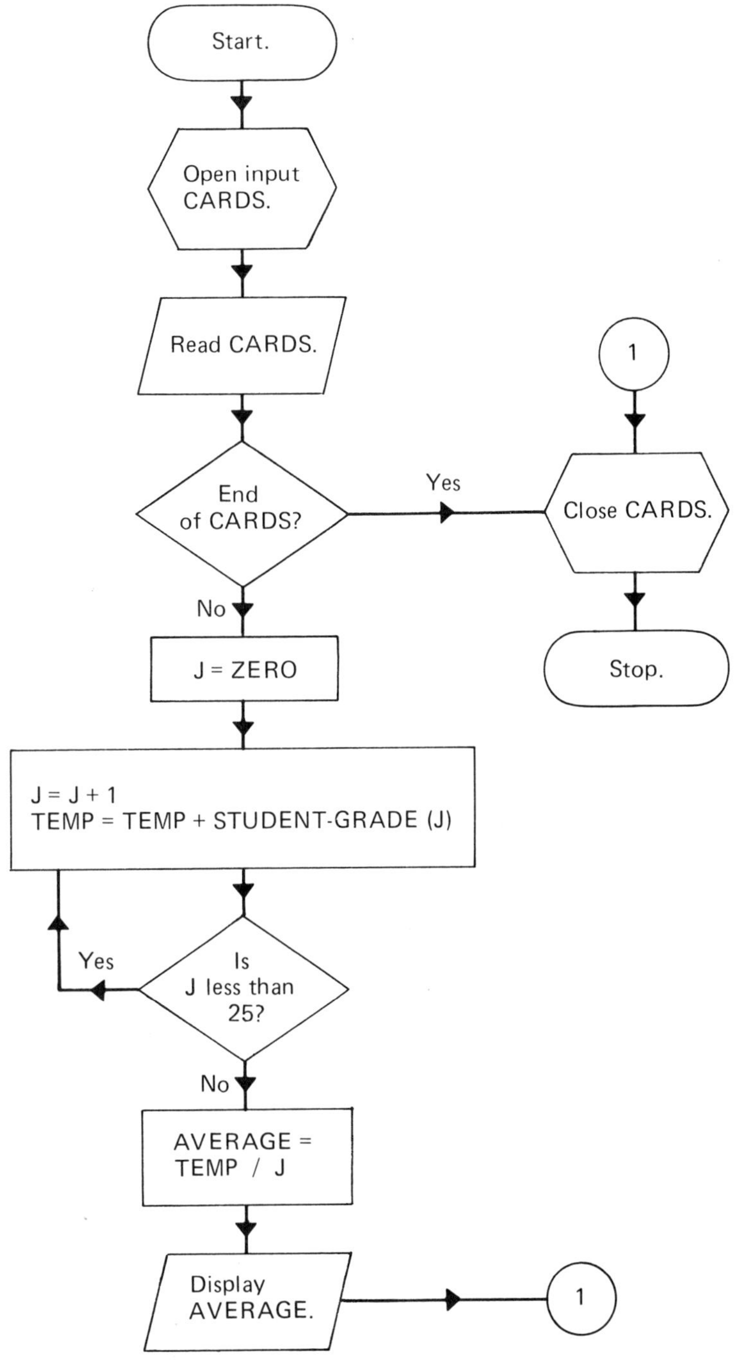

Figure 8.4 Printout of listing of AVERAGE-GRADES program for example 8.9 as run on the B1700.

```
 IDENTIFICATION DIVISION.
 PROGRAM-ID. AVERAGE-GRADES.
 ENVIRONMENT DIVISION.
 ************************************************************************
 *****IN THIS EXAMPLE THE CONFIGURATION SECTION IS OMITTED. THIS   *
 *****SECTION IS ALWAYS OPTIONAL.....                              *
 ************************************************************************
 INPUT-OUTPUT SECTION.
 FILE-CONTROL.
     SELECT CARDS, ASSIGN TO READER.
 DATA DIVISION.
 FILE SECTION.
 FD  CARDS, LABEL RECORDS ARE OMITTED.
 01  GRADE.
     02  STUDENT-GRADE OCCURS 25 TIMES PIC 9(3).
 WORKING-STORAGE SECTION.
 77  TEMP PIC 9(5) COMP VALUE 0.
 77  J PIC 9(2) COMP VALUE 0.
 77  AVERAGE PIC 9(3).9(2).
 PROCEDURE DIVISION.
 BEGIN.
     OPEN INPUT CARDS.
     READ CARDS AT END GO TO END-OF-PROGRAM.
 ************************************************************************
 *****THIS CAUSES ALL THE GRADES TO BE READ.....                  *
 ************************************************************************
 ADDITIONS-LOOP.
     ADD 1 TO J.
     COMPUTE TEMP = TEMP + STUDENT-GRADE (J).
     IF J IS LESS THAN 25, GO TO ADDITIONS-LOOP.
 AVERAGE-GRADE-PARAGRAPH.
 ************************************************************************
 *****ALL THE GRADES HAVE BEEN ADDED. WE CAN NOW COMPUTE THEIR    *
 *****AVERAGE...........                                          *
 ************************************************************************
     COMPUTE AVERAGE = TEMP / J.
 ************************************************************************
 *****FOR SUCH SIMPLE OUTPUT WE USE THE DISPLAY STATEMENT. FOR    *
 *****LARGER PRINTING NEEDS WE SHOULD USE THE WRITE STATEMENT FOR *
 *****A LINE PRINTER FILE SINCE THIS IS MUCH MORE EFFICIENT.....  *
 ************************************************************************
     DISPLAY 'AVERAGE GRADE IS ', AVERAGE, ' FOR ', J,
         ' STUDENTS.'.
 END-OF-PROGRAM.
     CLOSE CARDS.
     STOP RUN.
```

5. Given the values $A = 12$, $B = 10$, $C = 11$, and $D = 5$, compute the value of Y for each statement:

```
COMPUTE Y = (A + B) / 2 - C * D
COMPUTE Y = 5 * A - B ** 2 + (C + D) / 2
COMPUTE Y = ((A / 2) + B * 2) / 4 + 3 * C
COMPUTE Y = (D * 5 + (C - A * B / 2)) / 2
COMPUTE Y = B + 3 * C - A / 2 - 19
```

6. Assume that arithmetic expression is A + ((B / C) + (D * C)). What is the order of computation?

Figure 8.5 Modifications necessary in the program for example 8.9 to run it on the IBM-1130, the IBM-S3, and the DECSYSTEM-10.

---

a. For the IBM-1130:

```
FILE-CONTROL.
    SELECT CARDS ASSIGN TO RD-2501.
```

b. For the IBM-S3:

```
FILE-CONTROL.
    SELECT CARDS ASSIGN TO UR-2501-RD.
```

c. For the DECSYSTEM-10:

```
FILE-CONTROL.
    SELECT CARDS ASSIGN TO CDR.
```

---

7. Can the computer perform arithmetic calculations on numeric DISPLAY items? On numeric-edited items?
8. Since COBOL does not have the ability to perform exponentiation, except for positive integral powers, nor the ability to find logarithms, how can you compute these values if they are needed?

Suggested Projects

1. Write a COBOL program to instruct the computer to read the records of the employees of a certain company to find the federal, state, and city taxes for each employee and the sum of the federal taxes, the sum of the state taxes, and the sum of the city taxes paid by all the employees. Assume that all the employees are salary paid, and find the average of the salaries in this company. A typical input card is:

Card column	Content
1–5	employee number
6–25	employee name
30–54	employee address
55–60	salary XXXX.XX

Use the following formulas:
Federal tax = Salary × 0.18
State tax = (Salary − federal tax) × 0.05
City tax = (Salary − federal tax − state tax) × 0.01
The output headings are left to your imagination.

2. Complete the "after" quantity for each arithmetic statement below:
    a. Divide *A* by *B*

	A	*B*	*C*	*D*
Before	5	7	2	6
After				

b. Divide *A* by *B* giving *B*

Before	*A*	*B*	*C*	*D*
	5	7	2	6

After _______________________

c. Multiply *D* by *B* giving *A*

Before	*A*	*B*	*C*	*D*
	10	20	16	25

After _______________________

d. Divide *D* into *C* giving *B*

Before	*A*	*B*	*C*	*D*
	18	19	50	25

After _______________________

e. Subtract *A*, *B*, *C* from *D* giving *D*

Before	*A*	*B*	*C*	*D*
	17	10	5	12

After _______________________

f. Add *A*, *B*, *C*, *D* giving *D*

Before	*A*	*B*	*C*	*D*
	5	6	7	8

After _______________________

g. Subtract *D*, *B*, *C* from *A* giving *C*

Before	*A*	*B*	*C*	*D*
	9	10	12	16

After _______________________

3. Write a program to instruct the computer to read a card file containing the sales records of the Acme Shoe Company. Each card contains the following information.

Card column	*Content*
1–15	shoe style
16–25	color
26–30	number sold
31–35	price per shoe

The output should have the heading

```
SALES REPORT FOR THE ACME SHOE COMPANY
```

at the top of *each* page. For each card, skip two lines, print the heading

```
STYLE     COLOR     NUMBER SOLD      PRICE
```

Print the content of the card beneath the appropriate heading, compute the total sales for that shoe (TOTAL = NUMBER-SOLD * PRICE), skip a line, and print

```
TOTAL SALES FOR THIS SHOE IS $------.--
```

and print the total found. At the end of the card file, compute the total sales for all shoes and print

```
TOTAL SALES IS $-------.--
```

after skipping three lines. Make up 20 cards for your file and run your program.

4. One method to find a depreciation schedule is the *straight-line method*. In this method the yearly depreciation is assumed to be fixed, and this amount is determined by the formula DEPRECIATION-PER-YEAR = (COST − SCRAP-VALUE) / USE-LIFE.

   Write a COBOL program to use this method to figure a depreciation schedule for several items listed in a card file. An input card contains the following information.

Asset name	X(20)
Use-life	99
Scrap value	9(5)V99
Asset number	X(6)

   For each item a depreciation schedule should be printed showing for each year of the use-life of the item, the depreciation for that year, and the carrying value of the item at the end of that year. The carrying value is computed as COST − total depreciation up to and including the current year. The headings and arrangement of the table are left to your imagination. Run your program with at least five data cards.

5. The (s,S) doctrine is a well-known inventory policy. This type of inventory policy requires periodic reviews of current inventory levels. At the time of the review, if the current inventory level for an item is below its lower critical number, s, then S − the current inventory level numbers of this item are ordered. Otherwise, no order is placed for that item. Write a COBOL program that will create a randomly organized file in which each record contains item number, item name, item cost, address of the place from which the item can be ordered, s for the item, S for the item, and suggested sale price of the item. This information should be read from a card file in which two cards contain the information for each item.

   The program should also be capable of reading a card file in which each card contains item number, item name, and the current inventory level of the item. As each card of this file is read, the appropriate record of the random file should be read and the item names checked to see if they match. If they do not match, an appropriate message should be printed. If they do match, a check should be made to see if any of the items should be ordered. If such is the case, then the item number, item name, amount to order, cost of order, address from which to order, and suggested sale price of the item should be printed. At the end of the card file, print the total cost of all the orders. The headings are left to your imagination.

Note that your program must distinguish between which two procedures are to be done. We suggest a header card for the card files. Read this using an ACCEPT statement.

Run your program. In this case it will necessitate two runs: one to create the random file, and one to run the inventory cards. Be sure to DELETE any files you store permanently after you are finished.

6. Write a COBOL program to instruct the computer to read a list of numbers from cards and calculate their mean and variance. If the numbers are denoted by $x_1, \ldots, x_N$ and we use $\sum$ for summations, then

$$\text{MEAN} = \left(\sum_{i=1}^{N} x_i \right) / N \text{ and VARIANCE} = \left(\sum_{i=1}^{N} x_i^2 \right) / N - \left(\sum_{i=1}^{N} x_i / N \right)^2.$$

Run your program using at least 25 numbers.

7. Rewrite the student-grade program shown in figure 8.4 so that it will process a card file of separate cards. Each card contains the grades of 25 students in a class.

CHAPTER 9

Control Sequence Statements and the IF Statement

Control Sequence Statements

The control statements can change the normal sequential execution of the statements in a program. Two of these statements, EXIT and PERFORM, will be discussed in Chapter 10. IF, GO TO, ALTER, and STOP will be discussed in this chapter.

In the following discussion, *procedure name* will mean either a paragraph name or a section name in the PROCEDURE DIVISION.

GO TO Statement

The GO TO statement has three formats:

```
GO TO procedure-name
GO TO procedure-name-1, [procedure-name-2] , ... ,
     DEPENDING ON data-name
GO TO.
```

In the second format the data name is the name of an elementary numeric item described as an integer of two digits or less. Its USAGE may be COMPUTATIONAL or DISPLAY, and its value should be in the range of 1 through 99.

If the first format is used, the control transfers unconditionally to the procedure name, which is the operand of GO TO. If the second format is used, the control transfers to one of the procedure names—i.e., to one of the operands of GO TO—enclosed between the reserved words GO TO and the reserved word DEPENDING. If the value of the data name (the operand of DEPENDING) is, say 7, then control transfers to procedure-name-7. In general, if the value of the data name is i, then control transfers to procedure-name-i. (Note that procedure-name-i is the *i*th operand of the GO TO.)

Example 9.1

```
GO TO LOOP-1.
```

Example 9.1 shows an unconditional GO TO statement. After this statement is executed, control branches to LOOP-1.

```
GO TO 65.
```

Control transfers unconditionally to paragraph 65.

```
GO TO LP-1, 19, END-OF-JOB,
       LAST-P DEPENDING ON DEST.
```

If the value of the data name DEST, is

1, control transfers to LP-1;
2, control transfers to 19;
3, control transfers to END-OF-JOB; or
4, control transfers to LAST-P.

Note that LAST-P is the fourth operand and 19 is the second operand of GO TO.

Thus if the value of C is 3 and we write

```
GO TO L, M, N, Q, Z DEPENDING ON C,
```

then control transfers to the procedure N; and in

```
GO TO PAR-1, PAR-2, PAR-3 DEPENDING ON COUNT
```

if the value of COUNT is 2, the control transfers to PAR-2. But if the value of COUNT is not 1 or 2 or 3, the statement is ignored. Thus the GO TO statement is ignored if the current value of the data name is not in the range 1 through n where n is the number of operands of the GO TO.

The GO TO statement permits a transfer from one part of the program to another. In addition, the transfer point specified in a GO TO statement can be changed. This is done by means of the ALTER statement.

The ALTER Statement

```
ALTER procedure-name-1
      TO [PROCEED TO] procedure-name-2
      [procedure-name-3
      TO [PROCEED TO] procedure-name-4] ...
```

where procedure-name-1 and procedure-name-3, . . . are paragraph names. Each must contain only one statement, either the GO TO statement with one operand—i.e., the first format—or the GO TO statement without an operand—i.e., the third format; and procedure-name-2 or procedure-name-4, . . . can be any paragraph or section name in the PROCEDURE DIVISION.

The effect of using the ALTER statement is that when it is executed, it replaces the operand of the GO TO statement in procedure-name-1, procedure-name-3, . . . by procedure-name-2, procedure-name-4, . . . , respectively. If procedure-name-1 or procedure-name-3 contains a GO TO statement without an operand, then procedure-name-2, procedure-name-4, . . . will be assumed as the operand of GO TO. As a matter of fact, if the third format of GO TO—i.e., the GO TO without an operand—is used, an ALTER statement referring to the paragraph that has this GO TO must have been executed prior to the execution of the operandless GO TO. These concepts are clarified in the following examples.

Example 9.2

```
LP-1.
      GO TO LAST-P.
LP-2.
       ⋮
LP-3.
       ⋮
LP-4.
      ALTER LP-1 TO PROCEED TO END-OFF-JOB.
              ↑                      ↑
          procedure-1          procedure-2
       ⋮
END-OFF-JOB.   STOP RUN.
```

If we execute paragraph LP-4, then the next time control passes to LP-1, it will transfer to paragraph END-OFF-JOB. In other words, LAST-P, which was the operand of the GO TO in the paragraph of LP-1, is replaced by END-OFF-JOB—i.e., the paragraph LP-1 after the execution of the ALTER in LP-4 has been changed from

```
LP-1.
      GO TO LAST-P.
```

to

```
LP-1.
      GO TO END-OFF-JOB.
```

Example 9.3

```
PAR-1.
    ⋮
PAR-2.
      ALTER PAR-3 TO PROCEED TO PAR-5
            PAR-5 TO PROCEED TO PAR-1.
    ⋮
PAR-3.
      GO TO DISCOUNT.
PAR-4.
    ⋮
PAR-5.
      GO TO PAR-10.
PAR-6.
    ⋮
```

First, note that PAR-3 and PAR-5 contain only one statement—a GO TO statement. The ALTER statement of PAR-2 will change the GO TO DIS-COUNT of PAR-3 to GO TO PAR-5 and GO TO PAR-10 of PAR-5 to GO TO PAR-1. Thus when control reaches PAR-3, a transfer occurs to PAR-5; and when it reaches PAR-5, another transfer occurs to PAR-1. As you can see, the operands of the GO TO statement of procedure-name-1, procedure-name-3 can be replaced. It is reasonable to have a GO TO without an operand because the execution of an ALTER statement can provide an operand, as in example 9.4.

Example 9.4   If we omit the operands of the GO TO statements in PAR-3 and PAR-5 in example 9.3, we have

```
PAR-1.
    ⋮
PAR-2.
        ALTER PAR-3 TO PROCEED TO PAR-5,
              PAR-5 TO PROCEED TO PAR-1.
    ⋮
PAR-3.
        GO TO.
PAR-4.
    ⋮
PAR-5.
        GO TO.
PAR-6.
```

This sequence of statements has exactly the same effect as in example 9.3. When execution reaches PAR-3, a transfer occurs to PAR-5 (since the GO TO in PAR-3 will behave as a GO TO PAR-5), and in PAR-5 a transfer occurs on PAR-1.

Both operandless GO TO statements of PAR-3 and PAR-5 were valid because an ALTER was executed before control reached either PAR-3 or PAR-5. However, the operandless GO TO in PAR-1 in the following sequence of statements in example 9.5 is not valid because there is no ALTER statement before PAR-1. Thus there is no procedure name available when the GO TO is first encountered.

Example 9.5

```
PAR-1.
        GO TO.
PAR-2.
        ALTER PAR-1 TO PROCEED TO PAR-10,
              PAR-3 TO PROCEED TO PAR-1,
              PAR-5 TO PROCEED TO PAR-4.
    ⋮
PAR-3.
        GO TO.
PAR-4.
    ⋮
PAR-5.
        GO TO.
PAR-6.
    ⋮
PAR-10.
```

The STOP Statement

The format of the STOP statement is

$$\underline{\text{STOP}} \left\{ \begin{array}{l} \underline{\text{RUN}} \\ \text{literal} \end{array} \right\}$$

If the STOP RUN format is used, it causes the execution of the program to be terminated. If the STOP literal option is used, the computer will halt the execution of the program and display the literal to the computer operator. The operator may then cause the execution of the program to resume from the point at which it was halted. All files should be closed before STOP RUN is used.

Conditions

In COBOL, *conditions* can be created and then tested. There are five different conditions.

1. condition name
2. class condition
3. relation condition
4. sign condition
5. switch status condition

Condition Name

Condition names can be assigned to the values a variable can assume. The value of the conditional variable is tested to determine whether its value is equal to one of the values of its condition names. Recall that by means of level number 88, values are assigned to condition names.

Example 9.6

```
02 PLAYER-QUALITY  PICTURE 9.
   88 EXCELLENT     VALUE 1.
   88 GOOD          VALUE 2.
   88 AVERAGE       VALUE 3.
   88 POOR          VALUE 4.
```

In example 9.6, PLAYER-QUALITY is the conditional variable, and EXCELLENT, GOOD, AVERAGE, and POOR are condition names. Thus instead of the condition statement

```
IF PLAYER-QUALITY = 1
```

the equivalent clause IF EXCELLENT can be used and both have the same effect. Thus IF POOR is equivalent to

```
IF PLAYER-QUALITY = 4.
```

Class Condition

This test determines whether a data name is an alphabetic or a numeric item. Recall that an alphabetic item may contain any letter from A through Z and the blank. A numeric item consists of the digits 0 through 9 with or without an optional sign.

The format for this condition is

$$\text{name IS } [\underline{\text{NOT}}] \left\{ \begin{array}{l} \underline{\text{NUMERIC}} \\ \underline{\text{ALPHABETIC}} \end{array} \right\}$$

The item name must have usage DISPLAY. The NUMERIC test cannot be applied to a name if it has been described as alphabetic, and the ALPHA-BETIC test cannot be applied to a name if it has been described as numeric. Either test may be applied to a name if it is described as alphanumeric.

Example 9.7

```
     :
02 PAY  PIC 99V99.
02 BALANCE  PIC S9(5)V99.
02 BILL  PIC $$$$$.99.
     :
02 EMPLOYEE-NAME  PIC A(20).
02 EMPLOYEE-ADDR  PIC X(20).
```

The following condition statements are valid:

```
IF EMPLOYEE-ADDR NUMERIC
IF EMPLOYEE-ADDR ALPHABETIC
IF PAY NUMERIC
IF PAY NOT NUMERIC
IF BALANCE NUMERIC
IF BALANCE IS NOT NUMERIC
IF EMPLOYEE-NAME ALPHABETIC
IF EMPLOYEE-NAME IS NOT ALPHABETIC
IF EMPLOYEE-ADDR IS NOT ALPHABETIC
```

The following condition statements are not valid.

`IF PAY IS ALPHABETIC`	(because PICTURE of PAY is numeric)
`IF BALANCE IS NOT ALPHABETIC`	(because PICTURE of BALANCE is numeric)
`IF BILL NUMERIC`	(because BILL is an edited numeric item)
`IF EMPLOYEE-NAME NUMERIC`	(because the PICTURE for EMPLOYEE-NAME is alphabetic)

Relational Condition

A *relational condition* involves a comparison of expressions. The expressions may be a name of a data item, an arithmetic expression, or a literal. The format is

$$\begin{Bmatrix} \text{name-1} \\ \text{arithmetic-expression-1} \\ \text{literal-1} \end{Bmatrix} \text{relational-operator} \begin{Bmatrix} \text{name-2} \\ \text{arithmetic-expression-2} \\ \text{literal-2} \end{Bmatrix}$$

The first expression is called the *subject* and the last expression is called the *object*. Some basic rules for relational conditions follow.

1. The subject and object cannot both be literals.
2. If the subject and object are both numeric, then a comparison is allowed regardless of their USAGE.
3. If the subject and object are not both numeric, then they must have the same USAGE.
4. Numeric comparisons include the comparison of signs; however, +0 and −0 are considered equal. Unsigned expressions are considered nonnegative.
5. If two nonnumeric expressions with unequal size (the size is the total number of characters) are compared, the shorter value is extended to the right by spaces to permit comparison.

The format of the relational operator is one of the following:

```
IS [NOT] GREATER THAN
IS [NOT] LESS THAN
IS [NOT] EQUAL TO
IS [NOT] =
```

The meaning of relational conditions for numeric items is well known. For nonnumeric items the comparison is made character by character, proceeding from left to right. If all characters are the same, the expressions are considered equal. If one or more characters do not match, then a comparison is made of the first nonmatching characters. Figure 9.1 shows the EBCDIC collating sequence in ascending order. The expression whose character occurs first in the table is considered the "smaller" expression. For example, if the relational conditions are used in placing alphabetic items in ascending order, they would be in alphabetic order.

EBCDIC stands for Extended Binary Coded Decimal Interchange Code. Each character (numeric, alphabetic, or special character) is represented by a byte that contains eight bits. Each bit is either 0 or 1. The byte coding for each character is used for the purpose of the comparison.

Comparison of index names and index data items will be discussed in Chapter 11.

Example 9.8   If the alphanumeric items with values THREE and THROB are compared, then THREE is smaller than THROB since E precedes O in the collating sequence table. Similarly, 1 is greater than ONE since O precedes 1 in the table of collating sequence. If ONE is compared to ⌿ONE (with one preceding blank indicated by ⌿), then ⌿ONE is smaller than ONE since blank precedes O. If ONE is compared to ONE⌿⌿, then they are equal since ONE will be extended by two blanks on the right in order to make the comparison.

Sign Condition   This test determines whether the operand is positive, negative or equal to 0. Its format is

```
{name                 }           (POSITIVE)
{arithmetic-expression}  IS [NOT] {NEGATIVE}
                                  (ZERO    )
```

Figure 9.1 The EBCDIC collating sequence in ascending order.

1.	blank	8.	—
2.	.	9.	/
3.	(	10.	,
4.	+	11.	'
5.	$	12.	=
6.	*	13–38.	A through Z
7.	)	39–48.	0 through 9

where name is that of a numeric data item. Recall that arithmetic-expression was explained in Chapter 8.

Example 9.9

Suppose A, B, C, and D are described as elementary numeric items. Then the following are valid conditional statements.

```
IF A IS POSITIVE
IF D IS NOT ZERO
IF (A * C) IS NEGATIVE
IF (A + B) IS ZERO
IF (A + D) / 2 IS POSITIVE
```

Switch Status Condition

On the IBM-1130, the IBM-S3, and the DECSYSTEM-10, names can be assigned to the ON and OFF status of console switches. This was discussed in conjunction with the material on the SPECIAL-NAMES paragraph in Chapter 5. The switch status condition determines the ON or OFF status of a switch. The format for this condition is

```
condition-name
```

where condition-name is a name assigned to the status of a console switch. The result of the test is true if the switch is set to the position corresponding to the condition name.

Example 9.10

```
      :
SPECIAL-NAMES.
    SW07 ON STATUS IS GOOD.
```

This is an entry for a switch status on the IBM-1130. On an IBM-S3 the entry would be

```
SPECIAL-NAMES.
    UPSI-7 ON STATUS IS GOOD.
```

The entry for the DECSYSTEM-10 would be

```
SPECIAL-NAMES.
    SWITCH (7) ON STATUS IS GOOD.
```

Regardless of the computer used, writing IF GOOD in the PROCEDURE DIVISION will give a test whose result is true only if switch number 7 on the console is ON at the time the test is made.

Truth Tables

The determination of the result of the test of a simple condition is easily done. For example, in

    A GREATER THAN 5

the result of this test is true if the value of A is greater than 5; otherwise the result of the test is false. However, when more complicated conditions, such as compound conditions that are constructed by using parentheses and logical operators, are used, the result of the test of such a condition is not obvious. Truth tables provide a convenient method of determining the results of more complex kinds of conditions. To be able to use truth tables, you first have to understand logical operators in COBOL.

The logical operator AND has two operands. Each operand is a condition. The overall value of AND is true if and only if the value of both operands is true. Thus the format for AND is

    A AND B

where A and B are conditions, simple or compound. The truth table for AND is

A	B	A AND B
T	T	T
F	T	F
T	F	F
F	F	F

where T stands for true and F stands for false. Thus the result of A AND B is true if and only if both A and B are true.

Example 9.11   Suppose A and B are numeric and their values are 50 and 18, respectively. Then find the result of

$$(A + B) / 2 \text{ GREATER THAN } 10 \text{ AND } B \text{ LESS THAN } A$$

first operand   second operand

Observe that $(A + B)/2$ is 34 and thus, we have the following truth table.

$(A + B) / 2 > 10$	$B < A$	$(A + B) / 2 > 10$ AND $B < A$
T	T	T

The result of the compound condition

    (A + B) / 2 GREATER THAN B AND (A - 2 * B)
    LESS THAN 10

is given by the following truth table. Note that $(A + B)/2$ is 34 and $A - 2 \times B$ is 14.

$(A + B)/2 > B$	$A - 2 * B < 10$	$(A + B) / 2 > 10$ AND $A - 2 * B < 10$
T	F	F

The second logical operator is OR. This operator has two operands, and the result of the compound condition formed by OR is false if and only if both operands are false. Thus A OR B is true when at least one of A or B is true. The truth table for OR is

A	B	A OR B
T	T	T
T	F	T
F	T	T
F	F	F

Example 9.12   Suppose $A = 10$, $B = 18$, $C = 6$.

```
(A + B)  LESS THAN 60 OR (C * B GREATER THAN 100
         AND C EQUAL 0)
```

$(A + B) < 60$	$(C * B) > 100$	$C = 0$	$(C * B) > 100$ AND $C = 0$
T	T	F	F

$(A + B) < 60$ or $((C * B) > 100$ AND $C = 0)$
T

The last logical operator is NOT. NOT A is true if and only if the condition A is false. NOT has only one operand. The truth table for NOT is

A	NOT A
T	F
F	T

The operator NOT should not be applied to a condition that already contains NOT.

Example 9.13

```
A = 10,      B = -6,      D = 9

NOT (B IS POSITIVE)
```

The value of this compound test is true since we have

B IS POSITIVE	NOT (B IS POSITIVE)
F	T

```
(NOT (A LESS THAN 5) AND D = 0) OR B IS ZERO
```

$A < 5$	NOT (A LESS THAN 5)	$D = 0$	NOT (A LESS THAN 5) AND $D = 0$
F	T	F	F

$B = 0$	(NOT (A LESS THAN 5) AND $D = 0$) OR $B = 0$
F	F

and the overall result is false.

Thus you can create as complicated a condition as you want by using logical operators.

Evaluation Rules For Compound Conditions

The evaluation of a compound condition begins with the innermost parenthesis and proceeds to the outermost parenthesis. In the absence of parentheses, the expression is evaluated in the following order, proceeding from left to right.

1. arithmetic expression
2. relational operator
3. NOT condition
4. AND condition
5. OR condition

Example 9.14   In the expression

```
B IS EQUAL TO A OR B * 2 + A LESS THAN 55
AND K IS NEGATIVE
```

the evaluation will be in the following order.   )

1. B * 2 + A is evaluated; call the intermediate numeric result T1.
2. B IS EQUAL TO A is evaluated; call the intermediate truth value (true or false) T2.
3. T1 LESS THAN 55 is evaluated; call the intermediate truth value T3.
4. K IS NEGATIVE is evaluated; call the intermediate truth value T4.
5. T3 AND T4 is evaluated; call the intermediate result T5.
6. Finally, T2 OR T5 is evaluated; the result is the final truth value.

The IF Statement

The IF statement is used to test whether a condition is true or false and to prescribe the action to be taken in each case. Its format is

```
IF condition {statement-1 [, statement-2] ...}
             {NEXT SENTENCE                   }

   [ELSE {statement-3 [, statement-4] ...} ].
         {NEXT SENTENCE                   }
```

where condition is one of the five conditions: condition name, class condition, relational condition, sign condition, and switch status condition, or a compound condition.

If the condition is true, then the next sentence, or statement-1, statement-2 . . . etc., are executed, and the statements (operands of ELSE), statement-3, statement-4 . . . etc., are by-passed. However, if the condition is false, the statements statement-1, statement-2 . . . etc., following the condition are not executed; instead, the statements following the ELSE are executed.

The NEXT SENTENCE option specifies that the computer is to execute the next sentence. If the ELSE NEXT SENTENCE is used, and this phrase is followed immediately by a period, then the phrase can be omitted without changing the effect of the IF statement.

Example 9.15   Suppose $G = 5$ and we write

```
IF B LESS THAN 8 COMPUTE G = 9 ELSE COMPUTE G = 0.
MOVE G TO D.
```

Now, if the value of B is less than 8, then the test B LESS THAN 8 is true. Hence, the statement COMPUTE $G = 9$ is executed, and after that the control passes to the statement MOVE G TO D. In this case the value of D will be 9. But suppose B is 10; then the test B LESS THAN 8 is false, and control passes to the statement COMPUTE $G = 0$. After that, control passes to the statement MOVE G TO D. In this case the value of D will be zero.

Example 9.16   Suppose B is 5 and G is 77 and we write

```
IF B LESS THAN 8 NEXT SENTENCE ELSE COMPUTE G = 0.
MOVE G TO D.
```

Since the condition B LESS THAN 8 is true and we have NEXT SENTENCE after the condition, control will be transferred to the next sentence, which is MOVE G TO D; hence, the value of D will be 77. But, if the value of B were 16, the value of G and D would be 0.

Example 9.17   Suppose B is 10 and again G is 77, and we write

```
IF B LESS THAN 8 COMPUTE G = 9 ELSE NEXT SENTENCE.
MOVE G TO D.
```

Since the condition B LESS THAN 8 is false, the statement COMPUTE $G = 9$ is not executed. The control passes to the statement following ELSE; but since this statement is NEXT SENTENCE, the control passes to MOVE G TO D. Thus the value of D will be 77.

Since the ELSE NEXT SENTENCE becomes optional if it is immediately followed by a period, the effect of the above is exactly the same as

```
IF B LESS THAN 8 COMPUTE G = 9.
MOVE G TO D.
```

If we write

```
IF B LESS THAN 8 NEXT SENTENCE ELSE NEXT SENTENCE.
MOVE G TO D.
```

or

```
IF B LESS THAN 8 NEXT SENTENCE.
MOVE G TO D.
```

then in both cases control is passed to the statement MOVE G TO D, and the test does not have any effect.

Example 9.18   Suppose *B* is 10, *D* is 5, and *G* is 18, and we write

```
IF B LESS THAN 20 COMPUTE B = D * 10,
                  MOVE 0 TO D,
                  ADD 10 to G
ELSE MOVE D TO B
     COMPUTE D = 5 * G
     GO TO 18.
COMPUTE A = B + D + G.
```

This is a valid IF statement. As you can see the condition B LESS THAN 20 is true, so the statements following it—namely, COMPUTE B = D * 10, MOVE 0 to D, and ADD 10 TO G—are executed. Thus after these three statements are executed, the value of *B, D,* and *G* are 50, 0, and 28, respectively. After that, control transfers to COMPUTE A = B + D + G. Hence the value of *A* will be 78. However, if the value of *B* were greater than 20, the condition B LESS THAN 20 is false; therefore, the above three statements (COMPUTE B = D * 10, MOVE 0 TO D, ADD 10 TO G) are not executed. Instead, control passes to the three statements MOVE D TO B, COMPUTE D = 5 * G, GO TO 18. After these statements are executed, the value of *B, D,* and *G* will be 5, 90, and 18 respectively. Then control transfers to paragraph 18.

Example 9.19   For this example we shall rewrite example 8.9. Our new program will calculate the average of all the student grades as before, and now it will also find the largest and the smallest of the student grades.

Figure 9.2 shows the program flowchart for example 9.19; figure 9.3 shows the listing of the program run on the IBM-S3; and figure 9.4 shows the modifications necessary in the program to run it on the IBM-1130, the B1700, or the DECSYSTEM-10. If you run this program on the B1700, keep in mind that any displayed information will appear on the operator console, SPO, and that you cannot display information on the line printer.

Summary   Statements in COBOL are executed in the order in which they are listed unless a *control sequence statement* is used to change that order. The control sequence statements discussed in this chapter are GO TO, ALTER, IF, and STOP. There are three kinds of GO TO statements: the unconditional GO TO, the operandless GO TO, and the GO TO with the DEPEND-ING ON option. The ALTER statement is used to alter the operand of a GO TO statement. A GO TO statement that will be ALTERed must be the only statement in a paragraph, and the GO TO statement must not use the DEPENDING ON option. The IF statement is used to test a condition. In COBOL there are five different conditions: *condition names, class conditions, relational conditions, sign conditions,* and *switch status conditions.* Relational conditions are used to compare data items through the use of the operators EQUAL, GREATER and LESS. Any of the conditions can be combined to form compound conditions by using the *logical operators* AND, OR, and NOT.

Figure 9.2 Program flowchart for MIN-MAX-AVERAGE-GRADES program for example 9.19.

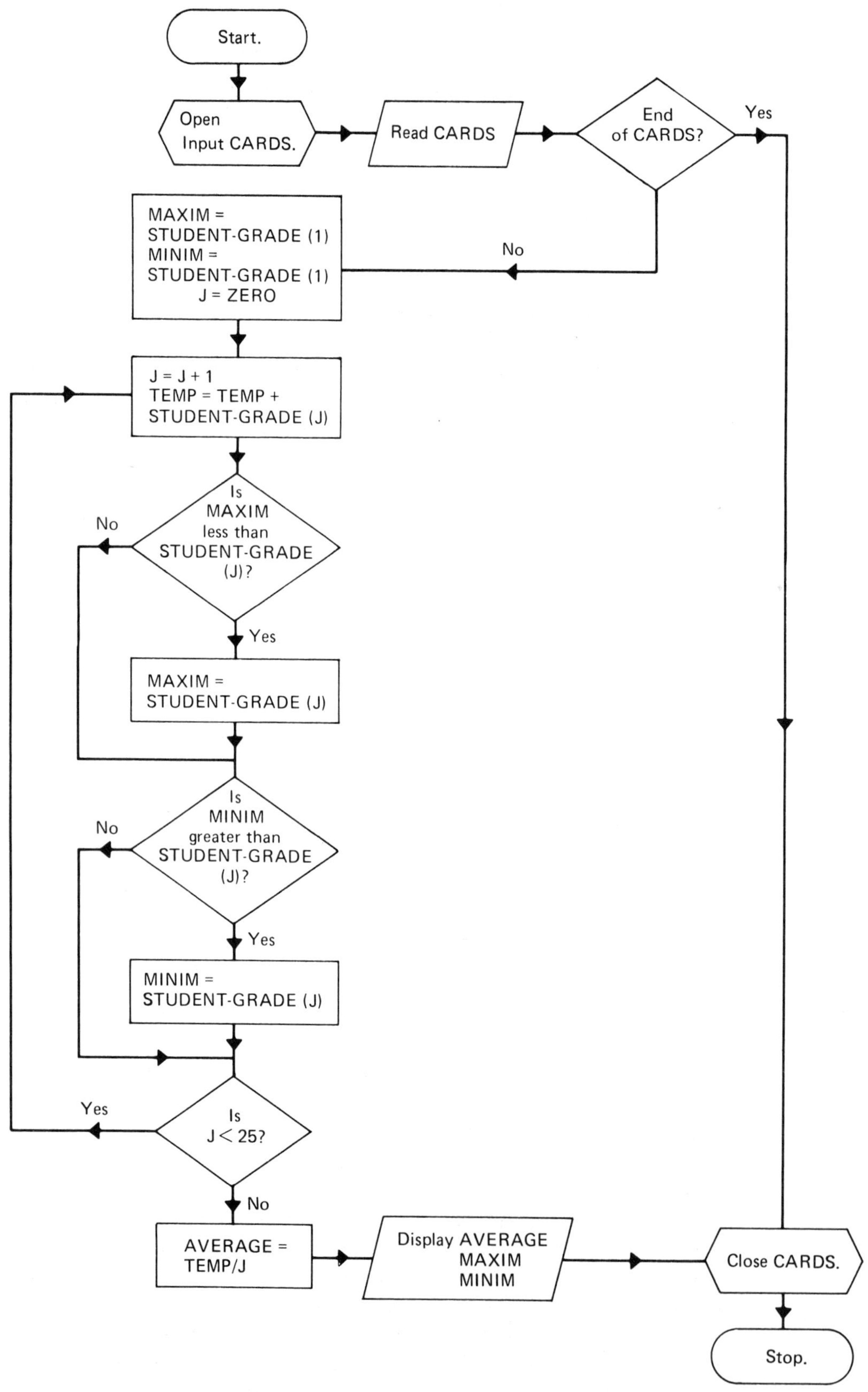

Figure 9.3 Listing for MIN-MAX-AVERAGE-GRADES program for example 9.19 run on the IBM-S3.

```
IDENTIFICATION DIVISION.
PROGRAM-ID. MIN-MAX-AVERAGE-GRADES.
ENVIRONMENT DIVISION.
CONFIGURATION SECTION.
SOURCE-COMPUTER. IBM-S3.
OBJECT-COMPUTER. IBM-S3.
INPUT-OUTPUT SECTION.
FILE-CONTROL.
    SELECT CARDS, ASSIGN TO UR-1442-RD.
DATA DIVISION.
FILE SECTION.
FD  CARDS, LABEL RECORDS ARE OMITTED.
01  GRADE.
    02  STUDENT-GRADE OCCURS 25 TIMES PIC 9(3).
WORKING-STORAGE SECTION.
77  TEMP PIC 9(5) COMP VALUE 0.
77  J PIC 9(2) COMP VALUE 0.
77  AVERAGE PIC 9(3).9(2).
77  MAXIM PIC 9(3).
77  MINIM PIC 9(3).
PROCEDURE DIVISION.
BEGIN.
    OPEN INPUT CARDS.
    READ CARDS AT END GO TO END-OF-PROGRAM.
***********************************************************************
*****THE FIRST STUDENT-GRADE IS MOVED TO MAXIM AND MINIM.....    *
***********************************************************************
    MOVE STUDENT-GRADE (1) TO MAXIM, MINIM.
WORK-LOOP.
    ADD 1 TO J.
    COMPUTE TEMP = TEMP + STUDENT-GRADE (J).
***********************************************************************
*****EACH TIME A GRADE GREATER THAN MAXIM IS FOUND IT BECOMES THE*
*****NEW VALUE OF MAXIM. WHEN FINISHED, MAXIM WILL BE EQUAL TO   *
*****THE VALUE OF THE LARGEST GRADE.....                         *
***********************************************************************
    IF MAXIM IS LESS THAN STUDENT-GRADE (J),
        MOVE STUDENT-GRADE (J) TO MAXIM.
***********************************************************************
*****EACH TIME A GRADE IS FOUND SMALLER THAN MINIM, IT BECOMES   *
*****THE NEW VALUE OF MINIM. WHEN FINISHED, MINIM WILL BE EQUAL   *
*****TO THE SMALLEST GRADE.....                                  *
***********************************************************************
    IF MINIM IS GREATER THAN STUDENT-GRADE (J),
        MOVE STUDENT-GRADE (J) TO MINIM.
    IF J IS LESS THAN 25, GO TO WORK-LOOP.
AVERAGE-GRADE-PARAGRAPH.
    COMPUTE AVERAGE ROUNDED = TEMP / J.
    DISPLAY 'AVERAGE GRADE IS ', AVERAGE, ' FOR ', J,
        ' STUDENTS.'.
    DISPLAY 'HIGHEST GRADE IS ', MAXIM,
        ', LOWEST GRADE IS ', MINIM.
END-OF-PROGRAM.
    CLOSE CARDS.
    STOP RUN.
```

Figure 9.4 Modifications necessary to run the program for example 9.19 on the IBM-1130, the B1700, or the DECSYSTEM-10.

a. For IBM-1130:

```
FILE-CONTROL.
          SELECT CARDS ASSIGN TO RD-2501.
```

b. For B1700:

```
FILE-CONTROL.
          SELECT CARDS ASSIGN TO READER.
```

c. For DECSYSTEM-10

```
FILE-CONTROL.
          SELECT CARDS ASSIGN TO CDR.
```

Review Questions

1. Suppose A is 9, B is 3, and D is 18.

```
IF A + B GREATER THAN D, MOVE 0 TO A, B, ADD D
TO D ELSE ADD B, A TO B, DIVIDE A INTO D,
MULTIPLY D BY 2. STOP RUN.
```

After the above segment is executed, the value of *A* is _______, *B* is _______, and *D* is _______.

2.
```
COMPUTE NOW = 3.
GO TO LP, TP, GP, KG DEPENDING ON NOW.
GP. MOVE 5 TO POCKET, STOP RUN.
KG. MOVE -2 TO POCKET, STOP RUN.
TP. MOVE 0 TO POCKET, STOP RUN.
LP. MOVE -10 TO POCKET, STOP RUN.
```

After execution of the preceding segment of the program, the value of POCKET is ———. If NOW had been 5, then the value of POCKET would be ———.

3.
```
LP-1.
          COMPUTE B = 5.
LP-2. ALTER LP-3 TO PROCEED TO LAST.
LP-3. GO TO LP-1.
LAST. MOVE 0 TO B. STOP RUN.
```

After the execution of the preceding segment, the value of *B* is _______.

4.
```
LP-1.
          ALTER LP-2 TO PROCEED TO LP-4.
LP-2. GO TO.
LP-3. MOVE 0 TO B. STOP RUN.
LP-4. COMPUTE B = 7.
          STOP RUN.
```

After execution of the preceding program, *B* is _______.

5. Is the following segment of a program correct? If not, why?

```
11.
    GO TO.
12. ALTER 11 TO PROCEED TO DISCOUNT.
DISCOUNT.
        COMPUTE PRICE = (0.99) * PRICE.
        STOP RUN.
```

6. What is the truth value of the following expression:

```
(A/2) LESS THAN B + K AND G IS NEGATIVE
OR B + D = C - F
```

where F is 18, C is 50, B is 20, D is 12, G is 0, K is 3, and A is 24.

7. What is wrong with the following statement?

```
IF COUNTER IS GREATER THAN 10, GO TO BEGIN, MOVE 0 TO
COUNTER.
```

Suggested Projects

1. Write a COBOL program to compute federal taxes. Each record of an input card file contains

```
TAXPAYER - X(25)
SOC-SEC-NUM - 9(9)
NUM-EXEMPTIONS - 9(2)
DEDUCTIONS - 9(5)V99
WITHHOLDING - 9(5)V99
INCOME - 9(8)V99
```

Then COMPUTE TAXABLE-INCOME = INCOME − DEDUC-TIONS − 750 ∗ NUM-EXEMPTIONS and TAX = 0.18 ∗ TAXABLE-INCOME. If TAX is negative, the tax owed is 0. If TAX is positive, then COMPUTE AMOUNT-DUE = TAX − WITHHOLDING. If AMOUNT-DUE is nonnegative, then it is the actual amount due. If AMOUNT-DUE is negative, then COMPUTE OVER-PAYMENT = −1 ∗ AMOUNT-DUE. Print each person's name (TAX-PAYER's content), social security number (SOC-SEC-NUM), AMOUNT-DUE, and OVER-PAYMENT. Provide headings for output and run the program with 10 data cards.

2. Suppose you have exactly 50 data cards. These data cards belong to a bank. On each data card there is a field, and its length is only one character. This field on some cards contains the number 1, and on others the field contains the number 2. The number 1 indicates that this is a checking account, and 2 indicates that this is a savings account. In addition to that, each card contains a customer's name, account number, amount of deposit, and amount of withdrawal. These 50 data cards represent transactions of one day in this bank. Write a COBOL program to do the following.

   a. Read exactly the 50 data cards.

   b. Find the average of deposits for saving, deposits for checking, with-drawals from saving, and withdrawals from checking.

    c. Print out a list of customers and their deposits and withdrawals with a heading on each page, double-spacing, and 10 lines per page.

    d. Use a condition name in the program for CHECKING and SAV-INGS.

    e. Print the averages of b.

3. The Harris Survey Company has just canvassed a consumer market to test their reaction to their new product GOTCHA. The results of the survey have been coded on cards. Each column of a card contains 1, 2, 3, or 4 to indicate consumer preferences. These correspond to a bad, poor, fair, or good reaction to the product. Write a flowchart and then a COBOL program to process these cards. The program should compute the total number of responses and the percentages of bad, poor, fair, and good consumer reactions. A blank column on a card should not be counted in any calculations. Use the EXAMINE statement in your program to tally the responses on each card. Round all percentage calculations. Print the results in the form of a table. Run your program with at least eight cards.

4. Your instructor has created a file of numbers on a disk. Each record of the file consists of one number whose picture is S9(3)V9. The file is sequentially organized and was created to hold up to 300 records. It is possible that less than 300 records were placed in the file. Write a COBOL program to read the file and print a list of all the negative numbers in the file with four numbers to each line of print. Next reread the file and count all the positive numbers in the file. Also, total the negative numbers in the file and the positive numbers in the file separately. Print a summary of your computations. Run your program. You will need a card (∗ FILES on the IBM-1130) to cause the computer to process the correct file. This is similar to the processing of a bank file of withdrawals and deposits.

5. COBOL does not provide easy methods for many computations. One commonly desired result is the square root of a positive number. There is a simple algorithm for approximating the value of the square root of a number.

Let A be a positive number. Let X be a positive number chosen arbitrarily. If possible, choose X close to the square root of A. If we repeatedly compute new values for X according to the arithmetic statement

```
COMPUTE X = (X + A / X)/ 2.0.
```

then the values of X will gradually approach the value of the square root of A.

Write a COBOL program to test this algorithm for different choices of A and X. Try using the above arithmetic formula in a loop so that the value of X is computed 20 times. Print the value of X each time it is computed. (*Hint:* The accuracy of the results is improved if you provide several decimal places in the picture of X.)

6. In actual practice it is very important that all programs provide careful checking of all input data to files. Despite precautions, key-punching errors do occur and misunderstandings are not uncommon. It is particularly important to check to see that numeric data items are really numeric and that if data items are restricted, then the restrictions are met. For

example, if a program assumes that no employee earns more than $1,300 monthly, then the program should check to see that this is the case if a violation would invalidate the results of the program.

Design a payroll file for the employees of a company. Each employee record should contain information such as employee name, number, address, seniority, etc. As records are stored in the employee disk file from cards, you should check numeric fields to make sure that they are numeric. This is done by reading the field with a PICTURE of X's, using the EXAMINE statement to replace the blanks in the field with zeros, and testing the result to see if it is numeric. Assume that no employee is paid more than $1,300 dollars monthly. Check the salary of each employee to make sure that this condition is fulfilled. Provide such other checks as you feel are necessary.

CHAPTER 10

The PERFORM Statement

In many programs a group of instructions is needed in several places in the PROCEDURE DIVISION. You could write this group of instructions in each place they are needed, but this would make a program unnecessarily long. Instead, you could put them in the form of a subprogram (see Chapter 12) and call the subprogram each time the instructions are needed; or you could place the instructions in a paragraph or section and PERFORM the paragraph or section when it was needed. Such a paragraph or section is called a *procedure*. By using the various forms of the PERFORM statement, you can execute a single procedure, execute a group of procedures, or cause the repeated execution of a procedure or group of procedures. This chapter is devoted to explaining the different forms of the PERFORM statement.

There are five different forms of the PERFORM statement:

1. the simple PERFORM statement,
2. the PERFORM statement with the THRU option,
3. the PERFORM statement with the TIMES option,
4. the PERFORM statement with the UNTIL option, and
5. the PERFORM statement with the VARYING option.

Even though we will discuss the options singly, you should realize that they may be combined in some cases.

The Simple PERFORM Statement

The simple PERFORM statement has the format

```
PERFORM name.
```

where name is the name of a procedure. This statement causes the computer to execute each and every instruction in the procedure and then return and begin executing the instructions immediately following the PERFORM statement. This means that the procedure cannot contain any instruction that causes the computer to go to statements outside the procedure. Be careful to avoid this error.

Example 10.1

```
          A    B
          ⋮
          PERFORM DISCOUNT.
```

Figure 10.1 IBM System 3 computer system.
On the right of the photograph are the IBM-5445 disk storage units.

```
          ADD PURCHASE TO OLD-BAL GIVING NEW-BAL.
       ⋮
       DISCOUNT.
             MULTIPLY 0.9 BY PRICE.
             COMPUTE PURCHASE = NUMBER-OF-ITEM * PRICE.
```

When the statement PERFORM DISCOUNT is encountered, the computer transfers control to paragraph DISCOUNT. After executing all the statements of DISCOUNT, control is returned to the statement 'ADD PURCHASE TO OLD-BAL GIVING NEW-BAL'. which immediately follows the PERFORM statement. The location of DISCOUNT in the PROCEDURE DIVISION does not affect the PERFORM statement. DISCOUNT may precede or follow the PERFORM statement. The flowchart in figure 10.2 shows the order in which the instructions are executed for example 10.1.

Throughout our remaining work on the PERFORM statement we shall use name or name-i to denote the names of procedures. Remember that a procedure name is the name of a paragraph or section in the PROCEDURE DIVISION.

Figure 10.2 Flowchart for example 10.1.

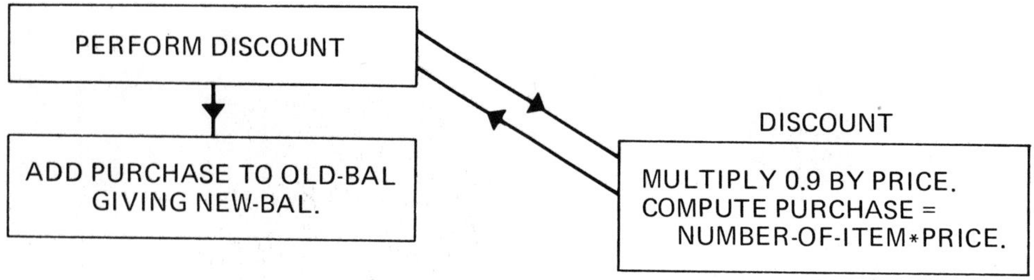

The PERFORM Statement with the THRU Option

The PERFORM statement with the THRU option has the format

```
PERFORM name-1 THRU name-2.
```

The *range* of this PERFORM statement includes the first statement of name-1, the last statement of name-2, and all statements between the first statement of name-1 and the last statement of name-2. When this PERFORM statement is executed, the computer executes all the statements in the range of the PERFORM statement and then returns control to the statement immediately following the PERFORM statement. Thus the statements in the range of the PERFORM cannot transfer control to a statement outside the range of the PERFORM.

Example 10.2

```
A    B
  ⋮
PAR-1.
  ⋮
PAR-2.
  ⋮
PAR-3.
  ⋮
PAR-4.
  ⋮
PAR-5.
      PERFORM PAR-1 THRU PAR-4.
      PERFORM PAR-1.
      PERFORM PAR-2 THRU PAR-3.
  ⋮
```

When PAR-5 is executed, the computer will execute the first PERFORM statement, which causes the execution of PAR-1, PAR-2, PAR-3, and PAR-4. Then control returns to the statement immediately following the PERFORM statement. This statement is also a PERFORM statement and causes the execution of PAR-1. Then control returns to the next statement, which is a PERFORM statement with the THRU option. This statement causes the execution of PAR-2 and PAR-3. Then control returns to the statement following this third PERFORM statement. The flowchart in figure 10.3 illustrates the concept.

Figure 10.3 Flowchart for example 10.2.

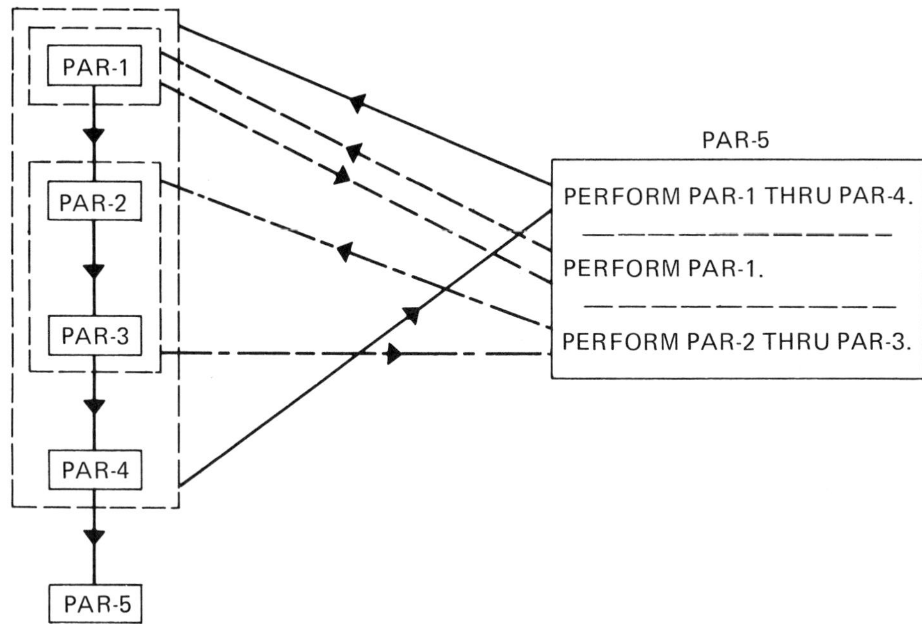

You can transfer control from one statement to another by using the GO TO statement. A GO TO statement can be in the range of a PERFORM statement if it does not transfer control to a statement outside the range of the PERFORM statement.

Example 10.3

```
A    B
  :
PAR-1.
  :
PAR-A.
  :
PAR-2.
  :
BEGIN.
  :
PAR-4.
  :
PAR-3.
  :
PAR-6.
      PERFORM PAR-A THRU PAR-3.
      COMPUTE INTEREST = UN-PAID-BALANCE * RATE.
  :
```

The range of the preceding PERFORM statement is all statements in PAR-A, PAR-2, BEGIN, PAR-4, and PAR-3. It would be permissible if PAR-A contained any of the following GO TO statements: GO TO PAR-2, GO TO BEGIN, GO TO PAR-4, or GO TO PAR-3. It would be permissible for BEGIN to contain any of the following GO TO statements: GO TO PAR-A, GO TO PAR-2, GO TO BEGIN, GO TO PAR-4, or GO TO PAR-3. It would not be permissible for PAR-A, PAR-2, BEGIN, PAR-4, or PAR-3 to contain GO TO PAR-1 or GO TO PAR-6, since the latter paragraphs are not in the range of the PERFORM statement.

Since you cannot transfer control outside the range of a PERFORM statement, a problem occurs when you are within the range of a PERFORM and desire to skip the rest of the range. You must reach the end of the range for control to return to the proper place in the program. Since you do not want to do any further operations while in the range of the PERFORM, you need to have a way to provide a paragraph at the end of the range that contains no instructions. The EXIT statement, which has no effect on a COBOL program, is used for this purpose. The statement is used most commonly in the last paragraph in the range of a PERFORM statement. Whenever it is used in a paragraph, it must be the only statement in the paragraph. As an example, suppose in example 10.3 that when the value of a variable, say N, is greater than 20, you wish to transfer control to the end of the range of the PERFORM statement. Suppose that you test the value of N in PAR-2. You could change example 10.3 as follows.

```
A    B
PAR-1.
  ⋮
PAR-A.
  ⋮
PAR-2.
    IF N GREATER THAN 20 GO TO PARX.
  ⋮
BEGIN.
  ⋮
PAR-4.
  ⋮
PAR-3.
  ⋮
PARX. EXIT.
PAR-6.
    PERFORM PAR-A THRU PARX.
    COMPUTE INTEREST = UN-PAID-BALANCE * RATE.
  ⋮
```

If the value of N is ever greater than 20, control will be passed to PARX. Control then passes to the next statement after the PERFORM statement.

PERFORM statements may have other PERFORM statements in their range. However, the range of the "inner" PERFORM statement must be entirely contained in the range of the "outer" PERFORM statement; or the range of the inner PERFORM statement must be completely separate from the range of the outer PERFORM statement. If the range of the inner PERFORM is wholly contained in the range of the outer PERFORM, then care must be taken to ensure that their ranges do not terminate on the same procedure.

Example 10.4

```
A   B
P1.
      PERFORM P2 THRU P3.
P2.
      PERFORM P4 THRU P8.
P3.
      PERFORM P6 THRU P7.
P4.
      PERFORM P5 THRU P7.
P5.
   .
   .
   .
P6.
   .
   .
   .
P7.
   .
   .
   .
P8.
   .
   .
   .
```

The PERFORM statement of P3 is valid because its range is completely separate from the range of the PERFORM statement in P1. The PERFORM statements in P2 and P4 are valid because the range of the PERFORM in P4 is completely included in the range of the PERFORM statement in P2, and the PERFORM in P2 has a range completely separate from the range of the PERFORM in P1. However, if in P4 we were to write PERFORM P1 THRU P6, the range of this statement would not be completely included in the range of the PERFORM statement in P2 nor completely separate from the range of that statement.

The PERFORM Statement with the TIMES Option

The format of the PERFORM statement with the TIMES option is

$$\underline{\text{PERFORM}}\ \text{name-1}\ [\underline{\text{THRU}}\ \text{name-2}]\ \begin{Bmatrix} \text{integer} \\ \text{data-name} \end{Bmatrix}\ \underline{\text{TIMES}}.$$

Data-name must be an elementary numeric item, and the value of data-name and of the integer must not exceed 9999 on the IBM-1130 and IBM-S3. The effect of this statement is similar to that of the preceding two forms of the PERFORM statement except that the procedures are executed several times. The number of repetitions is given by the value of integer or of data-name. After the procedures are executed, control returns to the statement following the PERFORM statement. If the value of integer or of data-name is 0 or a negative integer, the procedures are not executed, and control passes to the statement after the PERFORM statement. You should know that once the PERFORM statement initiates the execution of the procedures, you can change the value of data-name without affecting the number of times the procedures are executed.

Let the number of times specified by integer or data-name be denoted by N. The flowchart in figure 10.4 explains how the PERFORM statement with the TIMES option is executed.

Figure 10.4 Flowchart for the PERFORM statement with the TIMES option.

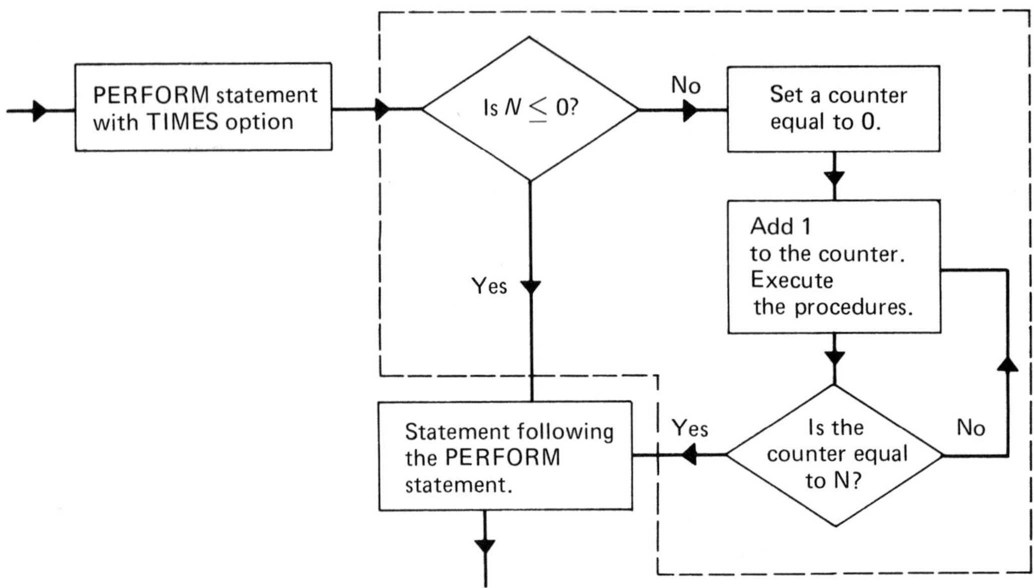

Example 10.5

```
PERFORM PARX 15 TIMES.
PERFORM PARX THRU PARZ 15 TIMES.
PERFORM PARX MANY TIMES.
PERFORM PARX THRU PARZ MANY TIMES.
```

All of the PERFORM statements in example 10.5 are correct provided that the value of the data name MANY is an integer. The first statement causes PARX to be executed 15 times, and the second statement causes all the statements from PARX through those of PARZ to be executed 15 times. In the third and fourth statements, the number of times the procedures are executed depends upon the value of MANY at the time the PERFORM statement is encountered.

Example 10.6

```
A    B
PROCEDURE DIVISION.
    ⋮
    MOVE 25 TO MANY.
    PERFORM PARX THRU PARZ MANY TIMES.
    ⋮
PARX.
    COMPUTE MANY = 50.
    ⋮
PARZ. EXIT.
```

The PERFORM statement in example 10.6 causes PARX through PARZ to be executed 25 times. Note that although the value of MANY is changed in PARX to 50, this does not have any effect upon the number of times the procedures are executed.

The PERFORM Statement with the UNTIL Option

The format of the PERFORM statement with the UNTIL option is

```
PERFORM name-1 [THRU name-2] UNTIL condition.
```

If the condition is true, the specified procedures will not be executed; otherwise, the procedures are repeatedly executed until the condition is true. Then control returns to the statement following the PERFORM statement as shown in the flowchart in figure 10.5.

Example 10.7

```
A   B
 ⋮
77  N   PICTURE 9(2) VALUE 0.
 ⋮
        PERFORM PR-1 THRU PR-5 UNTIL N IS GREATER
            THAN 10.
PAR-1.
        ADD 1 TO N.
 ⋮
PAR-5.
 ⋮
```

The procedures PAR-1 thru PAR-5 will be executed 11 times.

Figure 10.5 Flowchart for the PERFORM statement with the UNTIL option.

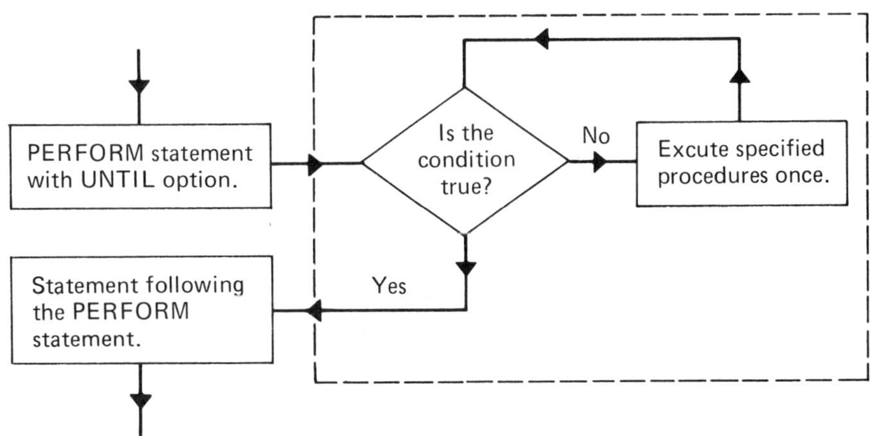

Example 10.8

```
A    B
:
02   CATEGORY   PICTURE 9.
     88 VERY-GOOD VALUE IS 1.
     88 GOOD VALUE IS 2.
     88 AVERAGE VALUE IS 3.
     88 POOR VALUE IS 4.
:
PROMOTION.
     READ EMPLOYEE-FILE AT END MOVE 4 TO CATEGORY.
     IF CATEGORY NOT EQUAL 4 COMPUTE RATE-PER-HOUR
     = RATE-PER-HOUR * 1.02.
:
MAKE-PROMOTIONS.
     PERFORM PROMOTION UNTIL POOR.
:
```

Assume that we are processing a card file of employee records and that each card contains an EMPLOYEE-NAME, RATE-PER-HOUR and CATEGORY. If the records of employees are arranged so that all the VERY-GOOD, GOOD, and AVERAGE employees precede the POOR employees and we MAKE-PROMOTIONS, then only the POOR employees do not receive the higher rate of pay given in PROMOTION. When the first POOR record is encountered, control passes to the first statement after the PERFORM statement.

Example 10.8 illustrates an important consideration. When using the PERFORM statement with the UNTIL option, be sure that a provision is made to guarantee that the condition will be true at least once. Otherwise, the program would execute PROMOTION endlessly. (If we had forgotten to add 1 to N each time the procedure was executed, then N would always be less than 10, and the program would be caught in an endless loop as in example 10.7.)

The PERFORM Statement with the VARYING Option

The PERFORM statement with the VARYING option has the following basic format:

```
PERFORM procedure-1 [THRU procedure-2]
VARYING  { index-1 }
         { name-1  }
FROM { index-2   }      { literal-2 }
     { literal-1 } BY   { name-3    } UNTIL condition.
     { name-2    }
```

Chapter 11 discusses index names, and we will discuss the PERFORM statement with the VARYING option for indices in that chapter. There is no essential difference between the cases where indices are used and the cases where they are not used.

Procedure-1 and procedure-2 must be the names of procedures in the PROCEDURE DIVISION. Literal-1 and literal-2 must be numeric literals which are integers not exceeding 9999. Name-1, name-2, and name-3 must be numeric items whose pictures contain only 9's or S, and their value may not exceed 9999. None of these may be subscripted or indexed variables, a concept that will be discussed more thoroughly in Chapter 11. If this statement appears in a subprogram, then none of name-1, name-2, or name-3 can appear in the FILE SECTION or the LINKAGE SECTION. (A subprogram is a program used to perform tasks for a main program. Chapter 12 discusses subprograms more thoroughly.) The value of index-2, literal-1, and name-2 must be positive at the time the PERFORM statement is begun. When the PERFORM statement is executed, the following steps occur.

1. The operand of VARYING is set to the initial value specified by the operand of FROM.
2. The condition is tested to see if it is true. If it is, control passes to the statement immediately after the PERFORM statement. If not, step 3 is executed.
3. The specified procedures are executed.
4. The operand of VARYING is augmented by the operand of BY. Control passes to step 2.

Figure 10.6 is a flowchart for this option that illustrates the process.

A change in the value of the FROM operand after execution of the PERFORM has begun will not affect the number of times the procedures are executed, but a similar change in the VARYING operand or the BY operand will affect the number of repetitions.

Example 10.9

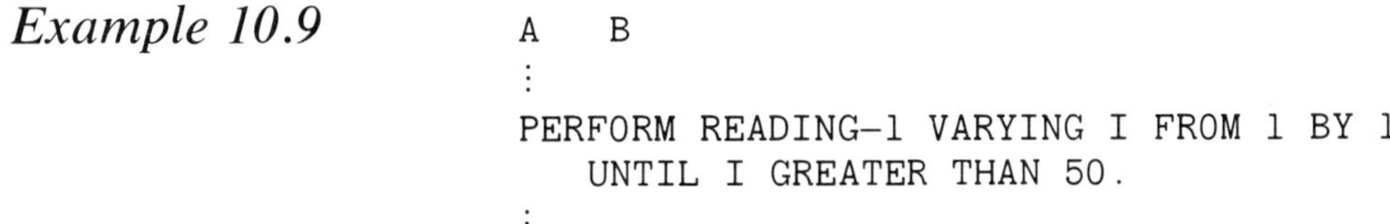
```
A    B
  :
PERFORM READING-1 VARYING I FROM 1 BY 1
    UNTIL I GREATER THAN 50.
  :
```

Figure 10.6 Flowchart for the PERFORM statement with the VARYING option.

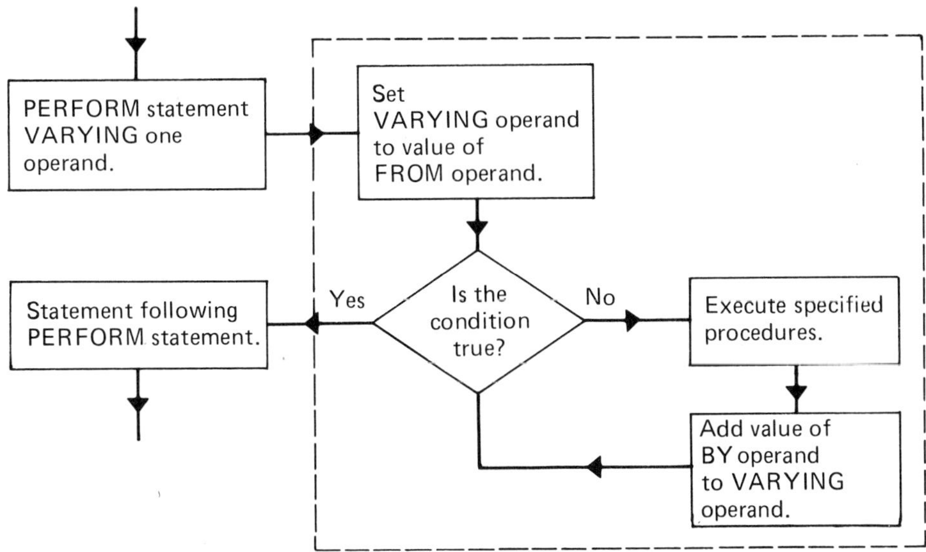

In example 10.9, the initial value of I is 1, the increment is 1, and the condition is I GREATER THAN 50. This PERFORM statement will cause the procedure READING-1 to be executed 50 times. Indeed, since I is initially 1, the condition is not true, and READING-1 is executed. Then 1 is added to I giving I a new value of 2; and since the condition is still false, READING-1 is again executed. This continues until I is 50. Then READING-1 is executed, I is increased to 51; and since the condition is true, control passes to the statement immediately following the PERFORM statement.

The statement

```
PERFORM READING-1 VARYING I FROM 51 BY -1
    UNTIL I IS EQUAL TO 1.
```

has the same effect as the preceding PERFORM statement. The starting value is 51, and I is repeatedly decreased by 1 until I is 1.

Example 10.10

```
A   B
:
WORKING-STORAGE SECTION.
77  I  PICTURE 9(3).
77  AGE  PICTURE 9(3).
77  J  PICTURE 9(2).
77  LAST-1  PICTURE 9(2).
77  INCR  PICTURE 9(2).
:
PROCEDURE DIVISION.
START.
:
    COMPUTE J = 1.
    COMPUTE LAST-1 = 50.
    COMPUTE INCR = 1.
:
    PERFORM READING-1 VARYING I FROM J BY INCR
        UNTIL I IS GREATER THAN LAST-1.
:
```

This PERFORM statement has the same effect as the PERFORM statement of example 10.9. If the value of J is changed in the paragraph READING-1, the change does not affect the number of times READING-1 is executed. Thus if we have

```
READING-1.
    MOVE 14 TO J.
```

READING-1 will still be executed 50 times, and the value of J will be 14 when the PERFORM is finished.

Example 10.11

```
A   B
:
PROCEDURE DIVISION.
    COMPUTE J = 1.
```

```
    COMPUTE LAST-1 = 50.
    COMPUTE INCR = 1.
    PERFORM LOOP-1 THRU LOOP-2 VARYING I FROM J
        BY INCR UNTIL I GREATER THAN LAST-1.
    ⋮
LOOP-1.
    ⋮
    MOVE 20 TO J.
    ⋮
LOOP-2.
    MOVE 5 TO INCR.
    SUBTRACT 5 FROM LAST-1.
    ⋮
```

The starting value of J is 1. The statement MOVE 20 TO J does not affect the starting value of the PERFORM statement because it occurs after the PERFORM statement begins execution. However, the statements MOVE 5 TO INCR and SUBTRACT 5 FROM LAST-1 affect the number of times the procedures LOOP-1 through LOOP-2 are executed. In fact, each time the paragraphs are executed, the value of LAST-1 decreases by 5 and the value of I increases by 5. You should be able to see that the procedures are executed five times, and the value of I in the last iteration is 26, whereas that of LAST-1 is 25.

If you know the FORTRAN language or PL/1, you may have realized that the PERFORM is very much like the DO loop in these languages. DO loops can be nested, and the same can be done with COBOL PERFORM statements. The presence of a PERFORM statement can be nested within the range of another PERFORM statement, as shown in example 10.4, or it can be done using an expanded format for the PERFORM statement, which is

$$
\underline{\text{PERFORM}} \text{ procedure-1 } [\underline{\text{THRU}} \text{ procedure-2}] \underline{\text{VARYING}}
$$

$$
\begin{Bmatrix} \text{index-1} \\ \text{name-1} \end{Bmatrix} \underline{\text{FROM}} \begin{Bmatrix} \text{index-2} \\ \text{literal-2} \\ \text{name-2} \end{Bmatrix}
$$

$$
\underline{\text{BY}} \begin{Bmatrix} \text{literal-3} \\ \text{name-3} \end{Bmatrix} \underline{\text{UNTIL}} \text{ condition-1}
$$

$$
[\underline{\text{AFTER}} \begin{Bmatrix} \text{index-3} \\ \text{name-4} \end{Bmatrix} \underline{\text{FROM}} \begin{Bmatrix} \text{index-4} \\ \text{literal-4} \\ \text{name-5} \end{Bmatrix}
$$

$$
\underline{\text{BY}} \begin{Bmatrix} \text{literal-5} \\ \text{name-6} \end{Bmatrix} \underline{\text{UNTIL}} \text{ condition-2}
$$

$$
[\underline{\text{AFTER}} \begin{Bmatrix} \text{index-5} \\ \text{name-7} \end{Bmatrix} \underline{\text{FROM}} \begin{Bmatrix} \text{index-6} \\ \text{literal-6} \\ \text{name-8} \end{Bmatrix}
$$

$$
\underline{\text{BY}} \begin{Bmatrix} \text{literal-7} \\ \text{name-9} \end{Bmatrix} \underline{\text{UNTIL}} \text{ condition-3}]]
$$

This format permits varying one or two additional variables in the PERFORM statement. When only name-1 and name-4 are varied, the following sequence of events takes place.

1. Set name-1 and name-4 to their initial values given in their respective FROM operands.
2. Test condition-1. If it is true, return control to the statement immediately following the PERFORM statement. Else go to step 3.
3. Test condition-2. If it is false, go to step 5; else go to step 4.
4. Set name-4 to its initial value. Augment name-1 by the operand of its BY. Go to step 2.
5. Execute procedure-1 through procedure-2 once. Augment name-4 by the operand of its BY. Go to step 3.

The flowchart in figure 10.7 illustrates these steps.

The effect of the PERFORM when all of name-1, name-4, and name-7 are used is essentially the same as in the case where only name-1 and name-4 are used. Now as the procedures are executed, name-7 is augmented until condition-3 is true, then name-4 is augmented. This continues until condition-2 is true. Then name-1 is augmented. This continues until condition-1 is true. The flowchart in figure 10.8 illustrates these steps.

Figure 10.7 Flowchart for the PERFORM statement VARYING with two operands.

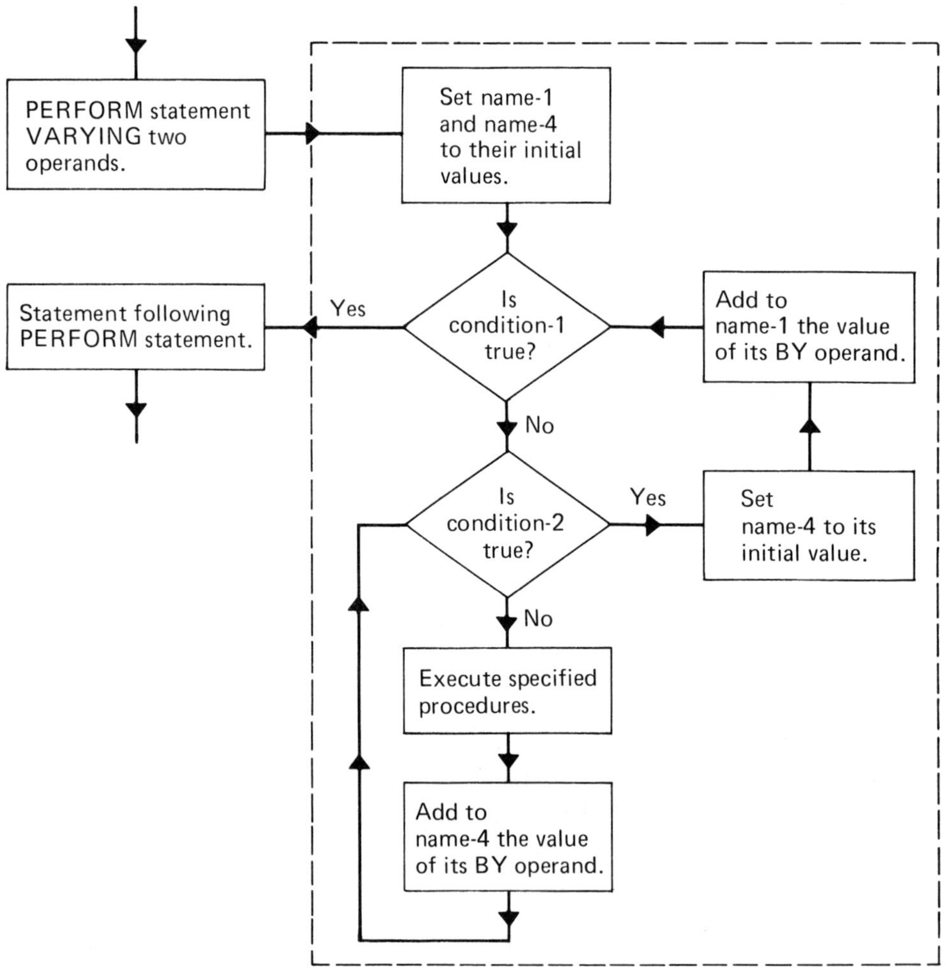

Figure 10.8 Flowchart for the PERFORM statement VARYING with three operands.

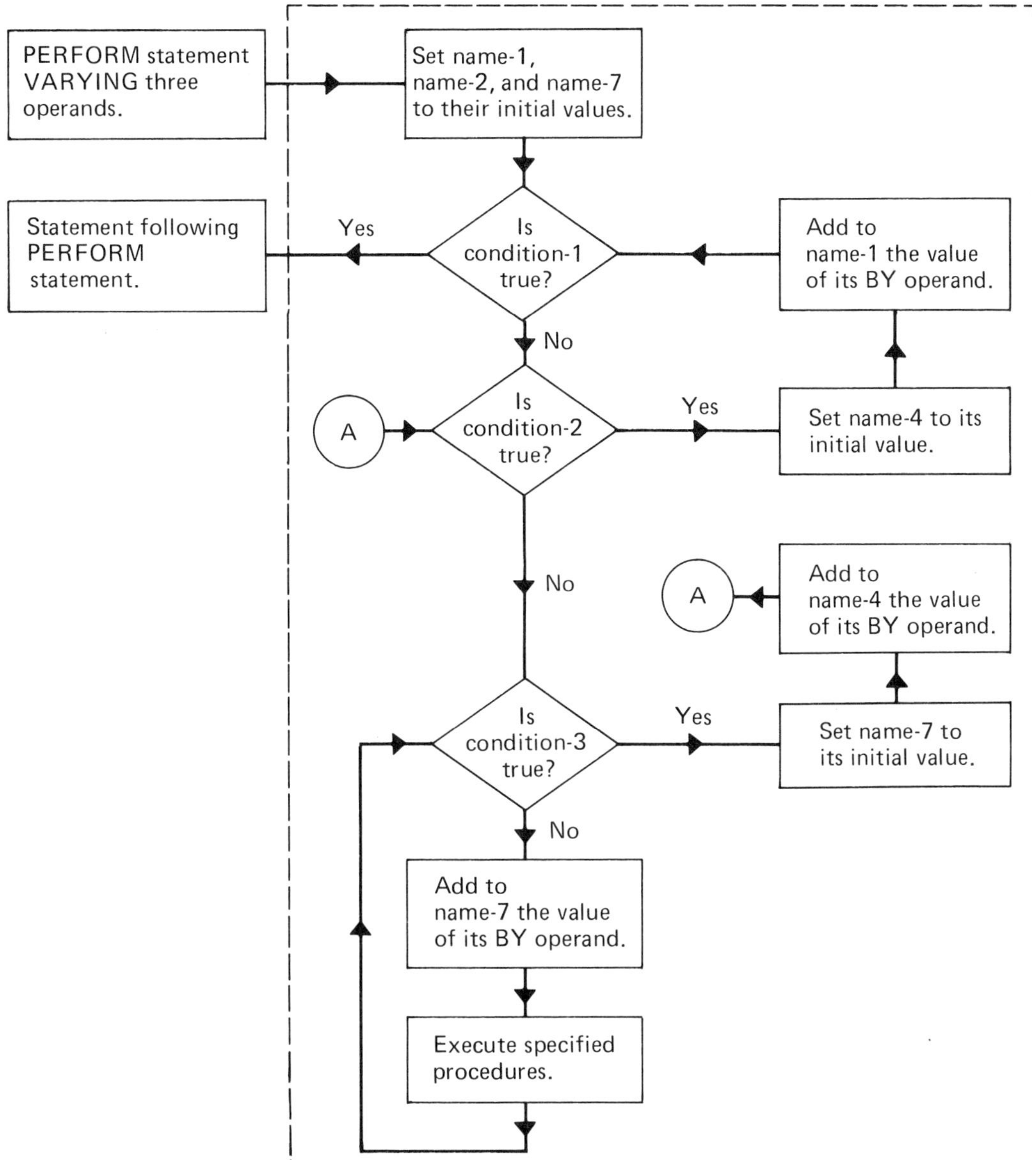

Example 10.12

```
A    B
:
     PERFORM MASTER-EVALUATION THRU MASTER-EXIT
     VARYING I FROM 10 BY 2 UNTIL I IS GREATER
     THAN 20, AFTER J FROM 25 BY -5 UNTIL J IS
     EQUAL TO 0, AFTER K FROM 1 BY 1 UNTIL K IS
     GREATER THAN 10.
:
```

The effect of the PERFORM statement in example 10.12 is that procedures MASTER-EVALUATION through MASTER-EXIT will be executed

300 times. When the PERFORM is finished, *I* will be 22. For each value of *I,* the value of *J* changes five times (from 25 to 0 by -5), and for each value of *J,* the value of *K* changes 10 times (from 1 to 11 by 1).

Example 10.13   Figure 10.9 is the listing of the program done for example 9.19 in which student grades are averaged. Note that the IDENTIFICATION, ENVI-RONMENT, and DATA divisions are unchanged, but the PROCEDURE DIVISION is changed to make use of a PERFORM statement.

Figure 10.9 Printout of listing for the program described in example 10.13.

```
IDENTIFICATION DIVISION.
PROGRAM-ID. MIN-MAX-AVERAGE-GRADES.
ENVIRONMENT DIVISION.
CONFIGURATION SECTION.
SOURCE-COMPUTER.  IBM-1130.
OBJECT-COMPUTER.  IBM-1130.
INPUT-OUTPUT SECTION.
FILE-CONTROL.
    SELECT CARDS, ASSIGN TO RD-2501.
DATA DIVISION.
FILE SECTION.
FD  CARDS, LABEL RECORDS ARE OMITTED.
01  GRADE.
    02  STUDENT-GRADE OCCURS 25 TIMES PIC 9(3).
WORKING-STORAGE SECTION.
77  TEMP PIC 9(5) COMP VALUE 0.
77  J PIC 9(2) COMP VALUE 0.
77  AVERAGE PIC 9(3).9(2).
77  MAXIM PIC 9(3).
77  MINIM PIC 9(3).
PROCEDURE DIVISION.
BEGIN.
    OPEN INPUT CARDS.
    READ CARDS AT END GO TO END-OF-PROGRAM.
    MOVE STUDENT-GRADE (1) TO MAXIM, MINIM.
*********************************************************************
*****THE PERFORM STATEMENT CAUSES WORK-LOOP TO BE EXECUTED 25   *
*****TIMES. THE COMPUTER WILL THEN PROCEED TO EXECUTE THE       *
*****STATEMENTS FOLLOWING THE PERFORM STATEMENT. WHEN THE PERFORM*
*****STATEMENT FINISHES THE VALUE OF J WILL BE 26......         *
*********************************************************************
    PERFORM WORK-LOOP VARYING J FROM 1 BY 1
        UNTIL J IS GREATER THAN 25.
    COMPUTE AVERAGE ROUNDED = TEMP / 25.
    DISPLAY 'AVERAGE GRADE IS ', AVERAGE, ' FOR ', J,
        ' STUDENTS.'.
    DISPLAY 'HIGHEST GRADE IS ', MAXIM,
        ', LOWEST GRADE IS ', MINIM.
END-OF-PROGRAM.
    CLOSE CARDS.
    STOP RUN.
WORK-LOOP
    COMPUTE TEMP = TEMP + STUDENT-GRADE (J).
    IF MAXIM IS LESS THAN STUDENT-GRADE (J),
        MOVE STUDENT-GRADE (J) TO MAXIM.
    IF MINIM IS GREATER THAN STUDENT-GRADE (J),
        MOVE STUDENT-GRADE (J) TO MINIM.
/*
```

Example 10.14   Example 10.14 uses the PERFORM statement in a program to create a permanent direct file on disk. Suppose there are 1,000 employees in Company X. Company X decides to give each employee an employee number consisting of four digits from 1000 through 1999. The maximum size of the file for employee records should be 1000. Each record of this file, MASTER-FILE, contains the following data.

Employee number	*Employee name*	*Employee address*	*Pay to date*	*Federal with. tax*	*State with. tax*
4 digits	20 characters	30 characters	9(6)V99	9(5)V99	9(4)V99

When MASTER-FILE is created initially, PAY-TO-DATE, FED-W-TAX, and STATE-W-TAX are set to 0 for all employees. Every month MASTER-FILE is updated by a program. Figure 10.10 is the system flowchart for example 10.14; figure 10.11 is the flowchart for that program; figure 10.12 is the listing for the program as it was run on the IBM-1130; and figure 10.13 lists the modifications necessary to run the program on the IBM-S3, B1700, or DECSYSTEM-10. In the program, we give the name FINDER to the file key.

We use the following procedure in determining the value of FINDER for each employee record.

$$\text{Remainder} = \text{employee number} - 999$$

Below are several values of FINDER corresponding to the respective employee numbers.

Employee number	*Value of FINDER*
1000	1
1678	679
1234	235
1999	1000

Figure 10.10 System flowchart for example 10.14.

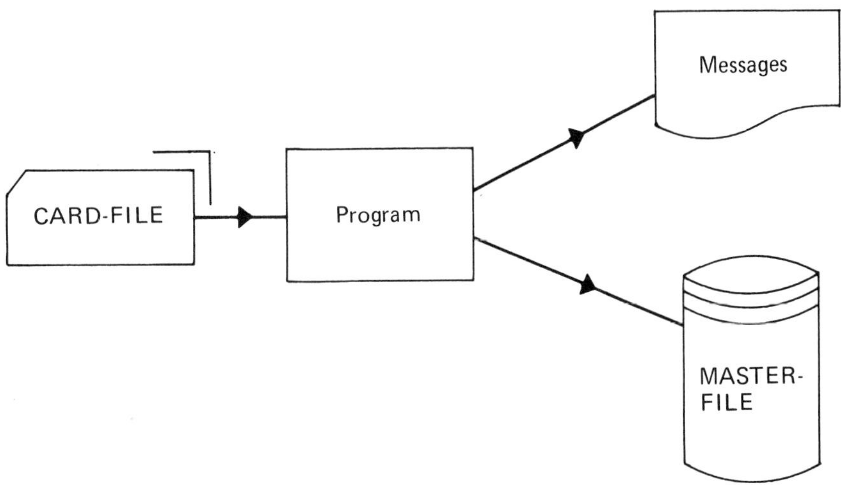

Figure 10.11 Program flowchart for MASTF program for example 10.14.

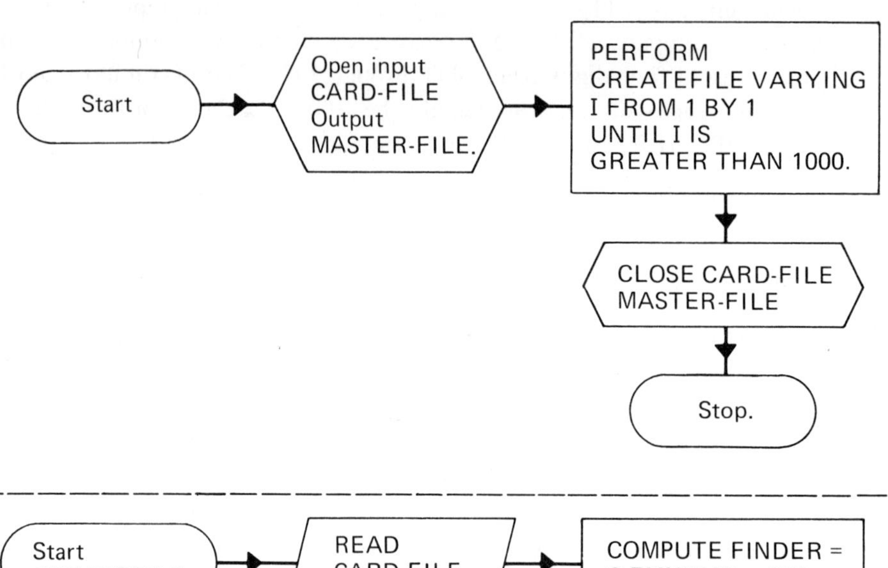

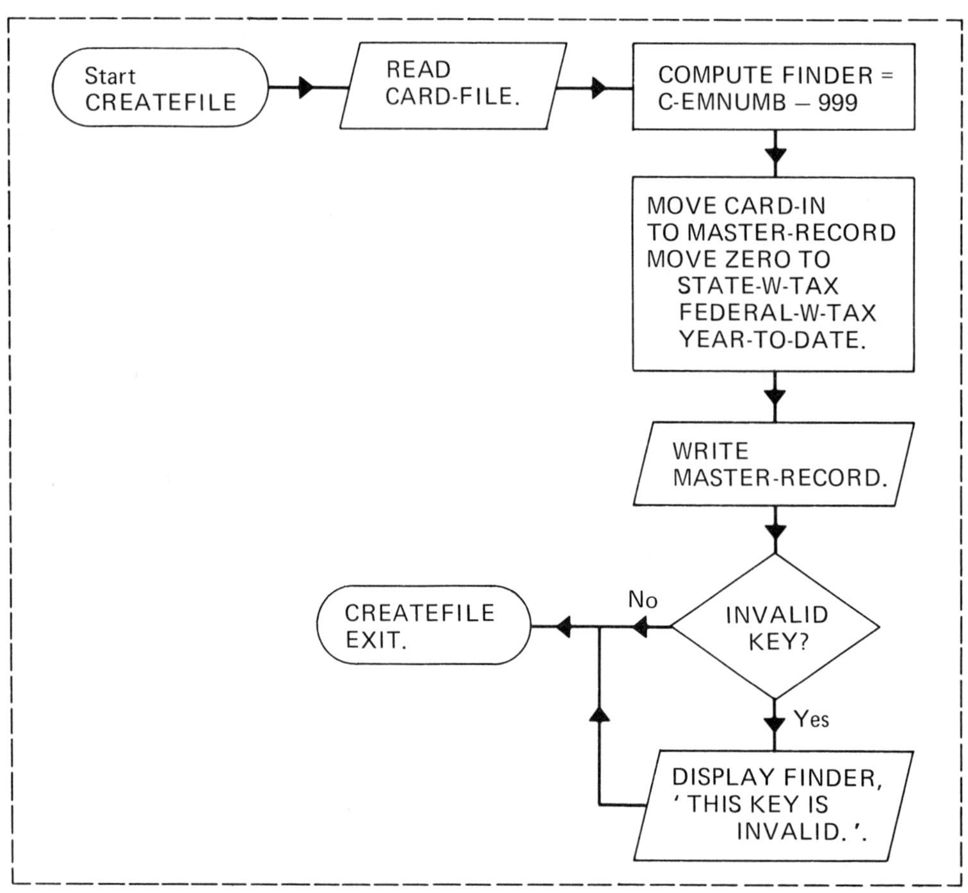

Figure 10.12 Printout of listing for program described in example 10.14.

```
// JOB T
// COBOL
*LIST,/O1FE,PMAP,DMAP,XREF
       IDENTIFICATION DIVISION.
       PROGRAM-ID. MASTF.
       REMARKS. THIS PROGRAM CREATES A PERMANENT EMPLOYEE
           FILE ON DISK. THIS FILE SHOULD BE UPDATED MONTHLY.
       ENVIRONMENT DIVISION.
       CONFIGURATION SECTION.
       SOURCE-COMPUTER. IBM-1130.
       OBJECT-COMPUTER. IBM-1130.
       FILE-CONTROL.
           SELECT MASTER-FILE, ASSIGN TO DF-18-1000,
               ACCESS IS RANDOM,
                   ACTUAL KEY IS FINDER.
           SELECT CARD-FILE, ASSIGN TO RD-2501.
       DATA DIVISION.
       FILE SECTION.
       FD  MASTER-FILE,
           LABEL RECORDS ARE STANDARD,
               DATA RECORD IS MASTER-RECORD.
       01  MASTER-RECORD.
           02 MASTER-EM-NUMB               PIC 9(4) COMP.
           02 MASTER-EM-NAME               PIC X(20).
           02 MASTER-EM-ADD                PIC X(30).
           02 YEAR-TO-DATE                 PIC 9(6)V99 COMP.
           02 FEDERAL-W-TAX                PIC 9(5)V99 COMP.
           02 STATE-W-TAX                  PIC 9(4)V99 COMP.
       FD  CARD-FILE,
           LABEL RECORDS ARE OMITTED,
               DATA RECORD IS CARD-IN.
       01  CARD-IN.
           02 C-EMNUMB                     PIC 9(4).
           02 C-EM-NAME                    PIC X(20).
           02 C-EM-ADD                     PIC X(30).
       WORKING-STORAGE SECTION.
       77  FINDER                          PIC S9(5) COMP.
       77  I                               PIC 999.
       PROCEDURE DIVISION.
       START-PROGRAM.
           OPEN INPUT CARD-FILE, OUTPUT MASTER-FILE.
       ****************************************************************
           PERFORM CREATEFILE VARYING I FROM 1 BY 1
               UNTIL I IS GREATER THAN 1000.
       ****************************************************************
           CLOSE CARD-FILE, MASTER-FILE.
           STOP RUN.
       CREATEFILE.
           READ CARD-FILE AT END
               DISPLAY 'MASTER-FILE IS NOT FILLED. RECORDS ARE MISSING',
               CLOSE CARD-FILE, MASTER-FILE,
                   STOP RUN.
       ****************************************************************
       *****FINDER DETERMINES THE LOCATION OF THE EMPLOYEE RECORD.    *
       *****     THE HASHING TECHNIQUE TO DETERMINE FINDER IS TO SUBTRACT*
       *****     999 FROM THE EMPLOYEE NUMBER.....                    *
       ****************************************************************
           COMPUTE FINDER = C-EMNUMB - 999.
           MOVE C-EMNUMB TO MASTER-EM-NUMB.
           MOVE C-EM-NAME TO MASTER-EM-NAME.
           MOVE C-EM-ADD TO MASTER-EM-ADD.
```

Figure 10.12 (Cont'd.)

```
            MOVE 0 TO YEAR-TO-DATE, FEDERAL-W-TAX, STATE-W-TAX.
            WRITE MASTER-RECORD INVALID KEY
                DISPLAY FINDER, '***THIS KEY IS INVALID***'.
/*
// XEQ
     DATA CARDS GO HERE
/*
// DUP
*STOREDATA  WS  UA  MDSKF  200
```

As you see, we used simple functions to determine the value of the file key from the employee number. Using a function to determine values for a file key is a *hash technique,* and the functions involved are called *hash functions.*

Note that the last three cards are monitor control cards to store the file after we have created it. It is stored under the name MDSKF. See Appendix II for further information on how to create disk files on an IBM-1130. This file occupies 200 sectors. The number of sectors was found as follows.

1. Each of the four fields MASTER-EM-NUMB, YEAR-TO-DATE, FEDERAL-W-TAX, and STATE-W-TAX have computational usage. Since MASTER-EM-NUMB has four digits, it occupies one word of storage. Each of the other numeric items have five through nine digits and occupy two words of storage. Thus the numeric items in MASTER-RECORD occupy seven words of storage. Since the remaining two fields have display usage, they occupy one word for each character for a total of fifty words. Thus MASTER-RECORD requires 57 words of storage in all.
2. The number of records which can be entirely stored in a sector is 5 since $320/57 = 5 + 35/57$.
3. The number of sectors required for storing 1,000 records is 1,000/5 or 200.

If you are not using an IBM-1130 in running your programs, you may find it instructive to perform the preceding calculations to determine the amount of storage required for MASTER-RECORD and MASTER-FILE on your computer.

Our final comment on the PERFORM statement involves sequence control. Recall that when a PERFORM is executed, control passes to the statements of the procedures in the range of the PERFORM; and when the PERFORM is finished, control passes to the statement immediately following the PERFORM statement. What would happen if we were not executing a PERFORM statement, and we transferred control to a statement included in the range of the PERFORM statement? The answer is that unless the PERFORM is active, the statements in the range of a PERFORM behave exactly as they would normally.

Figure 10.13 Modifications necessary in the program for example 10.14 to run it on the B1700, IBM-S3, and DECSYSTEM-10.

a. For a B-1700:

```
SOURCE-COMPUTER. B-1700.
OBJECT-COMPUTER. B-1700.
INPUT-OUTPUT SECTION.
FILE-CONTROL.
    SELECT MASTER-FILE ASSIGN TO DISK  ACTUAL KEY IS FINDER
        ACCESS IS RANDOM.
    SELECT CARD-FILE ASSIGN TO READER.
  ⋮
FD  MASTER-FILE, LABEL RECORDS ARE STANDARD,
                FILE CONTAINS 1000 RECORDS.
  ⋮
FD  CARD-FILE, LABEL RECORDS ARE OMITTED, VALUE OF ID
                IS "CARDF".
  ⋮
77  FINDER   PIC 9(8)  COMP.
```

b. For the IBM-S3:

```
SOURCE-COMPUTER. IBM-S3.
OBJECT-COMPUTER. IBM-S3.
INPUT-OUTPUT SECTION.
FILE-CONTROL.
    SELECT MASTER-FILE ASSIGN TO DA-5444-R-FILE18,
        ACTUAL KEY IS FINDER ACCESS IS RANDOM.
    SELECT CARD-FILE ASSIGN TO UR-2501-RD.
  ⋮
77  FINDER   PIC S9(7)  COMP.
```

c. For the DECSYSTEM-10:

```
SOURCE-COMPUTER. DECSYSTEM-10.
OBJECT-COMPUTER. DECSYSTEM-10.
INPUT-OUTPUT SECTION.
FILE-CONTROL.
    SELECT MASTER-FILE ASSIGN TO DSK, FILE-LIMIT IS 1000,
        ACTUAL KEY IS FINDER, ACCESS IS RANDOM.
  ⋮
```

Summary   The PERFORM statement is a powerful COBOL statement. There are five forms of the PERFORM statement:

1. the simple PERFORM
2. PERFORM with THRU option
3. PERFORM with TIMES option
4. PERFORM with UNTIL option
5. PERFORM with VARYING option

The statements all execute one or more procedures in the PROCEDURE DIVISION one or more times. The PERFORM statements may be nested under certain conditions. The range of nested PERFORM statements must not end on the same statement. To designate the end of the range of a PERFORM statement, it is good practice to use the EXIT statement.

In well-written programs each task is accomplished by a self-contained group of instructions. It is a good practice to place these instructions in a SECTION. By using the PERFORM statement, the programmer can cause the instructions to be carried out from any point in the logical flow of the program.

Review Questions   1. Consider

```
        PERFORM L VARYING I FROM 2 BY 3 UNTIL I
        GREATER 12.
    L.
        PERFORM M VARYING J FROM 8 BY -2 UNTIL J
        LESS 1.5.
    M.
        ADD 1 TO COUNTER.
```

where COUNTER has an initial value of 0. What is the value of COUNTER after the PERFORM is executed?

2. Which of the following are valid PERFORM STATEMENTS?

```
    PERFORM L THRU 1.
    PERFORM PARA VARYING I FROM 2 BY 3 UNTIL I
        EQUAL TO 11.
    PERFORM P VARYING H FROM 3 BY 5 UNTIL H
        EQUAL TO 19.
    PERFORM P THRU Q VARYING U BY 1 UNTIL U
        GREATER THAN 51.
    PERFORM P VARYING Q FROM 1 BY 2 UNTIL K
        GREATER THAN 67 AFTER K FROM 1 BY 2
        UNTIL K GREATER THAN 30.
    PERFORM P VARYING Q FROM 0 BY 1 UNTIL Q
        GREATER THAN 7.
```

3. What will the value of K be after the following statements are executed?

```
        PERFORM P VARYING K FROM 1 BY 2 UNTIL K EQUAL
            TO 9.
    P.
        COMPUTE I = I + 1.
    Q. COMPUTE K = K + 1.
```

4. Consider the following statements.

```
MOVE 1 TO K, J, I.
MOVE 100 TO B.
PERFORM LP VARYING K FROM J BY 1 UNTIL K IS
    GREATER THAN B.
LP.
    COMPUTE J = 60.
    ADD 3 TO I.
    SUBTRACT 10 FROM B.
    ⋮
```

a. Does the statement COMPUTE J = 60 affect the number of times that LP is executed?

b. How many times will LP be executed?

5. Consider the following statements from the PROCEDURE DIVISION of a program.

```
MOVE 0 TO TOTAL.
PERFORM ADD-LOOP VARYING I FROM 1 BY 1 UNTIL
    I IS GREATER THAN 3.
GO TO ADD-LOOP.
NEXT-P.
⋮
ADD-LOOP.
    COMPUTE TOTAL = TOTAL + I.
FINAL-P.
    STOP RUN.
```

What will be the value of TOTAL when the STOP RUN statement has been executed? Does the PERFORM statement have any effect on the ADD-LOOP paragraph when it is entered via the GO TO statement?

Suggested Projects

1. In example 10.14 we created a permanent file on disk by the name of MDSKF. Write a COBOL program that will accomplish the following.

   a. Read records from the card reader. (Each record contains an employee's number and monthly pay.)

   b. Calculate federal and state tax by using the following formulas: federal tax = monthly-pay × 0.18 and state tax = (monthly-pay − federal-tax) × 0.05.

   c. Update MDSKF by adding monthly pay, federal tax, and state tax to YEAR-TO-DATE, FEDERAL-W-TAX, and STATE-W-TAX, respectively.

   d. Print a list that gives for each employee the employee number, name, address, net monthly pay, federal tax, and monthly state tax. (Use MDSKF as an I-O file.)

2. Write a COBOL program to create a permanent random file for the customers of a bank. Include the information you feel should be included in a bank file.

3. Write a program to update the bank file of project 2 on a monthly basis. Make sure the program prints a record of each customer's account.

4. Suppose that a life insurance company has life insurance to sell to customers and that the amount of the premium (per thousand dollars of insurance) is determined only by the customer's age. Insurance is sold to customers from age 1 through age 100. Create a file on disk that permanently stores the age and premium charged to customers between 1 and 100 years old in 100 records.

5. Write a COBOL program that uses the file created for project 4. The program should instruct the computer to read a card file in which each record contains the name, amount of the policy, and age of a customer. The program should print a list of customers' names and the total cost of the premiums for their policies.

6. Random files are preferable when there is no need to access large numbers of records in the file. On the other hand, if access to the file regularly involves a high percentage of records in the file, a sequential file is preferred. Rewrite example 10.14 to create a sequential file on disk.

7. Following the lead of project 6, rewrite project 1 to work with the sequential file discussed in project 6.

8. One method of calculating the yearly depreciation on an investment is the sum-of-years digit method. If COST denotes the original value of an asset, N the estimated number of use-life years, and SCRAP the estimated scrap value of the asset at the end of its use-life, then the depreciation in the Mth year of its use is $(P/Q) * (COST - SCRAP)$ where $Q = N \times (N + 1) / 2$ and $P = N - M$. Write a COBOL program that uses the PERFORM statement to print a table showing the carrying value for each year. The carrying value is the original value of the asset minus the total depreciation in all preceding years. Your program should read the original value of the asset, the SCRAP value, and the expected use life, N, from a card. The printed table should extend from year 1 through year N.

Table Handling

A *table* is a collection of homogeneous data organized so that it can be collectively referenced by a single name and individually referenced by a name and one or more numbers. In mathematics, a table is referred to as a *matrix* or *array*. Each part of the matrix is an *element* of the matrix, and the numbers that identify a particular element of the matrix are *subscripts*.

For example, if we let X be the matrix

$$\begin{pmatrix} 5 & 18 \\ 0 & 19 \\ 22 & 26 \end{pmatrix}$$

then X has 6 elements. Note that the matrix X has 3 rows and 2 columns. Since each row has 2 elements, X must have 2×3, or 6 elements. To identify a particular element of X, we use subscripts to designate the row and column containing the element. Thus $X_{1,1}$ refers to the number 5 in the first row and first column, and we can state correctly that $X_{1,1} = 5$. Similarly, $X_{2,1} = 0$, $X_{3,1} = 22$, $X_{2,2} = 19$, and $X_{1,2} = 18$. Since we need two numbers or subscripts to identify a particular element of X, X is said to be a two-dimensional array.

In COBOL, matrix arrays are called tables. We cannot write subscripts on a punched card as we write them by hand, so a slightly different notation is used. Instead of $X_{2,1}$ we write X (2, 1). Similarly, X (3, 2) = 26 and X (1, 1) + X (3, 1) = 27.

A table in COBOL can have one, two, or three dimensions. Henceforth, we shall use the name array only for a table having one column and one or more rows. Thus an array will be a one-dimensional table. For example, suppose we have a class of eight students, and we wish to represent their scores on a test as an array.

Student Number	Grade
1	60
2	70
3	80
4	50
5	65
6	75
7	82
8	90

If we call our array GRADE, then

$$\text{GRADE} = \begin{pmatrix} 60 \\ 70 \\ 80 \\ 50 \\ 65 \\ 75 \\ 82 \\ 90 \end{pmatrix} \begin{matrix} \longleftrightarrow \text{GRADE} \ (1) \\ \longleftrightarrow \text{GRADE} \ (2) \\ \longleftrightarrow \text{GRADE} \ (3) \\ \longleftrightarrow \text{GRADE} \ (4) \\ \longleftrightarrow \text{GRADE} \ (5) \\ \longleftrightarrow \text{GRADE} \ (6) \\ \longleftrightarrow \text{GRADE} \ (7) \\ \longleftrightarrow \text{GRADE} \ (8) \end{matrix}$$

Note that an array permits you to refer conveniently to the data. For example, GRADE (4) is 50, which is the grade of the fourth student.

Creating Tables

The COBOL compiler is informed of a table in a COBOL program by an OCCURS clause in the DATA DIVISION. The format of the OCCURS clause is

```
data-name OCCURS integer TIMES [[INDEXED BY
index-name-1 [index-name-2] ...]
```

The level number of data-name, which is the subject of the OCCURS clause, cannot be 77 or 1. Except for condition names, the VALUE clause cannot be applied to the subject of an OCCURS clause nor to a data item that is a part of an item that is the subject of an OCCURS clause. The total amount of main storage for a table cannot exceed 4,095 words on the IBM-1130.

In the following examples we will present different kinds of tables and discuss table storage requirements on the IBM-1130.

Example 11.1   Write a DATA DIVISION entry describing a one-dimensional table having five elements. Each element is subdivided into the following fields:

field-1	faculty-number	five digits
field-2	faculty-name	twenty characters
field-3	faculty-address	thirty characters
field-4	faculty-salary	seven digits with two decimal places

The DATA DIVISION entry could be

```
01 DEPARTMENT.
    02 FACULTY OCCURS 5 TIMES.
        03 F-NUM  PIC  9(5).
        03 F-NAME PIC  X(20).
        03 F-ADD  PIC  X(30).
        03 F-SAL  PIC  9(5)V99.
```

The table is DEPARTMENT. The table is subdivided into five elements called FACULTY (1), FACULTY (2), . . . , FACULTY (5). Each element is subdivided into four DISPLAY items, and each element occupies 62 characters (words on the IBM-1130) of storage. Thus the table occupies 310 words of storage on the IBM-1130.

To name the items in each element of the table, consider that FACULTY (3) is subdivided into F-NUM (3), F-NAME (3), F-ADD (3), and F-SAL (3). You could also refer to F-SAL OF FACULTY (3) or F-SAL OF DE-PARTMENT (3) (the subscript applies to F-SAL).

One of the most powerful features of COBOL is the simplicity with which complex data structures can be created and manipulated. The structure described in example 11.1 is a good example of this feature. Its organization permits easy manipulation of different data levels. For example, the sentence MOVE SPACES TO DEPARTMENT. causes 310 words of storage to be filled with spaces. The statement MOVE SPACES TO FACULTY (4). fills 62 words of storage with spaces. The statement MOVE ZEROS TO F-NUM (2). fills 5 words of storage with zeros.

Subscripts

Let us assume that data-name is a subscripted variable. How would you name a particular element of data-name? The format is

$$\text{data-name}\ \left(\left\{\begin{array}{l}\text{integer-1}\\\text{name-1}\end{array}\right\}\ \left[,\ \left\{\begin{array}{l}\text{integer-2}\\\text{name-2}\end{array}\right\}\ \left[,\ \left\{\begin{array}{l}\text{integer-3}\\\text{name-3}\end{array}\right\}\right]\right]\right).$$

Each of integer-1, integer-2, and integer-3 must be positive. Each of name-1, name-2, and name-3 can be the special item TALLY or an elementary numeric data item whose PICTURE clause describes an integer. The smallest permissible value for name-1, name-2, and name-3 is 1. If the optional portions of the format are used because data-name is two-dimensional or three-dimensional, then the commas must be included and a space must follow each comma. No spaces should follow the left parenthesis or precede the right parenthesis.

Example 11.2   Examples of valid subscripting are

```
SALARY (MONTH, YEAR)
EMPLOYEE (FACTORY, DEPT, SHIFT)
GRADE (20)
INVENTORY (MONTH)
BOOK (MONTH, YEAR)
PAY (WEEK, MONTH, YEAR)
HOUSE (1, BLOK, 18)
```

if we assume appropriate restrictions on the types and values of the data items.

Examples of invalid subscripting are

```
SALARY(MONTH, YEAR)      (since no space follows SALARY)
SALARY (MONTH,YEAR)      (since no space follows the comma)
SALARY ( MONTH, YEAR)        (since a space follows the left
    parenthesis)
SALARY (MONTH, YEAR )        (since a space precedes the right
    parenthesis)
STUDENT (STATE, CITY, COUNTY, SCHOOL)      (since four-
    dimensional tables are not allowed)
SALARY (1 , YEAR)      (since a space precedes the comma)
SALARY (1 YEAR)      (since a comma is missing)
SALARY (0, 19)      (since 0 is not a positive integer.)
```

Example 11.3   To define a two-dimensional table in the DATA DIVISION, consider

```
01 A.
    02 B OCCURS 5 TIMES.
        03 C OCCURS 3 TIMES   PIC XX.
```

The independent data item A occupies 30 words of storage. A is divided into five parts: B (1), B (2), B (3), B (4), and B (5). Each element of B is further subdivided into three parts. B (1) is subdivided into C (1, 1), C (1, 2), and C (1, 3); and B (4) is subdivided into C (4, 1), C (4, 2), and C (4, 3). Each of the 15 elementary subdivisions of A occupies 2 words of storage.

Example 11.4   Consider

```
01 A USAGE IS COMPUTATIONAL.
    02 B OCCURS 2 TIMES.
        03 C OCCURS 3 TIMES.
            04 D OCCURS 7 TIMES   PIC S9(4).
```

This table is similar to the table in example 11.3 except that it is three-dimensional. Also the USAGE clause is used to cause every item of the table to have computational usage. On the IBM-1130 each of the 42 elementary computational items of the table occupies one word of storage, so that the entire table occupies 42 words of storage. Examples of correctly named parts of the table are A, B (1), B (2), C (1, 2), C (2, 3), D (1, 2, 5), D (2, 1, 1), and D (2, 2, 7). Examples of incorrect data names are A (1) (since A is not subscriptable), B (since B is subscripted), B (1, 1) (since B is a one-dimensional table), C (1, 4) (since C (1) has only three elements), D (1, 0, 6) (since 0 is not a valid subscript), D (1, 1) (since D is a three-dimensional table), and D (6, 1, 2) (since the first subscript cannot exceed 2).

Example 11.5   Consider

```
01 A.
    02 B OCCURS 10 TIMES.
        03 C PIC   X(7).
        03 D PIC   S99V99 COMP.
        03 E OCCURS 3 TIMES   PIC 99.
```

A is subdivided into B (1), B (2), . . . , B (10). Each of the B's is subdivided into five elementary items. For example, B (8) is subdivided into C (8), D (8), E (8, 1), E (8, 2), and E (8, 3). Thus on the IBM-1130 each of the B's occupies 14 words of storage, and A occupies 140 words of storage. Example 11.5 and the preceding examples illustrate clearly that when an OCCURS clause is used, you must subscript the item to which it applies *and all items subordinate to that item.*

Example 11.6   The primary advantage of tables is the ease with which you can create names for data items. Let us assume that we desire to read 3,000 numbers from punched cards. Each card contains 20 four-digit numbers. The program to accomplish this is outlined in figure 11.1.

Note that in the outline in figure 11.1, we are careful to move each number read to an element of B. If several numbers had been moved at once, we would have had a group move, and the conversion from DISPLAY to COMP format would not have been made. Note also that B must have computational usage; otherwise, the table would need 12,000 words of storage, which is far in excess of 4,095 words.

Figure 11.1 Outline of program for example 11.6.

```
IDENTIFICATION DIVISION.
    ⋮
ENVIRONMENT DIVISION.
    ⋮
DATA DIVISION.
FILE SECTION.
FD   CARD-IN LABEL RECORDS ARE OMITTED.
01   CARD.
     02 NUMB OCCURS 20 TIMES    PIC S9(4).
WORKING-STORAGE SECTION.
77   I   PIC 9(4)  COMP.
77   J   PIC 9(4)  COMP.
01   A.
     02 B OCCURS 3000 TIMES    PIC S9(4)   COMP.
PROCEDURE DIVISION.
1.
     OPEN INPUT CARD-IN. MOVE 0 TO I.
2.
     READ CARD-IN AT END GO TO 3.
     PERFORM 4 VARYING J FROM 1 BY 1 UNTIL J GREATER 20.
     IF I IS EQUAL TO 3000 GO TO 3 ELSE GO TO 2.
3.
     CLOSE CARD-IN. STOP RUN.
4.
     ADD 1 TO I. MOVE NUMB (J) TO B (I).
/*
```

Initializing Tabular Values

Many methods are available for specifying the initial values of a table. Example 11.6 demonstrates how card input can be used for this purpose. If all the table elements are to have the same value and the table has DISPLAY usage, then the MOVE statement can be used. If in example 11.3 we had written MOVE SPACES TO A, then the entire table would contain spaces. Writing MOVE ALL 'AB' TO A. would cause each element of A to contain AB. Writing MOVE 'ABCDEFGHIJKLMNOPQRSTUVWXYZ1234' TO A. would cause each element of A to have a different value. For example, the value of C (5, 2) would be 12.

Let us use the PERFORM statement to initialize the value of a computational table. The following statements show how this might be done.

```
77 H  PIC S99V99 COMP.
77 I  PIC S9(4) COMP.
77 J  PIC S9(4) COMP.
01 A    COMP.
   02   B OCCURS 30.
        03 EUPHRATES OCCURS 80 PIC S99V99.
PROCEDURE DIVISION.
1.  MOVE 99.99 TO H.
    PERFORM 2 VARYING I FROM 1 BY 1
        UNTIL I GREATER 30 AFTER J
        FROM 1 BY 1 UNTIL J GREATER 80.
2.
    MOVE H TO EUPHRATES (I, J).
```

If the table is not too large, the REDEFINES statement can be used to overcome the problem of not being able to use a VALUE clause on a table.

```
01 ALL-VALUE.
   02   FILLER  PIC S9(3)V99 VALUE 58.36.
   02   FILLER  PIC S9(3)V99 VALUE 125.78.
   02   FILLER  PIC S9(3)V99 VALUE -95.29.
01 TABLE-1 REDEFINES ALL-VALUE.
   02   ENTRI OCCURS 3 TIMES  PIC S9(3)V99.
```

This item in the DATA DIVISION causes ENTRI (1), ENTRI (2), and ENTRI (3) to have the values 58.36, 125.78, and −95.29, respectively.

All the material you need to work with tables is contained in the preceding pages of this chapter. However, the material which follows is important if you wish to work more efficiently with tables; and we therefore encourage you to read it.

Storing Tables Internally

Consider the following table

```
01 A.
   02 B OCCURS 3 TIMES PIC XX.
```

A is stored in memory as shown in figure 11.2. As you can see, on the IBM-1130 each element of A occupies two consecutive words of storage. Above each word of storage is written a number indicating the relative displacement of each word from the beginning of the table, which is the first word of B (1). To find the absolute address of each element of A, say element B (I), use the following formula:

$$\text{Absolute-address-of-B (I)} = \text{Absolute-address-of-A} + (I - 1) * \text{Length-of-elements}$$

For example, if the address of A is 4000, and we wish the address of B (2), then it is 4000 + (2 − 1) ∗ 2, or 4002. The address of B (1) would be 4000 + (1 − 1) ∗ 2, or 4000. Similarly, the address of B (3) is 4004 and B (3) occupies words 4004 and 4005 of main storage.

As another example consider the following two-dimensional table.

```
01 SUPPLIES.
   02  D OCCURS 3 TIMES.
      03 I OCCURS 2 TIMES  PIC 99.
```

Figure 11.3 shows how the preceding table can be stored in main storage.

The two-dimensional table is stored in memory as a one-dimensional array. It is stored by rows. Figure 11.3 shows the relative displacement (also known as the relative address) of each word used to store the table. Since D is a one-dimensional table, it is easy to determine the absolute address of each element of D. For example, on the IBM-1130, since each element of D occupies four words of storage, we see that the absolute address of D (3) is

$$\text{Absolute-address-of-SUPPLIES} + (3 - 1) * 4.$$

However, how would you determine the absolute address of one of the I's, say I (3, 2)? The formula for determining the absolute address of I (m, n) is

$$\text{Absolute-address-of-SUPPLIES} + (m - 1) * \text{size-of-D} + (n - 1) * \text{size-of-I}$$

where size-of-D is 4, and size-of-I is 2. Thus, the absolute address of I (3, 2) is absolute-address-of-supplies + (3 − 1) ∗ 4 + (2 − 1) ∗ 2. Similarly, the absolute address of I (1, 2) is absolute-address-of-supplies + (1 − 1) ∗ 4 + (2 − 1) ∗ 2.

Figure 11.2 Example of storage of a table and the relative displacements of its elements.

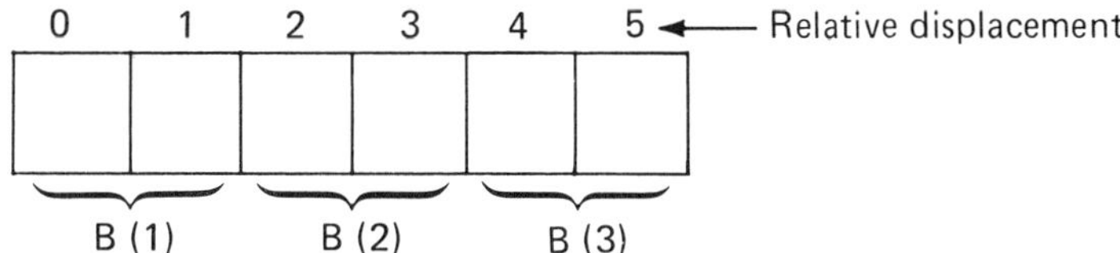

Figure 11.3 Example of the storage and relative displacements for a two-dimensional table.

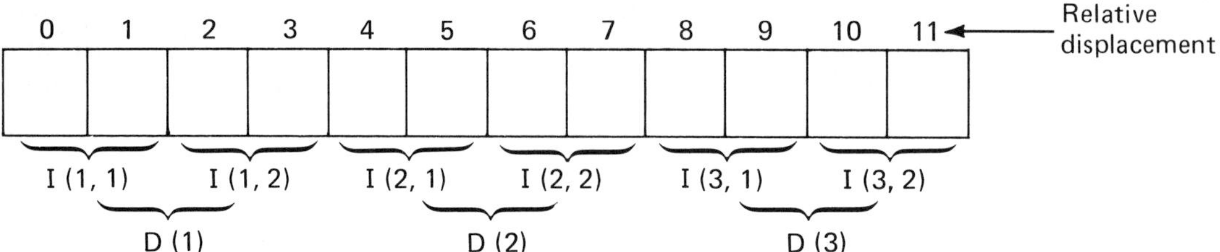

Indexing Tables

In our discussion on storing tables internally, we wanted to show how tables are stored in the computer memory and to show how you would locate the absolute addresses of table elements. Locating the absolute addresses of table elements is especially important because it shows the necessity of finding the relative address of table elements. Every time a subscript is used in a COBOL program, the computer must perform several arithmetic operations to determine the relative address of the named table element. The use of special data items called *indices* is designed to reduce this computation of relative addresses as much as possible. An *index* is always used to store the relative address of table elements.

The COBOL compiler on the DECSYSTEM-10 does not recognize any difference between an index name and a subscript. The subscripting and indexing are identical in use and can be used interchangeably. The following discussion that differentiates between subscripting and indexing is not applicable to DECSYSTEM-10 COBOL. However, note that on the DEC-SYSTEM-10 the clause INDEXED BY with the OCCURS clause can still be used, though there is no difference between indexing and subscripting.

Recall that a *subscript* is the special register TALLY, a numeric literal that is a positive integer, or a data item that is a numeric elementary item representing a positive integer. *Subscripting* is the referencing of table elements by use of subscripts as in TABLE (1, I). Subscripted data items cannot be used as subscripts.

An *index* is a special data item used for storing the relative addresses of table elements. An index is never defined explicitly by a PICTURE clause in the DATA DIVISION; instead, each level of a table is assigned one or more indices as a part of the table definition. This assignment automatically causes each index name to represent a one-word computational item on an IBM-1130. Each level of a table can have as many as 12 indices on the IBM-1130 and the IBM-S3.

Indexing is the referencing of table elements by use of indices as in ITEM (I, J, K) where I, J, and K are indices. In referencing table elements subscripting requires the use of subscripts and indexing requires the use of indices. Mixing the two processes as in TABLE (I, J), where I is a subscript and J is an index, is not permitted in COBOL.

An *index data item* is always defined in the DATA DIVISION by an entry of the form

```
level-number index-data-name [USAGE IS] INDEX.
```

The PICTURE, SYNCHRONIZED, JUSTIFIED, BLANK, and VALUE clauses cannot be applied to an index data item. Index data items are used for storing values of indices, i.e., relative displacements. It is important to distinguish between an index and an index data item since they are not used for the same purposes.

Example 11.7   A county decides to arrange its police force as follows.

a. The county is divided into two districts.
b. Each district is divided into three regions.
c. Two law enforcement officers are assigned to each region.

For each officer the following information is kept.

```
Information   Picture
RANK          X(10)
NAME          X(18)
CAR-PHONE     X(7)
AGE           9(2)
SALARY        9(4)V99
ADDRESS       X(30)
HOME-PHONE    X(7)
```

The following table description in the DATA DIVISION is used.

```
01 COUNTY-FORCE.
   02 DISTRICT OCCURS 2, INDEXED BY DST.
    03 REGION OCCURS 3, INDEXED BY RGN.
     04 OFFICER OCCURS 2, INDEXED BY J.
      08 RANK  PIC X(10).
      08 NAME  PIC X(18).
      08 CAR-PHONE  PIC X(7).
      08 AGE  PIC 9(2)
      08 SALARY  PIC 9(4)V99.
      08 ADDRESS  PIC X(30).
      08 HOME-PHONE  PIC X(7).
```

(Examine the format of the OCCURS clause and note the INDEXED BY option.)

Figure 11.4 is a three-dimensional table with 12 elements. On the IBM-1130 each element occupies 80 words of storage in that all elementary items in the table have DISPLAY usage. Thus each of REGION (1, 1), REGION (1, 2), . . . , REGION (2, 2), and REGION (2, 3) occupies 160 words of storage and DISTRICT (1) and DISTRICT (2) each occupy 480 words of storage.

Let us do some examples of calculating relative displacements. Henceforth in our discussions we will use *occurrence number* synonymously with subscript value.

The relative displacement of an element at the first level of the table is relative-address = size-level-1-element $* (O1 - 1)$, where $O1$ is the subscript or occurrence number of the element. Thus the relative address of DISTRICT (2) is $480 * (2 - 1)$ or 480.

Figure 11.4 Example of the storage and relative displacement of a three-dimensional table.

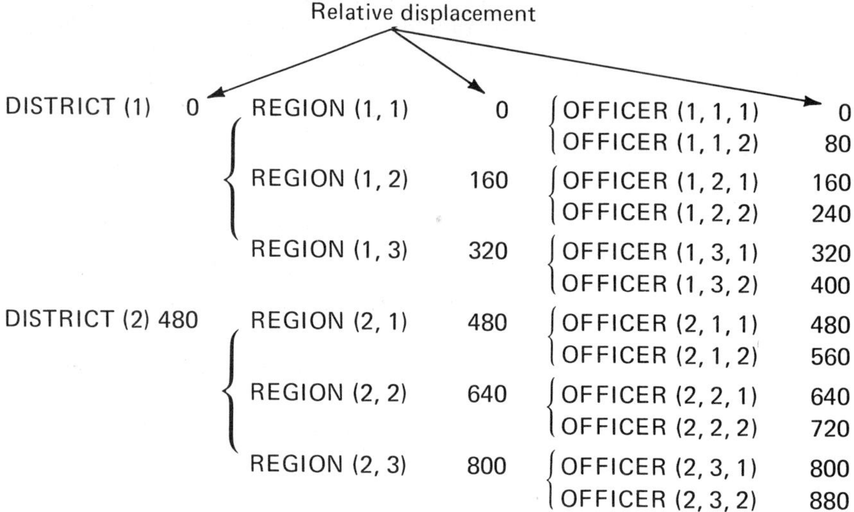

The relative displacement of an element on the second level of the table is relative-address = size-level-1-element $*$ (O1 − 1) + size-level-2-element $*$ (O2 − 1), where O1 and O2 are the first- and second-level occurrence numbers. Thus the relative address of REGION (2, 3) is 480 $*$ (2 − 1) + 160 $*$ (3 − 1), or 800.

The formula for the relative displacement of 1 a third-level element is relative-address = size-level-1-element $*$ (O1 − 1) + size-level-2-element $*$ (O2 − 1) + size-level-3-element $*$ (O3 − 1). Thus the relative address of OFFICER (1, 2, 2) is 480 $*$ (1 − 1) + 160 $*$ (2 − 1) + 80 $*$ (2 − 1) or 240.

The SET Statement

Since indices and index data items are used to store the relative addresses of table elements, we need a method of storing desired values in these items. Recall that indices and index data items cannot appear in a MOVE statement. Therefore, another statement, the SET statement, is used for this purpose.

One format of the SET statement is

```
SET index-name-1 [index-name-2...]
    TO  {integer-1}
        {data-name}
```

where data-name is an elementary numeric item whose value is a positive integer, and integer-1 is a positive integer. This statement takes the subscript value (or occurrence number) specified by integer-1 or data-name and stores the corresponding displacement in each index-name.

In example 11.7, the indices named were DST, RGN, and J. After execution of the statement SET DST RGN J TO 2., DST, RGN, and J are 480, 160, and 80, respectively. Observe that the relative address of OFFICER (2, 2, 2) is 480 + 160 + 80 or 720. After execution of SET RGN TO 3., RGN is 320. The relative address of REGION (DST, RGN, J)—that is, of REGION (2, 3, 2)—is 480 + 320 + 80 or 880.

To reverse this process, we can use the following format of the SET statement:

```
SET data-name-1 [data-name-2...] TO index-name
```

where the data names are of elementary numeric items. If RGN is 320 and K is an elementary numeric item, then execution of SET K TO RGN causes K to be 3. If J is 0, then execution of SET K TO J causes K to be 1.

Another format of the SET statement is

```
SET index-name-1 [index-name-2...]
    TO { index-name-2   }
       { index-data-name }
```

If index-data-name is used in this statement, then its content is moved without change to index-name-1. However, if index-name-2 is used, a very different process results. The value of index-name-2 corresponds to a certain subscript or occurrence number value, which is used to determine the relative address stored in index-name-1. For instance, suppose the value of J is 80. This corresponds to occurrence number 2. After execution of SET DST TO J., DST is 480, since this relative address corresponds to occurrence number 2 in the case of DST.

Another format of the SET statement is

```
SET index-data-item-1 [index-data-item-2 ...]
    TO { index-name      }
       { index-data-name }
```

This statement moves the content of the TO operand to the content of each SET operand.

The final format of the SET statement is

```
SET index-name-1 [index-name-2...]
    { UP BY   } { data-name }
    { DOWN BY } { integer   }
```

where integer is a positive integer, and data-name is an elementary numeric item representing a positive integer. Data-name and integer specify the amount of change to be made in the occurrence number of each index. For instance, suppose the occurrence number of RGN is 1. This implies that the value of RGN is 0. After execution of SET RGN UP BY 2., the occurrence number of RGN is 3 and the value of RGN is $(3 - 1) * 160$, or 320.

The format of the SET statement is actually somewhat more general than we have shown. For further information consult the COBOL language manual for your computer.

Indices and Index Data Items in Relational Conditions

Comparison of values involving indices can be tricky. Do you compare the actual value of the index or its occurrence number? The table in figure 11.5 summarizes the methods of comparison involving indices and/or index data items.

Two Indexing Methods

One method of indexing is *direct indexing*. This is the method we have used in all our examples of indexing. The format for direct indexing of a table element is

```
data-name (index-name-1
            [, index-name-2] [, index-name-3]).
```

A second method of indexing is *indirect indexing*. The format of this indexing is

```
data-name (index-1 [{±} integer-1]
            [, index-2 [{±} integer-2]]
            [, index-3 [{±} integer-3]])
```

where each integer is positive. This type of indexing causes each index to be adjusted by an amount corresponding to the occurrence number specified by the integer. If in example 11.7, RGN has the value 160 corresponding to occurrence number 2, then RGN + 1 would specify a displacement of 320 corresponding to occurrence number 3.

Figure 11.5 Summary of methods of comparison involving indices and/or index data items.

First operand	Second operand		
	Index	*Index data item*	*Numeric data item / Integer literal*
Index	Compare occurrence numbers	Compare actual value	Compare occurrence number with value
Index data item	Compare actual value	Compare actual value	Not permitted
Numeric data item / Integer literal	Compare occurrence number with value	Not permitted	See Chapter 9

Example 11.8   Suppose that in example 11.7, we added the statement

```
77 IND-DAT USAGE IS INDEX.
```

to the WORKING-STORAGE SECTION. Also assume that the following statements have been executed:

```
SET J TO 2.
SET IND-DAT TO J.
SET J DOWN BY 1.
SET DST, RGN TO IND-DAT.
MOVE 35 TO AGE (DIST, RGN, J).
```

The values of IND-DAT, DST, RGN, and J are 80, 80, 80, and 0, respectively. Thus the relative address of AGE (DST, RGN, J) is 80 + 80 + 0, or 160. This is the relative address of AGE (1, 2, 1) and not of AGE (2, 2, 1). Thus AGE (1, 2, 1) is now 35.

The PERFORM Statement in Index Manipulation

The SET statement and PERFORM statement with the VARYING option are the only statements that can be used for specifying values of indices and index data items. Recall that the simplest form of the PERFORM statement with the VARYING option is

$$\text{PERFORM procedure-name-1 VARYING} \begin{Bmatrix} \text{index-name-1} \\ \text{data-name-1} \end{Bmatrix}$$

$$\text{FROM} \begin{Bmatrix} \text{index-name-2} \\ \text{integer-2} \\ \text{data-name-2} \end{Bmatrix} \quad \text{BY} \begin{Bmatrix} \text{integer-3} \\ \text{data-name-3} \end{Bmatrix}$$

$$\text{UNTIL condition-1.}$$

Each data name should be for an elementary numeric data item. This excludes index data items.

When the PERFORM statement is begun, the initial value of the VARYING operand is established as though you had written

$$\text{SET} \begin{Bmatrix} \text{index-name-1} \\ \text{data-name-1} \end{Bmatrix} \text{TO} \begin{Bmatrix} \text{index-name-2} \\ \text{integer-2} \\ \text{data-name-2} \end{Bmatrix}.$$

Each time the VARYING operand is incremented, it is done as though you had written

$$\text{SET} \begin{Bmatrix} \text{index-name-1} \\ \text{data-name-1} \end{Bmatrix} \begin{Bmatrix} \text{UP} \\ \text{DOWN} \end{Bmatrix} \text{BY} \begin{Bmatrix} \text{integer-3} \\ \text{data-name-3} \end{Bmatrix}.$$

These remarks should enable you to determine the effect of a PERFORM statement using indices in the VARYING option.

Example 11.9   A county is divided into eight districts. Patrol cars are assigned to each district. The number of cars assigned to each district is no more than nine. Each car is assigned one or two police officers.

A card file is maintained on all officers. The number of officers does not exceed 144. Each officer has a card in the file containing the following:

Card column	Field	Picture
1	District number	9
2	car number	9
3–17	name	X(15)
18–20	rank	X(3)
21–27	car phone	X(7)
28–34	home phone	X(7)
35–54	street address	X(20)
55–67	city	X(13)
68–72	zip code	9(5)
73–74	age	99
75–80	salary	9(4)V99

Example 11.9 shows how tables are used in a tag-sort of a disk file. Sorting is one of the most common uses of tables in COBOL. The system flowchart in figure 11.6 summarizes the major steps for the program, and figure 11.7 shows the complete flowchart for the program. The program in figure 11.8 will read the card file and store it in a disk file. The program calculates the number of officers in each district in addition to the total number of officers. This information is stored in the first record of the disk file. Such a record is known as a *header record*. The program sorts the disk file in alphabetic order by officer name and prints the sorted list of names giving also the appropriate district, car number, and address. Figure 11.9 shows the modifications needed to run the program on the DECSYSTEM-10, the B1700, and the IBM-S3, and figure 11.10 shows a sample of the output from the STATFILE-CREATION program.

Figure 11.6 System flowchart for STATFILE-CREATION of example 11.9.

(Note that all the program steps are within a single program in figure 11.8; however, they can be a separate program if that is desired.)

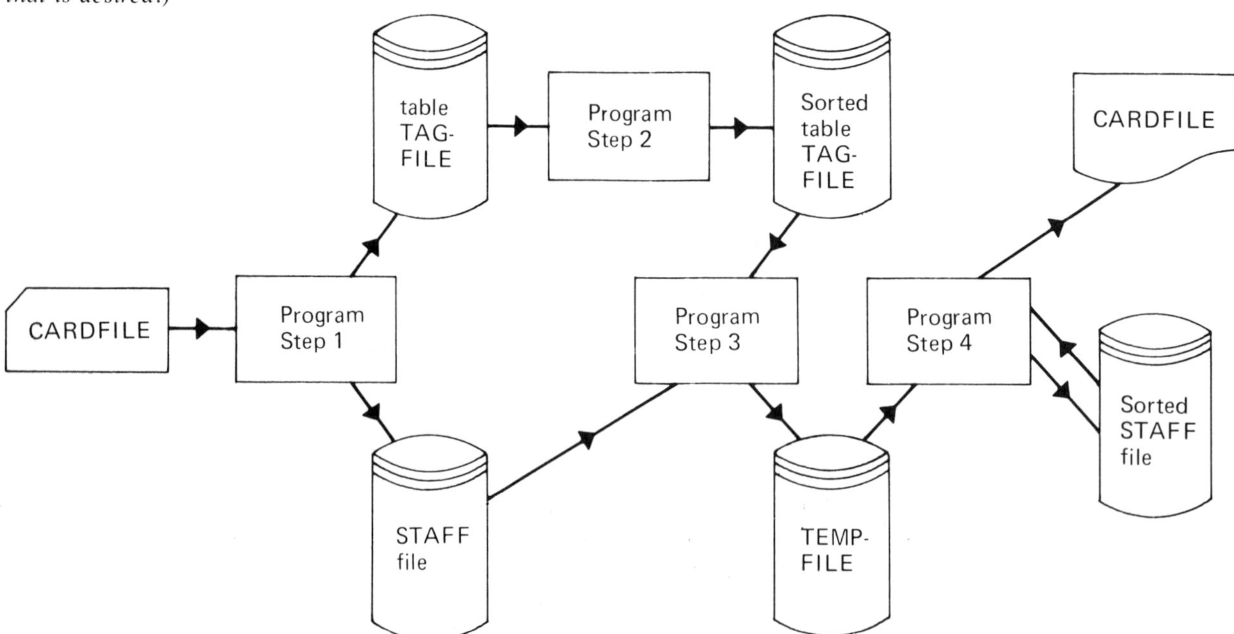

Figure 11.7 Flowchart for STATFILE-CREATION for example 11.9.

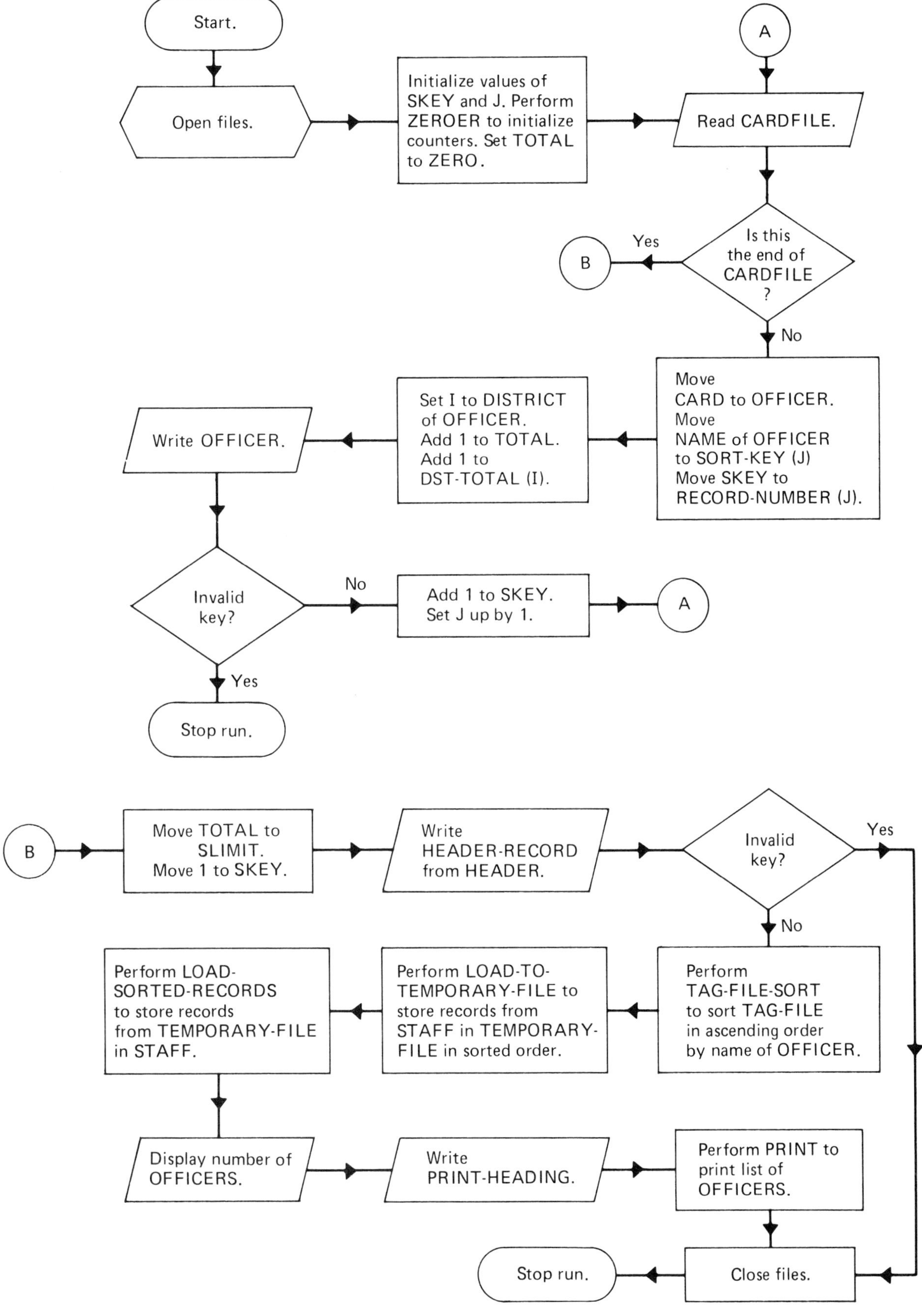

Figure 11.7 (Cont'd.)

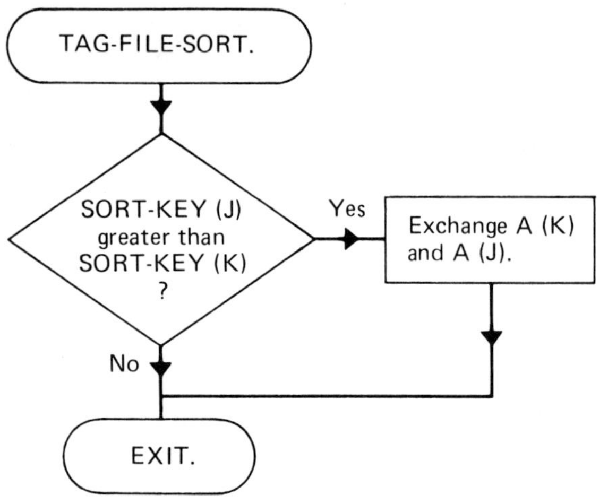

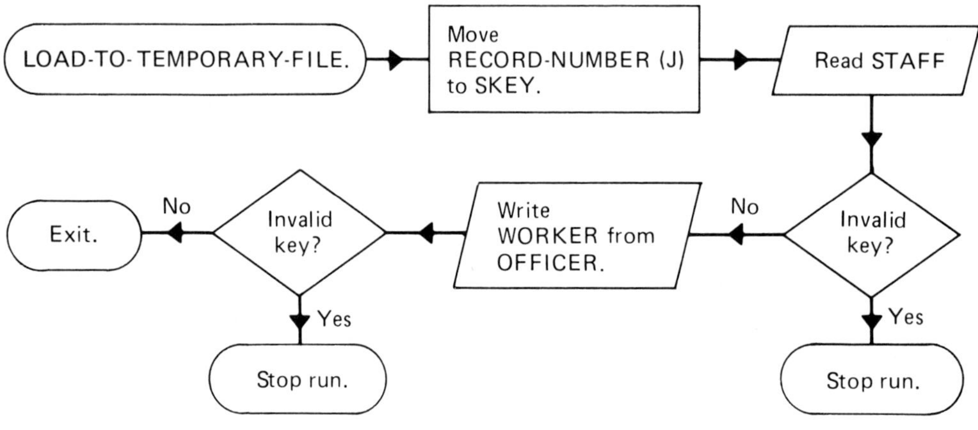

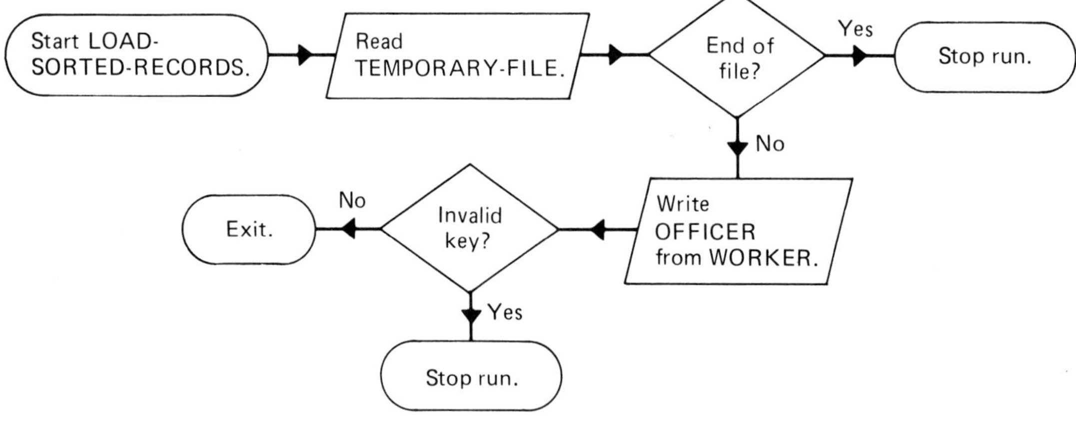

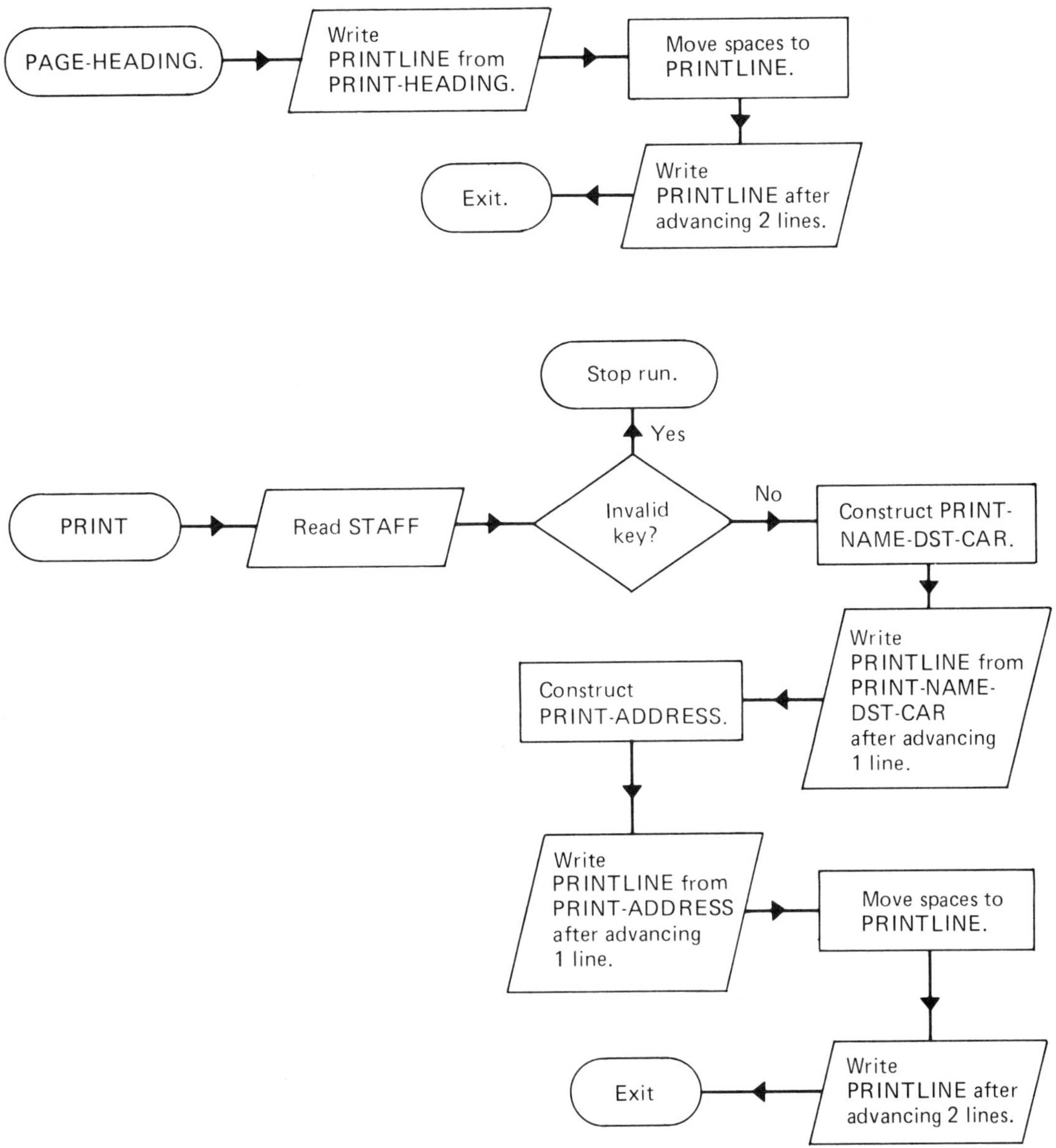

Figure 11.8 Listing of STATFILE-CREATION program of example 11.9.

```
// COBOL
*LIST
      IDENTIFICATION DIVISION.
      PROGRAM-ID. STATFILE-CREATION.
      AUTHOR. KHAILANY-DUPLISSEY.
      REMARKS.
          THIS PROGRAM SORTS AND STORES A DATA FILE ON COUNTY OFFICERS.
          THE SORTING TECHNIQUE USED IS VERY CRUDE, BUT ADEQUATE.
          THIS TYPE OF SORT IS A LINEAR SORT WITH EXCHANGE.
              PLEASE NOTE THAT EACH RECORD IS PROVIDED WITH AN UNUSED
          AREA FOR ADDITIONAL INFORMATION.
      ENVIRONMENT DIVISION.
      CONFIGURATION SECTION.
```

Figure 11.8 (Cont'd.)

```
      SOURCE-COMPUTER. IBM-1130.
      OBJECT-COMPUTER. IBM-1130.
      SPECIAL-NAMES.
          C01 IS TO-TOP, CSP IS NO-LINES.
      INPUT-OUTPUT SECTION.
      FILE-CONTROL.
          SELECT CARDFILE ASSIGN TO RD-2501,
              RESERVE 1 ALTERNATE AREA.
          SELECT STAFF ASSIGN TO DF-1-145
          ACCESS IS RANDOM
              ACTUAL KEY IS SKEY
                      FILE-LIMIT IS 2 THRU 145.
          SELECT TEMPORARY-FILE ASSIGN TO DF-2-144.
          SELECT PRINTFILE ASSIGN PR-1403.
      DATA DIVISION.
      FILE SECTION.
      FD  CARDFILE LABEL RECORDS ARE OMITTED.
      01  CARD.
          02  DISTRICT        PIC 9.
          02  CAR             PIC 9.
          02  NAME            PIC X(15).
          02  RANK            PIC X(3).
          02  CARPHONE        PIC X(7).
          02  HOMEPHONE       PIC X(7).
          02  ADDRESS.
              03  STREET-ADDRESS      PIC X(20).
              03  CITY                PIC X(13).
              03  ZIP-CODE            PIC 9(5).
          02  AGE             PIC 99.
          02  SALARY          PIC 9(4)V99.
      FD  STAFF LABEL RECORDS ARE STANDARD
          RECORD CONTAINS 106 CHARACTERS.
      01  HEADER-RECORD       PIC X(106).
      01  OFFICER.
          02  DISTRICT        PIC 9.
          02  CAR             PIC 9.
          02  NAME            PIC X(15).
          02  RANK            PIC X(3).
          02  CARPHONE        PIC X(7).
          02  HOMEPHONE       PIC X(7).
          02  ADDRESS.
              03  STREET-ADDRESS      PIC X(20).
              03  CITY                PIC X(13).
              03  ZIP-CODE            PIC 9(5).
          02  AGE             PIC 99.
          02  SALARY          PIC 9(4)V99.
          02  EXPAND-AREA     PIC X(26).
      FD  TEMPORARY-FILE LABEL RECORDS ARE STANDARD
          RECORD CONTAINS 106 CHARACTERS.
      01  WORKER PIC X(106).
      FD  PRINTFILE LABEL RECORDS ARE OMITTED.
      01  PRINTLINE           PIC X(120).
      WORKING-STORAGE SECTION.
      77  SKEY                PIC S9(5) COMP.
      77  SLIMIT              PIC S9(5) COMP.
      77  L PIC 99 COMP.
      77  EXCH                PIC X(17).
      77  D                   PIC ZZ9.
      77  PRINT-HEADING       PIC X(44) VALUE IS
          'OFFICER            DISTRICT CAR          ADDRESS'.
      01  HEADER.
          02  DISTRICT-TOTAL OCCURS 8 INDEXED BY I PIC S9(4) COMP.
          02  TOTAL PIC S9(4) COMP.
      01  TAG-FILE.
          02  A OCCURS 144 TIMES INDEXED BY J, K.
              03  SORT-KEY            PIC X(15).
              03  RECORD-NUMBER       PIC S9(5) COMP.
```

```
****************************************************************
*****NOTICE THE USE OF THE REDEFINES CLAUSE WHICH ALLOWS US TO   *
*****USE THE SAME STORAGE AREA FOR TWO TYPES OF DATA ITEMS. THESE*
*****TWO ITEMS, PRINT-NAME-DST-CAR AND PRINT-ADDRESS WILL BE USED*
*****TO PRINT A SUMMARY OF OUR FILE.....                         *
****************************************************************
 01   PRINT-ADDRESS.
      02   FILLER          PIC X(36).
      02   SADD            PIC X(20).
      02   CITY-ZIP REDEFINES SADD.
           03   C                    PIC X(14).
           03   Z                    PIC X(6).
 01   PRINT-NAME-DST-CAR REDEFINES PRINT-ADDRESS.
      02   NAME-P          PIC X(15).
      02   FILLER          PIC X(7).
      02   DISTRICT-P      PIC 9.
      02   FILLER          PIC X(6).
      02   CAR-P           PIC 9.
      02   FILLER          PIC X(26).
  PROCEDURE DIVISION.
  BEGIN-AND-INITIALIZE.
      OPEN INPUT CARDFILE, OUTPUT STAFF, TEMPORARY-FILE,
          PRINTFILE.
      MOVE 2 TO SKEY.
      SET J TO 1.
****************************************************************
*****THE NEXT PERFORM SETS ALL COUNTERS TO ZERO.....             *
****************************************************************
      PERFORM ZEROER VARYING I FROM 1 BY 1
          UNTIL I IS GREATER THAN 8.
      MOVE ZERO TO TOTAL.
  READ-LOOP.
      READ CARDFILE AT END GO TO PROCESS-OFFICERS.
****************************************************************
*****WE NEXT STORE THE OFFICER'S RECORD AND MAKE AN ENTRY FOR    *
*****THIS OFFICER IN THE TAG SORT ARRAY.....                     *
****************************************************************
      MOVE CARD TO OFFICER.
      MOVE NAME OF OFFICER TO SORT-KEY (J).
      MOVE SKEY TO RECORD-NUMBER (J).
      ADD 1 TO TOTAL.
      SET I TO DISTRICT OF OFFICER.
      ADD 1 TO DISTRICT-TOTAL (I).
      WRITE OFFICER INVALID KEY STOP RUN.
****************************************************************
*****WE HAVE STORED ALL INFORMATION FOR THIS OFFICER. NOW WE     *
*****PREPARE FOR THE NEXT OFFICER.....                           *
****************************************************************
      ADD 1 TO SKEY.
      SET J UP BY 1.
      GO TO READ-LOOP.
  PROCESS-OFFICERS.
      MOVE TOTAL TO SLIMIT.
      MOVE 1 TO SKEY.
****************************************************************
*****WE STORE THE DISTRICT TOTALS AND THE OVERALL TOTAL.....     *
****************************************************************
      WRITE HEADER-RECORD FROM HEADER INVALID GO TO LAST-P.
****************************************************************
*****WE SORT THE TAG ARRAY.....                                  *
****************************************************************
      PERFORM OUTER-SORT-LOOP VARYING J FROM 1 BY 1
          UNTIL J IS EQUAL TO SLIMIT.
****************************************************************
*****USING THE INFORMATION IN THE SORTED TAG ARRAY, WE WRITE THE *
*****RECORDS IN SORTED ORDER TO A TEMPORARY DISK FILE.....       *
****************************************************************
      CLOSE STAFF.
      OPEN INPUT STAFF.
      PERFORM LOAD-TO-TEMPORARY-FILE
```

Figure 11.8 (Cont'd.)

```
            VARYING J FROM 1 BY 1 UNTIL J IS GREATER THAN SLIMIT.
        CLOSE STAFF, TEMPORARY-FILE.
    **********************************************************************
    *****WE READ THE SORTED RECORDS IN THE TEMPORARY DISK FILE BACK  *
    *****TC THE PERMANENT STAFF FILE.....                            *
    **********************************************************************
        OPEN INPUT TEMPORARY-FILE, OUTPUT STAFF.
        MOVE SLIMIT TO D.
        ACD 1 TO SLIMIT.
        PERFORM LOAD-SORTED-RECORDS
        VARYING SKEY FROM 2 BY 1 UNTIL SKEY IS GREATER THAN SLIMIT.
    **********************************************************************
    *****WE PRINT INFORMATION GIVING THE NUMBER OF ALL OFFICERS..... *
    **********************************************************************
        DISPLAY 'THE NUMBER OF OFFICERS IN THE CCUNTY IS ', D.
        CLOSE STAFF.
    **********************************************************************
    *****WE PRINT A LISTING OF THE SORTED RECORDS.....              *
    **********************************************************************
        OPEN INPUT STAFF.
        PERFORM PAGEHEADING.
        PERFORM PRINTT
            VARYING SKEY FROM 2 BY 1 UNTIL SKEY IS GREATER THAN
            SLIMIT.
    LAST-P.
    **********************************************************************
    *****THE PROGRAM IS FINISHED.....                              *
    **********************************************************************
        CLOSE CARDFILE, STAFF, TEMPORARY-FILE, PRINTFILE.
        STOP RUN.
    OUTER-SORT-LOOP.
        SET L TO J.
        ACD 1 TO L.
        PERFORM TAG-FILE-SORT VARYING K FROM L BY 1
            UNTIL K IS GREATER THAN SLIMIT.
    TAG-FILE-SORT.
        IF SORT-KEY (J) IS GREATER THAN SORT-KEY (K),
            MOVE A (J) TO EXCH,
            MOVE A (K) TO A (J),
            MOVE EXCH TO A (K),
        ELSE NEXT SENTENCE.
    LOAD-TO-TEMPORARY-FILE.
        MOVE RECORC-NUMBER (J) TO SKEY.
        READ STAFF INVALID KEY GO TO LAST-P.
        WRITE WORKER FROM OFFICER INVALID KEY GO TO LAST-P.
    LOAD-SORTEC-RECORDS.
        READ TEMPORARY-FILE INTO OFFICER AT END GO TO LAST-P.
        WRITE OFFICER INVALID KEY GO TO LAST-P.
    PRINTT.
        READ STAFF INVALID GO TO LAST-P.
        MOVE SPACES TO PRINT-NAME-DST-CAR.
        MOVE NAME OF OFFICER TO NAME-P.
        MOVE DISTRICT OF OFFICER TO DISTRICT-P.
        MOVE CAR OF OFFICER TO CAR-P.
        MOVE PRINT-NAME-DST-CAR TO PRINTLINE.
        WRITE PRINTLINE AFTER ADVANCING 1
            AT EOP PERFORM PAGEHEADING.
        MOVE SPACES TO PRINT-ADDRESS.
        MOVE STREET-ADDRESS OF OFFICER TO SADD.
        MOVE PRINT-ACDRESS TO PRINTLINE.
        WRITE PRINTLINE AFTER ADVANCING NO-LINES
            AT EOP PERFORM PAGEHEADING.
        MOVE CITY OF OFFICER TO C.
        MOVE ZIP-CCDE OF OFFICER TO Z.
        MCVE PRINT-ADDRESS TO PRINTLINE.
        WRITE PRINTLINE AFTER ADVANCING 1
            AT EOP PERFORM PAGEHEADING.
```

```
            MOVE SPACES TO PRINTLINE.
            WRITE PRINTLINE AFTER ADVANCING 2
                AT EOP PERFORM PAGEHEADING.
        PAGEHEADING.
            MOVE PRINT-HEADING TO PRINTLINE.
            WRITE PRINTLINE AFTER ADVANCING TO-TOP.
            MOVE SPACES TO PRINTLINE.
            WRITE PRINTLINE AFTER ADVANCING 2.
        ZEROER.
            MOVE ZERO TO DISTRICT-TOTAL (I).
/*
// XEQ
    DATA CARDS GO HERE
/*
```

Figure 11.9 Modifications in the program for example 11.9 that are necessary to run the program on the DECSYSTEM-10, the B1700, and the IBM-S3.

a. For the DECSYSTEM-10:

```
SOURCE-COMPUTER. DECSYSTEM-10.
OBJECT-COMPUTER. DECSYSTEM-10.
SPECIAL-NAMES. CHANNEL (1) IS TO-TOP.
INPUT-OUTPUT SECTION.
FILE-CONTROL.
    SELECT CARDFILE ASSIGN TO CDR,
        RESERVE 1 ALTERNATE AREA.
    SELECT STAFF ASSIGN TO DSK, ACTUAL KEY IS SKEY,
        ACCESS IS RANDOM, FILE-LIMITS ARE 2 THRU 145.
    SELECT TEMPORARY-FILE, ASSIGN TO DSK.
    SELECT PRINT-FILE, ASSIGN TO PLT,
        RESERVE 1 ALTERNATE AREA.
  ⋮
FD  STAFF,
        VALUE OF IDENTIFICATION IS 'STAF1 DDD',
        BLOCK CONTAINS 5 RECORDS,
  ⋮
FD  TEMPORARY-FILE,
        VALUE OF IDENTIFICATION IS 'TEMP1 TTT',
  ⋮
```

b. For the B1700:

```
SOURCE-COMPUTER. B-1700.
OBJECT-COMPUTER. B-1700.
INPUT-OUTPUT SECTION.
FILE-CONTROL.
    SELECT CARDFILE ASSIGN TO READER, VALUE OF ID IS 'OFFICER',
        RESERVE 1 ALTERNATE AREA.
    SELECT STAFF ASSIGN TO DISK, ACTUAL KEY IS SKEY,
        ACCESS IS RANDOM.
    SELECT TEMPORARY-FILE ASSIGN TO PRINTER,
```

Figure 11.9 (Cont'd.)

```
        RESERVE 1 ALTERNATE AREA.
  ⋮
FD  STAFF, FILE CONTAINS 145 RECORDS,
  ⋮
FD  TEMPORARY-FILE, FILE CONTAINS 144 RECORDS,
  ⋮
```

And in the PROCEDURE DIVISION, you must use CHANNEL 01 in place of TO-TOP.

c. For the IBM-S3:

```
SOURCE-COMPUTER. IBM-S3.
OBJECT-COMPUTER. IBM-S3.
INPUT-OUTPUT SECTION.
FILE-CONTROL.
    SELECT CARDFILE ASSIGN TO UR-2501-RD,
        RESERVE 1 ALTERNATE AREA.
    SELECT STAFF ASSIGN TO DA-2544-R-STAFL,
        ACTUAL KEY IS SKEY, ACCESS IS RANDOM,
            FILE-LIMIT IS 2 THRU 145.
    SELECT TEMPORARY-FILE ASSIGN TO DA-2544-S-TEMP,
        FILE-LIMIT IS 1 THRU 144.
    SELECT PRINTFILE ASSIGN TO UR-1403-2-66.
  ⋮
FD CARDFILE, LINAGE IS 66 WITH FOOTING AT 61,
  ⋮
```

Figure 11.10 Sample of output from STATFILE-CREATION program for example 11.9.

OFFICER	DISTRICT	CAR	ADDRESS	
JABLONSKI CARL	1	5	12 KEY STREET LTTLE RCK	72203
SMITH JOE	1	5	303 MAIN LTTLE RCK	72200

The sorting procedure is known as a tag-sort because the sorting algorithm is not applied directly to the disk file. Instead it is applied to a table, A, containing the minimum information needed for sorting: the key field that determines the sorting order and the record number. The key field for our sort is the name of the officer. By sorting the table in main memory and avoiding disk reads and writes, a great amount of time is saved.

Summary   Tables are created in a COBOL program by means of the OCCURS clause in the DATA DIVISION. The format for this clause is

```
level-number data-name OCCURS integer TIMES
    [INDEXED BY index-name-1 [index-name-2] ...]
```

A table cannot have more than three dimensions; the total amount of main storage occupied by a table on an IBM-1130 must not exceed 4,095 words, and on an IBM-S3 it must not exceed 32,767 bytes of main storage. Whenever an OCCURS clause is used for a data item or one of its subordinate data items, the names of these items must be *subscripted* or *indexed*. The indexes that can be used are specified for each data item in its DATA DIVISION entry or in the entry for a data item of which it is a part. The indices specified for the items with the INDEXED BY clause must *not* be defined elsewhere in the DATA DIVISION.

The values of indices can be established only by use of the SET or PERFORM statements.

Indices should not be confused with *index data items*. Index data items are used to store the values of indices. These data items do not have PICTURE clauses in their definitions, nor can you use the SYN-CHRONIZED, JUSTIFIED, BLANK, or VALUE clauses in their definitions. Their values can be established only through the use of the SET statement.

COBOL permits *direct* and *indirect* indexing of data items, but it does not permit indirect subscripting. In general, it is more efficient to use indices than it is to use subscripts in COBOL programs.

Review Questions   1. Consider the following DATA DIVISION entries.

```
77  K INDEX.
77  L  PIC 99.
01   ATABLE.
    02  LEVEL1 OCCURS 3 INDEXED BY J1.
     03 LEVEL2 OCCURS 4 INDEXED BY J2.
      04 LEVEL3 OCCURS 5 INDEXED BY J3,M.
       05  CODE  PIC X(4).
       05  PRICE  PIC 9(4)V99.
```

a. Which of the following statements are invalid and why?

```
SET L TO 3.
MOVE 4 TO J3 K.
COMPUTE J2 = J3 + 1.
SET K TO L.
SET J2 UP BY 1.
SET J2 J3 TO 4.
MOVE 3 TO L.
SET J1 M TO 5.
```

b. After the following statements are executed, what is the value of *L*?

```
SET J3 TO 4.  SET J1 J2 TO 2.
SET K TO J2.  IF J3 GREATER 3
AND J1 LESS THAN 3 AND K
EQUAL TO 10, MOVE 67 TO L
ELSE MOVE 0 TO L.
```

c. Which element of ATABLE is filled by 0 after execution of the following instructions?

```
SET J3 TO 3.  SET L TO J3.
SET J1, J2 TO L.  MOVE 0 TO
PRICE (J1, J2, J3).
```

d. After the execution of the following statements, which element of ATABLE contains 555.7, and which contains CODE?

```
SET J3 TO 3.  SET J1, J2 TO J3.
SET J2 DOWN BY 2.
MOVE 555.7 TO PRICE (J3 − 2, J2 + 1, J3 − 1).
MOVE 'CODE' TO CODE (J3 − 1, J2, J3 + 1).
```

2. Consider the following DATA DIVISION entries.

```
01    TABLE-VALUES.
   02   FILLER   PIC X(16)
            VALUE '2345678102780571'.
   02   FILLER   PIC X(16)
            VALUE '9876598769111098'.
   02   FILLER   PIC X(16)
            VALUE '6543210098065400'.
01   RATE-TABLE REDEFINES TABLE-VALUES.
   08   AGE-GROUP OCCURS 3.
      12  SEX OCCURS 2.
         20 RATE-BY-CLASS OCCURS 2  PIC S99V99.
```

What is the value of RATE-BY-CLASS (3, 1, 2), RATE-BY-CLASS (1, 2, 1), and RATE-BY-CLASS (2, 2, 2)? MOVE SEX (2, 1) TO SOMEWHERE transfers what numeric digits? MOVE AGE-GROUP (1) TO ABOX transfers which numeric digits?

3. Can data-name-1 of a REDEFINES clause be the subject of an OCCURS clause or subordinate to an OCCURS clause?

4. Consider the DATA DIVISION entry:

```
01  A.
   02  C OCCURS 7.
      03 D OCCURS 3.
        04 PART1  PIC X(5).
        04 PART2  PIC S9(7).
```

How much main storage would this table require?

5. What type of PICTURE clauses can an index have? What about an index data item?

Suggested Projects   1. Commissions are paid to salespersons based upon the number of units sold. The following table gives the needed information on commissions.

Product	Selling price	Commission
1	$ 16.00	$ 1.60
2	17.00	1.70
3	18.00	1.80
4	20.00	3.00
5	25.50	3.50
6	28.50	4.00
7	30.50	4.50
8	35.00	5.00
9	50.50	7.50
10	40.50	6.00
11	50.00	7.50
12	60.00	8.00
13	70.00	10.50
14	75.50	11.00
15	100.50	15.00
16	95.00	14.00
17	85.50	13.00
18	89.50	13.50
19	65.60	8.50
20	45.30	6.50

There are 99 territories numbered 1 through 99. Certain products are difficult to sell in some territories. The table that follows shows which products are hard to sell in which territories.

Product	Territories
1	5, 7, 80, 60
7	14, 21, 99
13	13, 39, 65
18	45, 30, 1

On any sale made under these circumstances, the amount of the commission is increased by 3 percent of the selling price.

Write a program to process a file of at least 30 punched cards. Each card contains

Card column	Picture
territory	99
salesperson number	9(3)
date of sale	9(6)
name salesperson	X(19)
number units sold	9(5)
product number	99

The program should print a table giving product number, selling price, and commission similar to the table given at the beginning of the project.

Hint: In your program define a table in the following way.

```
01 VALUE-FOR-TABLE.
   02   FILLER   PIC 9(8)  VALUE 16000160.
   02   FILLER   PIC 9(8)  VALUE 17000170.
    ⋮
   02   FILLER   PIC 9(8)  VALUE 45300650.
01 PSC-TABLE, REDEFINES VALUE-FOR-TABLE.
   02   PRODUCT OCCURS 20.
      03   SELL  PIC 99V99.
      03   COMM  PIC 99V99.
```

The program should read the card file and then sort the file by the salesperson number in ascending order. Print a list of the sorted records. Each line is to show name, date, territory, product number, units sold, and amount paid in commissions on the sales. (*Hint:* To take the bonus commissions into account, use an IF statement.) Finally, print a list of salespersons, and give the total dollar amount of sales and commission for each. Note that most salespersons should have more than one data card in the deck. Also, be sure to provide headings as needed.

Run your program. Provide flowcharts.

2. The greatest rate of return on capital is achieved by minimizing the value of inventory and maximizing the value of sales. The rate of stock turnover is calculated from the formula RATE-STOCK-TURNOVER = NET-RETAIL-SALES / AVERAGE-VALUE-OF-INVENTORY. This ratio serves as a guide to management. It is desirable to maximize this ratio.

Write a program to read a file of up to 12 cards. Each card contains

Card column	*Field*	*Picture*
1–2	number of month	99
2–10	value of month's inventory	9(6)V99
11–18	value of month's net sales	9(6)V99

Your program should sort this file in ascending order by month. Print a table of the sorted file; however, instead of the number of the month, print the name of the month in the table. To do this, store the names of the months in a table as a part of your program (see the hint for project 1), and use the number of the month to obtain the correct name from the table. At the bottom of the table give the total of the inventory and sales columns and then print the rate of stock turnover. Be sure to provide good headings for your table and print all numbers in a well-edited format. Run your program with data cards for seven months. Provide a flowchart.

3. This project will teach you the fundamental method for sorting a file on the basis of three key fields. For this purpose, you need a card file of at least 50 and no more than 200 cards. Each card contains three fields: The first field in column 1 contains a letter of the alphabet; the second field in column 3 contains a numeric digit; and the third field in column 5 contains a + or a −. Read the card file and store it in an array. (Use indices, if possible.) The description of the array should be

```
01  A.
    02  REC OCCURS 200.
        03  ALP  PIC X.
        03  DIG  PIC X.
        03  PLMN  PIC X.
```

As the cards are read, print a listing of the file with appropriate headings. Sort the array A into *ascending* order as done in example 11.9. Print the sorted array elements. You should discover that the sorted records are in order by alphabetic character. All records with given alphabetic and numeric characters are in order determined by the third field. Run your program.

4. Do project 3 again, this time placing all records in *descending* order. Prepare a flowchart.

5. The XYZ Company makes five different products. From past experience the company has determined the upper and lower critical numbers of each product as shown in the following table.

Product	Lower	Upper
1	250	52534
2	980	50000
3	650	9000
4	900	12000
5	950	19000

At the end of each month the inventory level for each product is reviewed to see if it is below its critical number. If it is, an order is placed for the following amount: Upper critical-number − current inventory level = amount on order.

Write a COBOL program to read a card file in which each card contains the following information.

Field	Picture
item name	X(10)
item number	9
inventory level	9(5)
number on order	9(5)
unit wholesale price	9(3)V99

for each of the five products.

Print a table with headings giving the information on the cards, together with any orders that need to be placed and the dollar cost of the order. Run your program.

6. Do project 5 again and also store the information to be printed in a random file.

7. The Acme Furniture Company produces 20 products. Each sale of a product is recorded on a card as follows.

Card column	Field
1–20	product name
21–40	buyer name
41–45	filler

46–50	purchase price (read as 999V99)
51–55	filler
56–60	number units purchased
61–65	filler
66–70	invoice number

The first step in processing the sales cards would be to check the card file to be sure that the product purchased corresponds to one of the 20 products manufactured by the company. If the name of the product does not match the name of any product the company manufactures, the content of the offending card is printed in a list of file errors on the line printer.

Write a COBOL program to check a sales file. Invent your own list of 20 manufactured products, and use an array to store their names. Run your program with at least 10 data cards (including some erroneous cards), and provide a flowchart for your program.

CHAPTER 12
Sorting and Subroutines

The use of subroutines (also called *subprograms*) is not part of standard COBOL. However, the IBM-1130, IBM-S3, and the DECSYSTEM-10 have implemented the use of subroutines as an extension of standard COBOL. Although the B1700 does not permit the use of subroutines, it does permit the use of the ZIP statement that allows the programmer to perform some of the operations that are possible with the use of subroutines on the other computers. The reader who does not plan to use the IBM-1130, IBM-S3, or DECSYSTEM-10 may be tempted to skip some of this material, but we encourage you to read it. Most of our examples of subprograms deal with sorting techniques. *Sorting* is a fundamental process in data processing, and the techniques presented here will prove useful to the COBOL programmer.

This chapter also discusses the SORT statement. The SORT statement is part of standard COBOL, but the compilers for the IBM-1130 and the IBM-S3 do not permit the use of this statement. Nevertheless, we encourage the users of the IBM-1130 and the IBM-S3 to read the material on the SORT statement because the steps described are typical of all sorting processes and also because the IBM-1130 and the IBM-S3 do have subprograms that can be called upon to sort files. The use of these subprograms is very similar to the use of the SORT statement.

Subprograms

Your own programming attempts have probably indicated the value of dividing the PROCEDURE DIVISION into segments having separate, clearly defined purposes. By appropriate use of paragraph and section headers and the PERFORM statement, laborious tasks can be easily and clearly programmed. However, it can happen that the PROCEDURE DIVISION of a program is extremely complex or that a procedure used in a program is so common that you desire to make it accessible to other programs. The appropriate device for accomplishing this is the *subprogram* or *subroutine*. A subprogram is a program that is used only to perform tasks for a *main program*. Consequently, a subprogram must be compiled and stored on disk before it can be used by a main program.

The CALL Statement

A main program causes the execution of a subprogram by means of a CALL statement. When the computer encounters a CALL statement in a main program, the computer will transfer control to the subprogram that is being called. After the subprogram is executed, control of the computer returns to the main program unless a STOP RUN statement is executed in the subprogram. The execution of the main program resumes with the statement immediately following the CALL statement. The subprograms called may be written in FORTRAN, COBOL, or ASSEMBLER. We shall first discuss the use of COBOL subprograms.

The format of the CALL statement is

<u>CALL</u> literal [<u>USING</u> name-1 [name-2 ...]]

You can CALL only subprograms; you cannot call main programs. A subprogram may CALL another subprogram, but it may not directly or indirectly CALL itself.

The literal in the format for the CALL statement is the name of the subprogram being CALLed. However, on the IBM-1130 and the IBM-S3, the name is enclosed in quotation marks.

On the IBM-1130 the names in the USING option may be file names, record names for files, and WORKING-STORAGE items. If the CALLed subprogram is written in ASSEMBLER, the names in the USING option may also be procedure names. Any file used in a subprogram must be defined in the main program that CALLs it. The file name and at least one of its record names must appear after the USING option. If the file is a random-access file, then its ACTUAL KEY must appear after the USING option.

On the IBM-S3 the names in the USING option can be names of any data items except files. If the subprogram is written in a language other than COBOL, the names in the USING option can also be procedure names.

On the DECSYSTEM-10 the names in the USING option are as described for the IBM-S3.

The B1700 does not permit the CALL statement.

The names in the USING option of the CALL statement are commonly called *parameters*. They are the data items from the main program that will be available to the CALLed subprogram. If the CALL statement uses the USING option, then the header of the PROCEDURE DIVISION of the CALLed subprogram must have the format

<u>PROCEDURE</u> <u>DIVISION</u> <u>USING</u> name-1 [name-2] ...

The number of parameters in the USING option of the subprogram must be the same as the number of parameters in the USING option of the CALL statement for this subprogram. While the corresponding names in each of the parameter lists need not be identical, the *corresponding names in the parameter lists must have identical data descriptions.*

The parameter lists can contain as many as 15 parameters. The parameters in the USING option of a subroutine are dummy data names and do not really exist. At the time of execution, they are replaced by the corresponding data names in the USING option of the CALL statement in the main program. Thus any alteration of the values of the parameters in the USING option of the subroutine is really an alteration in the values of the corresponding parameters in the USING option in the main program.

Recall that in a main program the STOP RUN statement causes the computer to cease execution of a program and return control to the monitor program. This same statement can be used in a subprogram, but it stops the execution of both the subprogram and the main program that CALLed it. Normally you would use the EXIT PROGRAM statement to cause the computer to cease execution of a subroutine and return control to the main program that CALLed it. The main program resumes execution at the statement following the CALL statement. The format of the EXIT statement is

```
paragraph-name. EXIT PROGRAM.
```

and the EXIT statement must be the only statement in paragraph-name.

Figure 12.1 shows how to sort an array of numbers in ascending order. The main program reads in the values of 10 numbers and prints a list of the numbers in their original order. The subprogram, SUBSORT, is CALLed, and it sorts the numbers in ascending order using the method of *linear sort with exchange*. Control then returns to the main program and prints the numbers in sorted order. The listing shows all the cards needed to run this program on the IBM-1130. Figure 12.2 shows the output from the program when it was run with the data cards pictured in figure 12.1.

To run the program in figure 12.1 on the IBM-S3 or the DECSYSTEM-10, you need only change the control cards that are pictured in figure 12.1 and the device names used in the ASSIGN clauses.

All files and records used in subprograms are described in the subprogram exactly as in main programs. However, on the IBM-1130 all the files and records of files in subprograms must be parameters in the PROCEDURE DIVISION heading of the subprogram. Thus on the IBM-1130 these files in the subprogram are really dummy names for files in the main program. On the IBM-1130 if the file has random access, then you must include the ACTUAL KEY for the file as a parameter. On many computers you *cannot* include files as parameters to COBOL subprograms. On the IBM-1130 any file used as a parameter must be closed before a CALL is made to the subprogram and closed again in the subprogram before the return is made to the main program.

When a file name is in the parameter list of a subprogram, the file must be described in the FILE-CONTROL paragraph and the FILE SECTION of the subprogram. All other parameters will be WORKING-STORAGE-type items, and they must be described in the LINKAGE SECTION of the subprogram. The LINKAGE SECTION descriptions are done exactly as in the WORKING-STORAGE SECTION. A subprogram can also have a WORKING-STORAGE SECTION.

Figure 12.3 is a printout from the IBM-1130; it is the same program as in figure 12.1 except that a file name and its record name are included as parameters, along with the array that was a parameter in figure 12.1. Note that in all the examples in this chapter for the IBM-1130, we run with a JOB T card, which means that all files and subprograms stored on disk will be temporary and will be destroyed when the JOB is done. The output from the program in example 12.3 is exactly as it was in figure 12.1.

To run the program in figure 12.2 on the IBM-S3 you must change the control cards shown in figure 12.3, change the device names used in the ASSIGN clauses, and omit PRINT-FILE and A-LINE from the USING option in the subprogram and FILE-OUT and PRINT-LINE from the USING option in the main program.

In the program set up in figure 12.4, a file of up to 50 records can be sorted on a *key field* or *tag field,* which is a student number. Note the use of the COPY statement in the SPECIAL-NAMES paragraph.

Figure 12.1 Example of sorting an array of numbers in ascending order using linear sorting with exchange.

```
// COBOL
*LIST,SUBR
       IDENTIFICATION DIVISION.
       PROGRAM-ID. SUBSORT.
       ****************************************************************
       *****THE SORTING METHOD USED IN THIS SUBPROGRAM IS CALLED A    *
       *****LINEAR SORT WITH EXCHANGE. IT IS NOT A VERY GOOD SORT..... *
       ****************************************************************
       DATA DIVISION.
       WORKING-STORAGE SECTION.
       77  J                PIC 99 COMP.
       77  K                PIC 99 COMP.
       77  L                PIC 99 COMP.
       77  TEMP             PIC 9(5).
       ****************************************************************
       *****THE LINKAGE SECTION CONTAINS THE DATA DESCRIPTIONS OF      *
       *****WORKING-STORAGE LIKE ITEMS WHICH ARE PASSED TO THE         *
       *****SUBROUTINE FROM THE MAIN PROGRAM....                       *
       ****************************************************************
       LINKAGE SECTION.
       01  ARRAY-B.
           02  B OCCURS 10 TIMES PIC 9(5).
       PROCEDURE DIVISION USING ARRAY-B.
       BEGIN.
           PERFORM OUTERLOOP VARYING J FROM 1 BY 1
               UNTIL J IS GREATER THAN 10.
       ****************************************************************
       *****THE OUTER PERFORM DETERMINES WHICH MEMBER OF THE ARRAY IS  *
       *****THE  'FIXED' MEMBER OF THE ARRAY. THIS 'FIXED' MEMBER IS   *
       *****COMPARED TO ALL THE ARRAY MEMBERS 'BELOW' IT. THE COMPARISON*
       *****IS CAUSED BY THE INNER PERFORM STATEMENT.....             *
       ****************************************************************
       SORT-END. EXIT PROGRAM.
       OUTERLOOP.
           COMPUTE K = J + 1.
           PERFORM INNER-LOOP THRU INNER-LOOP-END VARYING L FROM K BY 1
               UNTIL L IS GREATER THAN 10.
       INNER-LOOP.
          IF B (J) IS GREATER THAN B (L),
              MOVE B (J) TO TEMP
              MOVE B (L) TO B (J)
              MOVE TEMP TO B (L).
       INNER-LOOP-END.          EXIT.
/*
// DUP
*STORE        WS  UA  SUBSO
// COBOL
*LIST
       IDENTIFICATION DIVISION.
       PROGRAM-ID. TEST-SUBROUTINES.
       INSTALLATION. EASTERN MICHIGAN UNIVERSITY.
       DATE-WRITTEN. 9/18/72.
       REMARKS.
           THIS PROGRAM IS WRITTEN TO SHOW HOW TO USE AND
           WRITE SUBROUTINES IN COBOL.
       ENVIRONMENT DIVISION.
       CONFIGURATION SECTION.
       SOURCE-COMPUTER. IBM-1130.
       OBJECT-COMPUTER. IBM-1130.
       SPECIAL-NAMES.
           C01 IS TO-NEW-PAGE.
       INPUT-OUTPUT SECTION.
       FILE-CONTROL.
           SELECT FILE-IN ASSIGN TO RD-2501.
           SELECT FILE-OUT ASSIGN TO PR-1403.
```

```
        DATA DIVISION.
        FILE SECTION.
        FD  FILE-IN, LABEL RECORDS ARE OMITTED,
                DATA RECORD IS CARD-IN.
        01  CARD-IN.
            02  INPUT-NUMBER  PIC 9(5).
        FD  FILE-OUT, LABEL RECORDS ARE OMITTED.
            DATA RECORD IS PRINT-LINE.
        01  PRINT-LINE          PIC X(120).
        WORKING-STORAGE SECTION.
        77  I                   PIC 99 COMP.
        01  PRINT-1.
            02  FILLER          PIC X(20) VALUE SPACES.
            02  TITLE-1         PIC X(16) VALUE IS
                'ORIGINAL NUMBERS'.
        01  PRINT-2.
            02  FILLER          PIC X(23) VALUE SPACES.
            02  TITLE-2         PIC X(14) VALUE IS
                'SORTED NUMBERS'.
        01  DETAIL-PRINT.
            02  FILLER          PIC X(37) VALUE SPACES.
            02  PRINT-NUMBER  PIC 9(5).
        01  ARRAY-A.
            02  A OCCURS 10 TIMES        PIC 9(5).
        PROCEDURE DIVISION.
        START-PROGRAM.
            OPEN INPUT FILE-IN, OUTPUT FILE-OUT.
            PERFORM READ-A-CARD VARYING I FROM 1 BY 1
                UNTIL I IS GREATER THAN 10.
            WRITE PRINT-LINE FROM PRINT-1 AFTER ADVANCING TO-NEW-PAGE.
            PERFORM PRINTING VARYING I FROM 1 BY 1
                UNTIL I IS GREATER THAN 10.
            CALL 'SUBSORT' USING ARRAY-A.
            WRITE PRINT-LINE FROM PRINT-2
                AFTER ADVANCING TO-NEW-PAGE.
            PERFORM PRINTING VARYING I FROM 1 BY 1
                UNTIL I IS GREATER THAN 10.
            CLOSE FILE-IN, FILE-OUT.
            STOP RUN.

        READ-A-CARD.
            READ FILE-IN AT END
                DISPLAY 'DATA IS MISSING FOR SORT.',
                CLOSE FILE-IN, FILE-OUT,
                STOP RUN.
            MOVE INPUT-NUMBER TO A (I).
        PRINTING.
            MOVE A (I) TO PRINT-NUMBER.
            WRITE PRINT-LINE FROM DETAIL-PRINT
                AFTER ADVANCING 1 LINES.
/*
// XEQ
    5
    7
    8
    1
    6
    2
    3
   10
    4
    9
/*
```

Figure 12.2 Output from program in figure 12.1.

```
ORIGINAL NUMBERS
                  00005
                  00007
                  00008
                  00001
                  00006
                  00002
                  00003
                  00010
                  00004
                  00009




SORTED NUMBERS
                  00001
                  00002
                  00003
                  00004
                  00005
                  00006
                  00007
                  00008
                  00009
                  00010
```

Figure 12.3 Example of sorting an array of numbers in ascending order using a file name and its record name as parameters.

```
// COBOL
*LIST,SUBR
      IDENTIFICATION DIVISION.
      PROGRAM-ID. SORTPRINT.
      ENVIRONMENT DIVISION.
      INPUT-OUTPUT SECTION.
      FILE-CONTROL.
          SELECT PRINT-FILE ASSIGN TO PR-1403.
      DATA DIVISION.
      FILE SECTION.
      FD  PRINT-FILE LABEL RECORDS ARE OMITTED,
              DATA RECORD IS A-LINE.
      01  A-LINE            PIC X(120).
      WORKING-STORAGE SECTION.
      77  J                 PIC 99 COMP.
      77  K                 PIC 99 COMP.
      77  L                 PIC 99 COMP.
      77  TEMP              PIC 9(5).
      01  SUBROUTINE-PRINT-DETAIL.
          02   FILLER       PIC X(37) VALUE SPACES.
          02   SUBROUTINE-NUMBER     PIC 9(5).
      LINKAGE SECTION.
      01  ARRAY-B.
          02  B OCCURS 10 TIMES PIC 9(5).
      PROCEDURE DIVISION USING ARRAY-B, PRINT-FILE, A-LINE.
      BEGIN.
          OPEN OUTPUT PRINT-FILE.
          PERFORM OUTERLOOP VARYING J FROM 1 BY 1
              UNTIL J IS GREATER THAN 10.
          CLOSE PRINT-FILE.
      SORT-END. EXIT PROGRAM.
```

```
     OUTERLOOP.
         COMPUTE K = J + 1.
         PERFORM INNER-LOOP THRU INNER-LOOP-END VARYING L FROM K BY 1
             UNTIL L IS GREATER THAN 10.
     *****************************************************************
     *****EACH TIME THE 'INNER' LOOP IS COMPLETED, B (J) IS THE       *
     *****MINIMUM OF THE LAST 11 - J MEMBERS OF THE ARRAY.....        *
     *****************************************************************
         MOVE B (J) TO SUBROUTINE-NUMBER.
         WRITE A-LINE FROM SUBROUTINE-PRINT-DETAIL AFTER
             ADVANCING 1 LINES.
     INNER-LOOP.
         IF B (J) IS GREATER THAN B (L),
             MOVE B (J) TO TEMP
             MOVE B (L) TO B (J)
             MOVE TEMP TO B (L).
     INNER-LOOP-END.         EXIT.
/*
// DUP
*STORE       WS  UA  SORTP
// COBOL
*LIST
     IDENTIFICATION DIVISION.
     PROGRAM-ID. TEST-SUBROUTINES.
     INSTALLATION. EASTERN MICHIGAN UNIVERSITY.
     DATE-WRITTEN. 9/18/72.
     REMARKS.
         THIS PROGRAM IS WRITTEN TO SHOW HOW TO USE AND
         WRITE SUBROUTINES IN COBOL.
     ENVIRONMENT DIVISION.
     CONFIGURATION SECTION.
     SOURCE-COMPUTER. IBM-1130.
     OBJECT-COMPUTER. IBM-1130.
     SPECIAL-NAMES.
         C01 IS TO-NEW-PAGE.
     INPUT-OUTPUT SECTION.
     FILE-CONTROL.
         SELECT FILE-IN ASSIGN TO RD-2501.
         SELECT FILE-OUT ASSIGN TO PR-1403.
     DATA DIVISION.
     FILE SECTION.
     FD  FILE-IN, LABEL RECORDS ARE OMITTED,
             DATA RECORD IS CARD-IN.
     01  CARD-IN.
         02  INPUT-NUMBER  PIC 9(5).
     FD  FILE-OUT, LABEL RECORDS ARE OMITTED,
             DATA RECORD IS PRINT-LINE.
     01  PRINT-LINE        PIC X(120).
     WORKING-STORAGE SECTION.
     77  I                 PIC 99 COMP.
     01  PRINT-1.
         02  FILLER        PIC X(20) VALUE SPACES.
         02  TITLE-1       PIC X(16) VALUE IS
             'ORIGINAL NUMBERS'.
     01  PRINT-2.
         02  FILLER        PIC X(23) VALUE SPACES.
         02  TITLE-2       PIC X(14) VALUE IS
             'SORTED NUMBERS'.
     01  DETAIL-PRINT.
         02  FILLER        PIC X(37) VALUE SPACES.
         02  PRINT-NUMBER  PIC 9(5).
     01  ARRAY-A.
         02  A OCCURS 10 TIMES      PIC 9(5).
     PROCEDURE DIVISION.
     START-PROGRAM.
         OPEN INPUT FILE-IN, OUTPUT FILE-OUT.
         PERFORM READ-A-CARD VARYING I FROM 1 BY 1
             UNTIL I IS GREATER THAN 10.
         WRITE PRINT-LINE FROM PRINT-1 AFTER ADVANCING TO-NEW-PAGE.
         PERFORM PRINTING VARYING I FROM 1 BY 1
             UNTIL I IS GREATER THAN 10.
```

Figure 12.3 (Cont'd.)

```
            WRITE PRINT-LINE FROM PRINT-2
                AFTER ADVANCING TO-NEW-PAGE.
            CLOSE FILE-IN, FILE-OUT.
        ***********************************************************************
        *****IF A FILE IN A MAIN PROGRAM IS TO ALSO BE USED IN A CALLED   *
        *****SUBPROGRAM, ONE SHOULD CLOSE THE FILE BEFORE THE CALL IS     *
        *****MADE TO THE SUBPROGRAM.....                                  *
        ***********************************************************************
            CALL 'SORTPRINT' USING ARRAY-A, FILE-OUT, PRINT-LINE.
            STOP RUN.
      READ-A-CARD.
            READ FILE-IN AT END
                DISPLAY 'DATA IS MISSING FOR SORT.',
                CLOSE FILE-IN, FILE-OUT,
                STOP RUN.
            MOVE INPUT-NUMBER TO A (I).
      PRINTING.
            MOVE A (I) TO PRINT-NUMBER.
            WRITE PRINT-LINE FROM DETAIL-PRINT
                AFTER ADVANCING 1 LINES.
/*
// XEQ
    5
    7
    8
    1
    6
    2
    3
   10
    4
    9
/*
```

*Figure 12.4 Program listing in which the main program calls a subprogram
to sort 50 records using the bubble sorting method.*

```
// COBOL
*SUBR,LIST
        IDENTIFICATION DIVISION.
        PROGRAM-ID. SRTPG.
        ***********************************************************************
        *****THE METHOD OF SORTING USED IN THIS PROGRAM IS CALLED THE     *
        *****BUBBLE SORT.  IT IS A MORE EFFICIENT SORT THAN THE LINEAR    *
        *****SORT WITH EXCHANGE FOR GENERAL PURPOSES.....                 *
        ***********************************************************************
        ENVIRONMENT DIVISION.
        DATA DIVISION.
        WORKING-STORAGE SECTION.
        77   FLAG              PIC 9(4) COMP.
             88  SORT-IS-COMPLETE VALUE IS 0.
        77   CTR               PIC 9(4) COMP.
        77   CTR1              PIC 9(4) COMP.
        77   CTR2              PIC 9(4) COMP.
        77   CTR3              PIC 9(4) COMP.
        77   TEMP              PIC X(80).
        LINKAGE SECTION.
          01 SORTE.
             05  CARDD OCCURS 50 TIMES.
                 10  KEYF      PIC X(5).
                 10  REST      PIC X(75).
        ***********************************************************************
        *****THE UNUSED MEMBERS OF THE ARRAY, SORTE, ARE PRESUMED TO BE   *
        *****FILLED WITH HIGH-VALUES.  THUS, WHEN THE SORT IN ASCENDING   *
```

```
     *****ORDER IS COMPLETED, THE UNUSED MEMBERS OF SORTE WILL BE AT  *
     *****THE 'BOTTOM' OF THE ARRAY.....                              *
     ****************************************************************
      PROCEDURE DIVISION USING SORTE.
     ****************************************************************
     *****TO DO THE SORT IN DECENDING ORDER, CHANGE THE WORD 'GREATER'*
     *****IN START-INNER-LOOP TO 'LESS'.....                         *
     ****************************************************************
      START-OF-SORT.
     ****************************************************************
     *****THE IDEA OF THE BUBBLE SORT IS TO COMPARE CONSECUTIVE      *
     *****MEMBERS OF THE ARRAY AND IF THEY ARE OUT OF ORDER, EXCHANGE *
     *****THEM.....                                                  *
     ****************************************************************
          MOVE 0 TO FLAG.
          PERFORM START-OUTER-LOOP THRU END-OUTER-LOOP
              VARYING CTR FROM 1 BY 1
                  UNTIL CTR IS GREATER THAN 49.
      END-OF-PROGRAM.          EXIT PROGRAM.
      START-OUTER-LOOP.
          COMPUTE CTR2 = 50 - CTR.
          PERFORM START-INNER-LOOP THRU END-INNER-LOOP
              VARYING CTR1 FROM 1 BY 1
                  UNTIL CTR1 IS GREATER THAN CTR2.
          GO TO END-OUTER-LOOP.
      START-INNER-LOOP.
          COMPUTE CTR3 = CTR1 + 1.
          IF KEYF (CTR1) IS GREATER THAN KEYF (CTR3),
              MOVE CARDD (CTR1) TO TEMP
              MOVE CARDD (CTR3) TO CARDD (CTR1)
              MOVE TEMP TO CARDD (CTR3)
              MOVE 1 TO FLAG.
      END-INNER-LOOP.         EXIT.
      END-OUTER-LOOP.
          IF SORT-IS-COMPLETE, PERFORM END-OF-PROGRAM
              ELSE MOVE 0 TO FLAG.
     ****************************************************************
     *****THE FLAG IS SET TO 0 BEFORE STARTING AN OUTER LOOP. IF ANY  *
     *****TWO CONSECUTIVE MEMBERS OF THE ARRAY ARE EXCHANGED, FLAG IS *
     *****SET TO 1. IF AN OUTER LOOP IS COMPLETED AND FLAG IS 0, THEN *
     *****NO EXCHANGES WERE MADE. IN THIS CASE THE ARRAY IS SORTED AND*
     *****ONE CAN HALT THE SORT IMMEDIATELY. IF FLAG IS 1, WE RESET   *
     *****FLAG TO 0 AND BEGIN ANOTHER OUTER LOOP.....                *
     ****************************************************************
  /*
 // DUP
 *STORE     WS  UA  SRTPG


 // COBOL
 *LIST
      IDENTIFICATION DIVISION.
      PROGRAM-ID. SIMPLE-SORT.
      REMARKS. THIS PROGRAM READS A CARD FILE, CALLS THE SUBROUTINE
          SRTPG WHICH SORTS THE FILE, AND THEN PRINTS THE SORTED FILE.
      ENVIRONMENT DIVISION.
      CONFIGURATION SECTION.
      SOURCE-COMPUTER. IBM-1130.
      OBJECT-COMPUTER. IBM-1130.
      SPECIAL-NAMES. COPY SPECNAMES.
     ****************************************************************
     *****WE USE THE COPY STATEMENT TO INSERT THE TEXT OF A SPECIAL-  *
     *****NAMES PARAGRAPH WHICH IS STORED IN THE COBOL SOURCE LIBRARY.*
     *****IN PARTICULAR, THE TEXT INCLUDES  C01 IS TO-TOP            *
     ****************************************************************
      INPUT-OUTPUT SECTION.
      FILE-CONTROL.
          SELECT CARDF, ASSIGN TO RD-2501.
          SELECT PRINTF, ASSIGN TO PR-1403.
      DATA DIVISION.
      FILE SECTION.
      FD  CARDF, LABEL RECORDS OMITTED.
```

Figure 12.4 (Cont'd.)

```
    01 CARD.
       02 KEYFIELD PIC X(5).
       02 REST PIC X(75).
   FD  PRINTF, LABEL RECORDS OMITTED.
    01  QUARTO.
       02  FILLER PIC X.
       02  KEYFIELD  PIC X(5).
       02  FILLER PIC X(3).
       02  LINER PIC X(75).
  WORKING-STORAGE SECTION.
    77  COUNTER PIC 9(4) COMP.
    77  CNT PIC 9(4) COMP.
    01 HEADER.
       02  FILLER PIC X.
       02 KEYF PIC X(5) VALUE ' KEY '.
       02 FILLER  PIC XXX   VALUE '   '.
       02 REST  PIC X(75) VALUE 'INFORMATION
 -        '.
    01  SORTARRAY.
       05  SORT-ITEM OCCURS 50 TIMES.
           10  KEYFIELD  PIC X(5).
           10  REST       PIC X(75).
   PROCEDURE DIVISION.
   START-OF-PROGRAM.
   ************************************************************************
   *****THE ITEMS TO BE SORTED ARE READ INTO SORTARRAY.  THE           *
   *****KEYFIELDS OF THE UNUSED ELEMENTS OF SORTE ARE FILLED WITH    *
   *****HIGH-VALUES. THUS WHEN THE ITEMS ARE SORTED IN ASCENDING      *
   *****ORDER, THE UNUSED ITEMS WILL BE LAST IN THE ARRAY. TO DO THE*
   *****SAME SORT IN DECENDING ORDER, CHANGE HIGH-VALUE TO LOW-VALUE*
   *****EVERYWHERE IT OCCURS IN THE PROGRAM AND MAKE THE CHANGES IN *
   *****SRTPG DESCRIBED THERE.....                                   *
   ************************************************************************
       OPEN INPUT CARDF, OUTPUT PRINTF.
       MOVE 0 TO COUNTER. MOVE SPACES TO QUARTO.
   READ-AND-COUNT-CARDS.
       COMPUTE COUNTER = COUNTER + 1.
       READ CARDF AT END
           PERFORM LOAD-HIGH-VALUE VARYING CNT FROM COUNTER BY 1
               UNTIL CNT IS GREATER THAN 50
           GO TO SORT-CALL.
       IF COUNTER IS GREATER THAN 50, GO TO ERROR-END.
       MOVE CARD TO SORT-ITEM (COUNTER).
       GO TO READ-AND-COUNT-CARDS.
   LOAD-HIGH-VALUE.
       MOVE HIGH-VALUE  TO KEYFIELD OF SORTARRAY (CNT).
   SORT-CALL.
       CALL 'SRTPG' USING SORTARRAY.
       WRITE QUARTO FROM HEADER AFTER ADVANCING TO-TOP.
       PERFORM PRINT-ARRAY VARYING CNT FROM 1 BY 1
           UNTIL CNT IS GREATER THAN 50.
   PRINT-ARRAY.
       IF KEYFIELD OF SORTARRAY (CNT) IS EQUAL TO HIGH-VALUE
           GO TO END-OF-PROGRAM.
       MOVE SPACE  TO QUARTO.
       MOVE KEYFIELD OF SORTARRAY (CNT) TO KEYFIELD OF QUARTO.
       MOVE REST OF SORTARRAY (CNT) TO LINER OF QUARTO.
       WRITE QUARTO AFTER ADVANCING 1, AT EOP
       WRITE QUARTO FROM HEADER AFTER ADVANCING TO-TOP.
   ERROR-END.
       MOVE SPACES TO KEYFIELD OF QUARTO.
       MOVE 'CARD FILE EXCEEDS 50 RECORDS. PROGRAM STOPS.' TO LINER.
       WRITE QUARTO AFTER ADVANCING 1.
   END-OF-PROGRAM.
       CLOSE CARDF, PRINTF. STOP RUN.
```

```
/*
// XEQ
     DATA CARDS GO HERE
/*
```

Figure 12.5 Sample output showing sorted records as described in program listing in figure 12.4.

```
 KEY      INFORMATION
07160    JONES THOMAS H      1812 RESERVOIR RD    LITTLE ROCK AR
07319    ENNIS REMONA        2109 S TAYLOR        LITTLE ROCK AR
07356    LOFTIS KATHY H      320 KNIGHTLER DR     LITTLE ROCK AR
  :
```

The text of the copied material was stored as described at the end of Chapter 7. Note how the figurative constants HIGH-VALUE and LOW-VALUE are used in working with files to give keys to unused records in a randomly organized file. Figure 12.5 shows sample output of the sorted records from the program in figure 12.4.

When a subprogram is called for the first time, the state of the called program is fresh. However, if the subprogram is called several times, then the parameters in the various CALL statements can be different. Moreover, the items in the WORKING-STORAGE SECTION of the subprogram and TALLY will have the same values as they did when the subprogram was last exited. Thus it is the responsibility of the programmer to reinitialize the following items: TALLY, GO TO statements that were altered, and data items as needed. Note the control cards in figure 12.4. The subroutine SRTPG is compiled and stored in the User Area of the disk, and then the program SIMPLE-SORT is compiled and executed. The JOB T causes SRTPG to be removed from the User Area when the next JOB card is encountered. To avoid cluttering the User Area with practice subroutines or disk files, you should always run your student programs under a temporary JOB card. If you wish the subroutine to be stored permanently, then store it under an ordinary job card.

The ENTER Statement on the DECSYSTEM-10

You can use the CALL statement on the DECSYSTEM-10 to transfer control to COBOL subprograms. By means of the ENTER statement, you can transfer control from COBOL main programs to subprograms written in other languages such as FORTRAN or MACRO. MACRO is the assembly language for DECSYSTEM-10. The ENTER statement is not permitted on the B1700, the IBM-1130, or the IBM-S3. The format for the ENTER statement on the DECSYSTEM-10 is

```
ENTER language-name, subprogram-name
      [USING name-1 [name-2] ...]
```

At the point in a main program where the ENTER statement is encountered, control transfers to subprogram-name written in language-name. Remember that program-name is *not* enclosed in quotation marks as on the IBM-1130 and the IBM-S3. The parameters of the USING option play the same role as they did with the CALL statement.

Example 12.1 shows the ENTER statement using a subprogram written in the FORTRAN language. If you are familiar with the FORTRAN language, then you are aware that arithmetic calculations are easier in FORTRAN than they are in COBOL and that FORTRAN provides many arithmetic functions not available in COBOL. For example, COBOL does not provide any means of calculating square roots of numbers, but FORTRAN makes calculating square roots very easy.

Example 12.1   We wish to write a Cobol program to read the grades of 20 students from cards, calculate the arithmetic mean of the grades in the COBOL program, and use a FORTRAN subroutine to calculate the standard deviation of the grades.

To calculate an arithmetic mean: Suppose we have N numbers named X_1, $X_2, \ldots, X_N$. We denote the arithmetic mean by M. Then the formula for the arithmetic mean is

$$M = \frac{\sum\limits_{i=1}^{N} X_i}{N}$$

If we denote the standard deviation by SD, then the formula for it is

$$SD = \sqrt{\frac{\sum\limits_{i=1}^{N} (X_i - M)^2}{N}}$$

where $\sum_{i=1}^{N} X_i$ is equal to $X_1 + X_2 + \cdots + X_N$ and $\sum_{i=1}^{N} (X_i - M)^2$ is calculated similarly. Since the standard deviation cannot be found without finding a square root, we shall use a FORTRAN subroutine to calculate the square root. Figure 12.6 shows the listing of the FORTRAN subroutine.

Figure 12.6 FORTRAN subroutine and COBOL main program for example 12.1.

```
Column 1

$JOB F[77,434] ; KHAILANY-DUPLISSEY
$PASSWORD ABCDE
$FORTRAN
      SUBROUTINE STANDV(JGR,ARM,NUM,STV)
CCCCCCCCCCCCCCCCCCCCCCCCCCCCCCCCCCCCCCCCCCCCCCCCCCCCCCCCCCCCCCCCCCCCCCCC
C IN FORTRAN, A CARD WITH C IN COLUMN 1 INDICATES A COMMENT CARD.....  C
CCCCCCCCCCCCCCCCCCCCCCCCCCCCCCCCCCCCCCCCCCCCCCCCCCCCCCCCCCCCCCCCCCCCCCCC
C THE NAME OF THE SUBPROGRAM IS STANDV, THE DUMMY ARGUMENTS JGR, ARM,  C
C NUM, AND STV CORRESPOND TO GRADE, ARITH-MEAN, NUMBER-OF-STUDENTS,    C
C AND TEMP-STNDV IN THE COBOL MAIN PROGRAM.....                        C
CCCCCCCCCCCCCCCCCCCCCCCCCCCCCCCCCCCCCCCCCCCCCCCCCCCCCCCCCCCCCCCCCCCCCCCC
```

```
      DIMENSION JGR(20)
      SUM = 0.0
      DO 15 I = 1, 20
      SUM = SUM + (JGR(I)-ARM)**2
   15 CONTINUE
      STV = SUM**0.5
CCCCCCCCCCCCCCCCCCCCCCCCCCCCCCCCCCCCCCCCCCCCCCCCCCCCCCCCCCCCCCCCCCCCCC
C THE DO LOOP IN THE PRECEDING STATEMENTS EXTENDS FROM THE LINE        C
C STARTING WITH THE WORD DO THRU THE LINE WHOSE LABEL IS 15. THE DO    C
C STATEMENT IS LIKE A PERFORM STATEMENT VARYING THE DATA ITEM I. WHEN  C
C THE DO STATEMENT HAS PERFORMED THE STATEMENTS IN THE DO LOOP 20 TIMESC
C VARYING I FROM 1 THRU 20, CONTROL TRANSFERS TO THE NEXT STATEMENT    C
C AFTER THE DO LOOP. THAT STATEMENT CALCULATES THE VALUE OF STV BY     C
C FINDING SUM RAISED TO THE ONE HALF POWER. RAISING A NUMBER TO THE    C
C ONE HALF POWER IS EQUIVALENT TO FINDING ITS SQUARE ROOT. WE ARE NOW  C
C DONE AND RETURN TO THE MAIN PROGRAM. THE END STATEMENT WHICH YOU     C
C WILL SEE IS USED TO MARK THE PHYSICAL END OF FORTRAN PROGRAMS.....   C
CCCCCCCCCCCCCCCCCCCCCCCCCCCCCCCCCCCCCCCCCCCCCCCCCCCCCCCCCCCCCCCCCCCCCC
      RETURN
      END
$COBOL /S
      IDENTIFICATION DIVISION.
      PROGRAM-ID. MAINPROGRAM.
      ENVIRONMENT DIVISION.
      CONFIGURATION SECTION.
      SOURCE-COMPUTER. DECSYSTEM-10.
      OBJECT-COMPUTER. DECSYSTEM-10.
      SPECIAL-NAMES. CHANNEL (1) IS TO-TOP.
      INPUT-OUTPUT SECTION.
      FILE-CONTROL.
          SELECT CARDFILE ASSIGN TO CDR.
          SELECT PRINTFILE ASSIGN TO LPT.
      DATA DIVISION.
      FILE SECTION.
      FD  CARDFILE LABEL RECORDS ARE OMITTED.
      01  GRADE.
          02  STUDENT-GRADE OCCURS 20 TIMES, PIC 9(3).
      FD  PRINTFILE LABEL RECORDS ARE OMITTED.
      01  LINE-P  PIC X(133).
      WORKING-STORAGE SECTION.
      77  ARITH-MEAN  PIC 9(3)V99  COMP VALUE 0.
      77  TEMP-STNDV  PIC 9(3)V99  COMP.
      77  I           PIC 9(2)     COMP.
      77  NUMBER-OF-STUDENTS PIC 9(2) COMP VALUE 20.
      01  GRADE-SUMMARY.
          05  FILLER PIC X(24) VALUE IS
                 "      ARITHMETIC MEAN IS ".
          05  ARITHMETIC-MEAN PIC ZZZ.99.
          05  FILLER PIC X(24) VALUE IS
                 " STANDARD DEVIATION IS ".
          05  STANDARD-DEVIATION PIC ZZZ.99.
```

Figure 12.6 (Cont'd.)

```
       PROCEDURE DIVISION.
       START-OF-PROGRAM.
           OPEN INPUT CARDFILE OUTPUT PRINTFILE.
           READ CARDFILE AT END GO TO END-OF-PROGRAM.
       ******************************************************************
       *THE READ STATEMENT HAS OBTAINED ALL 20 GRADES.....             *
       ******************************************************************
           PERFORM GRADE-SUMMER VARYING I FROM 1 BY 1
               UNTIL I IS GREATER THAN 20.
       ******************************************************************
       *THE PERFORM STATEMENT HAS ADDED ALL GRADES TO OBTAIN THE TOTAL *
       ******************************************************************
           DIVIDE ARITH-MEAN BY NUMBER-OF-STUDENTS GIVING ARITH-MEAN.
       ******************************************************************
       * WE HAVE FOUND THE ARITHMETIC MEAN AND NOW ENTER STANDV TO     *
       * OBTAIN THE STANDARD DEVIATION.....                            *
       ******************************************************************
           ENTER FORTRAN-IV STANDV USING GRADE, ARITH-MEAN,
               NUMBER-OF-STUDENTS, TEMP-STNDV.
       ******************************************************************
       *THE CONTROL HAS NOW RETURNED FROM STANDV. WE PRINT OUR RESULTS *
       *AND STOP THE PROGRAM.....                                      *
       ******************************************************************
           MOVE ARITH-MEAN TO ARITHMETIC-MEAN.
           MOVE TEMP-STNDV TO STANDARD-DEVIATION.
           WRITE LINE-P FROM GRADE-SUMMARY AFTER ADVANCING TO-TOP.
       END-OF-PROGRAM.
           CLOSE CARDFILE, PRINTFILE.
           STOP RUN.
       GRADE-SUMMER.
           ADD STUDENT-GRADE (I) TO ARITH-MEAN.
$DATA
$EOD
Data cards go here.
eof card goes here.
```

The $DATA card marks the end of your program and the beginning of
your data. It also causes your program to be executed. The eof card is a card
with punches in columns 1 and 80. In both columns one must have punches
in rows 12, 11, 0, 1, 6, 7, and 9.

The ZIP Statement on the B1700

The CALL and ENTER statements are not permitted on the B1700. The
B1700 has its own special statement, ZIP. The format of the ZIP statement
is

```
       ZIP data-name.
```

The data name must have a value that is a nonnumeric literal. This literal is a message that will be submitted to the *Master Control Program* that is the operating system for the B1700 system. For example, if the value of data-name were `'EXECUTE MASTERPROGRAM.'`, the ZIP statement would have the effect of asking the Master Control Program to schedule the program named MASTERPROGRAM for execution. In some ways this is similar to CALLing a subprogram; however, you cannot give parameters to the programs run in this way. Also, the ZIP statement asks the Master Control Program to *schedule* the requested operation, and once this has been done, control returns to the program containing the ZIP statement. In `'EXECUTE MASTERPROGRAM.'` it is quite likely that after the ZIP statement has been executed, control returns to the program before MAS-TERPROGRAM has been run.

There is a wide variety of functions you can request of the Master Control Program with the ZIP statement.

Subroutines Supplied with the IBM-1130

Many useful subroutines are supplied for use with COBOL on the IBM-1130. They are designed to carry out many useful tasks and to carry out tasks that are difficult to program in the COBOL language. Among the most useful are routines to sort disk files and routines to locate records in random-access disk files. The latter routines can be used to give the IBM-1130 the capabililty of handling files similar to indexed-sequential files. These subprograms can be used to perform many important data-processing functions, and they are fully described in the *IBM-1130 COBOL Programmer's Guide, Form SH20-0928*. We will describe nine of the subprograms here. In each case, where practical, we begin with the format of the CALL statement.

1. CALL `'QDUMP'` USING name-1 name-2. QDUMP will produce a hexadecimal core dump of all data physically located between name-1 and name-2. Name-1 and name-2 should name data items or procedures in the calling programs. They cannot be condition names or special names. Normally, the programmer would have obtained a map of the DATA and PRO-CEDURE divisions before using this subprogram to ensure that the desired information is obtained by the dump.

2. CALL `'QLINK'` USING data-name. Data-name should be a five-character DISPLAY item whose value is the name of a COBOL main program stored on disk. This call will load and execute the designated main program, and it will completely eliminate the calling program from main storage.

3. CALL $\left\{ \begin{array}{l} \text{'QCV12'} \\ \text{'QCV21'} \end{array} \right\}$ USING data-name-1, data-name-2, data-name-3.

In storing alphanumeric data using EBCDIC codes, COBOL assumes that one character is stored per unit of computer memory. Thus on the IBM-1130 one character is stored in each word of memory. However, a word is actually large enough to contain two characters in EBCDIC code. QCV12 converts data stored as one-character-per-word code to data stored as in two-characters-per-word codes. QCV21 reverses the process. In both subprograms data-name-1 is the one-character-per-word DISPLAY item, and data-name-2 is the name of the item containing two characters per word. Data-name-3 is a one- to four-digit computational item whose value is the number of *characters* to convert. This number can be odd and is normally the number of characters in data-name-1.

4. CALL $\left\{ \begin{array}{l} \text{'QCV13'} \\ \text{'QCV31'} \end{array} \right\}$ USING data-name-1, data-name-2, data-name-3.

By restricting alphanumeric data to a 39-character set, it is possible to use a special coding to store 3 characters per word memory. The characters are stored in collating sequence so that usual sorting techniques can be used. The 39 characters include A through Z, 0 through 9, the blank, period, comma, and hyphen. However, the computer installation can alter this selection of characters if desired.

5. CALL $\left\{ \begin{array}{l} \text{'QCVBP'} \\ \text{'QCVPB'} \end{array} \right\}$ USING binary-item, packed-item, number-of-digits-to-convert. These subprograms convert between the binary format used in COBOL and the packed-decimal format used in RPG. This enables both languages to be used for programming objectives.

6. Recall that each word on the IBM-1130 contains 16 bits that may be on or off; or, equivalently, 1 or 0. The subprograms QCVBC, QCVCB, QLAND, QLOR, QLXOR, QLSET, and QTEST permit the programmer to manipulate and test the values of bits within a word. QCVBC and QCVCB allow you to convert between a string of bits and an equivalent character string of 0's and 1's. This enables the programmer to examine values of bits and to place specified values in bits. The subprograms QLAND, QLOR, QLXOR, and QLSET allow the programmer to modify a string of bits according to one of several patterns. The subprogram QTEST allows the programmer to compare a string of bits against a fixed bit string and take one of several actions depending upon how the strings match.

7. QCBRN and QCBPC enable the programmer to read and punch in binary column mode. These subprograms permit the programmer to deal with nonstandard punched-card formats, such as those used for special applications.

8. One of the most important data-processing activities is sorting mass storage files. IBM provides programs that can be used to sort any direct disk file. Normally files are sorted on the basis of one or more key fields that appear in each record. Examples of key fields are names of individuals, identification numbers, and dates of transaction.

The first step in using the sorting program is the preparation of a data item that describes the key field(s) to be used in the sort. We call this data item SORT-INFORMATION, and it must be a level 01 item in the WORKING-STORAGE SECTION. SORT-INFORMATION contains three entries for *each* key field used in the sort as shown in the following formats:

```
01 SORT-INFORMATION COMP.
02 NUMBER-RECORDS-TO-SORT  PIC 9(5).
```

The preceding data item is used to determine the amount of disk space needed to perform the sort. If insufficient space is available, execution time error 43 occurs.

```
02 START-OF-KEY-FIELD  PIC 9(5).
```

The preceding data item specifies the word of the file record in which the key field begins. If the key field were at the beginning of each record, then the value of this item would be 1.

```
02 SEQ-TYPE-LENGTH  PIC S9(5).
```

If the preceding item is positive, the records are sorted in *ascending* order on the basis of this key; and if the value is negative, the sort is in *descending* order on the basis of this key. This value of this item is a four-digit number, nxxx. The value of n specifies the type of data in this key field.

$n = 1$ signifies a normal alphanumeric item

$n = 2$ signifies packed data (see items 3 and 4 in our list of subprograms)

$n = 3$ signifies numeric DISPLAY data

$n = 4$ signifies computational numeric data

The three lower-order digits specify the length of this key field as specified in its PICTURE clause. For example, $9(3) = 3$, $X(15) = 15$, $S9(5) = 5$, and $Z(2)V9(2) = 4$.

```
{ information for next key field
  ⋮
02 END-OF-TABLE  PIC 9(5) VALUE 0.
```

Note that several key fields can be specified. For example, you might sort the file of invoices first by company name and second by date of transaction.

In most cases the values of START-OF-KEY-FIELD and SEQ-TYPE-LENGTH do not change and can be specified by a VALUE clause. Since NUMBER-RECORDS-TO-SORT either is not generally known in advance or can change, its value is normally specified just prior to the sort.

The first step of the sort is the statement

```
CALL 'QSITL' USING FILE-NAME, SORT-INFORMATION.
```

FILE-NAME is the name of the file to be sorted. The next step is to present the records to be sorted to the subprogram QSREL. Recall that FILE-NAME must be a random disk file with an ACTUAL KEY. For each record to be sorted, the programmer must set the ACTUAL KEY for that record and read the file so that the desired record is available in the record area of the file. This is immediately followed by the statement CALL 'QSREL'.

After all records to be sorted have been presented to QSREL, the next step is the statement CALL 'QSORT'. QSREL will have prepared the information necessary to perform a tag sort for the specified records in the file. QSORT performs the tag sort. The final step is to place the actual file records in sorted order, since only the tag file has been sorted and not the records in the original file.

To obtain the order in which the records presented to QSREL should be placed if they are to be in sorted order, the program must repeatedly execute the statement

```
CALL 'QSRET'
```

Each time QSRET is called, the record number of the next record (in sorted sequence) is placed in the ACTUAL KEY for the disk file. The file can be read so that the record will be available for placing in a new file. After QSRET has returned the record number of all the records that were to be sorted, the ACTUAL KEY of the file will be set to 0 so that the INVALID KEY clause will be executed when the file is read. This can be used to end the sorting process. (*Note:* The values of START-OF-KEY-FIELD and SEQ-TYPE-LENGTH are altered during the execution of QSORT.)

Chapter 13 contains sample programs using these sorting subprograms.

9. Another important data-processing activity is locating records in a sorted mass storage file. This can be a slow process if the file is large, so IBM supplies subprograms for this purpose that are fast and versatile.

The method for locating a record is a *binary search*. In this method the portion of the file containing the desired record is steadily reduced until the desired record is located or it is determined that the file does not contain the record. Since the file is sorted sequentially, each iteration of the algorithm consists of examining the middle record of the remaining portion of the file. The half of the remaining portion of the file that cannot contain the desired record is ignored in succeeding iterations. Thus each iteration halves the portion of the file remaining to be searched.

The file to be searched must be a randomly accessed disk file organized as follows.

a. Header or label record(s): The first record(s) of the file must be a label *record(s)*. The total length of the label record(s) must be at least four words. The number of records used as label records is determined by this length requirement.
b. A block of sequentially sorted records.
c. A block of unsorted records.
d. An unused portion of the file to which additions can be made.

The label record(s) must contain the following information.

a. The first and second items must be defined as PICTURE 9(5) COMPU-TATIONAL.
b. The remaining portion of the label record(s) can contain any desired information, such as the date records that were last added to the file.
c. The value of the first computational item should be the relative position of the last record in the sorted portion of the file—i.e., the ACTUAL KEY value for that record.
d. The value of the second computational item should be the relative position of the last record in the unsorted portion of the file.

The record of the file is located on the basis of a key field in the file records. The subprogram to locate records will need to know where this key field is located in the file records. As in the use of the sorting program, this information is contained in a WORKING-STORAGE item whose description follows.

```
01 LOCATION-INFORMATION COMP.
02 START-OF-KEY  PIC 9(4).
```

The preceding format specifies the word of the record in which the key field begins.

```
02 NUMBER-OF-WORDS  PIC 9(4).
```

The preceding format specifies the number of words occupied by the key field.

```
02 START-OF-RECORDS  PIC 9(5).
```

The preceding format specifies the relative position of the record that begins the portion of the file to be searched. For example, if the label record(s) occupied only one record, then you might specify a value of 2 here.

```
02 NUMBER-LAST-SEQ-REC  PIC 9(5).
```

The preceding format specifies the position of the last record in the sorted portion of the file.

```
02 NUMBER-LAST-NONSEQ-REC  PIC 9(5).
```

The preceding format specifies the number of the last record in the nonsequential portion of the file.

LOCATION-INFORMATION provides the information necessary to search for a desired record. Note that the sequential portion of the file must be sorted on the basis of the key field described in LOCATION-INFOR-MATION.

To begin the search for records, the program should execute the statement

```
CALL 'QCORE' USING FILE-NAME,
    LOCATION-INFORMATION.
```

QCORE determines the amount of core storage not used by the calling program and clears each word in this area to hexadecimal /0000. QCORE also establishes certain constants in the area used by FORTRAN as a floating-point accumulator. If insufficient core storage is available, execution time error 82 results.

We are now ready to locate a desired file record. To locate the record, the program must execute the statement

```
CALL 'QFIND' USING NOMINAL-KEY.
```

NOMINAL-KEY must be a data item whose value matches the value of the key field in the desired record. QFIND first searches the sorted portion of the disk file, and if the record is not found, QFIND then searches the unsorted portion of the disk file. If the record *is* found, QFIND places its record number in the ACTUAL KEY of the disk file. If the record *is not* found, QFIND places a negative value in the ACTUAL KEY of the disk file. Thus a READ of the disk file after the call to QFIND will either bring the desired record to the record area of the file or cause the INVALID KEY clause of the READ statement to be executed because the record was not in the file.

The advantage of these IBM programs arises when several records must be located. As records are located by QFIND, an index of the records in the sorted portion of the file is built in the portion of main memory cleared by QCORE. As this index expands, QFIND uses this core storage information to lessen the number of disk READs that must be made to locate records. Since disk READs and WRITEs are the slow factor in the process of locating records, the subprograms become more efficient as successive records are located.

These programs can be used for only one disk file in a given mainline program. If a FORTRAN subprogram is called during the location of records, the content of the floating-point accumulator can be destroyed. Any subsequent attempt to locate records will cause execution time error 81. This can be overcome by calling QCORE before further attempts to locate records are made, but this will destroy the file index that was created in core storage.

If records are subsequently added to the unsorted portion of the file, QCORE need not be called to reinitialize the file index in core. You need only update the value of NUMBER-LAST-NONSEQ-REC to include the new records.

Records in the disk file can be marked as logically deleted (though not physically deleted) by placing hexadecimal /8000 in the first word of the record. However, if this capability is used, the key field by which the records are sorted cannot begin in this first word.

As stated earlier, the subprograms will locate records in a file of very general organization. It is worth observing that the sorting programs QCBRN and QCBPC can be used to sort this type of file. In fact, if the number of records in the unsorted portion of the file is large, the efficiency of the search algorithm is lowered, and a sort should be made to restore search efficiency.

The QFIND subprogram is illustrated in the sample application program in Chapter 13.

10. CALL $\begin{Bmatrix} \text{'QFRED'} \\ \text{'QFRIT'} \end{Bmatrix}$ USING FILENAME, COBOL-AREA, FORTRAN-CODING, ERROR-PARAGRAPH. The subroutines QFRED and QFRIT are supplied by IBM to allow the user to process a FORTRAN-created file through a COBOL program. The file may be sequentially or directly organized.

If QFRED is called and the requested record is not available in main storage, one sector of disk storage containing the record will be read into main storage (in the block area of FILENAME). The requested record is moved to the record area of FILENAME. This information is translated from FORTRAN data formats to COBOL data formats and stored in COBOL-AREA. The translation is performed according to the specifications in FORTRAN-CODING. ERROR-PARAGRAPH is the name of a paragraph to which the subroutine will branch if an invalid key is specified or the end of file is encountered.

If QFRIT is called, the information in COBOL-AREA is translated (according to the specifications in FORTRAN-CODING) into FORTRAN data formats and placed in the record area of FILENAME. If the next call to QFRIT refers to a record not in the sector containing this record or if FILENAME is closed, then this record is written on the disk file.

To use QFRED, FILENAME must be opened for INPUT or I-O. To use

QFRIT, FILENAME must be opened I-O and thus QFRIT can be used only for updating FILENAME.

FILENAME can have a special buffer (by specifying -X) only if it is blocked 320 words per sector.

FORTRAN-CODING is the name of a string of S9(4) computational items used to specify the data items in the disk record of the FORTRAN file and how they are to be changed to COBOL data items. COBOL-AREA is a group item containing the corresponding COBOL items. The valid values for the items in FORTRAN-CODING follow.

1. +0nnn to skip words in the FORTRAN record where nnn specifies the number of words to skip. The COBOL-AREA must contain an item of the same number of words. However, no translation is made for these words.
2. +1nnn to translate a one-word FORTRAN integer to a COBOL computational item. Set nnn = 000 for a 9(4) COMP picture and nnn ≠ 000 for a 9(5) COMP picture.
3. +2nnn to translate FORTRAN two-word integers to COBOL computational items. Set nnn = 000 for a 9(9) COMP picture and nnn ≠ 000 for a 9(10) COMP picture.
4. +4nnn to convert FORTRAN A1 to COBOL alphanumeric, X. nnn specifies the number of characters to convert.
5. +5nnn to convert FORTRAN A2 to COBOL alphanumeric, X. nnn specifies the number of characters to convert.
6. +6nnn to convert FORTRAN A3 to COBOL alphanumeric, X. nnn specifies the number of characters to convert.
7. −nnnn to repeat the next specification. nnnn specifies the number of repetitions.
8. 0000 to mark the end of the table.

If the +6nnn option was used to specify a conversion from A3 to COBOL alphanumeric, then immediately following the end-of-table marker must be a 40-character item whose VALUE clause specifies the accepted characters for conversion.

The use of these programs is illustrated in Chapter 13.

The SORT Statement

The SORT statement is not available on the IBM-1130 or the IBM-S3, since on these computers sorting is done by calling subprograms provided for this purpose. On the B1700 and the DECSYSTEM-10 you can sort a file by using the SORT statement. Every SORT statement causes three phases of actions.

1. The records to be sorted are placed in a sort disk file.
2. The sort disk file is sorted.
3. After being sorted, the records in the sort disk file are made available for storage in another file.

The first requirement for using the SORT statement is a sort disk file. You must provide a SELECT and ASSIGN clause for the sort disk file as usual. The name selected is the choice of the programmer. However, on the B1700 the file must be ASSIGNed to DISK, and on the DECSYSTEM-10 the file must be ASSIGNed to DSK, DSK, DSK. You must also provide an entry for the sort disk file in the FILE SECTION. The format of the entry is

```
SD sort-disk-file.
```

Notice that a LABEL RECORDS clause is not required nor is it permitted. The choice of a record name for the sort disk file and of its record description is the programmer's.

The format of the SORT statement is

```
SORT sort-disk-file

    ON {ASCENDING / DESCENDING} KEY data-name-1 [data-name-2] ...

    [ON {ASCENDING / DESCENDING} KEY data-name-3 [data-name-4] ...]

    {INPUT PROCEDURE IS section-name-1
         [THRU section-name-2]

     USING file-name-1 [LOCK / PURGE / RELEASE]}

    {OUTPUT PROCEDURE IS section-name-3
         [THRU section-name-4]

     GIVING file-name-2 [LOCK / RELEASE]}
```

If the USING or GIVING options are specified, then the files named in these options must be closed at the time the SORT statement is encountered in the program.

Example 12.2   Suppose that we have a file of student records on cards that we wish to be sorted to give a printed listing of the records. The program in figure 12.7 for the B1700 shows how to use the SORT statement for this purpose. The SORT statement in SAMPLE-SORT causes the READ-RECORDS section to be performed, the records in SORTFILE to be sorted, and the PRINT-RECORDS section to be performed. Note that a crucial step in the input procedure, READ-RECORDS, is the use of the RELEASE statement. The format of this statement is

```
RELEASE sort-record [FROM data-name]
```

The RELEASE statement informs the sort routines that the information in the sort-record area is to be included in the records to be sorted. If the

FROM option is used, then the information in data-name is moved to sort-record before the RELEASE is made to the sort file.

Figure 12.7 Program listing on the B1700 for example 12.2.

```
        IDENTIFICATION DIVISION.
        PROGRAM-ID. SAMPLE-SORT.
        ENVIRONMENT DIVISION.
        INPUT-OUTPUT SECTION.
        FILE-CONTROL.
            SELECT CARDFILE ASSIGN TO READER.
            SELECT SORTFILE ASSIGN TO DISK.
            SELECT PRINTFILE ASSIGN TO PRINTER.
        DATA DIVISION.
        FILE SECTION.
        FD  CARDFILE, LABEL RECORDS ARE OMITTED VALUE OF ID IS
                        "STUCARDS".
        01  STUDENT-RECORD.
            05  STUDENT-ID  PIC 9(5).
            05  STUDENT-NAME PIC X(30).
        SD  SORTFILE.
        01  SORT-RECORD.
            05  STUDENT-ID PIC 9(5).
            05  STUDENT-NAME PIC X(30).
        FD  PRINTFILE, LABEL RECORDS ARE OMITTED.
        01  PRINT-RECORD.
        05  STUDENT-NAME PIC 9(5).
        05  STUDENT-NAME PIC X(30).
    PROCEDURE DIVISION.
    START-OF-PROGRAM SECTION.
    PARAGRAPH-1.
        SORT SORTFILE ON ASCENDING KEY STUDENT-ID OF SORT-RECORD
            INPUT PROCEDURE IS READ-RECORDS
            OUTPUT PROCEDURE IS PRINT-RECORDS.
        STOP RUN.
    READ-RECORDS SECTION.
    1.
        OPEN INPUT CARDFILE.
    2.
        READ CARDFILE INTO SORT-RECORD AT END GO TO 3.
        RELEASE SORT-RECORD.
****************************************************************
*THE RELEASE STATEMENT MUST BE USED IN INPUT PROCEDURES FOR    *
*SORT FILES. THE RELEASE STATEMENT INFORMS THE SORT ROUTINES   *
*THAT THE RECORD AREA OF SORT FILE CONTAINS A RECORD TO BE IN- *
*CLUDED IN THE SORT.....                                       *
****************************************************************
```

Figure 12.7 (Cont'd.)

```
     GO TO 2.
 3.
     CLOSE CARDFILE.
 4.
     EXIT.
PRINT-RECORDS SECTION.
 1.
     OPEN OUTPUT PRINTFILE.
 2.
     RETURN SORTFILE RECORD INTO PRINT-RECORD,
         AT END GO TO 3.
     WRITE PRINT-RECORD AFTER ADVANCING 1 LINES.
     GO TO 2.
 3.
     CLOSE PRINTFILE.
 4.
     EXIT.
```

In the output procedure, PRINT-RECORDS, the RETURN statement is used. After the sort routines have finished the sorting, the statements in PRINT-RECORD are performed. The purpose of the RETURN statement is thus to place the sorted records in the sort-record area in sorted order. The first time the RETURN statement is used, the first of the sorted records is placed into SORT-RECORD. The second time the RETURN statement is used, the second of the sorted records is placed into SORT-RECORD. This continues until all the sorted records have been returned and then the AT END statement is performed.

The format of the RETURN statement is

```
RETURN sort-file RECORD[INTO data-name]
    AT END imperative-sentence.
```

If you use the SORT statement and specify input or output procedures, then the procedures names must be section names. If you use the THRU option for the input or output procedures, the computer will perform the specified sections and all sections located between them in the program.

The USING and GIVING options are often useful. For example, we could rewrite our program in figure 12.7 using the SORT statement by changing the PROCEDURE DIVISION to

```
PROCEDURE DIVISION.
 1.
         SORT SORTFILE ON ASCENDING KEY STUDENT-NUMBER
                 OF SORT-RECORD
                 USING CARDFILE,
                 GIVING PRINTFILE.
     STOP RUN.
```

The preceding single statement is equivalent to all the statements in the listing in figure 12.7. Specifically, this statement causes all the records of

CARDFILE to be read and presented to the SORTFILE for sorting. It also presents all the sorted records to PRINTFILE for output.

You can mix the various options of the SORT statement as desired. On the B1700 you can also use the LOCK, RELEASE, and PURGE options. These options cannot be used on the DECSYSTEM-10. Referring back to the format of the SORT statement; we see that

1. The LOCK option makes the specified file a permanent file if it is a file associated with a mass storage device,
2. The RELEASE option releases all main storage used by the specified file for processing its records,
3. The PURGE option removes the file if it is assigned to a mass storage device.

The SORT statement can be used to sort files in ascending or descending order. The SORT statement can also be used to sort a file on two or more keys. For example, suppose that we are processing customer transactions for a bank and wish to sort the transactions by ACCOUNT-NUMBER and within each account to have the transactions sorted by DATE-OF-TRANSACTIONS. To do this, we would create a sort file whose records will include the data items ACCOUNT-NUMBER and DATE-OF-TRANSACTION. Let us suppose that the file to be sorted is called CUSTOMER-FILE and the sort file is called SORTFILE. The statement

```
SORT SORTFILE ON ASCENDING KEY ACCOUNT-NUMBER,
     DATE-OF-TRANSACTION
     USING CUSTOMER-FILE,
     GIVING CUSTOMER-FILE.
```

will sort the records as desired. To sort the same file in ascending order by ACCOUNT-NUMBER and in DESCENDING order by DATE-OF-TRANSACTION, we would write

```
SORT SORTFILE ON ASCENDING KEY ACCOUNT-NUMBER
     ON DESCENDING KEY
     DATE-OF-TRANSACTION,
     USING CUSTOMER-FILE
     GIVING CUSTOMER-FILE.
```

The preceding examples should show you how powerful the SORT statement is on the B1700 and the DECSYSTEM-10. But, a word of caution: The SORT statement can be used to sort files of very large size and on a variety of keys. It should be clear that the routines that do the sort must be very general and quite complex. For very simple sorting requirements, a programmer can often write his own sort routines that are far more efficient for sorting files than are the SORT routines. It is largely a matter of opinion whether it is better to write your own sort routines or to use the SORT statement. This observation also applies to the sort subroutines supplied for the IBM-1130 and the IBM-S3.

Summary   The COBOL language as implemented on some computers has the ability to CALL subprograms. Subprograms are compiled separately from the main programs that call them. The format of the CALL statement is

    CALL subprogram-name [USING name-1 [name-2] ...]

where subprogram-name is the name appearing in the PROGRAM-ID paragraph. On the IBM-1130 and the IBM-S3, the name is enclosed in quotation marks. If the USING option is used, then the subprogram must have a PROCEDURE DIVISION header of the form

    PROCEDURE DIVISION USING name-1 [name-2] ...

On the DECSYSTEM-10 a subprogram written in a language other than COBOL can be called from a COBOL main program by use of the ENTER statement whose format is

    ENTER language-name subprogram-name
        [USING name-1 [name-2] ...]

A subprogram cannot call a main program, nor can a subprogram directly or indirectly call itself, although it may call other subprograms. When a subprogram is called, the subprogram has control of the computer. If the subprogram is terminated with the STOP RUN statement, execution of the subprogram will halt, and the main program that called it will also halt. If the subprogram is terminated with an EXIT PROGRAM, then the control of the computer returns to the statement in the main program after the CALL statement for the subprogram.

On the B1700 and the DECSYSTEM-10, a powerful statement is available for sorting files, the SORT statement. The format of the SORT statement is

$$
\text{SORT file-name-1 ON} \left\{ \begin{array}{l} \underline{\text{ASCENDING}} \\ \underline{\text{DESCENDING}} \end{array} \right\} \text{KEY}
$$

    data-name-1 [data-name-2] ...

$$
\left[\text{ON} \left\{ \begin{array}{l} \underline{\text{ASCENDING}} \\ \underline{\text{DESCENDING}} \end{array} \right\} \text{KEY data-name-3} \atop [\text{data-name-4}] ... \right]
$$

$$
\left\{ \begin{array}{l} \underline{\text{INPUT}} \ \underline{\text{PROCEDURE}} \ \text{IS section-name-1} \\ [\underline{\text{THRU}} \ \text{section-name-2}] \\ \underline{\text{USING}} \ \text{file-name-2} \end{array} \right\}
$$

$$
\left\{ \begin{array}{l} \underline{\text{OUTPUT}} \ \underline{\text{PROCEDURE}} \ \underline{\text{IS}} \ \text{section-name-3} \\ [\underline{\text{THRU}} \ \text{section-name-4}] \\ \underline{\text{GIVING}} \ \text{file-name-3} \end{array} \right\}
$$

The ASSIGN clause for a sort-file (file-name-1 in the SORT format) is

    ASSIGN sort-file TO device-name.

The device-name must be DISK for the B1700 and DSK, DSK, DSK for the DECSYSTEM-10. The FILE SECTION entry for a sort-file must be

    SD sort-file.

The RELEASE and RETURN statements are used to place records in a sort file before sorting begins and obtain the records in sorted order after the sorting is finished. The SORT command sorts the records placed in the sort file in order according to the ASCENDING and DESCENDING KEY clauses specified. The keys are presumed to be specified in order from most to least significant. If the USING and GIVING options are used, the effect is to place the records in file-name-2 into file-name-1, sort file-name-1, and to place the sorted records into file-name-3. The INPUT PROCEDURE option determines how the records are placed into file-name-1. The OUTPUT PROCEDURE determines what is done with the sorted records in file-name-1.

Review Questions

1. Consider the following list of data items.

   ```
   LAMB  C  A
   CLOUD  M  L
   MARKS  A
   TANNER  S  D
   DUPRE  L  G
   ```

   Sort this list manually and follow exactly the steps used in SRTPG to see how the subroutine works.

2. Consider the following list of data items.

   a. CLOUD M L
   b. DUPRE L G
   c. LAMB C A
   d. MARKS A
   e. TANNER S D

   Locate the record of this list containing CLOUD M L by using the search method described in project 2 of this chapter.

3. If an item is a parameter in the USING option of a subroutine, where will it be described in the subroutine? Consider files, records of files, and WORKING-STORAGE-type data items.

4. How does the compiler know whether or not it is compiling a subroutine?

Suggested Projects

1. Write a program to create a randomly organized disk file. The records of the file should each contain

   a. Name of person (last name, initials) X(25)
   b. Address X(40)
   c. Balance 9(6)V99

   When the records are read from a card file, they should be stored in the disk file, and the name item of each of the unused records should be filled with HIGH-VALUE. There should be a capacity for 200 records in the file. The program should call a subroutine which then sorts the file in ascending order using the name as the key field. Create 15 data cards to use as input and run the program using them.

2. Write a subroutine that will locate a record of the file described in project 1 after it has been sorted. The method of locating the record follows.

   Suppose we wish to find the record containing the name LAMB CA. We define two data items, BOTTOM and TOP, as numeric items. We give them the initial values 1 and 200, respectively. First we test to see if the record we want is record 1 or record 200. If it is one of them, we are finished. If it is not, then we select a record number, say 100, midway between 1 and 200. We then test to see if the name of this record precedes LAMB CA, follows LAMB CA, or is LAMB CA. Let us assume that the name of this record precedes LAMB CA. Then LAMB CA is between record 100 and record 200. Thus we give BOTTOM the value 100. Next we pick record 150, the record midway between 100 and 200, and compare the name of that record with LAMB CA. We discover that it follows LAMB CA. Therefore, we give TOP the value 150. By continuing in this way, we finally come across the record containing LAMB CA or we discover that the file does not contain a record for which the name is LAMB CA. It is important to remember that the file must be sorted for this method to work.

   Write a program similar to project 1 of this chapter to create the sorted file. Assume the cards of the file are sorted when they are read, if you wish. The program should print a list of the card file, and it should find one record (of your choice) in the file and print its record number. It should try to locate a record not in the file and print the number returned in that case. The location of the record is to be found by a subroutine; if it cannot find the requested record, it should return the number -1. Run your program with 15 data cards.

3. There are two methods to calculate the yearly depreciation for an asset:

   a. straight-line method
   b. sum-of-years digits method

   Suppose that COST denotes the original asset value, N denotes the estimated number of use-life years for the asset, and SCRAP denotes the estimated scrap value for the asset after its full use-life of N years. The two methods of calculating the yearly depreciation for an asset follow.

   a. straight-line method

      ```
      DEPRECIATION-PER-YEAR = (COST - SCRAP) / N
      ```

      The depreciation after M years is M $*$ DEPRECIATION-PER-YEAR.

   b. sum-of-years digit method

      The depreciation after M years is P $*$ (COST $-$ SCRAP)/Q. Q = N(N + 1)/2 and P = N $-$ M. For example, if the uselife N is 20, and we want to find the depreciation through the fifth year, then Q is 20(20 + 1)/2, or 210, and P is 15.

   Write a COBOL program and two subroutines for both methods of calculating depreciation. The main program reads an input card file in which each card contains

Card column	Item description	Type
1	method indicator	9
2–21	asset name	X(20)

22–26	asset code	X(5)
27–32	cost code	9(4)V99
33–38	scrap value	9(4)V99
39–41	use-life	999

Each time a card is read, the main program determines the type of depreciation method to use. The main program prints a table showing for each year from 1 through N, the depreciation, the carrying value (COST − total depreciation as of that year), and total depreciation as of that year. The subroutines are called to find the depreciation and total depreciation (as of that year) for each year. The method code should be a 1 or 2, and, if the code is neither of these, the program should print an error message. Run the program with at least two cards.

4. Rewrite project 5 of Chapter 9 in the form of a subprogram. Run it with a main program and compute the square roots of 10, 100, and 1,000.

5. Another method for calculating the depreciation of an asset is the declining-balance method. In this method

```
DEPRECIATION–PER–YEAR
   = DEPRECIATION–RATE * CARRYING–VALUE.
```

where

```
DEPRECIATION–RATE
   = 1 − (SCRAP–VALUE / COST) ** (1 / USE–LIFE).
```

The exponent in the second formula is a fraction. For example, if the USE-LIFE is 10, then the exponent will be 0.1.

Since COBOL does not permit fractional exponents, you must use a subprogram written in another language, such as FORTRAN, to calculate the DEPRECIATION-RATE needed in the declining-balance method. Use the information given in project 3 of this chapter to calculate the depreciation using the declining-balance method.

Due to technical problems that arise when using FORTRAN subprograms with COBOL programs on the IBM-1130, we do not advise trying to do this project on that computer.

6. Write a COBOL program to simulate the following game. The game is played in a casino. Anyone can play against the casino to win money. The maximum bet is $5,000. The rules for the game follow.

   a. Each outcome is determined by throwing two dice.
   b. If the sum of the faces is 12, you win three times the amount of your bet.
   c. If the sum of the faces is 2, you win twice the amount of your bet.
   d. If the sum of the faces is 11, you win only the amount of your bet.
   e. If the sum of the faces is 10, you throw the dice again. If you throw a sum of 12, 2, or 11, you win the amount of your bet.
   f. If the sum of the faces is other than 12, 2, 11, or 10, you lose your bet.

   To write the program, you must generate random numbers from 1 through 6. Most computers have a random-number generator that can be used with FORTRAN programs. Write your program to show how much money you would win or lose on 30 bets if you used one of two strategies. One strategy is to bet half your available money each time you bet. The other strategy is to bet half your available money after you lose, but bet only one-quarter of your available money if you win. Assume that you start with $1,000.

There is not a random-number generator provided with FORTRAN on the IBM-1130 or the IBM-S3. However, your instructor can probably provide a subprogram to generate random numbers for you.

7. A university has three schools, each of which has two departments. The registrar's office has decided to keep student information on cards as follows:

Card column	*Content*
1–3	Card 1: grade-point average
4–19	course name
20–39	student name
40–54	instructor name
55–68	department name
69–80	school name
1–7	Card 2: course code
8–17	phone number with area code of student
18–47	student address

Write a COBOL program to read the student records, store them in a direct disk file, and call the following subprograms.

a. Call a subprogram to print a listing of all students with a grade-point average of 2.75 or higher. The list should be printed in descending order according to grade-point average.

b. Call a subprogram to print lists for each of the schools. The lists for each school are sorted into departments. The list for each department is an alphabetical list of the students registered in the department.

c. Call a subprogram to list for each department all the students enrolled in courses for each instructor. Also compute the average grade point of the students of each instructor.

8. One general purpose sorting algorithm is the bubble sort. The bubble sort interchanges only adjacent records at each step. Thus, if two records that are six records apart are placed in order by the bubble sort, five interchanges of adjacent pairs are necessary to accomplish the task. Obviously, one interchange of items, the two records involved, could accomplish the same goal. A more efficient general-purpose sorting algorithm is the *shell sort,* which is an extended version of the bubble sort. Its advantage over the bubble sort is that the initial phases of the sort swap items that are out of order and that are far apart. Figure 12.8 is a flowchart for the shell sort.

Your project is to write a program implementing the shell sort and to run your program with 50 numbers. Print the original list of numbers and the sorted list of numbers. Let N be the number or items $X_1, X_2, \ldots, X_N$ to be sorted. Note that this sort places the items in descending order. Also, note that all data items, D, L, and K, are integers with no decimal places.

Figure 12.8 Flowchart of shell sort for project 8 of Chapter 12.

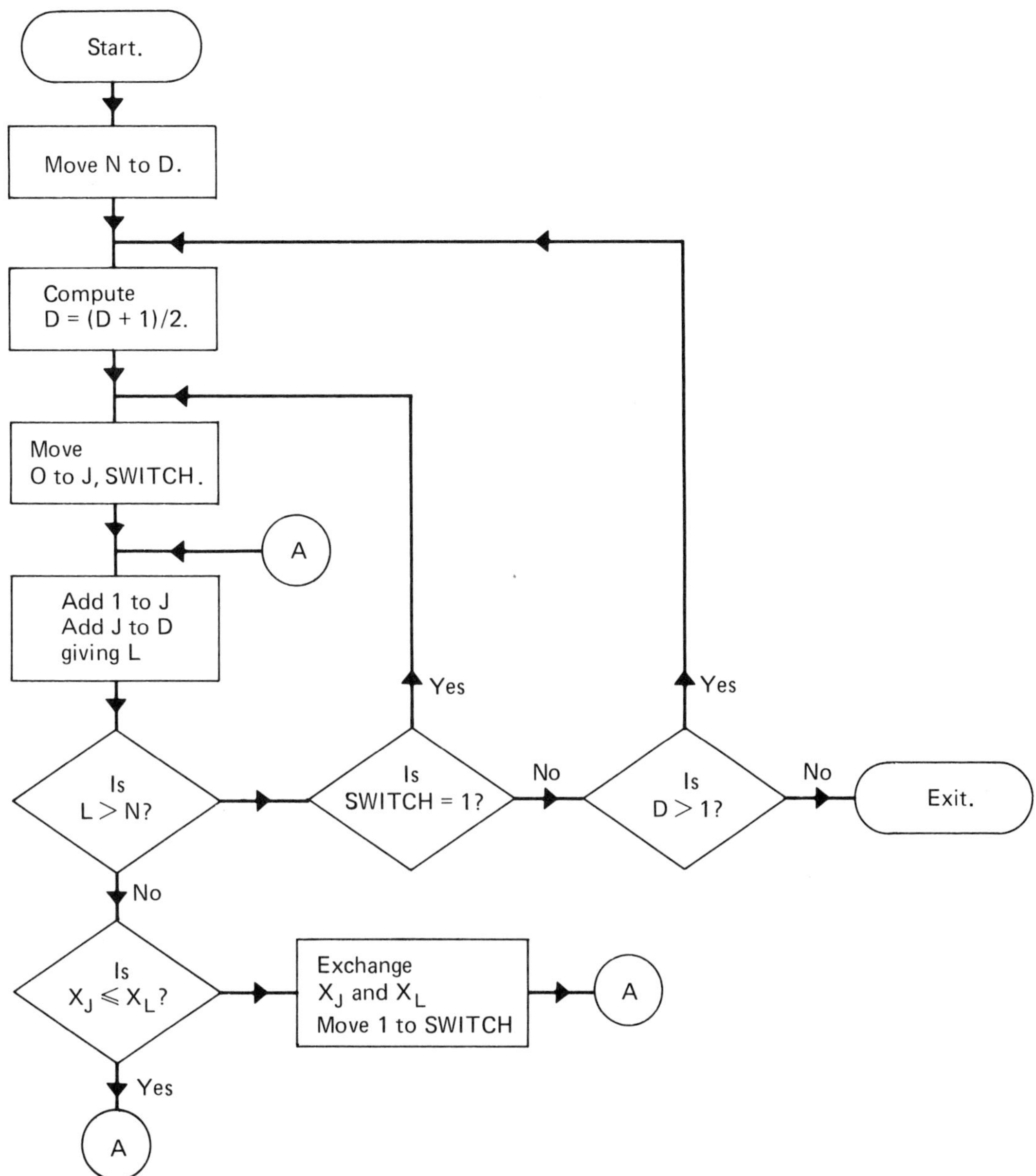

Programmer Goals and Some Sample Programs

Approaching A Programming Problem

There is probably no one best way to tackle a programming challenge. If there were, then there would be many more good programmers and many more good programs than there are. There are however, a few tips about writing good COBOL programs that you should keep in mind.

1. Define the problem precisely. Determine the information to be processed. Determine what must be done with the information. If you must create a file that will be the basis for future work, then you must decide what information will be stored in the file. When it is likely that the information in the file will expand, you must decide if an expansion area should be provided now or if the file will have to be recreated at a later date in order to provide for the necessary expansions. A primary consideration is how the file should be organized. For example, if records are added continually to the file and the file is large, then it may not be feasible to keep the file in sorted order. Sorting a large file could take hours on a computer. It may be wiser to allow the file to have a few unsorted records at its end, with most of the records in the file in sorted order. By writing programs that process the file with this type of organization, you could save many hours of sorting. Then, as the overhead in keeping track of the unsorted records became excessive, the file could be sorted to restore program efficiency. Our first sample Application Program will show how to work with such files on an IBM-1130.

2. After you have decided what information is to be processed and how it is to be stored, you can then decide how to program the processing steps. Sketch the major steps in the processing on a rough flowchart. Experienced programmers will try to make each major step as separate as possible from the other steps in the program. This helps to clarify the programming steps and also makes it easier to alter any step should it be necessary to do so in the future. It is always disheartening to discover that a program to be updated has been written so that a change in one of the major program steps requires altering several other parts of the program.

3. When you have the major outlines of the program in mind, you can begin to write the program. If possible, you should write and test each major part of the program separately. For example, the program might begin by adding records to an existing file. As each record is added, it must be checked against existing records to prevent storing duplicate records. Then it might process the records in some fashion. It is possible to write and check the storing phase of the program before beginning the remainder of the program.

4. Write all programs to guard against the "impossible" errors. Assume that if an error can happen, then it probably will some day. COBOL provides many ways for anticipating errors and handling them. The INVALID KEY and ON SIZE ERROR clauses are good examples of attempts to *force* the programmer to guard against errors. Less evident attempts include the class tests to see if the content of an alphanumeric field is alphabetic or numeric. Keep in mind that key-punching errors do occur despite all efforts to guard against them. If a program reads a supposedly numeric field from cards and the field contains nonnumeric characters, it is quite likely that an execution time error will result and the computer will halt the execution of the program. Simply by using the class test first, a program could always prevent such errors.

To summarize: Write all programs so that when the impossible error occurs, your files will be saved and recovery can be effected.

Tips on Style in COBOL Programs

The success of many programmers depends on both their ability to analyze a programming challenge and on their ability to write good programs that implement their ideas. We have just discussed how to approach a programming challenge. Here are some suggestions about how to reflect this approach in the program itself.

1. It is probable that the files used in one program will also be used in other programs. A standard file description and record description should be established for the use of all programs, which will make the programs easier to understand. It is a good idea to place the record description for the file in the COBOL Source Library so that it can be copied into various programs.

2. Make all names meaningful. The name of a data item should indicate its content or its use in a program. This saves a lot of time when you are trying to understand a program written by another person or when you are reading a program that you wrote some time ago.

3. Divide the PROCEDURE DIVISION into sections. Each section should have a separate and distinct purpose. Avoid statements that transfer control to the middle of a section rather than to the beginning.

4. Avoid placing more than one statement on a line in a COBOL program. Do not split names or numeric literals between lines. Split nonnumeric literals between lines only when the literal is too long for one line.

5. If main storage is in short supply, consider the use of the REDEFINES clause. If files are present that will not be open at the same time, use the SAME AREA clause.

6. Make all records for files as small as possible. This will use less main storage and decrease the time required for the input-output operations for the files. If your computer permits blocking of records, use the BLOCK CONTAINS clause to make the BLOCK size as large as possible. This will often increase execution speed dramatically.

7. Avoid using the ALTER statement.

8. Remember to specify COMPUTATIONAL usage for data items that will be used in frequent computations. Remember that using indexing for arrays is much faster than using subscripts.

9. Document the program extensively. Explain what the program does at each crucial step; and if the program statements are hard to follow, be sure to explain their purpose.
10. At the program beginning, explain the goals of the program. Describe the form of the input and the form of the output. If you anticipate that changes will be needed in the program to update it, then list the information that will be crucial in making changes.
11. Prepare a system flowchart for the program and a program flowchart showing the steps in the program.

Sample Application Programs

The first application program is written for the IBM-1130. It uses many special subprograms supplied by IBM for use on the 1130 to create and maintain a disk file. Figure 13.1 contains the flowcharts for the SALES-RECORDS program, and figure 13.2 shows the listing for the SALES-RECORDS program.

The file is organized so that we can use the IBM-supplied subprogram QFIND. Thus the file has a header record, a block of sorted records, a block of unsorted records, and finally a block of unused records. The file contains the sales records for our company, and each sales record contains an invoice number, the name of the company buying our product, the date of sale, the product name, the product number, and the unit price on a punched card.

Our program has five capabilities: creating the initial file, adding records to the file, sorting the file, deleting records from the file, and listing the content of the file.

Creating the File

The creation of the file requires three steps. First, the sales cards are read into the disk file starting at the second record position in the disk file. (We start at the second record position because the header record is the first record position.)

The second step is to initialize the values in the header record. The header record contains the number of the last record in the sorted portion of the file, the number of the last record in the unsorted portion of the file, the last date records were added, and the last date the file was sorted. When the file is created, the two record numbers are identical, and the two dates are identical.

The third step is to sort the records in the file. The records are sorted on the basis of three key fields. The first is the name of the company, the second is the date of the sale, and the third is the invoice number. The sorting routine was described in Chapter 12.

Adding Records

This section of the program is short. The ADDITIONS section of the program is used to add the new sales cards, and the header record is corrected to give the new value to the number of the last record in the unsorted portion of the file.

Figure 13.1 Flowcharts for SALES-RECORDS program illustrating the creation and maintenance of a disk file on the IBM-1130.

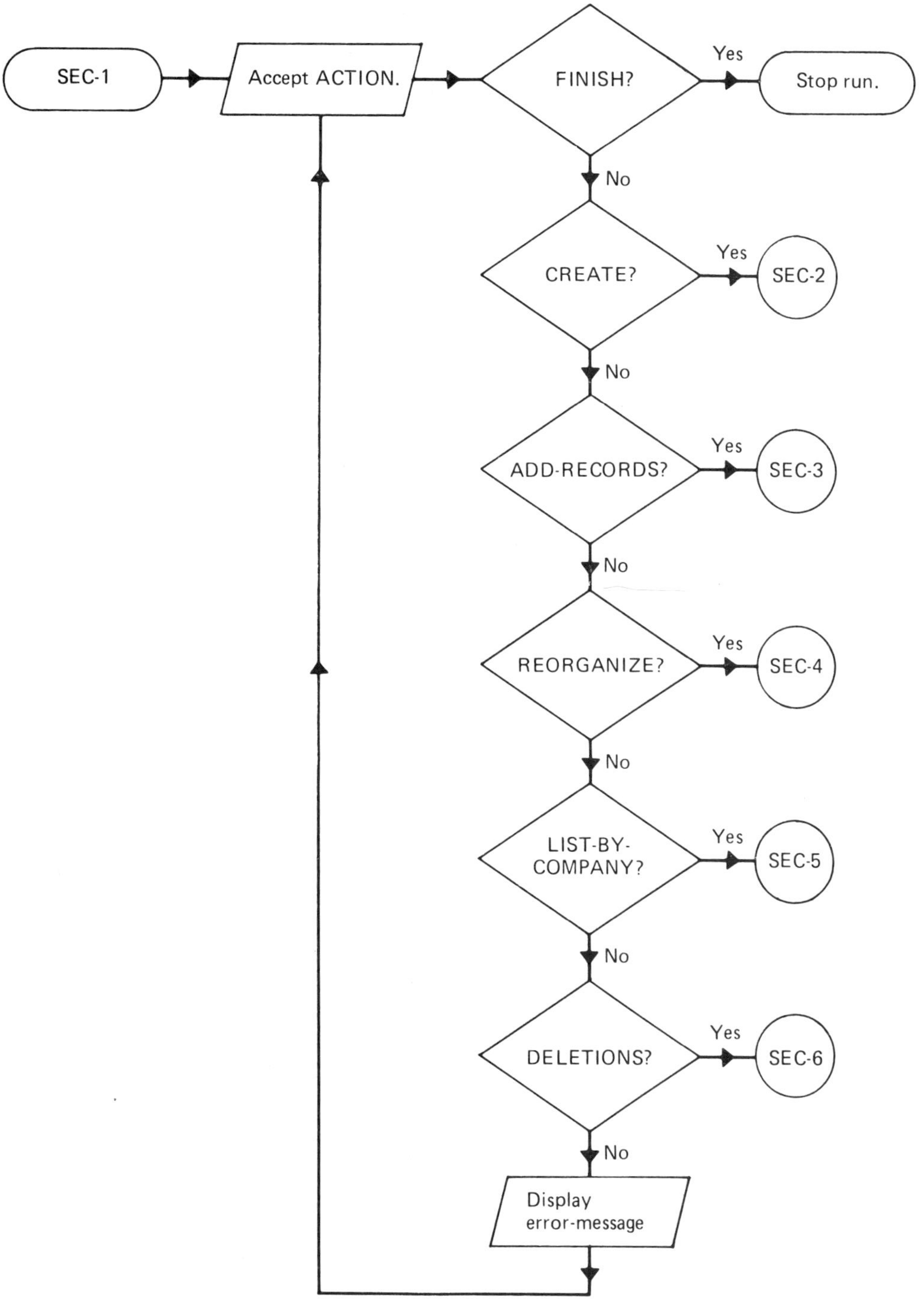

Figure 13.1 (Cont'd.)

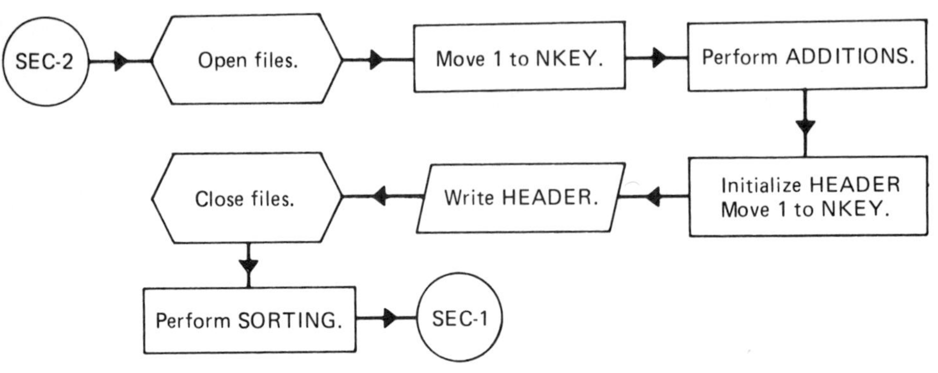

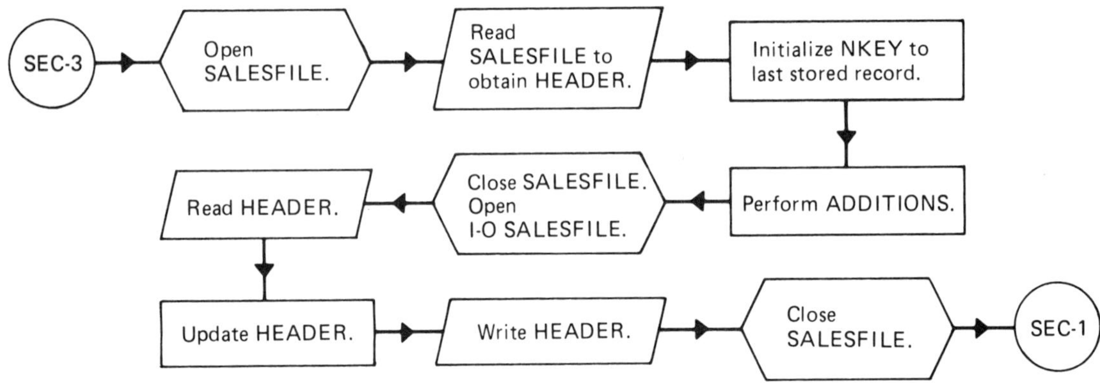

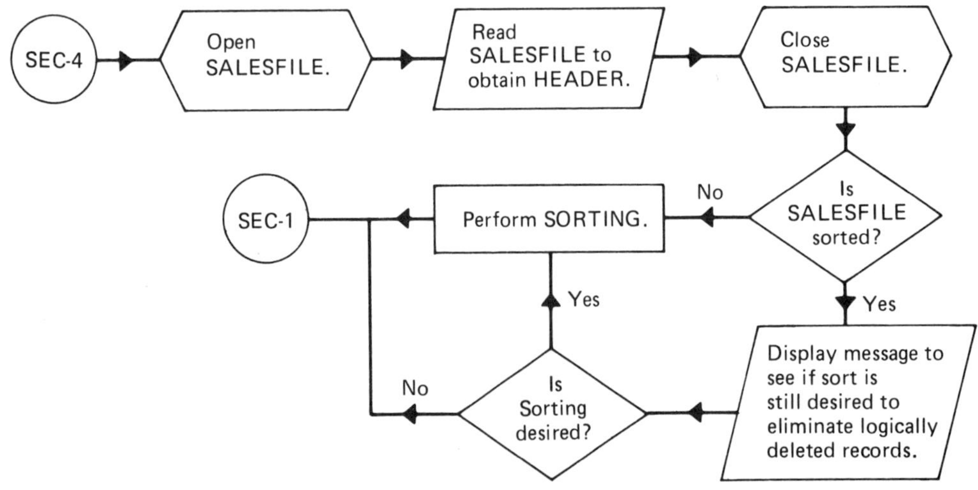

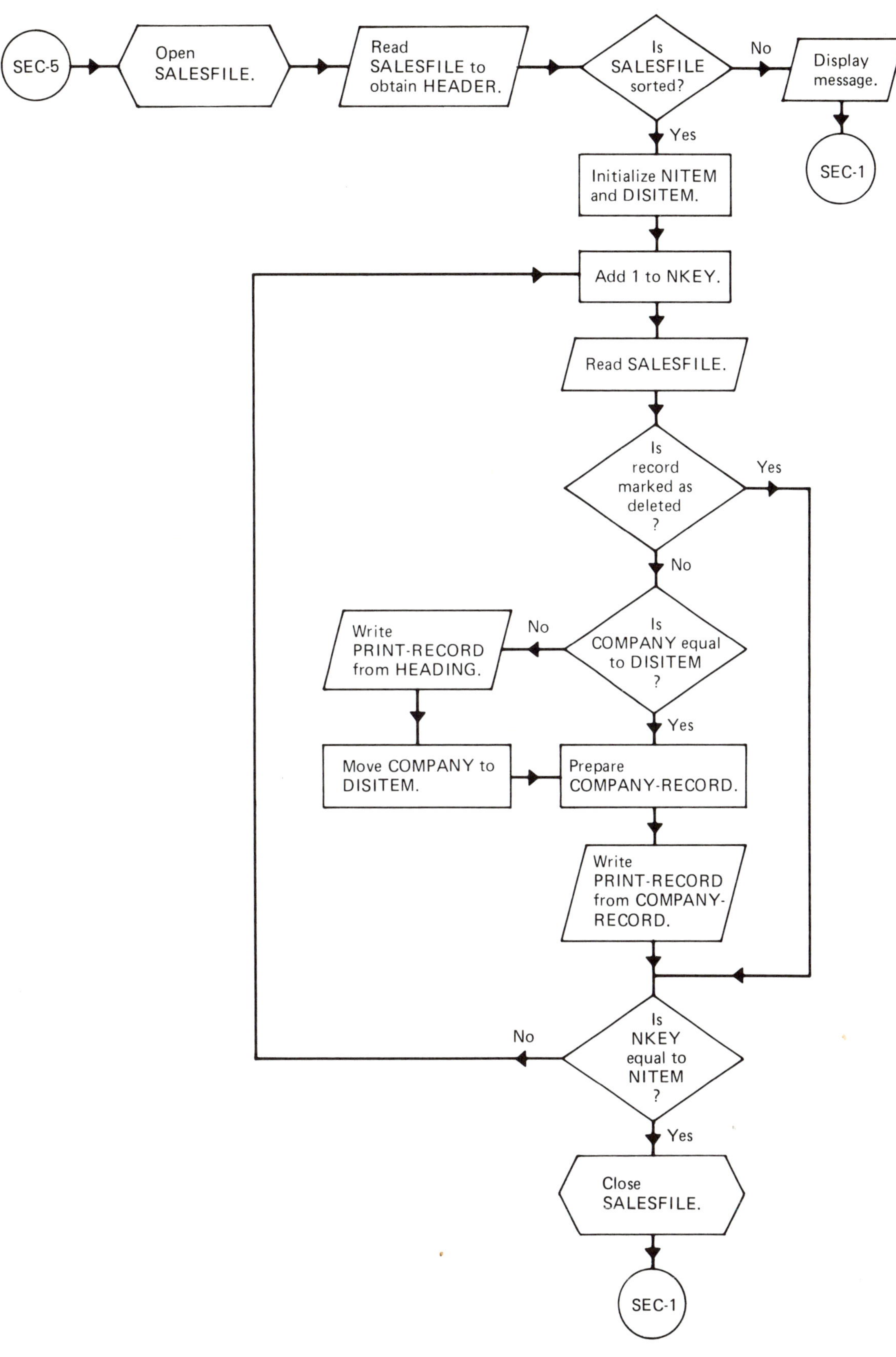

SEC-5
Open SALESFILE.
Read SALESFILE to obtain HEADER.
Is SALESFILE sorted?
No
Display message.
SEC-1
Yes
Initialize NITEM and DISITEM.
Add 1 to NKEY.
Read SALESFILE.
Is record marked as deleted ?
Yes
No
Is COMPANY equal to DISITEM ?
No
Write PRINT-RECORD from HEADING.
Move COMPANY to DISITEM.
Yes
Prepare COMPANY-RECORD.
Write PRINT-RECORD from COMPANY-RECORD.
Is NKEY equal to NITEM ?
No
Yes
Close SALESFILE.
SEC-1

Figure 13.1 (Cont'd.)

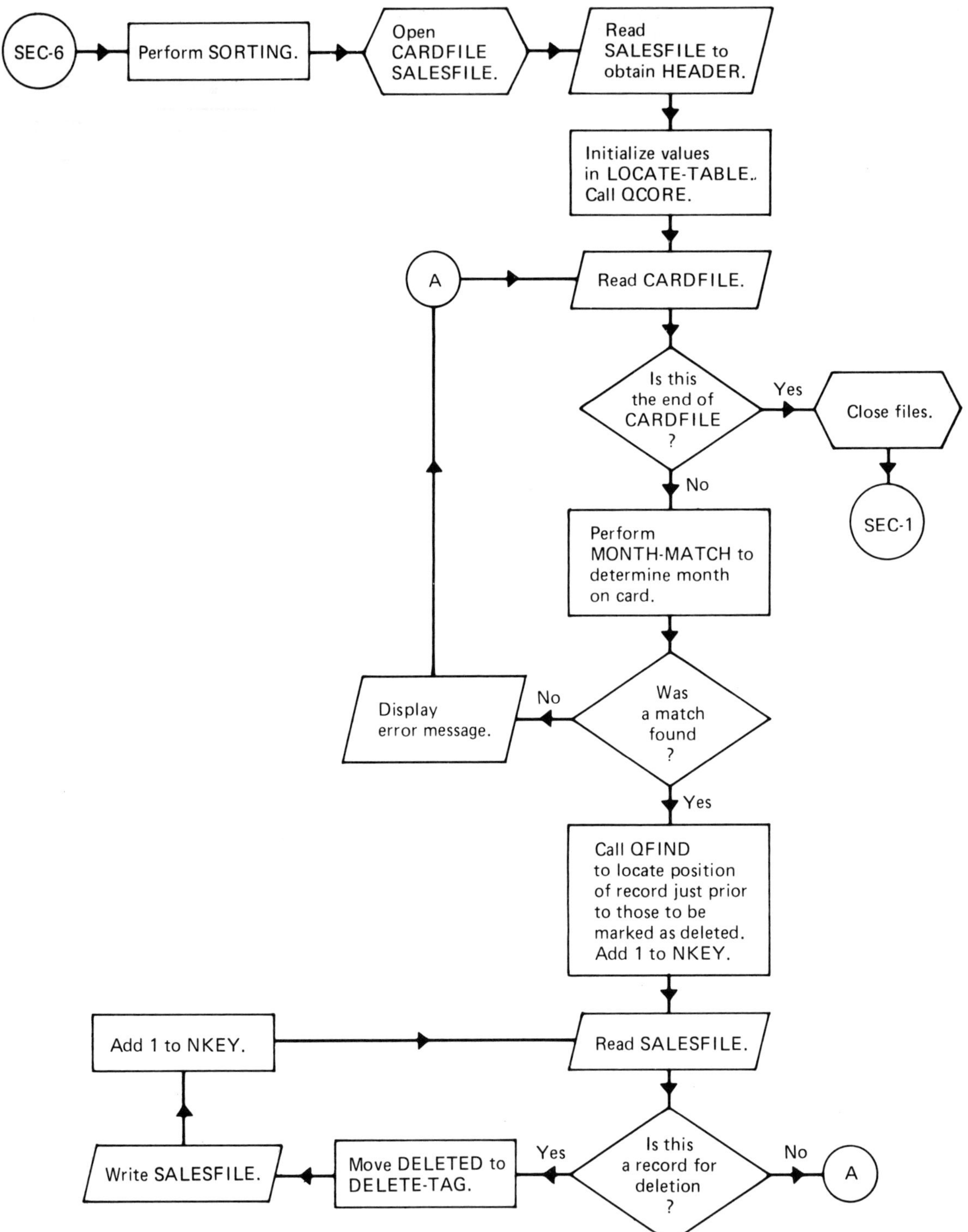

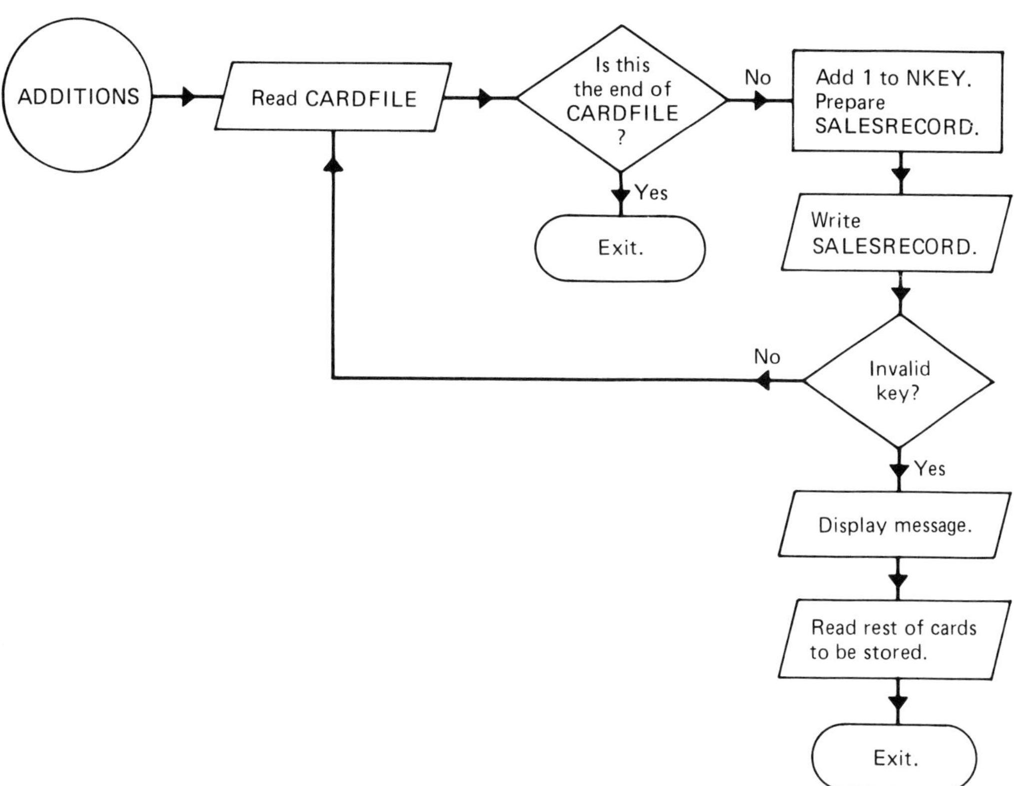
ADDITIONS
Read CARDFILE
Is this the end of CARDFILE ?
No
Yes
Exit.
Add 1 to NKEY. Prepare SALESRECORD.
Write SALESRECORD.
Invalid key?
No
Yes
Display message.
Read rest of cards to be stored.
Exit.

Figure 13.1 (Cont'd.)

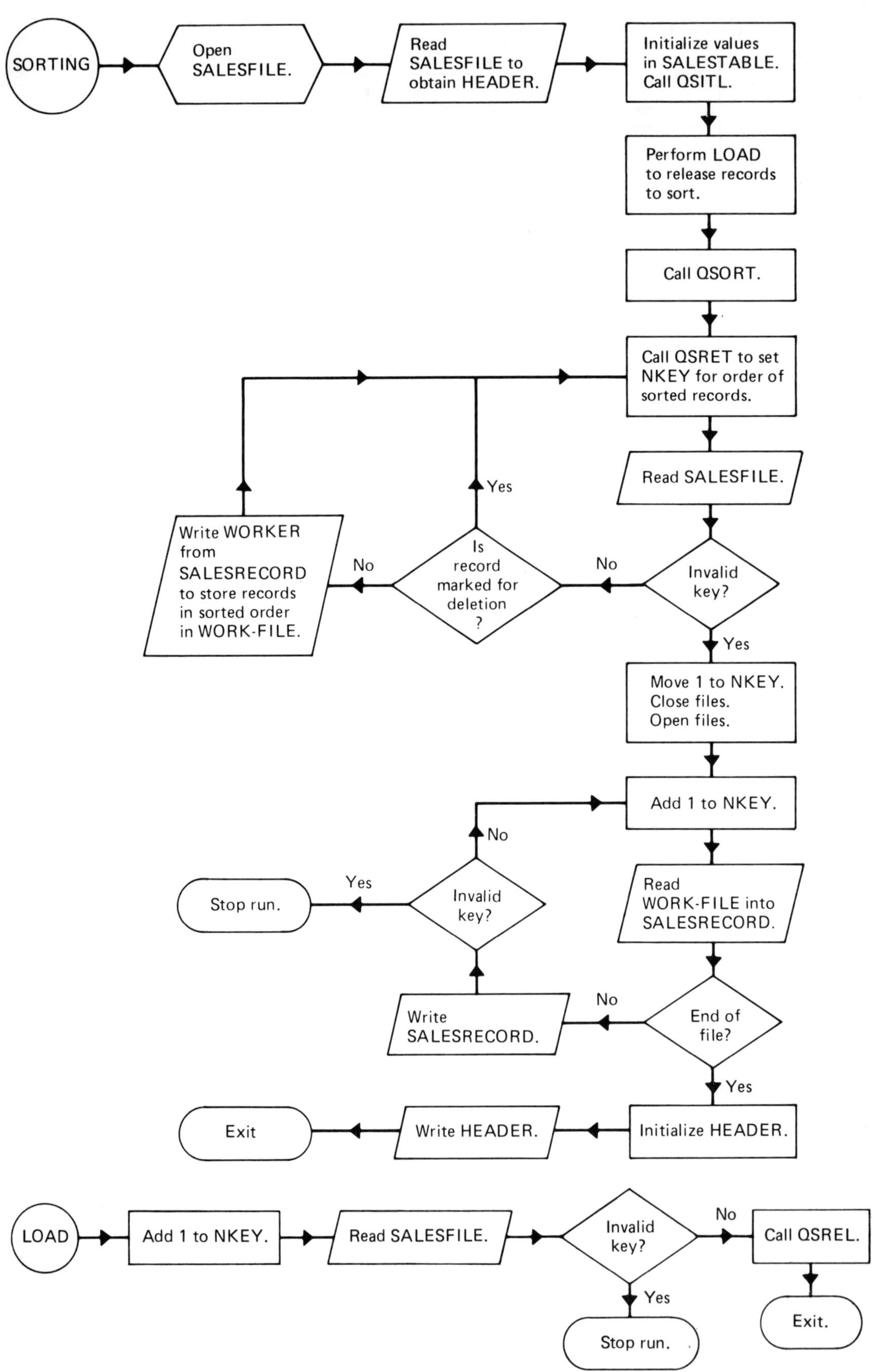

Figure 13.2 Listing of SALES-RECORDS program illustrating the creation and maintenance of a disk file on the IBM-1130.

```
// COBOL
*LIST,EJCT
      IDENTIFICATION DIVISION.
      PROGRAM-ID. SALES-RECORDS.
      AUTHOR. DUPLISSEY-KHAILANY.
      REMARKS.
          THIS PROGRAM COMBINES SEVERAL STANDARD FILE OPERATIONS.
          THESE OPERATIONS WOULD NORMALLY BE HANDLED BY SEVERAL
          SMALLER PROGRAMS.  IN THAT EVENT IT WOULD BE IMPORTANT TO
          STORE FILE AND RECORD DESCRIPTIONS IN THE COBOL LIBRARY
          TO ENSURE A STANDARD DESCRIPTION AND SELECTION OF DATA NAMES.
           TO SAVE SPACE IN THE TEXT, THE PROGRAMS ARE COMBINED.
          THIS PROGRAM CAN CERTAINLY BE IMPROVED IF GREATER EFFICIENCY
          IS DESIRED AND SOME OF ITS APPROACHES TO THE PROBLEM
          ARE UNREALISTIC.

      ENVIRONMENT DIVISION.
      CONFIGURATION SECTION.
      SOURCE-COMPUTER. IBM-1130.
      OBJECT-COMPUTER. IBM-1130.
      SPECIAL-NAMES.
          COPY SPECNAMES.
      INPUT-OUTPUT SECTION.
      FILE-CONTROL.
      ****************************************************************
      *****RECORDS ARE STORED IN THE SORTED PORTION OF SALESFILE    *
      *****AS SORTED ON THREE KEY FIELDS. THE FIRST IS THE NAME OF THE *
      *****COMPANY, THE SECOND IS THE DATE OF THE SALE, AND THE THIRD  *
      *****IS THE INVOICE NUMBER.....                              *
      ****************************************************************
          SELECT SALESFILE, ASSIGN TO DF-2-1000-X, ACCESS IS
          RANDOM, ACTUAL KEY IS NKEY.
      ****************************************************************
      *****WORK-FILE IS USED ONLY IN THE SORTING OPERATIONS.       *
      ****************************************************************
          SELECT WORK-FILE, ASSIGN TO DF-3-1000-X ACCESS IS SEQUENTIAL.
          SELECT CARD-FILE, ASSIGN TO RD-2501, RESERVE 1.
          SELECT PRINT-FILE, ASSIGN TO PR-1403, RESERVE 1.

      DATA DIVISION.
      FILE SECTION.
      FD  CARD-FILE   LABEL RECORDS OMITTED.
      ****************************************************************
      *****CARD-IN CONTAINS THE ORIGINAL INVOICE INFORMATION.      *
      ****************************************************************
      01  CARD-IN.
          02 INVOICE-NUMBER PIC 9(5).
          02 COMPANY PIC X(30).
      ****************************************************************
      *****DATE IS A RESERVED WORD IN IBM 1130 COBOL.              *
      ****************************************************************
          02 DAT   PIC 9(6).
          02 PRODUCT PIC X(20).
          02 PRODUCT-NUMBER PIC 9(4).
          02 UNIT-PRICE PIC 9(4)V99.
      ****************************************************************
      *****DELETE-RECORD IS USED TO SPECIFY THE RECORDS TO BE DELETED. *
      *****THUS, CARD-FILE IS USED FOR TWO PURPOSES. HENCE TWO RECORDS.*
      ****************************************************************
      01  DELETE-RECORD.
          02 CMPY PIC X(30).
          02 FILLER PIC X(10).
          02 MONTH PIC X(10).
          02 YEAR PIC 99.
```

Figure 13.2 (Cont'd.)

```
     ************************************************************************
     *****DATE OF YEAR IS ONLY LAST TWO DIGITS                            *
     ************************************************************************
          02 FILLER PIC X(19).
     FD   PRINT-FILE LABEL RECORDS OMITTED.
     01   PRINTE PIC X(121).

     FD   SALESFILE LABEL RECORDS STANDARD.
     ************************************************************************
     *****THE HEADER RECORD IS USED WITH QFIND TO LOCATE RECORDS.       *
     ************************************************************************
     01   HEADER.
          02 NO-LAST-SEQ-REC PIC 9(5) COMP.
          02 NO-LAST-NONSEQ-REC PIC 9(5) COMP.
          02 DATE-LAST-ADDITIONS PIC 9(6).
          02 DATE-LAST-SORT PIC 9(6).
          02 FILLER PIC X(17).

     01   SALESRECORD.
          02 DELETE-TAG    PIC X.
          02 C    PIC X(15).
          02 D    PIC 9(6) COMP.
          02 I    PIC 9(5) COMP.
          02 P    PIC X(10).
          02 PN   PIC 9(4) COMP.
          02 PR   PIC 9(4)V99 COMP.

     FD   WORK-FILE LABEL RECORDS STANDARD.
     01   WORKER PIC X(33).

     WORKING-STORAGE SECTION.
     77   ACTION PIC X(20).
          88 CREATE VALUE 'CREATE'.
          88 ADD-RECORDS VALUE 'ADD RECORDS'.
          88 DELETIONS VALUE 'DELETE RECORDS'.
          88 REORGANIZE VALUE 'SORT FILE'.
          88 LIST-BY-COMPANY VALUE 'LIST BY COMPANY'.
          88 FINISH VALUE 'FINISH'.
     77   TODAY PIC 9(6)  VALUE 0.
     77   SUBCPT PIC S9(4) COMP.
     77   MKEY PIC 9(5) COMP.
     77   NKEY PIC S9(5) COMP.
     77   NITEM PIC S9(5) COMP.
     77   NO-20 PIC 99 COMP VALUE 20.
     77   NO-30 PIC 99 COMP VALUE 30.
     77   DISITEM PIC X(50).
     77   DATE-IS-STORED    PIC 9 COMP VALUE 0.



     01    DOUBLE-DUMMY PIC 9(5) COMP VALUE 32767.
     01   DUMMI  REDEFINES DOUBLE-DUMMY.
          02 FILLER PIC X.
          02 DELETED PIC X.
     ************************************************************************
     *****        DELETED CONTAINS HEXIDECIMAL /8000.                    *
     ************************************************************************
     01   TAKE-DATE-APART.
          02 T1 PIC 99.
          02 T2 PIC 99.
          02 T3 PIC 99.
     01   T REDEFINES TAKE-DATE-APART PIC 9(6).
     01   NOMINAL-KEY COMP.
          02 COMPANY-NAME PIC X(15).
          02 SALE-DATE PIC 9(6).
          02 INVOICE PIC 9(5).
```

```
 01   HEADR  PIC X(120) VALUE  'INVOICE-NUMBER  COMPANY
-    '              DATE        PRODUCT                  PRODUCT-NUMB
-    'ER    UNIT-PRICE   '.
 01   COMPANY-REC.
      02 P1 PIC 9(5).
      02 FILLER PIC X(12) VALUE SPACES.
      02 P2 PIC X(30).
      02 FILLER PIC X(3) VALUE SPACES.
      02 P3 PIC 99.
      02 FILLER PIC X VALUE '/'.
      02 P4 PIC 99.
      02 FILLER PIC X VALUE '/'.
      02 P5 PIC 99.
      02 FILLER PIC X(3) VALUE SPACES.
      02 P6 PIC X(20).
      02 FILLER PIC X(3) VALUE SPACES.
      02 P7 PIC 9(4).
      02 FILLER PIC X(13) VALUE SPACES.
      02 P8 PIC $$$99.99.

 ******************************************************************
 *****SALESTABLE IS USED IN SORTING SALESFILE IN                 *
 *****SEQUENTIAL ORDER BY COMPANY NAME AND DATE OF TRANSACTION    *
 *****AND INVOICE NUMBER.....                                     *
 ******************************************************************
 01   SALESTABLE  COMP.
      02 NO-OF PIC 9(5).
      02  START-OF-KEY-1 PIC 9(5).
      02 TYPE-1 PIC S9(5).
 ******************************************************************
 *****KEYFIELD 1 IS THE COMPANY NAME                             *
 ******************************************************************
      02 START-OF-KEY-2 PIC 9(5).
      02 TYPE-2 PIC S9(5).
 ******************************************************************
 *****   KEYFIELD 2 IS THE DATE OF SALE                          *
 ******************************************************************
      02 START-OF-KEY-3 PIC 9(5).
      02 TYPE-3 PIC S9(5).
 ******************************************************************
 *****       KEYFIELD 3 IS THE INVOICE NUMBER.                   *
 ******************************************************************
      02 END-OF-TABLE PIC 9(5) COMP VALUE 0.


 01   LOCATE-TABLE COMP.
 ******************************************************************
 *****KEYFIELD IS COMPANY,DATE,INVOICE COMBINED                  *
 ******************************************************************
      02 KEY-START PIC 9(4) VALUE IS 2.
      02 KEY-LENGTH PIC 9(4) VALUE IS 18.
      02 FIRST-SEQ-REC PIC 9(5) VALUE IS 2.
      02 LAST-SEQ-REC PIC 9(5).
      02 LAST-NON-SEQ-REC PIC 9(5).


 01   MONTH-NAMES.
      02 FILLER PIC X(10) VALUE    'JANUARY    '.
      02 FILLER PIC X(10) VALUE    'FEBRUARY   '.
      02 FILLER PIC X(10) VALUE    'MARCH      '.
      02 FILLER PIC X(10) VALUE    'APRIL      '.
      02 FILLER PIC X(10) VALUE    'MAY        '.
      02 FILLER PIC X(10) VALUE    'JUNE       '.
      02 FILLER PIC X(10) VALUE    'JULY       '.
      02 FILLER PIC X(10) VALUE    'AUGUST     '.
      02 FILLER PIC X(10) VALUE    'SEPTEMBER  '.
      02 FILLER PIC X(10) VALUE    'OCTOBER    '.
      02 FILLER PIC X(10) VALUE    'NOVEMBER   '.
      02 FILLER PIC X(10) VALUE    'DECEMBER   '.
```

Figure 13.2 (Cont'd.)

```
   01   TABLE-OF-MONTHS REDEFINES MONTH-NAMES.
        02 MONTHS OCCURS 12 PIC X(10).


   PROCEDURE DIVISION.
   SEC-1 SECTION.
   1.
        GO TO 2 OF SEC-1 DEPENDING ON DATE-IS-STORED.
        ACCEPT TODAY FROM DATE.
        MOVE 1 TO DATE-IS-STORED.
   2.
        ACCEPT ACTION.
        IF FINISH, STOP RUN.
        IF CREATE, GO TO SEC-2.
        IF ADD-RECORDS GO TO SEC-3.
        IF REORGANIZE GO TO SEC-4.
        IF LIST-BY-COMPANY GO TO SEC-5.
        IF DELETIONS, GO TO SEC-6.
        DISPLAY 'THE FOLLOWING ACTION IS NOT RECOGNIZED-- ', ACTION.
        STOP RUN.
   ************************************************************************
   ************************************************************************
   ************************************************************************
    SEC-2 SECTION.
   ************************************************************************
   *     THIS SECTION CREATES SALESFILE INITIALLY.....
   ************************************************************************
    1.
        OPEN INPUT CARD-FILE OUTPUT SALESFILE.
   ************************************************************************
   *****WE INITIALIZE NKEY SO THE RECORDS WILL BE STORED IN            *
   *****SALESFILE STARTING IN RECORD 2. RECORD 1 IS HEADER.            *
   ************************************************************************
        MOVE 1 TO NKEY.
        PERFORM ADDITIONS.
        DISPLAY 'WITH TODAYS ADDITIONS, FIRST ' NKEY,
        ' RECORDS ARE FILLED INCLUDING HEADER.'
   ************************************************************************
   *****ADDITIONS DONE. TIME TO INITIALIZE HEADER RECORD.....          *
   ************************************************************************
        MOVE NKEY TO NO-LAST-SEQ-REC, NO-LAST-NONSEQ-REC.
        MOVE TODAY TO DATE-LAST-ADDITIONS, DATE-LAST-SORT.
        MOVE 1 TO NKEY.
        WRITE HEADER INVALID STOP RUN.
        CLOSE SALESFILE CARD-FILE.
   ************************************************************************
   *****FILE IS CREATED. RECORDS ARE IN ORIGINAL UNSORTED ORDER.....*
   ************************************************************************
    2.
   ************************************************************************
   *****NOW WE SORT SALESFILE.....                                     *
   ************************************************************************
        PERFORM SORTING.
        DISPLAY 'SORT COMPLETED'.
   ************************************************************************
   *****GO SEE IF MORE IS TO BE DONE.....                              *
   ************************************************************************
        GO TO SEC-1.
   ************************************************************************
   ************************************************************************
   ************************************************************************
    SEC-3 SECTION.
    COMMENT.
        NOTE THIS SECTION ADDS RECORDS TO THE UNSORTED ADDITIONS AREA
        OF SALESFILE.
```

```
1.
     OPEN INPUT CARD-FILE, SALESFILE.
     MOVE 1 TO NKEY.
     READ SALESFILE INVALID STOP RUN.
*********************************************************************
*****TO ADD RECORDS, WE MUST KNOW POSITION OF LAST RECORD IN FILE*
*****AND THIS NUMBER IS PLACED IN NKEY. ADDITIONS WILL PLACE     *
*****NEW RECORDS STARTING AT NKEY+1.....                         *
*********************************************************************
     MOVE NO-LAST-NONSEQ-REC TO NKEY.
     CLOSE SALESFILE.
     OPEN OUTPUT SALESFILE.
     PERFORM ADDITIONS.
*********************************************************************
*****SAVE VALUE OF NKEY WHICH IS NUMBER OF LAST RECORD IN FILE   *
*****NOW AND REVISE HEADER RECORD.....                           *
*********************************************************************
     MOVE NKEY TO MKEY.
     CLOSE SALESFILE.
     OPEN I-O SALESFILE.
     MOVE 1 TO NKEY.
     READ SALESFILE INVALID STOP RUN.
     MOVE MKEY TO NO-LAST-NONSEQ-REC.
     MOVE TODAY TO DATE-LAST-ADDITIONS.
     WRITE HEADER INVALID STOP RUN.
     CLOSE CARD-FILE SALESFILE.
     DISPLAY 'ADDITIONS COMPLETED. FILE HAS ' MKEY 'RECORDS.'.
*********************************************************************
*****ALL DONE. GO SEE IF MORE IS TO BE DONE.....                 *
*********************************************************************
     GO TO SEC-1.
*********************************************************************
*********************************************************************
*********************************************************************
  SEC-4 SECTION.
  COMMENT.
     NOTE THIS SECTION WILL CHECK TO SEE IF FILE NEEDS SORTING.
     IF IT DOES, THE SORTING SECTION IS PERFORMED.....

1.
     OPEN INPUT SALESFILE.
     MOVE 1 TO NKEY.
     READ SALESFILE INVALID STOP RUN.
     CLOSE SALESFILE.
     IF NO-LAST-SEQ-REC NOT = NO-LAST-NONSEQ-REC
         PERFORM SORTING
         GO TO 2 OF SEC-4.
*********************************************************************
*****SORT NOT NEEDED. TEST GAVE EQUALITY. SEE IF SORT IS STILL   *
*****DESIRED TO PHYSICALLY DELETE RECORDS.....                   *
*********************************************************************
     DISPLAY 'IS THIS SORT TO ELIMINATE DELETED RECORDS'
     UPON CONSOLE.
     DISPLAY 'REPLY WITH YES OR NO.' UPON CONSOLE.
     ACCEPT ACTION FROM CONSOLE.
     IF ACTION = 'NO'
         GO TO SEC-1.
*********************************************************************
*****SORT IS DESIRED TO DELETE RECORDS.....                      *
*********************************************************************
     PERFORM SORTING.
2.
*********************************************************************
*****GO SEE IF MORE IS TO BE DONE.                               *
*********************************************************************
     DISPLAY 'FILE SORTED.'.
     GO TO SEC-1.
*********************************************************************
```

Figure 13.2 (Cont'd.)

```
*************************************************************************
*************************************************************************
  SEC-5 SECTION.
  COMMENT.
     NOTE THIS SECTION LISTS THE CONTENT OF SALESFILE.
  1.
     OPEN INPUT SALESFILE, OUTPUT PRINT-FILE.
     MOVE 1 TO NKEY.
     READ SALESFILE INVALID STOP RUN.
*************************************************************************
*****DELETING RECORDS FROM A FILE DOES NOT AFFECT THE 'SORTED'    *
*****STATUS OF A FILE. ONE CAN STILL LIST THE RECORDS.....        *
*************************************************************************
     IF NO-LAST-NONSEQ-REC GREATER NO-LAST-SEQ-REC,
        DISPLAY 'FILES MUST BE SORTED BEFORE LISTING.'
         CLOSE SALESFILE PRINT-FILE
         GO TO SEC-1.
*************************************************************************
*****START DISITEM WITH FAKE VALUE OF SPACES.                    *
*****NORMALLY IT HOLDS NAME OF LAST COMPANY WHOSE RECORD WAS      *
*****PRINTED.....                                                *
*************************************************************************
     MOVE SPACES TO DISITEM.
     MOVE NO-LAST-SEQ-REC TO NITEM.
  2.
*************************************************************************
*****BEGIN READING RECORDS IN SALESFILE.....                     *
*************************************************************************
     ADD 1 TO NKEY.
     READ SALESFILE INVALID STOP RUN.
     IF DELETE-TAG IS EQUAL TO DELETED GO TO 3.
*************************************************************************
*****CONVERT PACKED ALPHANUMERIC TO STANDARD ALPHANUMERIC.....    *
*************************************************************************
     CALL 'QCV21' USING P2 C NO-30.
*************************************************************************
*****COMPARE COMPANY NAME WITH OLD COMPANY NAME....              *
*************************************************************************
     IF DISITEM NOT EQUAL TO P2,
*************************************************************************
*****NEW COMPANY. GO TO NEW PAGE AND PRINT HEADING.              *
*************************************************************************
         WRITE PRINTE FROM HEADR AFTER ADVANCING TO-TOP
         MOVE SPACES TO PRINTE
         WRITE PRINTE AFTER ADVANCING 1 LINES.
*************************************************************************
*****PRINT RECORD.....                                           *
*************************************************************************
     MOVE P2 TO DISITEM. MOVE I TO P1. MOVE D TO T.
     MOVE T1 TO P3. MOVE T2 TO P4. MOVE T3 TO P5.
     CALL 'QCV21' USING P6 P NO-20.
     MOVE PN TO P7. MOVE PR TO P8.
     WRITE PRINTE FROM COMPANY-REC AFTER ADVANCING 1 AT EOP
         MOVE SPACES TO PRINTE
         WRITE PRINTE AFTER ADVANCING TO-TOP.
  3.
*************************************************************************
*****IF THIS IS LAST RECORD, GET READY TO FINISH SECTION.....     *
*************************************************************************
     IF NKEY IS EQUAL TO NITEM,
         MOVE SPACES TO PRINTE
        WRITE PRINTE AFTER ADVANCING TO-TOP
         CLOSE PRINT-FILE SALESFILE
         GO TO 4 OF SEC-5
     ELSE
         GO TO 2 OF SEC-5.
```

```
 4.
 ****************************************************************
 *****ALL DONE. GO SEE IF MORE IS TO BE DONE.....              *
 ****************************************************************
      DISPLAY 'LISTING FINISHED.'.
      GO TO SEC-1.
 ****************************************************************
 ****************************************************************
 ****************************************************************
  SEC-6 SECTION.
  COMMENT.
      NOTE  THIS SECTION MARKS SELECTED RECORDS OF SALESFILE
      WITH A DELETE CODE (/8000). THESE RECORDS WILL STAY IN
      SALESFILE UNTIL A SORT IS MADE. THEN THEY ARE PHYSICALLY
      DELETED FROM SALESFILE.

  1.
 ****************************************************************
 *****RECORDS MUST BE IN SEQUENTIAL ORDER IF THIS IS TO WORK.  *
 ****************************************************************
      PERFORM SORTING.
      OPEN INPUT CARD-FILE, I-O SALESFILE.
 ****************************************************************
 *****THIS INITIALIZES LOCATE-TABLE.                           *
 ****************************************************************
      MOVE 1 TO NKEY.
      READ SALESFILE INVALID STOP RUN.
      MOVE NO-LAST-SEQ-REC TO LAST-SEQ-REC.
      MOVE NO-LAST-NONSEQ-REC TO LAST-NON-SEQ-REC.
 ****************************************************************
 *****THE WRITE IS ONLY BECAUSE SALESFILE IS OPENED I-O.       *
 ****************************************************************
      WRITE HEADER INVALID STOP RUN.
 ****************************************************************
 *****INITIALIZE UNUSED CORE STORAGE.                          *
 ****************************************************************
      CALL 'QCORE' USING SALESFILE, LOCATE-TABLE.
  2.
 ****************************************************************
 *     READ FIRST DELETE RECORD. TRY TO MATCH MONTH ON CARD.   *
 ****************************************************************
      READ CARD-FILE AT END GO TO ENDING OF SEC-6.
      MOVE 0 TO MKEY.
      PERFORM MONTH-MATCH VARYING SUBCPT FROM 1 BY 1 UNTIL SUBCPT
      GREATER 12.
      IF MKEY = 0  DISPLAY ' INCORRECT MONTH FOR '
      DELETE-RECORD  GO TO 2 OF SEC-6.
 ****************************************************************
 *****SUCCESSFUL MONTH MATCH PREPARE TO MARK RECORDS.          *
 ****************************************************************
      CALL 'QCV12' USING CMPY COMPANY-NAME NO-30.
      MOVE MKEY TO T1. MOVE 0 TO T2. MOVE YEAR TO T3.
      MOVE T TO SALE-DATE. MOVE 0 TO INVOICE.
 ****************************************************************
 *****THIS CALL GIVES THE NEGATIVE OF THE RECORD NUMBER        *
 *****PRECEDING THE RECORDS TO BE DELETE MARKED SINCE NO RECORD*
 *****HAS INVOICE NUMBER 0.                                    *
 ****************************************************************
      CALL 'QFIND' USING NOMINAL-KEY.
      IF NKEY IS POSITIVE DISPLAY 'QFIND ERROR' STOP RUN.
 *    NOW WE GET NUMBER OF RECORD PRECEDING RECORDS TO BE MARKED.
      MULTIPLY -1 BY NKEY.
  3.
      ADD 1 TO NKEY.
      READ SALESFILE INVALID GO TO 2 OF SEC-6.
      MOVE 0 TO T.
 ****************************************************************
 *****TEST TO SEE IF WE HAVE GONE PAST ALL RECORDS TO BE MARKED. *
 ****************************************************************
```

Figure 13.2 (Cont'd.)

```
        IF C GREATER COMPANY-NAME OR T1 GREATER MKEY  OR T3
        GREATER YEAR GO TO 2 OF SEC-6.
    ****************************************************************************
    *****SEE IF NEXT RECORD IS TO BE MARKED FOR DELETION.                      *
    ****************************************************************************
        IF COMPANY-NAME = C AND T3 = YEAR AND  T1 = MKEY,
        MOVE  DELETED TO  DELETE-TAG.
        WRITE SALESRECORD INVALID STOP RUN.
    ****************************************************************************
    *****GO BACK TO EXAMINE NEXT RECORD.                                       *
    ****************************************************************************
        GO TO 3 OF SEC-6.
    MONTH-MATCH.
        IF  MONTHS (SUBCPT) = MONTH MOVE SUBCPT TO MKEY.
    ENDING.
        CLOSE SALESFILE CARD-FILE.
        DISPLAY 'ALL SPECIFIED RECORDS HAVE BEEN MARKED FOR DELETION,
    -   ' A SORT MUST BE PERFORMED TO REMOVE RECORDS.'.
        GO TO SEC-1.
    ****************************************************************************
    *****GO SEE IF MORE IS TO BE DONE.                                         *
    ****************************************************************************
    ****************************************************************************
    ****************************************************************************
    ADDITIONS SECTION.
    1.
    ****************************************************************************
    *****ADD ONE RECORD TO SALEFILE.                                           *
    ****************************************************************************
        READ CARD-FILE AT END GO TO ENDING OF ADDITIONS.
        ADD 1 TO NKEY.
        MOVE 0 TO DELETE-TAG. MOVE INVOICE-NUMBER TO I.
        CALL 'QCV12' USING COMPANY, C, NO-30.
        MOVE DAT TO D.
    ****************************************************************************
    *****QCV12 IS USED TO CONVERT TO PACKED FORM.                              *
    ****************************************************************************
        CALL 'QCV12' USING PRODUCT, P, NO-20.
        MOVE PRODUCT-NUMBER TO PN. MOVE UNIT-PRICE TO PR.
        WRITE SALESRECORD INVALID GO TO 2 OF ADDITIONS.
        GO TO 1 OF ADDITIONS.
    2.
    ****************************************************************************
    *    WE GOT HERE IN ATTEMPT TO WRITE BEYOND END OF FILE.                   *
    ****************************************************************************
        DISPLAY 'FILES ARE FULL, FIRST INVOICE OF UNSTORED RECORDS IS
    -   'NUMBER ', INVOICE-NUMBER.
    3.
    ****************************************************************************
    *****GET PAST UNPROCESSED RECORDS TO SEE IF MORE IS TO BE DONE.  *
    ****************************************************************************
        READ CARD-FILE AT END GO TO ENDING OF SEC-6.
        GO TO 3 OF ADDITIONS.
    ENDING. EXIT.
    ****************************************************************************
    ****************************************************************************
    ****************************************************************************
    SORTING SECTION.
    COMMENT.
        NOTE THIS SECTION BRINGS ALL RECORDS IN THE FILE INTO THE
        SEQUENTIAL PORTION OF THE FILE AND SORTS THEM.  ANY RECORD
        WITH A DELETE TAG WILL BE REMOVED FROM THE FILES IN THIS
        SECTION.

    1.
    ****************************************************************************
    *****INITIALIZE SORTABLE.                                                  *
    ****************************************************************************
```

```
           OPEN INPUT SALESFILE. MOVE 1 TO NKEY.
           READ SALESFILE INVALID STOP RUN.
           SUBTRACT 1 FROM NO-LAST-NONSEQ-REC GIVING NO-OF.
           MOVE 2 TO START-OF-KEY-1. MOVE 2030 TO TYPE-1.
           MOVE 17 TO START-OF-KEY-2. MOVE 4006 TO TYPE-2.
           MOVE 19 TO START-OF-KEY-3. MOVE 4005 TO TYPE-3.
           MOVE 0 TO END-OF-TABLE.
      ******************************************************************
      *****LET QSITL CHECK SPECIFICATIONS AND PREPARE FOR SORT.       *
      ******************************************************************
           CALL 'QSITL' USING SALESFILE, SALESTABLE.
      ******************************************************************
      *****PRESENT RECORDS TO BE SORTED TO QSREL. SORT TAG FILE THUS  *
      *****CREATED.                                                   *
      ******************************************************************
           PERFORM LOAD NO-OF TIMES. CALL 'QSORT'. OPEN OUTPUT
           WORK-FILE.
       2.
      ******************************************************************
      *****QSRET GIVES RECORD NUMBERS FOR SORTED ORDER.              *
      ******************************************************************
           CALL 'QSRET'. READ SALESFILE INVALID GO TO 3 OF SORTING.
      ******************************************************************
      *****READ RECORDS INTO WORK-FILE IN THIS ORDER UNLESS MARKED    *
      *****FOR DELETION. IF MARKED, SKIP.                             *
      ******************************************************************
           IF DELETE-TAG EQUAL TO DELETED GO TO 2 OF SORTING.
           MOVE SALESRECORD TO WORKER. WRITE WORKER INVALID
               STOP RUN.
           GO TO 2 OF SORTING.
       3.
      ******************************************************************
      *****PREPARE TO PUT RECORDS BACK INTO SALESFILE IN SORTED ORDER. *
      ******************************************************************
           CLOSE WORK-FILE SALESFILE.
           OPEN INPUT WORK-FILE, OUTPUT SALESFILE.
           MOVE 1 TO NKEY.
       4.
      ******************************************************************
      *****PLACE RECORD IN SALESFILE.                                 *
      ******************************************************************
           ADD 1 TO NKEY. READ WORK-FILE INTO SALESRECORD AT END GO TO
           5 OF SORTING.
           WRITE SALESRECORD INVALID STOP RUN.
           GO TO 4 OF SORTING.
       5.
      ******************************************************************
      *****INITIALIZE HEADER.                                         *
      ******************************************************************
           SUBTRACT 1 FROM NKEY GIVING NO-LAST-SEQ-REC.
           MOVE NO-LAST-SEQ-REC TO NO-LAST-NONSEQ-REC.
           MOVE TODAY TO DATE-LAST-ADDITIONS,
           DATE-LAST-SORT. MOVE 1 TO NKEY. WRITE HEADER INVALID
           STOP RUN.
           CLOSE SALESFILE WORK-FILE.

       LOAD SECTION.
        1.
           ADD 1 TO NKEY. READ SALESFILE INVALID STOP RUN.
           CALL 'QSREL'.

/*
// XEQ          1
*FILES(2,SFLE)
      SAMPLE DATA CARDS ARE SHOWN AS FOLLOWS
CREATE
00147ACME BAKERIES            012572BAKERY CONVEYOR      0278973241
00247ALLIED VAN LINES         012572FORK LIFT           0125254756
00398ALLIED VAN LINES         062172FORK LIFT           0125254756
00345ALLIED VAN LINES         031872TWO-MAN DOLLY       0245078937
00478ALLIED VAN LINES         031472TWO-MAN DOLLY       0245078937
```

Figure 13.2 (Cont'd.)

```
03275GLADDINGS CORPORATION        090972TWO-MAN DOLLY        0089034599
00357GLADDINGS CORPORATION        040972TWO-MAN DOLLY        0089034599
04297GLADDINGS CORPORATION        120972TWO-MAN DOLLY        0089034599



00111UNITED FREIGHT INC           010272FORK LIFT            0125254756
/*
LIST BY COMPANY
DELETE RECORDS
ALLIED VAN LINES                       JANUARY   72
UNITED FREIGHT INC                     JANUARY   72
ALLIED VAN LINES                       MARCH     72
/*
SORT FILE
LIST BY COMPANY
FINISH
```

Sorting the File

The file is sorted using QSORT as described in Chapter 12. The only unusual feature of this section is that if a record has been marked for deletion, the record is physically removed from the file.

Marking File Records for Deletions

This section marks selected records for deletion. You must specify on a card a company name, month, and year—for example,

```
ACME SHOES   FEBRUARY   73
```

The program marks all that company's records in the specified month and year with a delete code of /8000.

This section first ensures that the file is sorted. Then using QFIND, as described in Chapter 12, the program locates the record in the file *just preceding* the records to be marked. The program marks the specified records with the delete code. It is important to note that the marked records are still in the file and can be processed by the program for desired purposes. However, the next time the file is sorted, these marked records will be physically removed from the file.

Listing the File

This section of the program is very simple. It prints a list of the sorted file with the records listed by company name.

You can learn a great deal by studying this program in detail.

Example 13.1

The XYZ Company has five different departments. Each department has 20 employees. We shall create a payroll system by writing a COBOL program to accomplish the following tasks.

a. Read the input cards from the card reader. The typical input card contains the following.

Card column   *Field*
1–20   employee name
21–25   employee number
26–32   pay (The last two digits are decimals.)

b. After each input card is read, the name, pay, and employee number must be checked from a permanent sequential disk file that was created previously and stored on the disk. If the name or the number or the pay is not found (or matched), a message should be printed, and the record should not be added to any calculations. A message must be generated to inform the authorized personnel about such a case.

c. Find: (1) for each department the average, total, maximum, and minimum number of employees and the salaries of these employees; and (2) for the company the average, total, maximum, and minimum number of employees and the salaries of these employees.

d. Print a list of the employees together with all the information in part c.

Figure 13.3 is a flowchart, and figure 13.4 is the complete program to create the payroll system.

Processing a FORTRAN Disk File on the IBM-1130

On the IBM-1130 there are special problems created by the incompatibilities of FORTRAN and COBOL. Example 13.1 demonstrated the difficulties of working with FORTRAN floating-point data. If you avoid the use of floating-point data, the difficulties that arise from the incompatibility of FORTRAN and COBOL are not as great. Processing disk files created by a FORTRAN program is quite simple if the files do not contain floating-point data. You can read the file using the QFRED subroutine and write to the file using the QFRIT subroutine. The following sample programs also use the MULTIPLE UNIT option for a COBOL sequential file to illustrate their use in a COBOL program.

The FORTRAN program in figure 13.5 stores a student card file in two disk files. Each record of the FORTRAN disk file is composed of the following items:

student id   (one-word integer);

student name   (stored in an array, three characters per word);

street address   (stored in an array, three characters per word);

city/state   (stored in an array, three characters per word);

zip code   (stored in an array, one numeric character per word);

tuition   (stored as a two-word integer); and

three unused words in the record   (for later expansion of the data in the file).

The first record of the FORTRAN file contains a header record specifying the number of records in the file (a one-word integer). The FORTRAN program in figure 13.5 is accompanied by a listing showing some of the records in the file.

Figure 13.3 Flowchart for PAYROLL program for example 13.1.

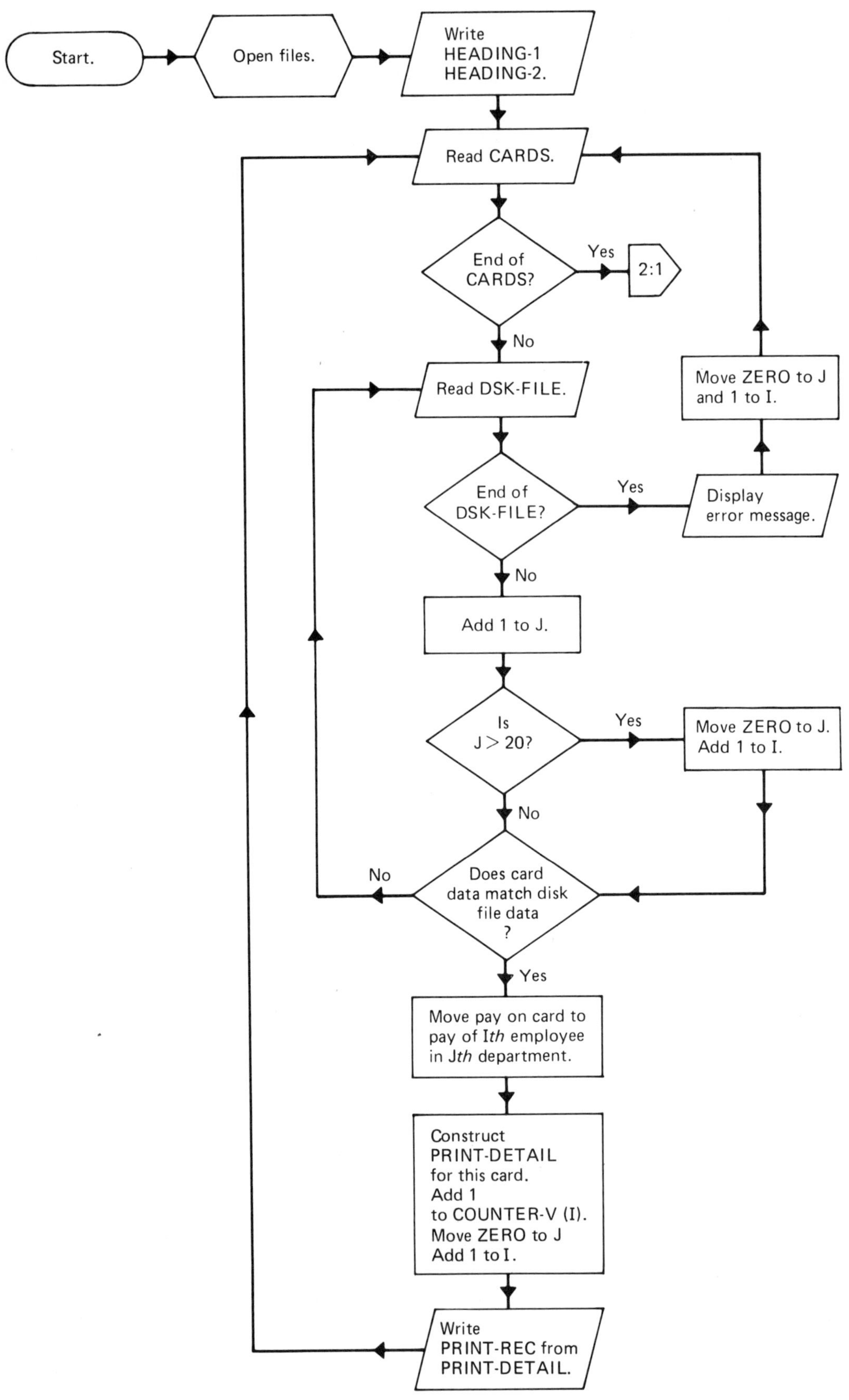

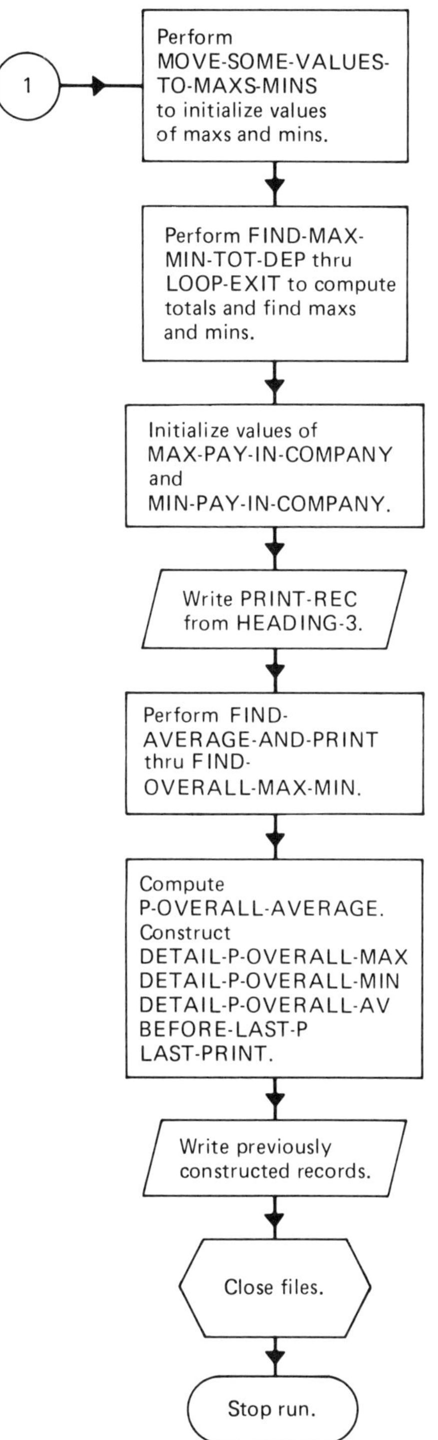

1
Perform MOVE-SOME-VALUES-TO-MAXS-MINS to initialize values of maxs and mins.
Perform FIND-MAX-MIN-TOT-DEP thru LOOP-EXIT to compute totals and find maxs and mins.
Initialize values of MAX-PAY-IN-COMPANY and MIN-PAY-IN-COMPANY.
Write PRINT-REC from HEADING-3.
Perform FIND-AVERAGE-AND-PRINT thru FIND-OVERALL-MAX-MIN.
Compute P-OVERALL-AVERAGE. Construct DETAIL-P-OVERALL-MAX DETAIL-P-OVERALL-MIN DETAIL-P-OVERALL-AV BEFORE-LAST-P LAST-PRINT.
Write previously constructed records.
Close files.
Stop run.

Figure 13.3 (Cont'd.)

MOVE-SOME-VALUES-TO-MAXS-MIN

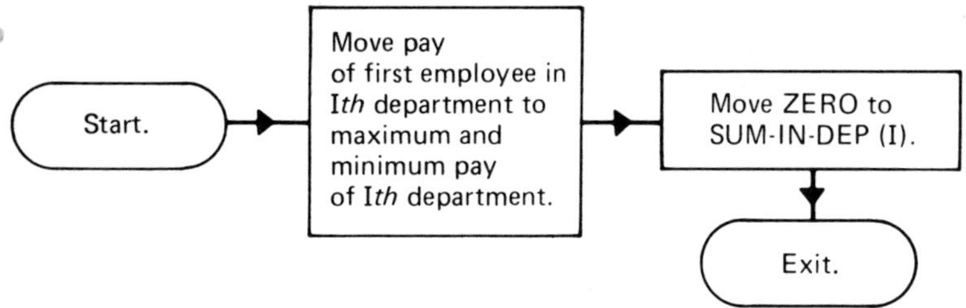

FIND-MAX-MIN-TOT-DEP thru LOOP-EXIT

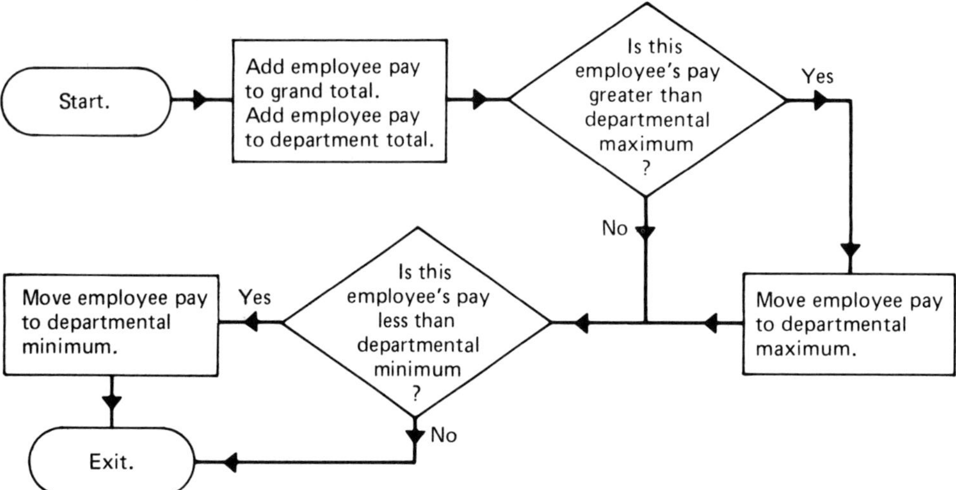

FIND-AVERAGE-AND-PRINT thru FIND-OVERALL-MAX-MIN

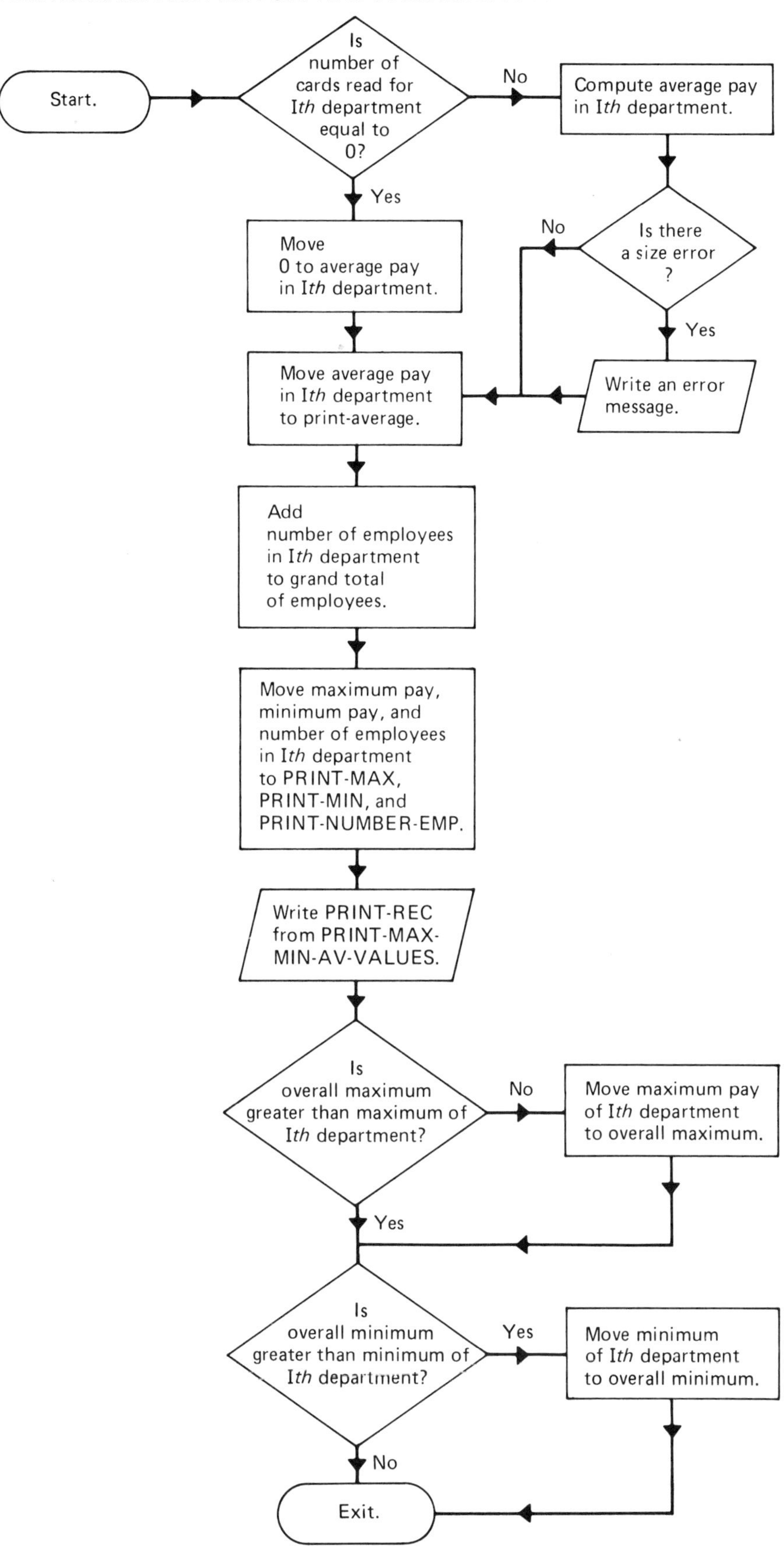

Figure 13.4 Listing of PAYROLL program for example 13.1.

```
// COBOL
*LIST,XREF,EJCT,/01FE,DMAP,PMAP
        IDENTIFICATION DIVISION.
        PROGRAM-ID. PAYROLL.
        ENVIRONMENT DIVISION.
        CONFIGURATION SECTION.
        SOURCE-COMPUTER. IBM-1130.
        OBJECT-COMPUTER. IBM-1130.
        SPECIAL-NAMES.
            C01 IS TO-NEW-PAGE.
        INPUT-OUTPUT SECTION.
        FILE-CONTROL.
            SELECT CARDS ASSIGN TO RD-2501 RESERVE 1.
            SELECT PRINTS ASSIGN TO PR-1403.
            SELECT DSK-FILE ASSIGN TO DF-17-100-X.
        DATA DIVISION.
        FILE SECTION.
        FD   CARDS,
             LABEL RECORDS ARE OMITTED,
             DATA RECORD IS CARD-IN.
        01   CARD-IN.
             02 E-NAME PIC X(20).
             02 E-NUMBER PIC 9(5).
             02 E-PAY PIC 9(5)V99.
        FD   PRINTS,
             LABEL RECORDS ARE OMITTED,
             DATA RECORD IS PRINT-REC.
        01   PRINT-REC PIC X(121).
        FD   DSK-FILE,
             LABEL RECORDS ARE STANDARD,
             DATA RECORD IS DISK-REC.
        01   DISK-REC.
             02 D-E-NAME PIC X(20).
             02 D-E-NUMBER PIC 9(5).
             02 D-E-PAY PIC 9(5)V99.
        WORKING-STORAGE SECTION.
        77   I PIC 99 COMP VALUE 1.
        77   J PIC 99 COMP VALUE 0.
        77   AVERAGE-PAY-IN-COMPANY PIC 9(5)V99.
        77   MAX-PAY-IN-COMPANY PIC 9(5)V99 COMP.
        77   MIN-PAY-IN-COMPANY PIC 9(5)V99 COMP.
        77   TEMP-1 PIC 9(5)V99 VALUE 0.
        77   TEMP-2 PIC 99.
        01   COUNTER-VARIABLES.
             02 C-VALUE PIC 9(10) VALUE ZEROES.
             02 COUNTER-V REDEFINES C-VALUE PIC 99 OCCURS 5 TIMES.
        ****************************************************************
        *****COUNTER-V (I) DATA-NAME IS USED TO HOLD THE NUMBER OF     *
        *****EMPLOYEES IN THE I-TH DEPT. THIS NUMBER MUST NOT BE MORE  *
        *****THAN 20......                                             *
        ****************************************************************
        01   MAX-TABLE.
             02 MAX-PAY-IN-DEP PIC 9(5)V99 COMP OCCURS 5 TIMES.
        01   MIN-TABLE.
             02 MIN-PAY-IN-DEP PIC 9(5)V99 COMP OCCURS 5 TIMES.
        01   AVERAGE-TABLE.
             02 AVERAGE-PAY-IN-DEP PIC 9(5)V99 COMP OCCURS 5 TIMES.
             02 SUM-PAY-IN-DEP PIC 9(5)V99 COMP OCCURS 5 TIMES.
        01   COMPANY-ORGANIZATION.
             02 DEPARTMENT OCCURS 5 TIMES.
                03 E-PAY-DEP PIC 9(5)V99 COMP OCCURS 20 TIMES.
        01   HEADING-1.
             02 FILLER PIC X(20) VALUE SPACES.
             02 FILLER PIC X(12) VALUE 'PAYROLL LIST'.
        01   HEADING-2.
             02 FILLER PIC X(10) VALUE SPACES.
```

```
        02 FILLER PIC X(15) VALUE 'EMPLOYEE-NUMBER'.
        02 FILLER PIC X(10) VALUE SPACES.
        02 FILLER PIC X(13) VALUE 'EMPLOYEE-NAME'.
        02 FILLER PIC X(10) VALUE SPACES.
        02 FILLER PIC X(7) VALUE 'PAYMENT'.
    01  HEADING-3.
        02 FILLER PIC X(20) VALUE SPACES.
        02 FILLER PIC X(14) VALUE 'HIGH PAY TABLE'.
        02 FILLER PIC X(20) VALUE SPACES.
        02 FILLER PIC X(13) VALUE 'LOW PAY TABLE'.
        02 FILLER PIC X(15) VALUE SPACES.
        02 FILLER PIC X(13) VALUE 'AVERAGE TABLE'.
        02 FILLER PIC X(2) VALUE SPACES.
        02 FILLER PIC X(19) VALUE 'NUMBER OF EMPLOYEES'.
    01  DETAIL-P-OVERALL-MAX.
        02 FILLER PIC X(20) VALUE SPACES.
        02 FILLER PIC X(35) VALUE 'THE HIGHEST PAY IN THE COMPANY IS
 -     ' '.
        02 P-MAX-COMPANY PIC *(6).99.
    01  BEFORE-LAST-P.
        02 FILLER PIC X(20) VALUE SPACES.
        02 FILLER PIC X(28) VALUE 'TOTAL AMOUNT PAY IN THIS RUN'.
        02 PRINT-TOTAL-PAY-IN-COMPANY PIC $(13)9.99.
    01  DETAIL-P-OVERALL-MIN.
        02 FILLER PIC X(20) VALUE SPACES.
        02 FILLER PIC X(33)
           VALUE 'THE LOWEST PAY IN THE COMPANY IS '.
        02 P-MIN-COMPANY PIC $(6).99.
    01  DETAIL-P-OVERALL-AV.
        02 FILLER PIC X(20) VALUE SPACES.
        02 FILLER PIC X(20) VALUE 'OVERALL AVERAGE IS  '.
        02 P-OVERALL-AVERAGE PIC $(6).99.
    01  PRINT-MAX-MIN-AV-VALUES.
        02 FILLER PIC X(6) VALUE SPACES.
        02 FILLER PIC X(11) VALUE 'DEPARTMENT-'.
        02 DEPT-NUMBER PIC X.
        02 PRINT-MAX PIC $(6).99.
        02 FILLER PIC X(27) VALUE SPACES.
        02 PRINT-MIN PIC $(6).99.
        02 FILLER PIC X(15) VALUE SPACES.
        02 PRINT-AVERAGE PIC $(6).99.
        02 FILLER PIC X(10) VALUE SPACES.
        02 P-NUMBER-EMP PIC Z9.
    01  LAST-PRINT.
        02 FILLER PIC X(20) VALUE SPACES.
        02 FILLER PIC X(29) VALUE 'TOTAL NUMBER OF EMPLOYEES IS '.
        02 PRINT-TOTAL-EMPLOYEE PIC Z(4)9.
    01  PRINT-DETAIL.
        02 FILLER PIC X(10) VALUE SPACES.
        02 PRINT-NUMBER PIC 9(5).
        02 FILLER PIC X(19) VALUE SPACES.
        02 PRINT-NAME PIC X(20).
        02 FILLER PIC X(3) VALUE SPACES.
        02 PRINT-PAY PIC $(5)9.99.
PROCEDURE DIVISION.
BEGIN.
    OPEN I-O DSK-FILE INPUT CARDS OUTPUT PRINTS.
    NOTE DSK-FILE WAS PREVIOUSLY CREATED AND STORED ON THE DISK.
*****************************************************************
*****WRITE THE MAIN TITLE......                                *
*****************************************************************
    WRITE PRINT-REC FROM HEADING-1, AFTER ADVANCING TO-NEW-PAGE.
*****************************************************************
*****WRITE COLUMNS HEADINGS FOR THE EMPLOYEE NUMBER,           *
*****EMPLOYEE NAME, AND EMPLOYEE PAY......                     *
*****************************************************************
    WRITE PRINT-REC FROM HEADING-2 AFTER ADVANCING 2 LINES.
*****************************************************************
*****READ INPUT CARDS.....                                     *
```

Figure 13.4 (Cont'd.)

```
      ***********************************************************************
       READ-A-CARD.
           READ CARDS AT END GO TO SECOND-LOOP.
       READ-DISK-REC.
           READ DSK-FILE AT END GO TO ERROR-ROUTINES.
      ***********************************************************************
      *****DATA-NAME J REPRESENTS THE J-TH EMPLOYEE IN A DEPARTMENT     *
      *****AND DATA-NAME I DENOTES THE I-TH DEPARTMENT......
      ***********************************************************************
           ADD 1 TO J.
      ***********************************************************************
      *****CHECK WHETHER ALL 20 RECORDS OF EMPLOYEES IN ONE DEPARTMENT *
      *****HAVE BEEN READ......                                        *
      ***********************************************************************
           IF J IS GREATER THAN 20, MOVE 0 TO J ADD 1 TO I.
      ***********************************************************************
      *****COMPARE THE INFORMATION FROM THE CARDS WITH INFORMATION     *
      *****FROM THE DISK.....                                          *
      ***********************************************************************
           IF E-NAME  IS EQUAL TO D-E-NAME, AND E-NUMBER IS EQUAL TO
           D-E-NUMBER, AND E-PAY IS EQUAL TO D-E-PAY, GO TO
           CALCULATIONS-AND-MOVES.
           GO TO READ-DISK-REC.
        CALCULATIONS-AND-MOVES.
           MOVE E-PAY TO E-PAY-DEP (I, J), PRINT-PAY.
           MOVE E-NAME TO PRINT-NAME.
           MOVE E-NUMBER TO PRINT-NUMBER.
      ***********************************************************************
      *****THIS EMPLOYEE BELONGS TO THE I-TH DEPT,                     *
      ***** THEREFOR COUNTER-V SHOULD BE INCREMENTED BY 1.....         *
      ***********************************************************************
           ADD 1 TO COUNTER-V (I).
      ***********************************************************************
      *****SINCE THE DSK-FILE IS SEARCHED EVERY TIME FROM THE FIRST    *
      *****RECORD, 1 MUST BE MOVED TO BOTH I AND J. NOTICE THAT        *
      *****I IS THE ROW AND J THE COLUMN OF TABLE COMPANY-ORGANIZATION.*
      ***********************************************************************
           MOVE 1 TO I.
           MOVE 0 TO J.
           WRITE PRINT-REC FROM PRINT-DETAIL AFTER ADVANCING 1 LINES.
           GO TO READ-A-CARD.
        SECOND-LOOP.
           PERFORM MOVE-SOME-VALUES-TO-MAXS-MINS, VARYING I FROM 1 BY
           1 UNTIL I IS GREATER THAN 5.
      ***********************************************************************
      *****THE FOLLOWING PERFORMS FINDS MAX, MIN, FOR ALL DEPARTMENTS. *
      ***********************************************************************
           PERFORM FIND-MAX-MIN-TOT-DEP THRU LOOP-EXIT
           VARYING I FROM 1 BY 1 UNTIL I IS GREATER THAN 5 AFTER
                   J FROM 1 BY 1 UNTIL J IS GREATER THAN 20.
      ***********************************************************************
      *****NOW MOVE SOME INITIAL VALUES TO OVERALL MAX AND OVERALL MIN.*
      *****USUALLY IF YOU WANT TO FIND THE HIGHEST OR LOWEST VALUE IN  *
      *****AN ARRAY, YOU MOVE THE VALUE OF THE FIRST ELEMENT TO THE MAX*
      *****OR MIN AND THEN COMPARE  THAT VALUE WITH THE VALUES OF ALL  *
      *****ELEMENTS IN THE TABLE. THE NEXT PERFORM DOES THAT COMPARISON*
      *****IT ALSO FINDS THE AVERAGE PAY IN EACH DEPARTMENT AND ALSO   *
      *****PRINTS THOSE VALUES......                                   *
      ***********************************************************************
           MOVE MAX-PAY-IN-DEP (1) TO MAX-PAY-IN-COMPANY.
           MOVE MIN-PAY-IN-DEP (1) TO MIN-PAY-IN-COMPANY.
           WRITE PRINT-REC FROM HEADING-3 AFTER ADVANCING TO-NEW-PAGE.
           PERFORM FIND-AVERAGE-AND-PRINT THRU FIND-OVERALL-MAX-MIN
           VARYING I FROM 1 BY 1 UNTIL I IS GREATER THAN 5.
      ***********************************************************************
      *****TEMP-1 CONTAINS TOTAL PAY IN THE COMPANY.                   *
      *****TEMP-2 CONTAINS TOTAL MUMBER OF EMPLOYEES IN THE COMPANY.   *
```

```
************************************************************************
************************************************************************
*****FIND OVERALL AVERAGE.....                                        *
************************************************************************
      DIVIDE TEMP-1 BY TEMP-2 GIVING P-OVERALL-AVERAGE.
      MOVE TEMP-1 TO PRINT-TOTAL-PAY-IN-COMPANY.
      MOVE TEMP-2 TO PRINT-TOTAL-EMPLOYEE.
      MOVE MAX-PAY-IN-COMPANY TO P-MAX-COMPANY.
      MOVE MIN-PAY-IN-COMPANY TO P-MIN-COMPANY.
      WRITE PRINT-REC FROM DETAIL-P-OVERALL-MAX
          AFTER ADVANCING TO-NEW-PAGE.
      WRITE PRINT-REC FROM DETAIL-P-OVERALL-MIN AFTER ADVANCING
          3 LINES.
      WRITE PRINT-REC FROM DETAIL-P-OVERALL-AV
          AFTER ADVANCING 3 LINES.
      WRITE PRINT-REC FROM BEFORE-LAST-P
          AFTER ADVANCING 3 LINES.
      WRITE PRINT-REC FROM LAST-PRINT
          AFTER ADVANCING 3 LINES.
************************************************************************
*****END OF THE PROGRAM.....                                          *
************************************************************************
      CLOSE CARDS PRINTS DSK-FILE. STOP RUN.
  ERROR-ROUTINES.
      DISPLAY 'THE RECORD FOR  ', E-NAME,
          ' IS NOT IN THE DISK-FILE'.
      DISPLAY 'THE EMPLOYEE NUMBER ', E-NUMBER, ' FOR ', E-NAME,
      ' WAS READ FROM CARDS'.
      DISPLAY 'THIS MUST BE CHECKEC WITH CONTROLLER, UNTIL THEN DIS
      'REGARD THIS CARD'.
      MOVE 1 TO I, J.
      GO TO READ-A-CARD.
  MOVE-SOME-VALUES-TO-MAXS-MINS.
      MOVE E-PAY-DEP (I, 1) TO MAX-PAY-IN-DEP (I), MIN-PAY-IN-DEP
      (I).
      MOVE 0 TO SUM-PAY-IN-DEP (I).
  FIND-MAX-MIN-TOT-DEP.
      ADD E-PAY-DEP (I, J) TO TEMP-1.
      ADD E-PAY-DEP (I, J) TO SUM-PAY-IN-DEP (I).
      IF MAX-PAY-IN-DEP (I) IS GREATER THAN E-PAY-DEP (I, J),
      OR MAX-PAY-IN-DEP (I) IS EQUAL TO E-PAY-DEP (I, J) GO TO
          LP-1.
      MOVE E-PAY-DEP (I, J) TO MAX-PAY-IN-DEP (I).
      GO TO LOOP-EXIT.
  LP-1.
      IF MIN-PAY-IN-DEP (I) IS LESS THAN E-PAY-DEP (I, J) OR
      MIN-PAY-IN-DEP (I) IS EQUAL TO E-PAY-DEP (I, J) GO TO
      LOOP-EXIT.
      MOVE E-PAY-DEP (I, J) TO MIN-PAY-IN-DEP (I).
  LOOP-EXIT.
      EXIT.
  FIND-AVERAGE-AND-PRINT.
************************************************************************
*****CHECK IF THERE IS 0 EMPLOYEES READ FOR A DEPARTMENT.            *
*****IF THERE ARE, MOVE 0 TO THE CORRESPONDING  AVERAGE......        *
************************************************************************
      IF COUNTER-V (I)  IS EQUAL TO 0
          MOVE 0 TO AVERAGE-PAY-IN-DEP (I), GO TO 16.
      COMPUTE AVERAGE-PAY-IN-DEP (I)  ROUNDED =
      SUM-PAY-IN-DEP (I) / COUNTER-V (I) ON SIZE ERROR DISPLAY
      'THERE IS A SIZE ERROR IN THE ', I, '-TH DEPARTMENT-AVERAGE'.

  16.
      ADD COUNTER-V (I) TO TEMP-2.
      ADD SUM-PAY-IN-DEP (I) TO TEMP-1.
      MOVE I TO DEPT-NUMBER.
      MOVE MAX-PAY-IN-DEP (I) TO PRINT-MAX.
      MOVE MIN-PAY-IN-DEP (I) TO PRINT-MIN.
      MOVE AVERAGE-PAY-IN-DEP (I) TO PRINT-AVERAGE.
      MOVE COUNTER-V (I) TO P-NUMBER-EMP.
```

Figure 13.4 (Cont'd.)

```
        WRITE PRINT-REC FROM PRINT-MAX-MIN-AV-VALUES BEFORE
            ADVANCING 1 LINES.
    FIND-OVERALL-MAX-MIN.
        IF MAX-PAY-IN-COMPANY LESS THAN MAX-PAY-IN-DEP (I) MOVE
        MAX-PAY-IN-DEP (I) TO MAX-PAY-IN-COMPANY.
        IF MIN-PAY-IN-COMPANY GREATER THAN MIN-PAY-IN-DEP (I)
        MOVE MIN-PAY-IN-DEP (I) TO MIN-PAY-IN-COMPANY ELSE NEXT
        SENTENCE.
/*
// XEQ
```

Figure 13.5 Listing of COBOL-FORTRAN-COMBO programs.

```
// JOB T   4000 4001
// DUP
*STOREDATA   WS   UA   STUF1    5
*STOREDATA   WS   UA   STUF2   15        4001
// FOR
*LIST SOURCE PROGRAM
*ONE WORD INTEGERS
*ICCS(2501 READER,1403 PRINTER,DISK)
      INTEGER*4 TUIT
CCCCCCCCCCCCCCCCCCCCCCCCCCCCCCCCCCCCCCCCCCCCCCCCCCCCCCCCCCCCCCCCCCCCC
C THE DIMENSION STATEMENT IS LIKE AN OCCURS IN COBOL.              C
CCCCCCCCCCCCCCCCCCCCCCCCCCCCCCCCCCCCCCCCCCCCCCCCCCCCCCCCCCCCCCCCCCCCC
      DIMENSION ICARD(75),INAME(7),ISTRT(7),ICTST(7)
CCCCCCCCCCCCCCCCCCCCCCCCCCCCCCCCCCCCCCCCCCCCCCCCCCCCCCCCCCCCCCCCCCCCC
C THE DEFINE FILE STATEMENT IS LIKE AN ASSIGN CLAUSE IN COBOL.     C
CCCCCCCCCCCCCCCCCCCCCCCCCCCCCCCCCCCCCCCCCCCCCCCCCCCCCCCCCCCCCCCCCCCCC
      DEFINE FILE 2(10,32,U,I1),3(100,32,U,I2)
      DATA IB/' '/
CCCCCCCCCCCCCCCCCCCCCCCCCCCCCCCCCCCCCCCCCCCCCCCCCCCCCCCCCCCCCCCCCCCCC
C ANY STATEMENT WITH AN '=' MEANS MOVE RIGHT SIDE TO LEFT SIDE.    C
CCCCCCCCCCCCCCCCCCCCCCCCCCCCCCCCCCCCCCCCCCCCCCCCCCCCCCCCCCCCCCCCCCCCC
CCCCCCCCCCCCCCCCCCCCCCCCCCCCCCCCCCCCCCCCCCCCCCCCCCCCCCCCCCCCCCCCCCCCC
C ICNTR COUNTS THE NUMBER OF RECORDS.                              C
CCCCCCCCCCCCCCCCCCCCCCCCCCCCCCCCCCCCCCCCCCCCCCCCCCCCCCCCCCCCCCCCCCCCC
      TUIT = 0
      ICNTR=0
      IFLE=1
      I1=2
      I2=1
CCCCCCCCCCCCCCCCCCCCCCCCCCCCCCCCCCCCCCCCCCCCCCCCCCCCCCCCCCCCCCCCCCCCC
C READ A CARD. AT END GO TO 10.                                    C
CCCCCCCCCCCCCCCCCCCCCCCCCCCCCCCCCCCCCCCCCCCCCCCCCCCCCCCCCCCCCCCCCCCCC
1     READ(8,2,END=10) ID,ICARD
CCCCCCCCCCCCCCCCCCCCCCCCCCCCCCCCCCCCCCCCCCCCCCCCCCCCCCCCCCCCCCCCCCCCC
C THE FORMAT STATEMENTS PLAY THE ROLE OF PICTURE CLAUSES IN COBOL  C
CCCCCCCCCCCCCCCCCCCCCCCCCCCCCCCCCCCCCCCCCCCCCCCCCCCCCCCCCCCCCCCCCCCCC
2     FORMAT(I5,80A1)
      ICNTR=ICNTR+1
CCCCCCCCCCCCCCCCCCCCCCCCCCCCCCCCCCCCCCCCCCCCCCCCCCCCCCCCCCCCCCCCCCCCC
C CRAM CONVERTS FROM 1 CHARACTER PER WORD TO 3 CHARACTERS PER WORD. C
CCCCCCCCCCCCCCCCCCCCCCCCCCCCCCCCCCCCCCCCCCCCCCCCCCCCCCCCCCCCCCCCCCCCC
      CALL CRAM(ICARD,1,21,INAME,1)
      CALL CRAM(ICARD,26,46,ISTRT,1)
      CALL CRAM(ICARD,49,69,ICTST,1)
CCCCCCCCCCCCCCCCCCCCCCCCCCCCCCCCCCCCCCCCCCCCCCCCCCCCCCCCCCCCCCCCCCCCC
C GO TO 20 OR 30 DEPENDING ON IFLE                                 C
CCCCCCCCCCCCCCCCCCCCCCCCCCCCCCCCCCCCCCCCCCCCCCCCCCCCCCCCCCCCCCCCCCCCC
      GO TO (20,30),IFLE
C WRITE A RECORD TO DISK FILE 2.
```

```
20      WRITE(2'I1) ID,INAME,ISTRT,ICTST,(ICARD(J),J=70,74),TUIT
        IF(I1.GE.11) IFLE =2
        GO TO 1
CCCCCCCCCCCCCCCCCCCCCCCCCCCCCCCCCCCCCCCCCCCCCCCCCCCCCCCCCCCCCCCCCCCCC
C WRITE A RECORD TO DISK FILE 3 .                                   C
CCCCCCCCCCCCCCCCCCCCCCCCCCCCCCCCCCCCCCCCCCCCCCCCCCCCCCCCCCCCCCCCCCCCC
30      WRITE(3'I2) ID,INAME,ISTRT,ICTST,(ICARD(J),J=70,74)
        GO TO 1
CCCCCCCCCCCCCCCCCCCCCCCCCCCCCCCCCCCCCCCCCCCCCCCCCCCCCCCCCCCCCCCCCCCCC
C WRITE A HEADER RECORD CONTAINING VALUE OF ICNTR.                  C
CCCCCCCCCCCCCCCCCCCCCCCCCCCCCCCCCCCCCCCCCCCCCCCCCCCCCCCCCCCCCCCCCCCCC
10      WRITE(2'1) ICNTR
CCCCCCCCCCCCCCCCCCCCCCCCCCCCCCCCCCCCCCCCCCCCCCCCCCCCCCCCCCCCCCCCCCCCL
C  GO TO THE TOP OF A NEW PAGE.                                     C
CCCCCCCCCCCCCCCCCCCCCCCCCCCCCCCCCCCCCCCCCCCCCCCCCCCCCCCCCCCCCCCCCCCCC
        WRITE(5,6)
6       FORMAT('1 ')
        IFLE=1
        I1=2
        I2=1
35      DO 40 J = 1,75
40      ICARD(J)= IB
50      GO TO (70,80),IFLE
70      READ(2'I1)             ID,INAME,ISTRT,ICTST,(ICARD(J),J=70,74)
        IF(I1.GE.11) IFLE =2
        GO TO 90
80      READ(3'I2)             ID,INAME,ISTRT,ICTST,(ICARD(J),J=70,74)
90      CALL UNCM(ICARD,1,21,INAME,1)
        CALL UNCM(ICARD,26,46,ISTRT,1)
        CALL UNCM(ICARD,49,69,ICTST,1)
CCCCCCCCCCCCCCCCCCCCCCCCCCCCCCCCCCCCCCCCCCCCCCCCCCCCCCCCCCCCCCCCCCCCC
C WRITE A LINE ON PRINTER                                           C
CCCCCCCCCCCCCCCCCCCCCCCCCCCCCCCCCCCCCCCCCCCCCCCCCCCCCCCCCCCCCCCCCCCCC
        WRITE(5,3) ID,ICARD
3       FORMAT(1X,I5,75A1)
        IF(I2.GT.ICNTR-9) GO TO 200
        GO TO 35
20C     CONTINUE
        WRITE(5,6)
CCCCCCCCCCCCCCCCCCCCCCCCCCCCCCCCCCCCCCCCCCCCCCCCCCCCCCCCCCCCCCCCCCCCC
C THE CALL EXIT IS EQUIVALENT TO STOP RUN IN COBOL                  C
CCCCCCCCCCCCCCCCCCCCCCCCCCCCCCCCCCCCCCCCCCCCCCCCCCCCCCCCCCCCCCCCCCCCC
        CALL EXIT
CCCCCCCCCCCCCCCCCCCCCCCCCCCCCCCCCCCCCCCCCCCCCCCCCCCCCCCCCCCCCCCCCCCCC
C THE END MARKS THE PHYSICAL END OF THE FORTRAN PROGRAM.            C
CCCCCCCCCCCCCCCCCCCCCCCCCCCCCCCCCCCCCCCCCCCCCCCCCCCCCCCCCCCCCCCCCCCCC
        END
// XEQ           1
*FILES(2,STUF1),(3,STUF2)
    DATA CARDS GO HERE
/*


// COBOL
*LIST,EJCT,XREF,/01FE,PMAP
        IDENTIFICATION DIVISION.
        PROGRAM-ID. COBOL-FORTRAN-COMBO.
        REMARKS.
            THIS PROGRAM WILL PRINT THE CONTENT OF THE FILE CREATED IN
            THE ACCOMPANYING FORTRAN PROGRAM. WE USE QFRED TO READ
            THE FILE.  WE ALSO ARE PROCESSING A MULTIPLE CARTRIDGE FILE.
        ENVIRONMENT DIVISION.
        CONFIGURATION SECTION.
        SOURCE-COMPUTER. IBM-1130.
        OBJECT-COMPUTER. IBM-1130.
        SPECIAL-NAMES. COPY SPECNAMES.
        INPUT-OUTPUT SECTION.
        FILE-CONTROL.
        ****************************************************************
        *****NOTE THAT DISK-FILE WILL EXTEND ACROSS TWO DISK CARTRIDGES. *
        ****************************************************************
```

Figure 13.5 (Cont'd.)

```
    SELECT DISK-FILE ASSIGN TO DF-1-10, DF-2-100
        FOR MULTIPLE UNIT.
    SELECT PRINT-FILE ASSIGN TO PR-1403.
    DATA DIVISION.
    FILE SECTION.
    FD  DISK-FILE LABEL RECORDS ARE STANDARD.
    01  DREC PIC X(32).
    FD  PRINT-FILE LABEL RECORDS ARE OMITTED.
    01  PREC.
        02  FILLER PIC X.
        02  NAMN PIC X(21).
        02  STREET-ADDRESS REDEFINES NAMN PIC X(21).
        02  CITY REDEFINES NAMN PIC X(21).
        02  ZPP PIC X(5).
    WORKING-STORAGE SECTION.
    77  NUMBER-OF-RECORDS PIC 9(5) COMP.
    *  ICNTR WILL COUNT THE NUMBER OF RECORDS READ FROM THE FILE.
    77  ICNTR PIC 9(4) COMP     VALUE 0.
    **************************************************************************
    *****NOW WE GIVE THE INFORMATION FOR TRANSLATING THE FORTRAN     *
    *****RECORDS INTO COBOL FORMATS.                                 *
    **************************************************************************
    01  FORTRAN-DESCRIPTION.
        02 I PIC S9(4) COMP     VALUE 1005.
        02 INAME PIC S9(4) COMP     VALUE 6021.
        02 ISTRT PIC S9(4) COMP     VALUE 6021.
        02 ICTST PIC S9(4) COMP     VALUE 6021.
        02 IZIP PIC S9(4) COMP     VALUE 4005.
        02 TUIT PIC S9(4) COMP     VALUE 2001.
        02 SKIP PIC S9(4) COMP VALUE 0003.
        02 ENDD PIC S9(4) COMP     VALUE 0000.
        02 A3-TABLE PIC X(40)    VALUE
           ' -.,ABCDEFGHIJKLMNOPQRSTUVWXYZ0123456789'.
    **************************************************************************
    *****THE NEXT ITEM WILL RECEIVE THE TRANSLATION OF THE FORTRAN   *
    *****RECORD.                                                     *
    **************************************************************************
    01  COBOL-RECEIVING-AREA.
        02  ID PIC S9(5) COMP.
        02  NAME PIC X(21).
        02  STREET PIC X(21).
        02  CITY-STATE PIC X(21).
        02  ZIP PIC X(5).
        02  TUITION PIC S9(10) COMP.
        02  FILLER PIC XXX VALUE SPACES.
    PROCEDURE DIVISION.
    1.
        OPEN INPUT DISK-FILE OUTPUT PRINT-FILE.
    **************************************************************************
    *****NOTE THAT THE FIRST RECORD IN THE FORTRAN FILE CONTAINS     *
    *****ONLY THE COUNT OF THE NUMBER OF RECORDS IN THE FILE AND     *
    *****SO WE PROCESS THAT RECORD SEPARATELY.                       *
    **************************************************************************
        CALL 'QFRED' USING DISK-FILE COBOL-RECEIVING-AREA
            FORTRAN-DESCRIPTION, ERROR-PROCEDURE.
        MOVE ID TO NUMBER-OF-RECORDS.
        MOVE SPACES TO PREC. WRITE PREC AFTER ADVANCING TO-TOP.
    2.
    **************************************************************************
    *****          WE NOW READ AND PRINT ONE RECORD FROM THE FILE.   *
    **************************************************************************
        CALL 'QFRED' USING DISK-FILE COBOL-RECEIVING-AREA
            FORTRAN-DESCRIPTION, ERROR-PROCEDURE.
        ADD 1 TO ICNTR.
        MOVE NAME TO NAMN.
        WRITE PREC BEFORE ADVANCING 1.
```

```
        MOVE STREET TO STREET-ADDRESS.
        WRITE PREC BEFORE ADVANCING 1.
        MOVE CITY-STATE TO CITY. MOVE ZIP TO ZPP.
        WRITE PREC BEFORE ADVANCING 2 AT EOP GO TO 4.
    3.
        MOVE SPACES TO ZPP.
        IF ICNTR NOT LESS THAN NUMBER-OF-RECORDS
            GO TO ERROR-PROCEDURE.
        GO TO 2.
    4.
        MOVE SPACES TO PREC.
        WRITE PREC AFTER ADVANCING TO-TOP.
        GO TO 3.
    ERROR-PROCEDURE.
    ********************************************************************
    *****ERROR-PROCEDURE SIMPLY TERMINATES THE PROGRAM. NORMALLY THIS*
    *****IS NOT AS THE RESULT OF AN ERROR.                           *
    ********************************************************************
        CLOSE PRINT-FILE DISK-FILE.
        STOP RUN.
/*
// XEQ        L 1
*FILES(1,STUF1),(2,STUF2)
```

The COBOL program, COBOL-FORTRAN-COMBO, prints a listing of the records of the FORTRAN file. It is very similar to other programs we have presented, so we have not provided a flowchart for the program. The only unusual feature of the program is the MULTIPLE UNIT option that allows us to process the two parts of the FORTRAN file as though they were parts of the same sequentially organized COBOL file. Note that the FILES card after the XEQ card assigns DISK-FILE to two disk files on disks 4000 and 4001. If we have only one disk drive available, then the COBOL program will process DISK-FILE; and when it reaches the end of the part of the file on disk 4000, it will automatically request the computer operator to replace disk 4000 by disk 4001 so that processing can continue. Since this program was run using two disk drives, there was no need for such a request. The program processed DISK-FILE as though it were an ordinary single-disk file, and there were no interruptions of the program execution. The listing of the COBOL program is accompanied by a listing of some of the records printed from the FORTRAN file.

Summary   The beginning COBOL programmer is concerned with learning the details of the COBOL language; but knowledge of the language is only the first step in writing good programs. Writing good programs requires patience and careful planning, planning that must include determination of the major steps of the program, the file design, and the descriptions of all major WORKING-STORAGE SECTION items.

Since programs are usually maintained and used over long periods of time by many people, it is important that they be written clearly and documented well. In a well-written program, the names of the items reflect their purpose in the program and are not chosen simply for their brevity; the instructions in the PROCEDURE DIVISION are divided into separate sections that have clearly defined purposes; and documentary comments are used liberally to explain programming steps.

Review Questions

1. In COBOL the names of data items can be up to 30 characters long. Why is this an advantage in a programming language?

2. In COBOL the names of paragraphs and sections in the PROCEDURE DIVISION can be up to 30 characters long. Why is this an advantage in a programming language?

3. Why is it advantageous to write the PROCEDURE DIVISION as a sequence of separate, major programming steps?

4. Why is the determination of file designs so important in writing good programs?

Suggested Projects

1. Write a COBOL program to read a card file of header records for the customers of an accounting firm. Each card contains the following information.

Card column	*Field*
1–6	account number
7–27	name of customer
28–34	balance (using S9(4)V99)

The records are to be read into a random disk file. The account number should be stored as a computational item. The name of the customer should be stored as a packed alphanumeric item if your computer permits this. (On the IBM-1130 you should use QCV13 and QCV31 for this purpose.) After the items are stored, sort the file by account number using the sort options provided for your computer. After the file is sorted, print a listing of the file to verify the success of the program.

Prepare a flowchart for your program and run the program with at least 10 data cards. Your program cannot assume that the number of customers is known, but it can assume that there are no more than 200 customers.

2. This project is a continuation of project 1. Expand the program you wrote for project 1 to process a second card file and store it in a second disk file. Each card record contains

Card column	*Field*
1–6	account number
7	transaction code
8–13	date of transaction six-digits, MMDDYY
14–20	amount of transaction to be read as 9(5)V99

As each card is read, the account number is compared with the account numbers in the header file described in project 1. If no header record is found to match the transaction record, an error message is printed showing the content of the card and the position of the card in the deck—i.e., card 5 or card 107, etc. If the transaction record matches a header record, then the transaction record is stored in the transaction disk file.

After all the transaction records are stored, the transaction file is sorted by account number and date of transaction.

After sorting, a ledger is printed. Each account listing begins at the top of a new page. The listing begins with the account number, customer name, and old balance. Beneath this should be printed a record of transactions for the customer. One column should show amounts of deposits (transaction code 1), and another column should show withdrawals (transaction code 0). The date is shown to the left. At the end of the ledger is printed the new balance. An example is shown below.

```
Account: 123456     Customer: R. J. Smith     Old balance: $10.00
Date            Deposit      Withdrawal
9/9/73          600.00
9/15/73                      100.00
10/1/73         400.00
10/1/73                       60.00

New balance is $800.00
```

Write the program. If possible, use the routine provided with your computer to perform the comparison of transaction and header records. Run the program with at least 20 transaction records and 3 header records.

3. The sample file maintenance program for the IBM-1130 (figures 13.1 and 13.2) uses subroutines designed to process a file with a special design. The file is considered to be broken into two logically separate parts. The first part of the file contains records in sorted order on the basis of the sort keys. The second part of the file contains additional records of the file that are not in sorted order. The remainder of the file contains space for expanding the second part of the file.

   An important step in working with this type of file is locating records within the file. An efficient method for locating records in the file uses a binary search. When we wish to locate a record in the file, we search the sorted first part of the file using a binary search, and if the record is not in the first part of the file, then we search the second part of the file by examining the records in that half in their natural order. If the record is located, we provide the location of the record in the file as the result of the search. If the record is not in the file, we return a value of zero to signal that fact.

   Write a subroutine (or program) that will carry out this search process given the position of the last record in the first part of the file, the location of the last record in the second half of the file, and the keys for the record to be located.

4. A very powerful type of file organization is the indexed file. Records in this type of file are stored in logically sorted order even though they might not be in physically sorted order. This is possible because each record in the file contains a data item whose value indicates the position of the record in the file that logically follows the record on the basis of the sort keys. For example, when we create the file, we normally store the records in physically sorted order. In this case, the first record in the file points to the second record in the file, the second record points to the third, the third record points to the fourth, and the last record points to an invalid location, say zero, in the file to signal the end of the records in the

file. Write a program that would create such a file. You can assume any type of data you desire.

5. When working with indexed files, you will have to consider the problem of adding and deleting records to and from the file. Suppose you need to add a record to the file. You first must find an unfilled location in the file in which to place the record. Then by comparing sort keys, you must determine the location of the record in the file that is the logical predecessor of the record. Let us suppose that this predecessor is in position 7 in the file and that it points to the record in position 11 in the file as its logical successor. To place the record in the file, we place it in the unfilled location we found, set its pointer to indicate the record in position 11, and change the pointer in the seventh record to point to the position of the new record.

Write a program (or subroutine) to add records to an indexed file. You may assume any type of data you desire. Assume in your program that the file has already been created.

Burroughs B1700 Systems

The B1700 systems are disk-operating systems. They offer support for a wide variety of peripheral equipment useful in data processing. These systems are widely used in banks.

The B1700 systems are operated under control of a Master Control Program (MCP). This program is on disk and manages all the resources of the computer. The MCP supports multiprogramming, spooling of output, and virtual memory allocation.

The B1700 systems are characterized by the ease with which they are used. This is accompanied by a somewhat higher cost than some competing systems, but the cost is offset greatly by increased programmer productivity. The ease of use of the B1700 systems is phenomenal and should cause many firms to consider their use.

The B1700 systems use the concept of the S-language that is unique to Burroughs. In these machines, software instructions (the S-language) are stored in fast memory. Each high-level language (COBOL, FORTRAN, BASIC) has its own individual S-language. The S-language is designed to carry out the instructions in the high-level language *efficiently* and to represent the most frequently used high-level instructions in the shortest available S-language codes. Implicit in this approach is the ability of the B1700 systems to address to the bit level, which results in rapid program execution and lessened storage requirements for programs.

The following list gives *some* of the differences between IBM-1130 COBOL and COBOL on any of the B1700 systems.

For debugging purposes, the MONITOR statement can be used to trace the steps of the program. Its format is

$$\underline{\text{MONITOR}} \ [\underline{\text{DEPENDING}}] \ \text{print-file} \ \underline{(}[\text{data-name}] \ \ldots$$

$$\underline{:}\left[\left\{\begin{array}{c} \text{ALL} \\ \text{paragraph-name}\ldots \end{array}\right\}\right]\underline{)}$$

Only one such statement is allowed per program, and it must immediately precede the IDENTIFICATION DIVISION header card. Print-file must be assigned to a line printer. The data names will be printed together with their value each time the value is changed by a MOVE statement or an arithmetic statement. The paragraph names will be printed together with the number of times they have been reached each time they are encountered during execution. If ALL is specified, then all section and paragraph names will be monitored. If DEPENDING is specified, monitoring will occur only if console switch 6 is up. Monitoring will not occur if print-file is closed. Note that the parentheses and colon are required.

IDENTIFICATION DIVISION

The DATE-COMPILED paragraph is allowed. At the time of compilation, the entry in this paragraph is replaced in the listing by the date and time as kept by the MCP.

ENVIRONMENT DIVISION

The SOURCE-COMPUTER and OBJECT-COMPUTER paragraphs may be omitted. For purposes of segmenting the PROCEDURE DIVISION, the OBJECT-COMPUTER paragraph should be included. The computer name must be B-1700.

In the SPECIAL-NAMES paragraph, an important difference occurs. Channels on the line printer cannot be given mnemonic names. Any input-output device can be given a mnemonic name, and these names may be used in ASSIGN clauses.

In the FILE-CONTROL paragraph, the system names for devices can be chosen from the following list:

SPO	console typewriter
READER	80-column card reader
CARD96	96-column read/punch
PRINTER	line printer
DISK	

The integer in the RESERVE clause may be 1 or greater. The first 10 characters in the name of a file identify it to the MCP and must identify it uniquely. The KEY for a random file must be described by PICTURE 9(8) COMP.

DATA DIVISION

There is no LINKAGE SECTION because Burroughs does not allow subprograms. (ANSI COBOL does not include subprograms.)

In the FILE SECTION each file description entry must include the clause

```
FILE CONTAINS integer RECORDS
```

for each disk or tape file. This is how the compiler knows the size of a file.

In the FILE SECTION there are several important differences between COBOL on the B1700 and on the IBM-1130. We shall explain the most important aspects of this entry on the B1700. The basic format of the FD entry is

```
FD file-name [FILE CONTAINS integer-1 RECORDS]

              [BLOCK CONTAINS integer-2

                { RECORDS    }
                { CHARACTERS }  ]
```

```
[RECORD CONTAINS integer-3
    CHARACTERS]


⎡       ⎧RECORD IS  ⎫ ⎧OMITTED ⎫⎤
⎢ LABEL ⎨           ⎬ ⎨        ⎬⎥
⎣       ⎩RECORDS ARE⎭ ⎩STANDARD⎭⎦


⎡      ⎧RECORD IS  ⎫
⎢ DATA ⎨           ⎬
⎣      ⎩RECORDS ARE⎭

    data-name-1 [data-name-2 ...]⎤.
                                 ⎦
```

The FILE CONTAINS clause is required for disk and tape files and is used by the MCP to determine the actual size of the file. The FILE CONTAINS clause is optional for other types of files. The remaining clauses are treated exactly as on an IBM-1130 except for the BLOCK CONTAINS clause. On the IBM-1130 this clause has no real effect, since blocking is done automatically and is beyond the control of the programmer. On the B1700 the size of the blocks for a file is controllable. For disk and tape files the size of blocks is limited only by the size of the main memory. Generally, the size of the blocks for disk and tape files should be made as large as possible. However, for student programs it is unlikely that blocking will be needed, and the BLOCK CONTAINS clause may be omitted.

The B1700 supports COBOL sort files. These disk files are used for sorting purposes only. The FILE SECTION entry for such files is

```
SD sort-file-name
   [FILE CONTAINS integer-1 RECORDS]


⎡                           ⎧RECORDS   ⎫⎤
⎢ BLOCK CONTAINS integer-2  ⎨          ⎬⎥
⎣                           ⎩CHARACTERS⎭⎦


⎡      ⎧RECORD IS  ⎫
⎢ DATA ⎨           ⎬
⎣      ⎩RECORDS ARE⎭

    data-name-1 [data-name-2 ...]⎤.
                                 ⎦
```

The FILE-CONTROL entry for a sort file is somewhat special. It must have the format

```
SELECT sort-file-name ASSIGN TO SORT DISK.
```

In record descriptions a variety of USAGEs are permitted. You can choose from among COMP, COMPUTATIONAL-1, COMPUTATIONAL-3, INDEX, DISPLAY, and ASCII. COMPUTATIONAL-1 is equivalent to COMPUTATIONAL, and both USAGEs specify storing each digit of the item in four bits (one-half byte). In COMPUTATIONAL-3 any sign is stored as part of the rightmost digit of the item, and thus the sign is not included in determining the storage requirements of the item. With COMPUTATIONAL or COMPUTATIONAL-1, the sign is stored as a separate character and must be counted in determining the storage requirements of such a data item. Any item with USAGE DISPLAY is stored one character per byte. The ASCII USAGE is used primarily in working with ASCII files, which we shall not discuss.

The VALUE clause for data items that are condition names is more general. For example, you could write

```
88 PERMISSIBLE-CODES VALUE IS 1 THRU 6,
   8 THRU 10, 13.
```

or

```
88 PERMISSIBLE-VALUE VALUE IS 'A', 'B', 'F', 'R'.
```

PROCEDURE DIVISION

In the ACCEPT and DISPLAY statements, you must specify SPO (the console typewriter) or a mnemonic name for SPO. The card reader and line printer cannot be used in these statements.

END-OF-JOB is a reserved word for this compiler. It is considered to be a statement. The statement is optional, but if used, it must be the last statement of the program.

The WRITE statement for the line printer is handled somewhat differently. As we have observed, mnemonic names cannot be assigned to channels 01 through 12 in the SPECIAL-NAMES paragraph. Instead, you can write the name of the channel after the word ADVANCING. For example, you could write

```
WRITE PRINT-LINE BEFORE ADVANCING TO CHANNEL 01.
```

As on the IBM-1130, channel 01 signifies the top of a page, and channel 12 signifies the bottom of a page.

The OPEN statement is more complex on the B1700. By writing

```
                                  [ [WITH LOCK ACCESS] ]
OPEN INPUT tape-file-name         | {REVERSED         | |
                                  [ [WITH NO REWIND  ] ]
```

or

```
OPEN OUTPUT tape-file-name [WITH NO REWIND]
```

you can specify a number of actions associated with tape files. For example, the WITH NO REWIND option causes the tape file to be opened without rewinding the tape to position it at the beginning of the file. The REVERSED option causes the records of the file to be processed in reverse order.

When a file on disk is opened I-O or INPUT, the MCP of the B1700 checks the Disk File Directory to see if the file is present on disk. If it is not, then the MCP checks to see if the file was opened and closed previously in the program. If neither is true, then the MCP will ask the computer operator to store the file on disk or cancel the program being run. You can also open a file O-I on the B1700 to create a new file.

The CLOSE statement is also more complex on the B1700 than on many other computers. The format of this statement is

```
                              [ [ LOCK      ] ]
                              | | PURGE     | |
CLOSE file-name [REEL]  | WITH { RELEASE   } |
                              | | NO REWIND | |
                              [ [ REMOVE    ] ]
```

The NO REWIND option is used to specify the closing of tape files without rewinding the tape. The REEL option is used to close a reel of a magnetic tape file. The LOCK option is used to close a disk file and make it a permanent file by entering it in the Disk File Directory. The name entered for the file is its name as given in the program unless a VALUE OF ID clause is specified; in which case the specified value becomes the name for the file in the directory. The PURGE option closes a disk or tape file, and if the file is permanent, makes it no longer so. The RELEASE option can be used with any file. It closes the file and releases the area in main memory used for processing the file. The REMOVE option is used with disk files. This option causes the MCP to see if there is a file in the Disk File Directory whose name matches the output disk file that was just closed. If there is, then that file is deleted. Then the file being closed is made a permanent file.

The SORT verb is included in COBOL for the B1700. This verb allows you to sort any file stored on a mass storage device. However, this verb must be used cautiously. In many cases, the programmer can write easily his own sort routines, and by taking into account particular characteristics of the file to be sorted, he can produce better results than the SORT verb can provide. These remarks apply to all computers on which the SORT verb is included.

The SEARCH verb is available on the B1700.

We have only dealt with a few of the aspects of COBOL on the B1700 systems. They support ANSI COBOL fully and include many excellent features not mentioned in this text.

Some Basic Control Cards

A card with ? in column 1 followed by the word END is used to mark the physical end of COBOL source decks and data decks.

To compile a COBOL source program, one uses the following cards:

```
?    COMPILE program-id WITH COBOL SYNTAX
?    DATA CARDS
          source cards for program
?    END
```

To compile a COBOL source program, SAMPLE, and execute the program with one card file named STUDENT-FILE, one could use

```
?    COMPILE SAMPLE WITH COBOL
?    DATA CARDS
          source cards for program
?    END
?    DATA STUDENT-FILE
          data cards
?    END
```

If you are compiling a COBOL program, then you can specify compilation options on one or more cards following the compile card. These cards should have a $ in column 7. The options are listed in columns 8 through 80. Some of the options are

```
     LIST (list source program with single spacing)
     SINGLE (use single-spacing in listing source program)
```

DOUBLE (use double-spacing in listing source program)
CHECK (check for sequencing errors in source deck)
SUPPRESS (suppress all warning messages)
SPEC (If syntax errors occur, do not list source program, but do list errors together with the associated source statements.)

Any of the preceding options can be negated by prefacing it with the word NO. This can be used to override the default options on the computer.

COBOL Syntax for B1700

```
[MONITOR [DEPENDING] file-name ([data-name] ... :
[{ALL              }]).]
[{paragraph-name...}
```

IDENTIFICATION DIVISION

```
IDENTIFICATION DIVISION.
[PROGRAM-ID. Any COBOL word.]
[AUTHOR. Any entry.]
[INSTALLATION. Any entry.]
[DATE-WRITTEN. Any entry.]
[DATE-COMPILED. Any entry. Replaced by the current
               date and time as maintained by the
               MCP.]
[SECURITY. Any entry.]
[REMARKS. Any entry. Continuation lines must be
          coded in area B of the coding form.]
```

ENVIRONMENT DIVISION

```
ENVIRONMENT DIVISION.
CONFIGURATION SECTION.
[SOURCE-COMPUTER. {B-1700     } .]
                 {any entry. }

[OBJECT COMPUTER. [{B-1700}]

                                    [{WORDS     }]]
[MEMORY SIZE integer-1 [{CHARACTERS}]]
                                    [{MODULES   }]]
```

[<u>DATA SEGMENT-LIMIT</u> IS integer-2 CHARACTERS]

[<u>SEGMENT-LIMIT</u> IS priority number] .

[<u>SPECIAL-NAMES</u>. [<u>CURRENCY</u> SIGN <u>IS</u> literal]

[implementor-name <u>IS</u> mnemonic-name ...]

[<u>DECIMAL-POINT</u> <u>IS</u> <u>COMMA</u>].

[<u>INPUT-OUTPUT</u> <u>SECTION</u>.]

Option 1:

[<u>FILE-CONTROL</u>.

<u>SELECT</u> [<u>OPTIONAL</u>] file-name-1
    <u>ASSIGN</u> TO hardware-name-1

        [{ <u>NO</u> <u>BACKUP</u> }] [<u>FORM</u>] [FOR <u>MULTIPLE</u> <u>REEL</u>]
        [{ <u>BACKUP</u>   }]

[<u>RESERVE</u> { <u>NO</u>   } ALTERNATE { AREA }]
            { integer-1 }   { AREAS }

[{ <u>FILE-LIMIT</u> IS   } { literal-1   } { <u>THRU</u>   }
  { <u>FILE-LIMITS</u> ARE } { data-name-1 } { <u>THROUGH</u> }
        { <u>END</u>   }
        { literal-2   } ...
        { data-name-2   }

        { literal-m   } { <u>THRU</u>   } { literal-n   }]]
        { data-name-m } { <u>THROUGH</u> } { data-name-n }

[<u>ACCESS</u> MODE IS { <u>RANDOM</u>   }]
                 { <u>SEQUENTIAL</u> }
    [<u>ACTUAL</u> KEY IS data-name-3]

            [<u>PROCESSING</u> MODE <u>IS</u> <u>SEQUENTIAL</u>].]

Option 2:

[<u>FILE-CONTROL</u>.
  <u>SELECT</u> sort-file-name <u>ASSIGN</u> TO SORT <u>DISK</u>.]

<u>I-O-CONTROL</u>.

[<u>RERUN</u> EVERY { [<u>END</u> OF] <u>REEL</u>   } OF file-name-1] ...
               { integer-1 RECORDS }

[<u>SAME</u> [RECORD] AREA FOR file-name-2 file-name-3
                [file-name-4] ...] ...

[<u>MULTIPLE</u> <u>FILE</u> "multi-file-id" CONTAINS

  file-name-list [<u>POSITION</u> integer-2 ...].]

<u>DATA DIVISION</u>.

[<u>FILE</u> <u>SECTION</u>.]

Option 1:

<u>FD</u> file-name <u>COPY</u> "library-name".

Option 2:

$$\underline{FD} \text{ file-name-1} \left[\underline{RECORDING} \text{ MODE IS} \left\{ \begin{array}{l} \underline{ASCII} \\ \underline{STANDARD} \\ \underline{NON-STANDARD} \end{array} \right\} \right]$$

$$\underline{FILE} \text{ CONTAINS integer-1 } [\underline{BY} \text{ integer-2}] \text{ RECORDS}$$

$$\left[\underline{BLOCK} \text{ CONTAINS } [\text{integer-3 } \underline{TO}] \quad \text{integer-4} \left\{ \begin{array}{l} \underline{RECORDS} \\ CHARACTERS \end{array} \right\} \right]$$

$$\left[\underline{RECORD} \text{ contains } [\text{integer-5 } \underline{TO}] \text{ integer-6 CHARACTERS} \right]$$

$$\left[\underline{LABEL} \left\{ \begin{array}{l} \underline{RECORD} \text{ IS} \\ \underline{RECORDS} \text{ ARE} \end{array} \right\} \left\{ \begin{array}{l} \underline{OMITTED} \\ \underline{STANDARD} \end{array} \right\} \right]$$

$$\left[\left\{ \begin{array}{l} \underline{VA} \\ \underline{VALUE} \end{array} \right\} \text{ OF } \left\{ \begin{array}{l} \underline{ID} \\ \underline{IDENTIFICATION} \end{array} \right\} \text{ IS } \left\{ \begin{array}{l} \text{"literal-1"} \\ \text{data-name-1} \end{array} \right\} \right.$$

$$\left. [\underline{SAVE-FACTOR} \text{ IS literal-2} \right]$$

$$\left[\underline{DATA} \left\{ \begin{array}{l} \underline{RECORD} \text{ IS} \\ \underline{RECORDS} \text{ ARE} \end{array} \right\} \text{ data-name-2 } [\text{data-name-3} \ldots] \right]$$

Option 3:

<u>SD</u> sort-file-name <u>COPY</u> "library-name".

Option 4:

<u>SD</u> sort-file-name
  <u>FILE</u> CONTAINS integer-1 [<u>BY</u> integer-2] <u>RECORDS</u>

$$\left[\underline{RECORD} \text{ CONTAINS } [\text{integer-3 } \underline{TO} \text{ integer-4 CHARACTERS}] \right]$$

$$\left[\underline{BLOCK} \text{ CONTAINS } [\text{integer-5 } \underline{TO}] \text{ integer-6} \left\{ \begin{array}{l} \underline{RECORDS} \\ CHARACTERS \end{array} \right\} \right]$$

$$\left[\underline{DATA} \left\{ \begin{array}{l} \underline{RECORD} \text{ IS} \\ \underline{RECORDS} \text{ ARE} \end{array} \right\} \text{ data-name-1 } [\text{data-name-2}] \ldots \right].$$

Option 1:

```
01 data-name-1 COPY "library-name".
```

Option 2:

```
{01            } {FILLER      }
{level-number } {data-name-1 }
   [REDEFINES data-name-2]

[ {PC     }                                       ]
[ {PIC    } IS (allowable PICTURE characters)     ]
[ {PICTURE}                                       ]

[{BZ              }] [{OC     }
[{BLANK WHEN ZERO }] [{OCCURS }

              {integer-1 TIMES                  }
              {integer-2 TO integer-3 TIMES     }

              [DEPENDING ON data-name-3]]

[{ASCENDING  } KEY IS data-name-4
[{DESCENDING }
    [data-name-5] ...] ...

[INDEXED BY index-name-1 [index-name-2] ...]

                 (DISPLAY          )
                 (CMP              )
                 (CMP-1            )
                 (COMP             )  {JS        }
[USAGE IS]       (COMPUTATIONAL    )  {JUST      } RIGHT
                 (COMPUTATIONAL-1  )  {JUSTIFIED }
                 (COMPUTATIONAL-3  )
                 (INDEX            )
                 (ASCII            )

[{VA    } IS literal-1 [{THRU    } literal-2
[{VALUE }               {THROUGH }

    [literal-3] [{THRU    } literal-4] ...]
                {THROUGH }

[{SY           }  {LEFT  }
[{SYNC         }  {RIGHT }
[{SYNCHRONIZED }
```

Option 3:

```
66 data-name-1 RENAMES data-name-2
        [{THRU    } data-name-3] .
        [{THROUGH }
```

Option 4:

    88 condition-name {VA / VALUE} IS literal-1

    [literal-2... [{THRU / THROUGH}] literal-n...].
    [WORKING-STORAGE SECTION.]

Same level number syntax as shown in the FILE SECTION
except that 77 level numbers can be used to reflect
noncontiguous data areas, if used, must precede all
other level number entries.

PROCEDURE DIVISION.

    ACCEPT data-name [FROM {SPO / mnemonic-name}]

Option 1:

    ADD {literal-1 / data-name-1} [{literal-2 / data-name-2} ...] TO

    data-name-n [ROUNDED] [ON SIZE ERROR any statement]

Option 2:

    ADD {literal-1 / data-name-1} {literal-2 / data-name-2} [{literal-3 / data-name-3} ...]

    GIVING data-name-n [ROUNDED] [ON SIZE ERROR any
    statement]

Option 3:

    ADD {CORR / CORRESPONDING} data-name-1 TO data-name-2
        [ROUNDED]

    [ON SIZE ERROR any statement]
    ALTER procedure-name-1 TO [PROCEED TO]
        procedure-name-2

    [procedure-name-3 [TO PROCEED TO]
        procedure-name-4 ...]

    CLOSE file-name-1 [REEL] [WITH {LOCK / PURGE / RELEASE / NO REWIND}]

```
[file-name-2...]
COMPUTE data-name-1 [ROUNDED]
         ⎧data-name-2           ⎫
   =     ⎨numeric-literal       ⎬
         ⎩arithmetic-expression ⎭

[ON SIZE ERROR any statement]
```

Option 1:

```
COPY "library-name".
```

Option 2:

```
COPY "library-name"

⎡          ⎧word-1      ⎫    ⎧word-2      ⎫
⎢REPLACING ⎨            ⎬ BY ⎨            ⎬
⎢          ⎩data-name-1 ⎭    ⎩data-name-2 ⎭
⎢              ⎡⎧word-3      ⎫    ⎧word-4      ⎫    ⎤   ⎤
⎢              ⎢⎨            ⎬ BY ⎨            ⎬ ...⎥ . ⎥
⎢              ⎣⎩data-name-3 ⎭    ⎩data-name-4 ⎭    ⎦   ⎦
        ⎧literal-1   ⎫ ⎡⎧literal-2   ⎫    ⎤
DISPLAY ⎨            ⎬ ⎢⎨            ⎬ ...⎥
        ⎩data-name-1 ⎭ ⎣⎩data-name-2 ⎭    ⎦
    ⎡     ⎧SPO           ⎫⎤
    ⎢Upon ⎨              ⎬⎥
    ⎣     ⎩mnemonic-name ⎭⎦
```

Option 1:

```
DIVIDE [MOD] ⎧literal-1   ⎫ INTO
             ⎨            ⎬
             ⎩data-name-1 ⎭
   data-name-2 [ROUNDED]

   [ON SIZE ERROR any statement]
```

Option 2:

```
DIVIDE [MOD] ⎧literal-1   ⎫ ⎧BY  ⎫ ⎧literal-2   ⎫
             ⎨            ⎬ ⎨    ⎬ ⎨            ⎬
             ⎩data-name-1 ⎭ ⎩INTO⎭ ⎩data-name-2 ⎭

   GIVING data-name-3 [ROUNDED]
   ⎡REMAINDER data-name-4 [ROUNDED]⎤

   [ON SIZE ERROR any statement]
END-OF-JOB.
EXAMINE data-name
                 ⎧ALL         ⎫ ⎧literal-1   ⎫
   TALLYING      ⎨LEADING     ⎬ ⎨            ⎬
                 ⎩UNTIL FIRST ⎭ ⎩data-name-1 ⎭
```

$$\left\{ \begin{array}{l} \left[\underline{\text{REPLACING}} \ \underline{\text{BY}} \ \begin{array}{l} \text{literal-2} \\ \text{data-name-2} \end{array} \right] \\[2ex] \text{REPLACING} \left\{ \begin{array}{l} \underline{\text{ALL}} \\ \underline{\text{LEADING}} \\ [\underline{\text{UNTIL}}] \ \underline{\text{FIRST}} \end{array} \right\} \left\{ \begin{array}{l} \text{literal-3} \\ \text{data-name-3} \end{array} \right\} \\[3ex] \underline{\text{BY}} \left\{ \begin{array}{l} \text{literal-4} \\ \text{data-name-4} \end{array} \right\} \end{array} \right\}$$

$\underline{\text{EXIT}}$.

Option 1:

$\underline{\text{GO}}$ TO [procedure-name].

Option 2:

$\underline{\text{GO}}$ TO procedure-name-1 procedure-name-2
  [procedure-name-3 ...]
$\underline{\text{DEPENDING}}$ $\underline{\text{ON}}$ data-name.

Option 1:

$\underline{\text{IF}}$ condition-1 statement-1

Option 2:

$\underline{\text{IF}}$ condition $\left\{ \begin{array}{l} \text{statement-1} \\ \underline{\text{NEXT}} \ \underline{\text{SENTENCE}} \end{array} \right\}$ $\left\{ \begin{array}{l} \underline{\text{OTHERWISE}} \\ \underline{\text{ELSE}} \end{array} \right\}$
$\left\{ \begin{array}{l} \text{statement-2} \\ \underline{\text{NEXT}} \ \underline{\text{SENTENCE}} \end{array} \right\}$

Option 3:

$\underline{\text{IF}}$ $\left\{ \begin{array}{l} \text{literal-1} \\ \text{data-name-1} \\ \text{arithmetic expression-1} \end{array} \right\}$

IS [$\underline{\text{NOT}}$] $\left\{ \begin{array}{l} = \\ > \\ < \\ \underline{\text{EQUAL}} \ \text{TO} \\ \underline{\text{LESS}} \ \text{THAN} \\ \underline{\text{GREATER}} \ \text{THAN} \\ \underline{\text{EQUALS}} \end{array} \right\}$

$\left\{ \begin{array}{l} \text{literal-2} \\ \text{data-name-2} \\ \text{arithmetic expression-2} \end{array} \right\}$

Option 4:

$$\text{IF} \begin{Bmatrix} \text{data-name} \\ \text{arithmetic expression} \end{Bmatrix} \text{IS} [\underline{\text{NOT}}] \begin{Bmatrix} \underline{\text{ZERO}} \\ \underline{\text{POSITIVE}} \\ \underline{\text{NEGATIVE}} \end{Bmatrix}$$

Option 5:

$$\underline{\text{IF}} \text{ data-name IS} [\underline{\text{NOT}}] \begin{Bmatrix} \underline{\text{NUMERIC}} \\ \underline{\text{ALPHABETIC}} \end{Bmatrix}$$

Option 6:

$$\underline{\text{IF}} [\underline{\text{NOT}}] \text{ condition-name}$$

Option 1:

$$\underline{\text{MOVE}} \begin{Bmatrix} \text{literal-1} \\ \text{data-name-1} \end{Bmatrix} \underline{\text{TO}} \text{ data-name-2 [data-name-3...]}$$

Option 2:

$$\underline{\text{MOVE}} \begin{Bmatrix} \underline{\text{CORR}} \\ \underline{\text{CORRESPONDING}} \end{Bmatrix} \text{data-name-1} \underline{\text{TO}} \text{ data-name-2}$$

$$\underline{\text{MULTIPLY}} \begin{Bmatrix} \text{literal-1} \\ \text{data-name-1} \end{Bmatrix} \underline{\text{BY}} \begin{Bmatrix} \text{literal-2} \\ \text{data-name-2} \end{Bmatrix}$$

[<u>GIVING</u> data-name-3] [<u>ROUNDED</u>] [ON <u>SIZE</u> <u>ERROR</u> any statement]
label. <u>NOTE</u> any comment.

Option 2—Paragraph NOTE:

<u>NOTE</u>. any comment.

Option 3—Sentence NOTE:

<u>NOTE</u>. any comment.

$$\underline{\text{OPEN}}$$

$$\left[\underline{\text{INPUT}} \text{ file-name-1} \left[\begin{Bmatrix} \text{WITH } \underline{\text{LOCK}} \text{ } [\underline{\text{ACCESS}}] \\ \underline{\text{REVERSED}} \\ \text{WITH } \underline{\text{NO}} \text{ } \underline{\text{REWIND}} \end{Bmatrix} \right] \right.$$

$$\left. [\text{file-name-2...}] \right]$$

$$
\left[\underline{\text{OUTPUT}} \text{ file-name-3 } [\text{WITH } \underline{\text{NO}} \ \underline{\text{REWIND}}] \\ [\text{file-name-4}\ldots] \right]
$$

$$
\left[\left\{ \begin{array}{l} \underline{\text{INPUT-OUTPUT}} \\ \underline{\text{I-O}} \end{array} \right\} \text{ file-name-5 } [\text{file-name-6}\ldots] \right]
$$

$$
\left[\underline{\text{O-I}} \text{ file-name-7 } [\text{file-name-8}] \right]
$$

Option 1:

$$
\underline{\text{PERFORM}} \text{ procedure-name-1 } \left[\left\{ \begin{array}{l} \underline{\text{THRU}} \\ \underline{\text{THROUGH}} \end{array} \right\} \right.
$$

$$
\left. \text{procedure-name-2} \right]
$$

Option 2:

$$
\underline{\text{PERFORM}} \text{ procedure-name-1 } \left[\left\{ \begin{array}{l} \underline{\text{THRU}} \\ \underline{\text{THROUGH}} \end{array} \right\} \right.
$$

$$
\left. \text{procedure-name-2} \right]
$$

$$
\left\{ \begin{array}{l} \text{integer-1} \\ \text{data-name-1} \end{array} \right\} \underline{\text{TIMES}}
$$

Option 3:

$$
\underline{\text{PERFORM}} \text{ procedure-name-1 } \left[\left\{ \begin{array}{l} \underline{\text{THRU}} \\ \underline{\text{THROUGH}} \end{array} \right\} \right.
$$

$$
\left. \text{procedure-name-2} \right]
$$

$$
\underline{\text{UNTIL}} \text{ condition-1}
$$

Option 4:

$$
\underline{\text{PERFORM}} \text{ procedure-name-1}
$$

$$
\left[\left\{ \begin{array}{l} \underline{\text{THRU}} \\ \underline{\text{THROUGH}} \end{array} \right\} \text{ procedure-name-2} \right]
$$

$$
\underline{\text{VARYING}} \left\{ \begin{array}{l} \text{index-name-1} \\ \text{data-name-1} \end{array} \right\} \underline{\text{FROM}} \left\{ \begin{array}{l} \text{index-name-2} \\ \text{data-name-2} \\ \text{numeric-literal-1} \end{array} \right\} \underline{\text{BY}}
$$

$$
\left\{ \begin{array}{l} \text{data-name-3} \\ \text{numeric-literal-2} \end{array} \right\} \underline{\text{UNTIL}} \text{ condition-1}
$$

$$
\left[\underline{\text{AFTER}} \left\{ \begin{array}{l} \text{index-name-3} \\ \text{data-name-4} \end{array} \right\} \right.
$$

$$
\underline{\text{FROM}} \left\{ \begin{array}{l} \text{index-name-4} \\ \text{data-name-5} \\ \text{numeric-literal-3} \end{array} \right\} \underline{\text{BY}} \left\{ \begin{array}{l} \text{data-name-6} \\ \text{numeric-literal-4} \end{array} \right\}
$$

UNDERLINE notation for COBOL syntax:

        UNTIL condition-2] [AFTER {index-name-5} FROM
                                  {data-name-7 }

        {index-name-6   }   {data-name-9   }
        {data-name-8   } BY {numeric-literal-6}
        {numeric-literal-5}

        UNTIL condition-3]

        READ file-name RECORD [INTO data-name]
          [{AT END   }
          [{INVALID KEY }

              any imperative statement]

        RELEASE record-name [FROM data-name]
        RETURN file-name RECORD [INTO data-name]
            [AT END any statement]

Option 1:

        SEARCH data-name-1 [VARYING {index-name-1}]
                                    {data-name-2 }

            [AT END imperative-statement-1]

                WHEN condition-1 {imperative-statement-2}
                                 {NEXT SENTENCE   }

                [WHEN condition-2 {imperative-statement-3} ...]
                                  {NEXT SENTENCE   }
        SEARCH ALL data-name-3
            [AT END imperative-statement-4]

                WHEN condition-3 {imperative-statement-5}
                                 {NEXT SENTENCE   }
        SEEK file-name RECORD / [WITH KEY CONVERSION]

Option 1:

        SET {index-name-1} [{index-name-2} ...]
            {data-name-1 } [{data-name-2 }   ]

            TO {index-name-3}
               {data-name-3 }
               {literal-1   }

Option 2:

        SET index-name-4 [index-name-5 ...]

            {UP BY } {data-name-4}
            {DOWN BY} {literal-2 }

        SORT file-name-1

```
            FROM data-name-2
     [ROUNDED] [ON SIZE ERROR any statement]
```

Option 1:

```
     USE AFTER STANDARD ERROR PROCEDURE
              ┌ file-name...  ┐
              │ INPUT         │
          ON ┤ OUTPUT         ├
              │ INPUT-OUTPUT  │
              │ I-O           │
              └ O-I           ┘
```

Option 2:

```
     USE ┌ AFTER  ┐ STANDARD ┌ BEGINNING ┐
         └ BEFORE ┘          └ ENDING    ┘

       ┌┌ REEL ┐┐                        ┌ file-name... ┐
       │└ FILE ┘│ LABEL PROCEDURE ON    ┤ INPUT         ├
       └        ┘                        └ OUTPUT        ┘
```

Option 3:

```
     USE FOR KEY CONVERSION ON file-name-1
         [file-name-2...].
```

Option 1:

```
     WRITE record-name [FROM data-name-1]
         ┌┌ AFTER  ┐            ┌┌ integer-1    ┐           ┐┐
         │└ BEFORE ┘ ADVANCING ┤│ data-name-2  │ LINES     ││
         │                      └[ TO CHANNEL integer-2 ]   ┘┘
         ┌    ┌ END-OF-PAGE ┐                              ┐
         │ AT ┤ EOP         ├ imperative-statement         │
         └    └             ┘                              ┘
         ┌         ┌ ERROR                       ┐┐
         │ TO      │ AUXILIARY                    ││
         │         │ STACKER ┌ literal-1    ┐     ││
         └         └         └ data-name-4  ┘     ┘┘
```

Option 2:

```
     WRITE record-name [FROM data-name]

         [INVALID KEY any statement]
```

Option 3:

```
     ZIP data-name
```

IBM-1130

Using Control Cards

The following material describes the use and purpose of several monitor control cards for the IBM-1130.

The JOB card

The JOB card informs the IBM-1130 monitor program of the beginning of a job. The most commonly used form of the card is

Card column	Content
1–2	/ /
4–6	JOB
8	T
11–14	four-digit number of disk required for job

The / / JOB characters are required. The optional character T causes all programs and files created in the job to be temporary. The temporary programs and files will be destroyed when the next job is processed.

Each disk of the computer center is identified by a four-digit number. If you know that your job will require a disk, perhaps the one containing the COBOL compiler, then specify its number in columns 11 through 14. Additional disks may be specified in columns 16 through 19, 21 through 24, 26 through 29, and 31 through 34.

Columns 46 through 53 may be used to give header information, such as your name, at the top of each page of line printer output.

You can speed the compilation of your program greatly by observing the following steps, which require that your computer have at least two disk drives. Let us assume that the COBOL compiler is on disk 4000 and that disk 1000 is normally on a disk drive as well as disk 4000 on another disk drive. On your JOB card, place 4000 in columns 11 through 14, 1000 in columns 16 through 19, and 1000 in columns 41 through 45. This can cut compilation time in half inasmuch as two working-storage areas can be used during compilation.

The COBOL card

The COBOL card causes the monitor to load the COBOL compiler and begin the compilation of the COBOL source program following it. The compiled program will be stored in the working-storage area of a disk. The format of the card is as shown.

Card column	Content
1–2	/ /
4–8	COBOL

Note that when the next JOB card is encountered, the object program is destroyed in the WORKING-STORAGE area. You could execute the program in the same job, or you could store the object program permanently and execute it under a later job card.

The XEQ card

The execute card (XEQ card) loads an object program from disk to main memory and executes the program. Its format is as shown.

Card column	Content
1–2	/ /
4–6	XEQ
8–12	name of program
14	L
16–17	two-digit number

If the program to be executed has just been compiled and not stored permanently, then columns 8 through 12 should be blank. Otherwise, columns 8 through 12 should contain the (left-justified) name assigned to the program when it was stored permanently. The number of LOCAL, NOCAL, FILES, and G2250 cards following the XEQ card should appear (right-justified) in columns 16 and 17. (Blanks are read as 0.) The L is optional and is explained in this appendix in the section on debugging a program. If your program has disk records more than 320 words long, then placing N in column 19 will make it more efficient.

The end of a COBOL program to be compiled or a card file to be read is indicated by a card having /* in columns 1 and 2. Thus a sample COBOL deck could be

```
//ƀJOBƀTƀƀ4002        (ƀ indicates a blank.)
//ƀCOBOL
            COBOL source program
/*
//ƀXEQ
            card-file-1
/*
            card-file-2
/*
            blank card
```

This job uses disk 4002, compiles and stores a program temporarily, and executes the program; and the program reads two card files. The blank card is used because of the method of operation of the card reader.

The Disk Monitor System

As you can see, many of the control cards involve the monitor system, so we will digress long enough to explain some of its capabilities.

The IBM-1130 Disk Monitor System is a collection of programs that provide a continuous control of the 1130 computing system. These programs follow.

1. **Supervisor**   The supervisor program is the heart of the monitor system. The program provides the linkage between the user program and/or other programs of the monitor system. The supervisor reads and analyzes the control records and causes the proper program to assume control of the CPU temporarily, or forces the program that currently has control of the CPU to relinquish its control. The supervisor always resides in the memory, and a copy of the supervisor is kept on disk in case the supervisor in main storage is inadvertently destroyed. The process of copying the supervisor from disk into main storage is called a *cold start*.

2. **Disk Utility Program (DUP)**   This group of programs performs operations such as moving, deleting, and dumping data and/or programs to or from a disk.

3. **FORTRAN Compiler**   This program translates the source program written in the FORTRAN language into an object program in machine language.

4. **ASSEMBLER**   This program translates a source program in the ASSEMBLER language into a machine-language object program.

5. **COBOL Compiler**   This program translates a source program in the COBOL language into a machine-language object program.

6. **System Library**   This is a group of disk resident programs that perform input/output, arithmetic, data conversion, and disk initialization and maintenance functions.

7. **Core Load Builder**   When a source program is converted to machine language, an object program is produced in disk system format. This object program is not executable. The Core Load Builder constructs from this object program a core image program that is in Disk Core Image format. Core image programs can be executed immediately or they can be stored on disk for later execution.

8. **Core Image Loader**   This serves as both a loader for core image programs and as an interface for the monitor programs.

Disk Cartridges

The following list elaborates on some of the disks available for use on the IBM-1130.

1. **System cartridge**   The system cartridge is the cartridge containing the monitor system program. This cartridge has been initialized by the Disk Cartridge Initialization program before the monitor system was loaded on it by the system loader.

2. **Master cartridge**   The system cartridge on logical drive 0 is called the master cartridge. The cold start establishes the physical drive on which the system cartridge resides as logical drive 0. The Job Card can be used to select the system cartridge by specifying its identification in columns 11 through 14.

3. **Satellite cartridge**   After the master cartridge is established, all other cartridges are called *satellite* cartridges. To use these in a JOB, you must specify them in columns 16 through 19, 21 through 24, 26 through 29, and 31 through 34 of the JOB card.

A description of the layout of a disk cartridge follows. The system cartridge is divided into three logical areas:

1. IBM area,
2. User area,
3. Working-storage area.

In addition to the first three logical areas, the user may define a fixed area for the purpose of storing programs and/or data files in permanent locations so that they may be referenced by a sector address.

The layout of a system cartridge is

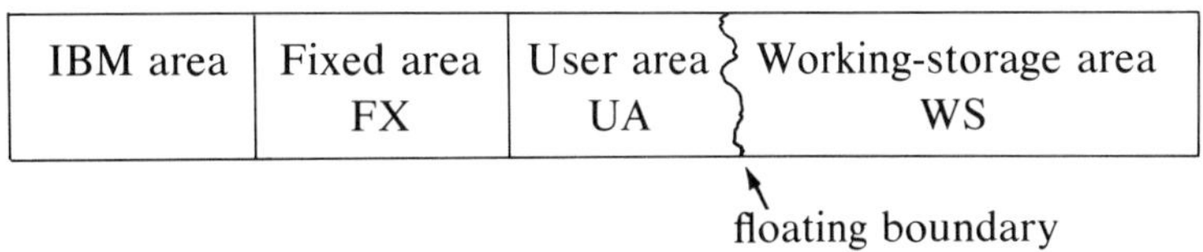

1. **Fixed area**   This area can be used to store data files in disk-data format, DDF, and core image programs in disk-core image format, DCI.

2. **User area**   This area can be used to store main programs in disk system format, DSF, subroutines in DSF, data files in DDF, and core image programs in DCI.

3. **Working-storage area**   This area can be used to store information temporarily for a job. The size of the working-storage area decreases as the user area increases.

There are several optional cards that can immediately follow the COBOL card. The first type of card begins with ** in columns 1 and 2 and a heading in columns 3 through 58. The heading will be printed at the top of each page of output.

The second type of card begins with * in column 1 followed by one or more of the following words separated by commas and no spaces between words.

1. **LIST, CSUP, NOLIST**   LIST causes a listing of the source program. CSUP lists the source program except for COPIED modules. NOLIST suppresses all listing.

2. EJCT or NOEJCT   EJCT causes a skip to a new page before printing a source program, a map, or diagnostics. NOEJCT is the negation of EJCT.

3. DMAP or NODMAP   DMAP prints a map of the DATA DIVISION showing the relative hexadecimal addresses of all data items relative to an origin of 0000 unless 5 is specified. NODMAP is the negation of DMAP.

4. PMAP or NOPMAP   PMAP causes the listing of the relative hexadecimal addresses of all PROCEDURE DIVISION paragraphs and sections. NOPMAP is the negation of PMAP.

5. /xxxx   This symbol causes all MAP addresses to be printed relative to an origin of xxxx (four hexadecimal digits). Omitting the symbol causes an assumed origin of 0000.

6. KP26 or NOKP26   KP26 allows the use of card decks punched on a 024/026 or 029 punch. NOKP26 is the negation of KP26.

7. 2501 or 1442   The principal card device is the 2501 or 1442. This specifies the card device for the ACCEPT statement only.

8. 1403 or 1132   The principal printer is a 1403 or 1132. This specifies the line printer for the DISPLAY statement only.

9. SUPX or NOSUPX   If C-level errors are present, the options suppress execution of DUP functions and source-program execution.

10. DUMP or NODUMP   DUMP prints all content of main storage if an execution time error occurs. NODUMP is the negation of DUMP.

11. STNO or NOSTNO   These include statement numbers in the object program. These options are used in the event of an execution time error. The options should be omitted after a program is debugged since they require extra main memory above the normal program requirements.

12. SUBR   The program to be compiled is a subroutine.

13. S =nnnn   When a main program uses a subroutine and the subroutine is compiled, a message stating that stack depth is nnnn is printed; then S =nnnn must be included as an option for the main program. Otherwise, an R20 error message will occur.

14. XREF or NOXREF   XREF causes a listing of all data items, paragraph names, and section names. Following each will be the numbers of all statements where the name occurred. An * marks the statement where the name was first used. NOXREF is the negation of XREF.

15. **DDMP** Prints all contents of the DATA DIVISION if an execution time error occurs.

The following example illustrates compiler options.

```
//ƀJOBƀTƀƀ4000
//ƀCOBOL
*LIST,STNO,EJCT,DMAP,PMAP,DUMP,/01FE


             Cards for source program


/*
//ƀXEQƀƀƀƀƀƀL
```

The DUP program

Compiled programs and disk files created by a program are stored temporarily in the WORKING-STORAGE (abbreviated WS) area of a disk. They can be stored permanently in the User area or Fixed area. The Disk Utility program performs operations involving a disk.

The format of the card to load and execute the Disk Utility program is

Card column	Content
1–2	/ /
4–6	DUP

When the supervisor encounters this card, it loads a copy of DUP in main storage, and DUP assumes control of the CPU.

Following this card can be one or more cards requesting action. The format of these cards is basically the same.

Card column	Content
1	*
2–12	name (left-justified) of action desired
13–14	code for FROM device or area
17–18	code for TO device or area
21–25	name (left-justified) of program or file
27–30	number (right-justified) giving size of file
31–34	number of FROM disk
37–40	number of TO disk

The codes for columns 13 through 14 and 17 through 18 can be

UA	User area of disk
WS	Working-Storage area of disk
FX	Fixed area of disk
CD	card reader
PR	principal printing device
PT	paper tape

There are many possible actions that DUP can perform, but we will discuss only a few of them.

Suppose you wish to compile a program and store the object program permanently. You must select a name for the program to use when it is stored. The name should contain no more than five characters, start with an alphabetic character, and contain no special characters or hyphens. Let's suppose we choose ANAME. (For a subprogram, this name must be identical with the first five characters of the name given in the PROGRAM-ID paragraph.)

```
//ƀJOBƀƀƀƀ4002
//ƀCOBOL


            deck for source program
/*

//ƀDUP
*STOREƀƀƀƀƀWSƀƀUAƀƀANAMEƀƀƀƀƀƀƀƀƀ4002
            blank card
```

Note that we specified 4002 as the TO disk, and so our program is stored on the same disk as the COBOL compiler.

If we wish to execute the program as a part of the same job, we would add the following cards:

```
//ƀXEQƀANAME


            card file (if used by program)

/*

            blank card
```

Suppose that later we wish to execute ANAME using two card files. The deck needed would be

```
//ƀJOBƀƀƀƀ4002
//ƀXEQƀANAME


            card file 1


/*

            card file 2

/*

            blank card
```

Suppose we have a program that will use disk files for storage. We may want these files to be permanent. To do this, we first select a name for the file in the way just described for programs. Note that the names for the program or disk file need not be the same as those given in the source program. Next we must know how many sectors the file will contain. Recall that a sector contains 320 words. First calculate (from the file description) how many words a file record will occupy. Next consider two cases:

1. If a record occupies more than 320 words, then calculate how many sectors are needed to store one record and multiply that result by the number of records in the file.
2. If a record occupies no more than 320 words, calculate the number of records that can be stored (in their entirety) in one sector. Next divide the number of records in the file by the number of records per sector. If there is no remainder, the result is the number of sectors required to store the file. If there is a remainder, increase the result to the next larger integer to obtain the number of sectors required.

For example, suppose a file contains 56 records, each of which needs 106 words of storage. Each sector can hold 3 records. Thus 18 sectors can hold 54 records, and 19 sectors can hold the entire file.

Or suppose that a file contains 63 records, each of which needs 500 words of storage. Each record needs 2 sectors of storage, and the entire file will occupy 126 sectors of storage.

The card to provide permanent storage for a file, named AFILE on disk, occupying 41 sectors on disk 4002 is

```
*STOREDATAᵇᵇWSᵇᵇUAᵇᵇAFILEᵇ0041ᵇᵇᵇᵇᵇᵇ4002
```

Suppose we want to remove a program or file that has been stored permanently. The format of the card for this is

```
*DELETEᵇᵇᵇᵇᵇᵇᵇᵇᵇᵇᵇNAME1
```

where NAME1 is the name of the item to be deleted.

Suppose we wish a list of the programs and files stored by the computer users in the user area or fixed area. (This is where your programs and files are stored permanently.) The format of the card to obtain the listing is

```
*DUMPLET
```

or

```
*DUMPFLET
```

The first card will list the names of the items stored in the user area, and the second does the same for the fixed area. If you desire only a listing for one disk, then place its number in columns 31 through 34. Otherwise, the listing is done for all disks mounted on a drive at the time the dump is done.

The LOCAL and NOCAL cards

If you believe that memory may not be large enough to contain your program and the subprograms it calls, you may LOCAL some of the subprograms. The localed subprograms will be loaded only when they are called by the main program. The format of the card is

```
*LOCALMPROG,SUB1,SUB2, . . .
```

if the main program MPROG is stored on disk or

```
*LOCAL,SUB1,SUB2, . . .
```

if the main program is only temporarily stored in the working-storage area. SUB1, SUB2, . . . are the names of the subprograms to be localed. Note that you cannot local a subprogram that calls a localed subprogram. No spaces between items are permitted in a LOCAL card.

The NOCAL card has the format

```
*NOCALMPROG,SUB1,SUB2, . . .
```

or

```
*NOCALSUB1,SUB2, . . .
```

and causes subroutines SUB1, SUB2, . . . to be loaded with the main program even if they are not called by the main program.

The FILES card

The FILES card is the most-used execution time option. As you have seen, we can store files on disk under an assigned name. When a COBOL program is executed, the FILES card established which disk files named in the program are only temporary and which files are permanently stored on disk. Let us suppose that our program, MPROG, has three files: PAYROLL, EMPLOYEE, and FEDERAL-TAX. Let us assume that FEDERAL-TAX is a permanent file, that 2 is its file number in the program, and that EMPLOYEE is a permanent file whose file number is 1.

```
FILE-CONTROL.
      SELECT PAYROLL ASSIGN TO DF-3-2000
         ACCESS IS RANDOM ACTUAL KEY IS EMNO.
      SELECT EMPLOYEE ASSIGN TO DF-1-1000
         ACCESS IS RANDOM ACTUAL KEY IS EMNO.
      SELECT FEDERAL-TAX ASSIGN TO DF-2-1000
         ACCESS IS SEQUENTIAL ACTUAL KEY IS EMNO2.
```

Suppose that FEDERAL-TAX is stored on disk under the name TAX, and EMPLOYEE is stored on disk under the name ENAME. Let PAYROLL be a temporary disk file. To execute MPROG with the files as described, we would use these cards:

```
//ƀJOB
//ƀXEQƀMPROGƀƀƀ01
*FILES(2,TAX),(1,ENAME)
```

If the file needed is not on the system cartridge, you should add the number of the disk where it is located as in (2,TAX,4003), for example.

Remember that all LOCAL, NOCAL, and FILES cards follow the XEQ card.

Monitor Control Cards for Sample Jobs

The following cards will create storage for a file name DFILE occupying 15 sectors on disk.

```
//ƀJOB
//ƀDUP
*STOREDATAƀƀWSƀƀUAƀƀDFILEƀ0015ƀƀƀƀƀƀ1000
```

```
blank card
```

The following cards will create storage for the file TAX occupying 20 sectors on disk 2000, compile PAYROLL, store PAYROLL, and execute PAYROLL using TAX (file number 5 in PAYROLL) and one card file.

```
//ƀJOB
//ƀDUP
*STOREDATAƀƀWSƀƀUAƀƀTAXƀƀƀ0020ƀƀƀƀƀƀ2000
//ƀCOBOL


              PAYROLL source program

/*
//ƀDUP
*STOREƀƀƀƀƀƀWSƀƀUAƀƀPAYRLƀƀƀƀƀƀ4002
//ƀXEQƀPAYRLƀƀƀ01
*FILES(5,TAX,2000)


              card file

/*

              blank card
```

The following cards will delete MPROG from disk and replace it by a new version.

```
//ƀJOB
//ƀCOBOL


              source program for new version of MPROG

/*
//ƀDUP
*DELETEƀƀƀƀƀƀƀƀƀƀƀƀMPROG
*STOREƀƀƀƀƀƀWSƀƀUAƀƀMPROGƀƀƀƀƀƀƀƀƀ4002
```

The following cards will execute PAYRL, stored on disk, using TAX as file number 1 of the program and using one card file.

```
//ƀJOB
//ƀXEQƀPAYRLƀƀƀ01
*FILES(1,TAX)


              card file

/*

              blank card.
```

There are many other control cards, and the ones we have discussed can be used in ways other than those mentioned here. If you need these functions in later work, consult the appropriate IBM manual, such as the latest version of the *IBM-1130 Disk Monitor System Reference Manual (Form C26-3750)*.

Debugging Programs

Step 1: Think before you run the program.

Step 2: Compile the program. If errors are found, they will be listed on the line printer. In rare instances, a message will be displayed on the console typewriter, which indicates a compiler malfunction. If these messages do not occur, then execute the program and proceed to step 3.

Step 3: The program may have errors that can be discovered only during execution. If such an error occurs, a message is printed of the form

$$**STNO=xxxx**ERR=YY**LOC=zzzz**ITEM=wwww$$

or

$$**ERR=YY**LOC=zzzz**ITEM=wwww$$

depending upon whether the STNO option was used or not.

YY is a two-digit code specifying the type of error. xxxx is the number of the statement where the error occurred. zzzz is the hexadecimal address of the instruction that caused the error. wwww is the hexadecimal address of the data, if any, involved in the error.

The meaning of the error codes follows.

Code	wwww	Meaning
01	None	RERUN clause in a program containing LOCALS or SOCALS
02	File number of checkpoint file	Checkpoint file is too small for rerun
03	File number of checkpoint or checkpoint file	Checkpoint file or checkpoint is in working-storage
05	None	Last statement of program did not lead to a STOP RUN
06	Address of subscript or index	A subscript or index has an illegal value
07	Address of data	A numeric display field contains nonnumeric characters
08	None	An exponent is not an integer from 1 through 32,767
09	None	A format 3 GO TO was not preceded by an ALTER statement
10	Address of file control block	An attempt was made to open a locked file
11	Address of file control block	An attempt was made to open an opened file
12	Address of file control block	An attempt was made to close a closed file
13	Address of file control block	An attempt was made to read an output file
14	Address of file control block	An attempt was made to write an input file
15	Address of file control block	An attempt was made to read, write, or seek a closed file
16	Address of file control block	A return was made to read or write a sequential file after EOF; examine action in EOF sentence

Code	wwww	Meaning
17	Address of file control block	Abnormal data was presented for punching
18	Address of file control block	A file passed between program, and sub-program was open at the time
19	Address of file control block	An attempt was made to do two successive WRITEs on an I-O file
21	Address of file control block	A column binary read was called for a file without an alternate area reserved
22	Address of file control block	A column binary punch was attempted for a file without an alternate area reserved
23	None	DATA has not been given by executing QNDTE
40	Address of file control block	An attempt was made to sort an unopened file
41	Address of parameter	An invalid parameter was presented to QSITL
42	Length of tag	Total length of tags for sort exceeds 319 word
43	Number of records that can be sorted	Too many records to sort for available space
44	Number of records processed	Disk space exceeded during sort
45	None	Abnormal condition encountered in sort mainline program
46	Address of actual key	Actual key for file being sorted is invalid
47	None	QSORT called before any records released via QSREL
50	Address of the parameter	Invalid parameter encountered in the list presented to QFRED or QFRIT
51	Address of the parameter	FORTRAN record area exceeded while processing the parameter at wwww
52	Address of the file control block referenced	File presented to QFRED or QFRIT is not blocked 320 words, but the -X specification was used in the SELECT for this file; remove the -X specification
81	None	Floating-point accumulator contents destroyed; eliminate use of floating-point arithmetic in called FORTRAN sub-routine, or execute QCORE after each call
82	None	Insufficient core available for the index; try localing subroutines
83	None	Invalid specification in parameter list; kcy length is 0, or invalid key occurred
84	Address of refer-enced relative record number	An out-of-sequence key exists in the file sequential portion
90-9F	None	The operator caused program termination; YY code is determined by computer center for these errors

As you see, by use of the STNO option and the execution time error messages you can obtain a fairly clear picture of the cause of the error. However, in some cases the knowledge of the immediate cause of the error does not always explain how it occurred. There are still a variety of possibilities open to you.

Step 4: We assume that you now need further information than was provided by the execution time error that you received. You can obtain further information about the state of your program at the time the error occurred by specifying the DDMP or the DUMP options on your compiler option card. If an execution time error occurs and the DDMP option is in effect, then the computer will print a hexadecimal listing of the values of all the data in your program at the time of the error. If the DUMP option is in effect at the time of the error, then the computer will print a hexadecimal listing of the content of all of main storage at the time of the error. To make proper use of these dumps, you should also specify the PMAP, DMAP, and XREF options on your compiler option card. These will print a list of all the data items in your program, the procedure names in your program, and the file areas for your program. The listings will include the hexadecimal addresses of all these items relative to an origin of /0000. In nearly all cases, by specifying the option /01FE on the compiler option card, you will have provided the compiler with the actual execution time address of the program. Then all the listings printed by the PMAP, DMAP, and XREF options will have the actual addresses of the items. Since the dumps printed by the DDMP or DUMP options have the actual (absolute) addresses of these items, it is a simple matter to determine the state of any part of your program at the time of the error from the dump. On some cases the execution address of the program is not /01FE. Then you need to place an L in column 14 of your XEQ card. this will cause the computer to print additional information that you can use in interpreting the dump. We will now show you how to find the content of each data item from a core dump. First, we must discuss hexadecimal notation and arithmetic.

Hexadecimal Notation and Addition

Hexadecimal is a number system based on 16. The hexadecimal symbols for the decimal numbers 0 through 15 are

0 for 0	8 for 8
1 for 1	9 for 9
2 for 2	A for 10
3 for 3	B for 11
4 for 4	C for 12
5 for 5	D for 13
6 for 6	E for 14
7 for 7	F for 15

If a number, say 1,243, is written in decimal (base 10), then this stands for (starting from left to right) $1 \cdot (10^3) + 2 \cdot (10^2) + 4 \cdot (10) + 3$. The number 1,243 as a hexadecimal number stands for $1 \cdot (16^3) + 2 \cdot (16^2) + 4 \cdot (16) + 3$, or the decimal number 5,275. The hexadecimal number 35B is equivalent to the decimal number $3 \cdot (16^2) + 5(16) + 11$, or 859.

To add two decimal numbers, say 136 and 75, you would find $6 + 5 = 11$ and subtract 10, which leaves 1, and carry 1. Then $1 + 3 + 7 = 11$. You subtract 10 and carry 1 to get

$$\begin{array}{r} {\scriptstyle 1\ 1} \\ 136 \\ \underline{75} \\ 211 \end{array}$$

To add the hexadecimal numbers 6 and C, you could do the following. $6 + C$ is 18 in decimal notation. Subtract 16 from 18, which leaves 2, and carry 1 to get

$$\begin{array}{r} {\scriptstyle 1} \\ 6 \\ \underline{C} \\ 12 \end{array}$$

We can check to see that in decimal notation 12 is $1 \cdot (16) + 2$ or 18.

To add C1 and 1F, you add 1 and F to get 16 in decimal notation. You subtract 16, which leaves 0, and carry a 1. Adding the 1 to C and 1, we obtain E. Thus

$$\begin{array}{r} C1 \\ \underline{1F} \\ E0 \end{array}$$

Some other examples follow.

$$\begin{array}{r} 0ED \\ +\ \ 14 \\ \hline 101 \end{array} \qquad \begin{array}{r} 0ED \\ +\ \ \ 1 \\ \hline 0EE \end{array} \qquad \begin{array}{r} 1FE \\ +\ \ 35 \\ \hline 233 \end{array}$$

We also need an easy way of converting a decimal integer to an equivalent hexadecimal integer. We will show you how to use the easy method of remainders. Suppose we want to convert the decimal integer 375 to an equivalent hexadecimal integer. The steps are:

> Divide 375 by 16 to get a quotient of 23 and a remainder of 7.
> Divide the quotient 23 of the first step by 16 to get a quotient of 1 and a remainder of 7.
> Divide the quotient 1 of the preceding step by 16 to get a quotient of 0 (the signal to stop this process) and a remainder of 1.
> Write the remainders obtained, in order from right to left to, get 177, which is the answer.

We will do another example to obtain the equivalent of the decimal integer 4,664.

> Divide 4,664 by 16 to get a quotient of 291 and a remainder of 8.
> Divide 291 by 16 to get a quotient of 18 and a remainder of 3.
> Divide 18 by 16 to get a quotient of 1 and a remainder of 2.
> Divide 1 by 16 to get a quotient of 0 and a remainder of 1.
> Write the remainders, in order from right to left, to get the answer of 1,238.

We can now explain how to use the main storage dump for debugging. Let us suppose that our program listing has the following information:

```
PROGRAM-SIZE  =  TALLY  +  FILE SECTION
    1,814           2           532

        +  W-S SECTION  +  CONSTANTS   +  TEMP-LOCNS
              55              284              60

        +  PROCEDURES  +  ARITH-STACK
              857             24
```

and that, from the inclusion of the L option on the XEQ card, we obtain

```
05A3 (HEX) IS THE EXECUTION ADDR.
```

The execution address corresponds to the beginning of the PROCE-DURES in our program. By adding the number of words preceding the PROCEDURES, we see that 2 + 532 + 55 + 284 + 60, or 933 words are required preceding the beginning of the execution address of our program. The first instruction of our program occurs 934 words from the storage for TALLY. Now TALLY begins in relative address 0 of our program and therefore occupies words 0 and 1 (relative addresses). The other data items and procedures follow consecutively. Since the numbering starts with 0, the first instruction occurs in word 933 (relative address). We convert 933 to hexadecimal to obtain 3A5. Since this is the location of the relative address of the execution address and since the actual execution address is 5A3, we see that the actual address of our program origin is 5A3 − 3A5, or 1FE. Thus TALLY occupies the words whose addresses are 1FE and 1FE + 1. Suppose that our DATA DIVISION MAP or CONCORDANCE shows the relative address of COMPANY-TABLE to be 23E. What is its actual address? It is 1FE + 23E, or 43C. Thus to get the actual address of a data item, you add the actual address of the program origin (the actual address of TALLY) to the relative address of the data item.

Alternately, if you know the actual address of the program origin (which is nearly always 01FE), you can specify it as a compiler option in the form /xxxx.

The dumps specify the actual address of the items and their hexadecimal content. If the item is a COMPUTATIONAL integer, you can convert its hexadecimal value to a decimal equivalent. For example, to convert 3A5 to a decimal equivalent, we compute $3 \cdot (16)^3 + 10(16) + 5$ to get 933. The conversion for data items stored as EBCDIC characters can be done with the use of the following table.

Character	EBCDIC Hex Code	Character	EBCDIC Hex Code
Blank	40	L	D3
¢	4A	M	D4
.	4B	N	D5
(	4D	O	D6
+	4F	P	D7
&	50	Q	D8
!	5A	R	D9
$	5B	S	E2
*	5C	T	E3

Character	EBCDIC Hex Code	Character	EBCDIC Hex Code
)	5D	U	E4
–	60	V	E5
/	61	W	E6
,	6B	X	E7
=	7E	Y	E8
A	C1	Z	E9
B	C2	0	F0
C	C3	1	F1
D	C4	2	F2
E	C5	3	F3
F	C6	4	F4
G	C7	5	F5
H	C8	6	F6
I	C9	7	F7
J	D1	8	F8
K	D2	9	F9

Example of a Program Dump

In the sample program (figure A.1), we have produced a dump of the DATA DIVISION at the time of an execution time error. We caused the error by trying to write to a file that was not open at the time. Examine the listing, paying particular attention to the dump of the DATA DIVISION. In particular, we arranged for certain data items to have values that are easily recognized.

The dump of the DATA DIVISION has a column labeled ADDR. Beneath this label are hexadecimal addresses. Next to the ADDR label is a string containing ∗∗∗ 0 ∗∗∗ 1 ∗∗∗ 2 ··· ∗∗∗ E ∗∗∗ F. These provide offsets to the addresses beneath the label. Thus to locate the entry in the dump for address 01F5 you would go down the first column to 01F0 and then go across that row until you are beneath the ∗∗∗ 5 entry at the top. The entry in the dump at this location is 0680. Now you should examine the CONCORDANCE LISTING just before the dump. This contains an alphabetic listing of all the data items and procedure names in our program. Since we specified the compiler option /01FE, the addresses listed beside each name in the listing are the actual addresses of the data items. For example, the WORKING-STORAGE item ALPHA begins at address 0372. It is 26 words long. Looking at the dump, we see that in location 0372 the hexadecimal value listed there is 00C1, which is the coding for an A. The value in the next word, 0373, is 00C2, which is the hexadecimal code for a B. These alphabetic characters extend through 038B, where the value E9 indicates a Z. This is exactly what we would expect the value of ALPHA to be at the time of the error in view of the MOVE statement in the program that determincs the value of ALPHA. See if you can locate the part of the dump for STUDENT-MAJOR. If you found it in addresses 021E through 0227 with a value of COMPUTER-S, then you are proceeding correctly. Note that STUDENT-NUMBER should be located in 0208 and 0209 since it is a six-digit *computational* item. The value in those locations is 00000025 or simply 25. Yet in the program we moved 37 to that location. The reason for the differences is that this number, 25, is the hexadecimal equivalent of 37, as you can easily verify.

$$\left[\left\{ \begin{array}{l} \underline{\text{PURGE}} \\ \underline{\text{RUN}} \\ \underline{\text{END}} \end{array} \right\} \text{ ON } \underline{\text{ERROR}} \right]$$

$$\text{ON } \left\{ \begin{array}{l} \underline{\text{DESCENDING}} \\ \underline{\text{ASCENDING}} \end{array} \right\} \text{KEY data-name-1 } [\text{data-name-2} \ldots]$$

$$\left[\text{ON } \left\{ \begin{array}{l} \underline{\text{DESCENDING}} \\ \underline{\text{ASCENDING}} \end{array} \right\} \text{KEY data-name-3} \right.$$

$$\left. [\text{data-name-4} \ldots] \right]$$

$$\left\{ \begin{array}{l} \underline{\text{INPUT}} \text{ } \underline{\text{PROCEDURE}} \text{ IS section-name-1} \\ \quad \left[\left\{ \begin{array}{l} \underline{\text{THRU}} \\ \underline{\text{THROUGH}} \end{array} \right\} \text{section-name-2} \right] \\ \underline{\text{USING}} \text{ file-name-2} \left[\left\{ \begin{array}{l} \underline{\text{PURGE}} \\ \underline{\text{LOCK}} \\ \underline{\text{RELEASE}} \end{array} \right\} \right] \end{array} \right\}$$

$$\left\{ \begin{array}{l} \underline{\text{OUTPUT}} \text{ } \underline{\text{PROCEDURE}} \text{ IS section-name-3} \\ \quad \left[\left\{ \begin{array}{l} \underline{\text{THRU}} \\ \underline{\text{THROUGH}} \end{array} \right\} \text{section-name-4} \right] \\ \underline{\text{GIVING}} \text{ file-name-3} \left[\left\{ \begin{array}{l} \underline{\text{LOCK}} \\ \underline{\text{RELEASE}} \end{array} \right\} \right] \end{array} \right\}$$

$$\underline{\text{STOP}} \left\{ \begin{array}{l} \underline{\text{RUN}} \\ \text{literal} \end{array} \right\}$$

Option 1:

$$\underline{\text{SUBTRACT}} \left\{ \begin{array}{l} \text{literal-1} \\ \text{data-name-1} \end{array} \right\} \left[\left\{ \begin{array}{l} \text{literal-2} \\ \text{data-name-2} \end{array} \right\} \ldots \right] \underline{\text{FROM}}$$

$$\text{data-name-m } [\underline{\text{ROUNDED}}]$$

$$\left[\text{data-name-n } [\underline{\text{ROUNDED}}] \ldots \right]$$

$$[\text{ON } \underline{\text{SIZE}} \text{ } \underline{\text{ERROR}} \text{ any statement}]$$

Option 2:

$$\underline{\text{SUBTRACT}} \left\{ \begin{array}{l} \text{literal-1} \\ \text{data-name-1} \end{array} \right\} \left[\left\{ \begin{array}{l} \text{literal-2} \\ \text{data-name-2} \end{array} \right\} \ldots \right] \underline{\text{FROM}}$$

$$\left\{ \begin{array}{l} \text{literal-m} \\ \text{data-name-m} \end{array} \right\} \underline{\text{GIVING}} \text{ data-name-n } [\underline{\text{ROUNDED}}]$$

$$[\text{ON } \underline{\text{SIZE}} \text{ } \underline{\text{ERROR}} \text{ any statement}]$$

Option 3:

$$\underline{\text{SUBTRACT}} \left\{ \begin{array}{l} \underline{\text{CORR}} \\ \underline{\text{CORRESPONDING}} \end{array} \right\} \text{data-name-1}$$

Figure A.1 Example of a dump of the DATA DIVISION produced at the time of an execution time error.

```
PAGE   1

// JOB

LOG DRIVE     CART SPEC     CART AVAIL    PHY DRIVE
  COOO          4000          4000          0002


V2 M11    ACTUAL 16K   CONFIG 16K


// COBOL
*LIST,STNO,DMAP,PMAP,XREF,/01FE,DDMP


OPTIONS-LIST,XREF,DMAP,PMAP,STNO,NOSUPX,NOKP26,NOSUBR,NOEJCT,2501,1403,DDMP,/01FE



STNO - A...B... C O B O L    S O U R C E    S T A T E M E N T S .......... IDENTFCN   PAGLIN

    1      IDENTIFICATION DIVISION.
    2      PROGRAM-ID. DUMPER.
    3      ENVIRONMENT DIVISION.
    4      INPUT-OUTPUT SECTION.
    5      FILE-CONTROL.
    6          SELECT DF ASSIGN TO DF-1-1000.
    7      DATA DIVISION.
    8      FILE SECTION.
    9      FD  DF, LABEL RECORDS ARE STANDARD
               DATA RECORD IS DOUT.
   10      01  DOUT.
   11          02 STUDENT-NUMBER PIC 9(6) COMP.
   12          02 STUDENT-NAME PIC X(20).
   13          02 STUDENT-MAJOR PIC X(10).
   14      WORKING-STORAGE SECTION.
   15      77  ALPHA PIC X(26).
   16      77  OTHER-NUMBER PIC 99.
   17      PROCEDURE DIVISION.
   18      BEGIN.
   19          MOVE 37 TO STUDENT-NUMBER, OTHER-NUMBER.
   20          MOVE 'ABCDEFGHIJKLMNOPQRSTUVWXYZ' TO ALPHA.
   21          MOVE 'KHAILANY-DUPLISSEY' TO STUDENT-NAME.
   22          MOVE 'COMPUTER-SCIENCE' TO STUDENT-MAJOR.
   23          WRITE DOUT INVALID KEY STOP RUN.
   25          STOP RUN.
/*
```

                              DATA DIVISION MAP

ADDR NAME   ADDR NAME   ADDR NAME

0228 *FILE=DF   0208 *** RECORD AREA FOR THIS FILE 0230 *** BLOCK AREA FOR THIS FILE

0372 ALPHA   038C OTHER-NUMBER

03EE *BEGINNING OF LITERALS AND EDIT MASKS

                              PROCEDURE DIVISION MAP

ADDR STNO   ADDR STNO   ADDR STNO   ADDR STNO   ADDR STNO   ADDR STNO   ADDR STNO   ADDR STNO   ADDR STNO   ADDR STNO

PAGE 2   ... U.A.L.R. COMPUTER CENTER -- COBOL COMPILATION ...
                              PROCEDURE DIVISION MAP

ADDR STNO   ADDR STNO   ADDR STNO   ADDR STNO   ADDR STNO   ADDR STNO   ADDR STNO   ADDR STNO   ADDR STNO   ADDR STNO

03E1 18   03E3 19   03F1 20   03F7 21   03FE 22   0404 23   040B 24   040E 25   0411 26   0413 27

                          D I A G N O S T I C S

STNO   ERR LVL   TEXT

  22   489   W   SOURCE ITEM SIZE EXCEEDS /STUDENT-MAJOR/
  26   458   C   MISSING OPEN OR CLOSE FOR FILE /DF/

  NO E LEVEL MESSAGES   1 C LEVEL MESSAGE   1 W LEVEL MESSAGE

                       C O N C O R D A N C E   L I S T I N G

 *   ITEM NAME / ADDRESS   *   STATEMENT NUMBER REFERENCES   * ATTRIBUTES   *LGTH* DEC *

ALPHA   0372   15*   20   D AN   26

BEGIN   03E1   18*   P PARAGRAPH

DF   0228   9*   F DF SEQL   32
DOUT   0208   9   10*   23   D GR   32

Figure A.1 (Cont'd.)

```
OTHER-NUMBER          038C   16*  19                    D ND    2

STUDENT-MAJOR         021E   13*  22                    D AN   10
STUDENT-NAME          020A   12*  21                    D AN   20
STUDENT-NUMBER        0208   11*  19                    D NC    6

TALLY                 0205                              D NC    5


PROGRAM-SIZE = TALLY + FILE SECTION + W-S SECTION + CONSTANTS + TEMP-LOCNS + PROCEDURES + ARITH-STACK
     562       2         370            28          61          18            59             24

END OF COBOL COMPILATION

// XEQ

**STNO=0023**ERR=15**LOC=0406**ITEM=0228



PAGE   3

ACCUMULATOR  C000     EXTENSION 0000     XR1  0000   XR2 0018   XR3  3F68     OVERFLOW OFF     CARRY OFF

ADDR ***0 ***1 ***2 ***3 ***4 ***5 ***6 ***7 ***8 ***9 ***A ***B ***C ***D ***E ***F

01E0 03DD 0018 FFFF 0001 001E 0C00 01E0 0C00 0030 0A9C 3F68 0091 0091 00B3 0091 00C4 *.....................D*
01F0 0091 0091 0091 0091 0091 0678 0091 0091 0091 0091 0000 4000 0000 0000 0001 03E8 *.....................Y*
02C0 0020 0000 8000 000A 0640 0000 0000 0000 0000 0025 00D2 00C8 00C1 00C9 00D3 00C1 *.................K.H.A.I.L.A*
0210 00D5 00E8 0060 00C4 00E4 00D7 00D3 00C9 00E2 00E2 00C5 00E8 0040 0040 00C3 00D6 *.N.Y.-.D.U.P.L.I.S.S.E.Y. . .C.O*
0220 00D4 00C7 00E4 00E3 00C5 00D9 0060 00E2 0020 0000 0208 0230 01FE 0000 0000 4374 *.M.P.U.T.E.R.-.S..............*
0230 0000 0000 0000 0000 0000 0C0C 0000 0C00 0000 0C00 0000 0000 0000 0000 0000 0000 *...........................*

02E0 0000 0000 0000 0000 0000 0C0C 0000 0C00 0000 0C00 0000 0000 5246 1307 5408 407F *.........................*
02F0 7E4A 7D0B 614C 5015 6B16 4D57 6061 5B62 5C23 4E6D 4B6E 5D2F 1234 5678 0000 0000 *=.'./.&.,.(.-/$.*.+...).......*
03C0 0000 0000 0000 0000 0000 0C0C 0000 0000 0000 0000 0000 0000 0001 0E63 0064 0E79 *.........................*
0310 00C8 0EBC 00FA 0EEE 0118 0F07 011D 0F09 012D 0F0B 01C7 0F47 7FFF 3569 3571 3577 *.H..........................G......*
0320 1810 D0A6 74FF 0032 1000 70B8 C8D7 D900 C0E1 70D0 C0E6 4400 0028 7038 7401 0032 *...........HPR.......W.........*
0330 6211 6A96 6500 0004 C900 D8C8 D8D1 1810 1084 D00E 80DC D01C 80DB D034 80D7 8008 *.........I.QHQJ.............P..*
0340 8007 D006 62FD 69BE C101 E0CC D101 9400 00A4 4828 7007 C101 80C3 7401 016E 7201 *........A...J.......A..C....*
0350 70F5 D101 6600 00F2 C23D E249 D250 C400 009F EA4E D23A EA43 D239 EA50 9247 D237 *.5J....2B.S.K&D....+K...K..&..K.*
0360 EA42 8247 D24D EA48 D23B CA3C 0A3A D2EB 4828 70BC 1002 4828 70BD 1002 4828 7010 *....K(..K)....K.............*
0370 C101 9400 00C1 00C2 00C3 00C4 00C5 00C6 00C7 00C8 00C9 00D1 00D2 00D3 00D4 00D5 *A.....A.B.C.D.E.F.G.H.I.J.K.L.M.N*
0380 00D6 00D7 00D8 00D9 00E2 00E3 00E4 00E5 00E6 00E7 00E8 00E9 00F3 00F7 0025 00C1 *.O.P.Q.R.S.T.U.V.W.X.Y.Z.3.7...A*
```

We hope that this short introduction to the use of dumps will help you in perfecting your programs.

The CONCORDANCE Produced by the XREF Option

The XREF option could be of value, since it shows the hexadecimal address of an item relative to the origin you specified. It also shows the statement number of the program statement defining the item (followed by an asterisk), the numbers of all other program statements referencing the item, and codes describing the item. The codes follow.

C	condition name
D	data name
F	file name
M	mnemonic name assigned in SPECIAL-NAMES
P	procedure name

Data names are further described as follows.

GR	group item
AL	alphabetic
AN	alphanumeric
NC	numeric computational
ND	numeric display
NE	numeric-edited
JR	justified right
S	signed
BZ	blank when zero
OCR	subject to the scope of an OCCURS clause.

An asterisk in column 1 indicates that the name is reserved on some IBM ANS COBOL compilers.

Step 5: If you still have not discovered why your program does not run as you expected, then you probably need to analyze the logic of your program. To do this, we suggest the liberal use of DISPLAY statements to show the value of data items at crucial points in the program. For example, the statement

DISPLAY 'STUDENT-GRADE ', STUDENT-GRADE.

will print the value of STUDENT-GRADE and also print STUDENT-GRADE to identify which data item is being DISPLAYed.

In addition to showing the values of data items, it is also worthwhile to be able to follow the actions of your program. The READY TRACE and RESET TRACE statements are ideal for this purpose. You may include the READY TRACE statement anywhere in the PROCEDURE DIVISION of your COBOL program. When the computer encounters this statement, it will begin to print the statement of each paragraph or section as it begins the statement. In order for the computer to be able to do this, you must have asked for the STNO option. The computer will continue printing the statement numbers of these procedures until it encounters a RESET TRACE statement or until it reaches the end of your program. You can use these statements as often as you like, and you can also use them in subprograms.

Formats of COBOL Statements for the IBM-1130

The general format of a COBOL program is illustrated in these format
summaries. Included within the general format is the specific format for each
valid COBOL statement. All clauses are shown as though they were required by the COBOL source program, although many are optional within a
given context. Repetition of clauses has not been indicated. Several formats
are included under special headings, which are different from or additions to
the general format. Under these special headings are included formats peculiar to the following COBOL features: Table Handling, Source Program
Library Facility, Debugging Language.

IDENTIFICATION DIVISION—*Basic formats*

```
    IDENTIFICATION DIVISION.
    PROGRAM-ID. program-name.
    AUTHOR. [comment-entry]...
    INSTALLATION. [comment-entry]...
    DATE-WRITTEN. [comment-entry]...
    SECURITY. [comment-entry]...
    REMARKS. [comment-entry]...
```

ENVIRONMENT DIVISION—*Basic formats*

```
    ENVIRONMENT DIVISION.
    [CONFIGURATION SECTION.
    SOURCE-COMPUTER. computer-name.

    OBJECT-COMPUTER. computer-name
        ⎡                        ⎧ WORDS      ⎫ ⎤
        ⎢ MEMORY SIZE integer    ⎨ CHARACTERS ⎬ ⎥.
        ⎣                        ⎩ MODULES    ⎭ ⎦
    SPECIAL-NAMES. [function-name-1 IS mnemonic-name]...
        [function-name-2 [IS mnemonic-name]
    ⎡ ⎧ ON STATUS IS condition-name-1            ⎫ ⎤
    ⎢ ⎪    [OFF STATUS IS condition-name-2]      ⎪ ⎥...
    ⎢ ⎨ OFF STATUS IS condition-name-2           ⎬ ⎥
    ⎣ ⎩    [ON STATUS IS condition-name-1]       ⎭ ⎦
        [CURRENCY SIGN IS literal]

        [DECIMAL-POINT IS COMMA].]
    INPUT-OUTPUT SECTION.
    FILE-CONTROL.
        [SELECT file-name
        ASSIGN TO [integer] system-name-1
            [system-name-2] ...
            [FOR MULTIPLE UNIT]

        ⎡          ⎧ NO      ⎫           ⎡ AREA  ⎤ ⎤
        ⎢ RESERVE  ⎨ integer ⎬ ALTERNATE ⎢ AREAS ⎥ ⎥
        ⎣          ⎩         ⎭           ⎣       ⎦ ⎦

        ⎡ ⎧ FILE-LIMIT IS   ⎫                          ⎤
        ⎢ ⎨ FILE-LIMITS ARE ⎬ integer-1 THRU integer-2 ⎥
        ⎣ ⎩                 ⎭                          ⎦
```

$$\left[\underline{\text{ACCESS}}\ \text{MODE}\ \underline{\text{IS}}\ \left\{\begin{array}{l}\underline{\text{SEQUENTIAL}}\\ \underline{\text{RANDOM}}\end{array}\right\}\right]$$

[<u>PROCESSING</u> MODE <u>IS</u> <u>SEQUENTIAL</u>]
[<u>ACTUAL</u> KEY <u>IS</u> data-name.]]...
<u>I-O-CONTROL</u>.
   [<u>RERUN</u> <u>ON</u> system-name EVERY integer
      <u>RECORDS</u> OF file-name]...
   [<u>SAME</u> AREA FOR file-name-1 file-name-2...]...

DATA DIVISION—*Basic formats*
  <u>DATA</u> <u>DIVISION</u>.
  <u>FILE</u> <u>SECTION</u>.
  <u>FD</u> file-name

$$\left[\underline{\text{BLOCK}}\ \text{CONTAINS}\ \text{integer-1}\ \left\{\begin{array}{l}\text{CHARACTERS}\\ \underline{\text{RECORDS}}\end{array}\right\}\right]$$

[<u>RECORD</u> CONTAINS [integer-1 <u>TO</u>]
    integer-2 CHARACTERS]

$$\underline{\text{LABEL}}\ \left\{\begin{array}{l}\underline{\text{RECORD}}\ \text{IS}\\ \underline{\text{RECORDS}}\ \text{ARE}\end{array}\right\}\ \left\{\begin{array}{l}\underline{\text{STANDARD}}\\ \underline{\text{OMITTED}}\end{array}\right\}$$

$$\left[\underline{\text{VALUE}}\ \underline{\text{OF}}\ \text{data-name-1}\ \text{IS}\ \left\{\begin{array}{l}\text{data-name-2}\\ \text{literal-1}\end{array}\right\}\right.$$
$$\left.\left[\text{data-name-3}\ \text{IS}\ \left\{\begin{array}{l}\text{data-name-4}\\ \text{literal-2}\end{array}\right\}\right]...\right]$$

$$\left[\underline{\text{DATA}}\ \left\{\begin{array}{l}\underline{\text{RECORD}}\ \text{IS}\\ \underline{\text{RECORDS}}\ \text{ARE}\end{array}\right\}\ \text{data-name-1}\ [\text{data-name-2}]...\right].$$

$$\text{01-49}\ \left\{\begin{array}{l}\text{data-name-1}\\ \underline{\text{FILLER}}\end{array}\right\}$$

[<u>REDEFINES</u> data-name-2]
[<u>BLANK</u> WHEN <u>ZERO</u>]

$$\left[\left\{\begin{array}{l}\underline{\text{JUSTIFIED}}\\ \underline{\text{JUST}}\end{array}\right\}\ \text{RIGHT}\right]$$

$$\left[\left\{\begin{array}{l}\underline{\text{PICTURE}}\\ \underline{\text{PIC}}\end{array}\right\}\ \text{IS character string}\right]$$

$$\left[\left\{\begin{array}{l}\underline{\text{SYNCHRONIZED}}\\ \underline{\text{SYNC}}\end{array}\right\}\ \left[\begin{array}{l}\underline{\text{LEFT}}\\ \underline{\text{RIGHT}}\end{array}\right]\right]$$

$$\left[\underline{\text{USAGE}}\ \text{IS}]\ \left\{\begin{array}{l}\underline{\text{INDEX}}\\ \underline{\text{DISPLAY}}\\ \left\{\begin{array}{l}\underline{\text{COMPUTATIONAL}}\\ \underline{\text{COMP}}\end{array}\right\}\\ \left\{\begin{array}{l}\underline{\text{COMPUTATIONAL-4}}\\ \underline{\text{COMP-4}}\end{array}\right\}\end{array}\right\}\right]$$

88 condition-name <u>VALUE</u> <u>IS</u> literal-1

Note: Formats of the OCCURS clause are included with formats for the table handling feature.

<u>WORKING-STORAGE</u> <u>SECTION</u>.
77 data-name-1

01-49 $\begin{Bmatrix} \text{data-name-1} \\ \underline{\text{FILLER}} \end{Bmatrix}$

[<u>REDEFINES</u> data-name-2]
[<u>BLANK</u> WHEN <u>ZERO</u>]

$\left[\begin{Bmatrix} \underline{\text{JUSTIFIED}} \\ \underline{\text{JUST}} \end{Bmatrix} \text{RIGHT} \right]$

$\left[\begin{Bmatrix} \underline{\text{PICTURE}} \\ \underline{\text{PIC}} \end{Bmatrix} \text{IS character string} \right]$

$\left[\begin{Bmatrix} \underline{\text{SYNCHRONIZED}} \\ \underline{\text{SYNC}} \end{Bmatrix} \begin{bmatrix} \underline{\text{LEFT}} \\ \underline{\text{RIGHT}} \end{bmatrix} \right]$

$\left[\text{[}\underline{\text{USAGE}}\text{ IS]} \begin{Bmatrix} \underline{\text{INDEX}} \\ \underline{\text{DISPLAY}} \\ \begin{Bmatrix} \underline{\text{COMPUTATIONAL}} \\ \underline{\text{COMP}} \end{Bmatrix} \\ \begin{Bmatrix} \underline{\text{COMPUTATIONAL-4}} \\ \underline{\text{COMP-4}} \end{Bmatrix} \end{Bmatrix} \right]$

[<u>VALUE</u> IS literal]
88 condition-name <u>VALUE</u> IS literal-1

<u>LINKAGE</u> <u>SECTION</u>.
77 data-name-1

01-49 $\begin{Bmatrix} \text{data-name-1} \\ \underline{\text{FILLER}} \end{Bmatrix}$

[<u>REDEFINES</u> data-name-2]
[<u>BLANK</u> WHEN <u>ZERO</u>]

$\left[\begin{Bmatrix} \underline{\text{JUSTIFIED}} \\ \underline{\text{JUST}} \end{Bmatrix} \text{RIGHT} \right]$

$\left[\begin{Bmatrix} \underline{\text{PICTURE}} \\ \underline{\text{PIC}} \end{Bmatrix} \text{IS character string} \right]$

$\left[\begin{Bmatrix} \underline{\text{SYNCHRONIZED}} \\ \underline{\text{SYNC}} \end{Bmatrix} \begin{bmatrix} \underline{\text{LEFT}} \\ \underline{\text{RIGHT}} \end{bmatrix} \right]$

$\left[\text{[}\underline{\text{USAGE}}\text{ IS]} \begin{bmatrix} \begin{Bmatrix} \underline{\text{INDEX}} \\ \underline{\text{DISPLAY}} \\ \begin{Bmatrix} \underline{\text{COMPUTATIONAL}} \\ \underline{\text{COMP}} \end{Bmatrix} \\ \begin{Bmatrix} \underline{\text{COMPUTATIONAL-4}} \\ \underline{\text{COMP-4}} \end{Bmatrix} \end{Bmatrix} \end{bmatrix} \right]$

88 condition-name <u>VALUE</u> IS literal-1

PROCEDURE DIVISION—*Basic formats*
  <u>PROCEDURE</u> <u>DIVISION</u>.

$\begin{Bmatrix} \underline{\text{PROCEDURE}}\ \underline{\text{DIVISION}}\ \underline{\text{USING}} \begin{Bmatrix} \text{identifier-1} \\ \text{file-name-1} \end{Bmatrix} \\ \quad \begin{bmatrix} \text{identifier-2} \\ \text{file-name-2} \end{bmatrix} \cdots \end{Bmatrix}$

Note: Formats of the OCCURS clause are included with formats for the table handling feature.

ACCEPT Statement

ACCEPT identifier [FROM { mnemonic-name / DATE / CONSOLE }]

ADD Statement

Format 1

    ADD { identifier-1 / literal-1 } [identifier-2 / literal-2] ...
        TO identifier-m [ROUNDED]
                        [ON SIZE ERROR
                            imperative-statement]

Format 2

    ADD { identifier-1 / literal-1 } { identifier-2 / literal-2 }
        [identifier-3 / literal-3] ...
        GIVING identifier-m [ROUNDED]
           [ON SIZE ERROR imperative-statement]

ALTER Statement

    ALTER procedure-name-1 TO [PROCEED TO]
        procedure-name-2
        [procedure-name-3 TO [PROCEED TO]
        procedure-name-4] ...

CALL Statement

CALL literal [USING { identifier-1 / file-name-1 } [identifier-2 / file-name-2] ...]

CLOSE Statement

    CLOSE file-name-1 [UNIT] [WITH LOCK]
            [file-name-2 [UNIT] [WITH LOCK]] ...

COMPUTE Statement

    COMPUTE identifier-1 [ROUNDED]
        = { arithmetic-expression / identifier-2 / literal-1 }
              [ON SIZE ERROR imperative-statement]

DISPLAY Statement

    DISPLAY { identifier-1 / literal-1 } [identifier-2 / literal-2] ...
        [UPON { mnemonic-name / CONSOLE }]

DIVIDE Statement

Format 1

    DIVIDE { identifier-1 / literal-1 } INTO identifier-2 [ROUNDED]
            [ON SIZE ERROR imperative-statement]

Note: Formats of the OCCURS Clause are included with formats for the table handling feature.

Format 2

    DIVIDE {identifier-1} {INTO} {identifier-2}
           {literal-1   } {BY } {literal-2   }
        GIVING identifier-3 [ROUNDED]
        [ON SIZE ERROR imperative-statement]
ENTER Statement
    ENTER language-name [routine-name].
EXAMINE Statement

Format 1

                                        (UNTIL FIRST)
    EXAMINE identifier TALLYING {ALL   } literal-1
                                (LEADING   )

        [REPLACING BY literal-2]

Format 2

                                         (ALL   )
    EXAMINE identifier REPLACING {LEADING   }
                                 {FIRST   }
                                 (UNTIL FIRST)

           literal-1 BY literal-2

EXIT Statement
    paragraph-name. EXIT [PROGRAM].
GO TO Statement

Format 1
    GO TO procedure-name-1

Format 2
    GO TO procedure-name-1 [procedure-name-2] ...
        DEPENDING ON identifier

Format 3
    GO TO.
IF Statement

    IF condition {NEXT SENTENCE   }
                 {statement-1, statement-3}

        [ELSE {NEXT SENTENCE   }]
        [{statement-2, statement-4}]
MOVE Statement

Format 1
    MOVE {identifier-1} TO identifier-2
         {literal   }
        [identifier-3]...
MULTIPLY Statement

Format 1

    MULTIPLY {identifier-1 / literal-1} BY identifier-2 [ROUNDED]
             [ON SIZE ERROR imperative-statement]

Format 2

    MULTIPLY {identifier-1 / literal-1} BY {identifier-2 / literal-2}
        GIVING identifier-3
          [ROUNDED] [ON SIZE ERROR imperative-statement]

NOTE Statement
    NOTE character string
OPEN Statement
    OPEN [INPUT file-name...]
         [OUTPUT file-name...]
         [I-O file-name...]
PERFORM Statement

Format 1

    PERFORM procedure-name-1 [THRU procedure-name-2]

Format 2

    PERFORM procedure-name-1 [THRU procedure-name-2]
              {identifier-1 / integer-1} TIMES

Format 3

    PERFORM procedure-name-1 [THRU procedure-name-2]
        UNTIL condition-1

Format 4

    PERFORM procedure-name-1 [THRU procedure-name-2]
        VARYING {index-name-1 / identifier-1} FROM {index-name-2 / literal-2 / identifier-2} BY
              {literal-3 / identifier-3} UNTIL condition-1
        [AFTER {index-name-4 / identifier-4} FROM {index-name-5 / literal-5 / identifier-5} BY
              {literal-6 / identifier-6} UNTIL condition-2
        [AFTER {index-name-7 / identifier-7} FROM {index-name-8 / literal-8 / identifier-8} BY
              {literal-9 / identifier-9} UNTIL condition-3]]

READ Statement
    <u>READ</u> file-name RECORD [<u>INTO</u> identifier]
        {AT <u>END</u>   }
        {<u>INVALID</u> KEY} imperative-statement
SEEK Statement
    <u>SEEK</u> file-name RECORD
STOP Statement
    <u>STOP</u> {<u>RUN</u>   }
         {literal}
SUBTRACT Statement

Format 1
    <u>SUBTRACT</u> {identifier-1} [identifier-2] ...
             {literal-1   } [literal-2   ]
        <u>FROM</u> identifier-m
            [<u>ROUNDED</u>] [ON <u>SIZE</u> <u>ERROR</u>
                imperative-statement]

Format 2
    <u>SUBTRACT</u> {identifier-1} [identifier-2] ...
             {literal-1   } [literal-2   ]
        <u>FROM</u> {identifier-m} <u>GIVING</u>
             {literal-m   }
        identifier-n [<u>ROUNDED</u>] [ON <u>SIZE</u> <u>ERROR</u>
                imperative-statement]
WRITE Statement

Format 1
    <u>WRITE</u> record-name [<u>FROM</u> identifier-1] [{<u>BEFORE</u>}]
                                                [{<u>AFTER</u> }]
            ADVANCING {identifier-2 LINES}]
                      {integer LINES   }]
                      {mnemonic-name   }]
        [AT {<u>END-OF-PAGE</u>} imperative-statement]
            {<u>EOP</u>   }

Format 2
    <u>WRITE</u> record-name-[<u>FROM</u> identifier-1]
        <u>INVALID</u> KEY imperative-statement

TABLE HANDLING—*Basic formats*
Data Division Table Handling Formats
    OCCURS Clause
        <u>OCCURS</u> integer TIMES [<u>INDEXED</u> BY index-name-1
            [index-name-2]...]
    USAGE Clause
        [<u>USAGE</u> IS] <u>INDEX</u>

PROCEDURE DIVISION—*Table handling formats*

   SET Statement

Format 1

$$\underline{SET} \quad \begin{Bmatrix} \text{index-name-1 [index-name-2] ...} \\ \text{identifier-1 [identifier-2] ...} \end{Bmatrix}$$

$$\underline{TO} \quad \begin{Bmatrix} \text{index-name-3} \\ \text{identifier-3} \\ \text{literal-1} \end{Bmatrix}$$

Format 2

$$\underline{SET} \text{ index-name-4 [index-name-5]...} \quad \begin{Bmatrix} \underline{UP} \ \underline{BY} \\ \underline{DOWN} \ \underline{BY} \end{Bmatrix}$$

$$\begin{Bmatrix} \text{identifier-4} \\ \text{literal-2} \end{Bmatrix}$$

DEBUGGING FACILITY
   TRACE Statement

$$\begin{Bmatrix} \underline{READY} \\ \underline{RESET} \end{Bmatrix} \quad \underline{TRACE}$$

SOURCE PROGRAM LIBRARY FACILITY—*Basic formats*
   COPY Statement
      <u>COPY</u> library-name

IBM System 3

The System 3 is the successor to the 1130. The System 3 uses many of the operating concepts of System 360/370 while enjoying the simplicity inherent in the 1130 operating system.

COBOL on the System 3 is similar to that on the 1130 except that a wider variety of peripherals are available, and indexed files are supported. We will describe some of the details of COBOL on the System 3 that differ from COBOL on the 1130.

IDENTIFICATION DIVISION

There are no differences in the IDENTIFICATION DIVISION between COBOL on the System 3 and that on the 1130.

ENVIRONMENT DIVISION

In the SOURCE-COMPUTER and OBJECT-COMPUTER paragraphs, the entry should be IBM-S3. The MEMORY SIZE clause may be used to specify the amount of main storage available for the execution of the object program.

The SPECIAL-NAMES paragraph may be used to provide mnemonic names for CONSOLE, C01, CSP, S01, S02, S03, S04, and S05. The latter names are associated with the pocket select options on the card units. The IBM-1442 has two available pockets, which are S01 and S02. The IBM-5424 has pockets S01, S02, S03, and S04 available for holding the cards after they are processed. All five pockets are available for the IBM-2560. Additionally, the SPECIAL-NAMES paragraph can be used to assign names to eight switches and their ON and OFF status. The switch names are UPSI-0, UPSI-1, . . . , UPSI-7.

In the FILE-CONTROL paragraph of the INPUT-OUTPUT SECTION, a wide variety of system devices are available for use in the ASSIGN clause.

For card devices the form of the system name is

Class-Device-Function [-Association].

The class is always UR for unit record. The device may be one of

    1442 for reader/puncher,
    5424P for MFCU primary hopper,
    5424S for MFCU secondary hopper,
    2560P for MFCU primary hopper,
    2560S for MFCU secondary hopper, and
    2501 for reader.

The function is

        RD for a card read file,
        PU for a card punch file,
        PR for a card print file on the 5424, and
        PI for a punch/interpret file on the 5424.

The association is an integer from 1 through 9 and is optional. It is used to allow multiple card file processing on the 5424 and 2560.

  For line printer files the form of the system name is

        Class-Device-Linewidth-Pagesize.

The class is always UR. The device may be 5203 or 1403. The linewidth is

        1 for 96 print positions,
        2 for 120 print positions, and
        3 for 132 print positions.

The pagesize is an integer in the range 7 through 66. If the pagesize is omitted, then 66 is assumed. The pagesize indicates the number of lines per page.

  The form for the system name for disk files is

```
Class-Device-Organization-Name[-Mode].
```

The class is UT for sequentially organized files and DA for files that are not sequentially organized. (This includes indexed files.) The device is 5444 or 5445. The organization is S for sequential, R for direct, and I for indexed. The name is a one- through eight-character name specifying the external name of the file. It is not necessarily the file name in the source program. The mode is always U and is specified only when the file is updated through the I-O option.

  The form of the system name for tape devices is

```
Class-Device-Recordformat-Name
    [-Fileformat[-Offset]].
```

The class is always UT. The device is always 3400. The recordformat is F for fixed-length records and V for variable-length records. The name is one through eight characters and is the external name of the file. The fileformat is C for ASCII and S for EBCDIC files. The offset is 0 - 99 for ASCII input files and 0 - 4 for variable-length ASCII output files.

  We would now like to comment on the clauses for the FILE-CONTROL paragraph. The RESERVE clause cannot specify alternate buffer areas for output card files, for files on MFCU or MFCM devices, or for printer files. The clause may be used only for sequential files or for the creation of an indexed file. The ACTUAL KEY clause should name a data item whose picture is S9(7) COMP. Since indexed files are permitted, there are two new clauses that are allowed. The first is the RECORD KEY clause whose format is <u>RECORD</u> KEY IS data-name. Data-name must name a field in the record of the indexed file. The indexed file is assumed to be in sequential order with respect to the content of this data name. The format of the other clause is <u>NOMINAL</u> KEY IS data-name. In this clause data-name is a WORKING-STORAGE item, no longer than 29 bytes. Its picture must match that of the RECORD KEY. If a value is assigned to the

NOMINAL-KEY, a COBOL program can be asked to locate the record in an indexed file whose content in the RECORD KEY field matches the NOMINAL KEY.

In the I-O-CONTROL paragraph, a new clause is available for the processing of randomly accessed indexed files. The format of the clause is APPLY CORE-INDEX TO data-name ON file-name. File-name is the name of the indexed file. Data-name is the name of an unedited data item in WORKING-STORAGE and must not exceed 9,997 bytes in length. This clause optimizes the location of records in the indexed file. (Processing indexed files with this option is very similar to processing files on the IBM-1130 with the QFIND subprogram.) Data-name should be long enough to contain a RECORD KEY and track number for each track of the file.

DATA DIVISION

There are several differences in this division. We begin with some comments about the clauses for file description entries.

The BLOCK CONTAINS clause is not required, but it is very important for the efficient processing of tape files.

The LABEL RECORDS CLAUSE is unchanged except for tape files. For unlabeled files, OMITTED is specified. For files with standard labels, STANDARD is specified.

For line printer files a special clause is available. The format of this clause is LINAGE IS integer-1 LINES [WITH FOOTING AT integer-2]. The value of integer-1 specifies the total number of lines per page. The value of integer-2 (which cannot exceed integer-1) determines the beginning of the footing area of the page. If the FOOTING clause is omitted, then integer-2 is assumed to be integer-1. The footing area is used in conjunction with the END-OF-PAGE option. If vertical spacing causes the line printer to position for printing in the footing area (integer-2 lines through integer-1 lines), then the EOP option would cause advancing to a new page. In any event, if spacing causes the printer to position on or beyond integer-1 lines, the printer will automatically advance to a new page.

The clauses that can be applied to data items in the DATA DIVISION are not changed greatly. We will mention the significant ones here.

The format of the SIGN clause is

$$[\underline{\text{SIGN}} \ \underline{\text{IS}}] \ \left\{ \begin{array}{l} \underline{\text{LEADING}} \\ \underline{\text{TRAILING}} \end{array} \right\} \ [\underline{\text{SEPARATE}} \ \text{CHARACTER}].$$

This clause is applicable only to numeric display items with an S in their picture clauses. If the SEPARATE CHARACTER option is omitted, then the TRAILING option specifies that a minus sign is treated as an overpunch in the rightmost digit of the item. The LEADING option specifies that the minus sign is treated as an overpunch in the leftmost digit of the item. If the SEPARATE CHARACTER option is used, then the + or − signs are separate characters, rightmost or leftmost according to whether TRAILING or LEADING is specified. Since the character is separate, it must now be counted in the storage requirements for the item. Note that a + or − sign *must* be present in the item if this option is used.

For numeric data items, USAGE may be COMP, COMP-3, or COMP-4. COMP is stored in zoned decimal and uses one byte per digit. COMP-3 is stored as packed decimal and uses one byte for each pair of digits. COMP-4 is stored in binary and uses the same storage requirements as the IBM-1130. COMP should be specified for arithmetic items. COMP-4 should be specified if storage requirements must be minimized. COMP-4 should be used for subscripts.

PROCEDURE DIVISION

The WRITE statement for the line printer or card unit has the format

```
WRITE record-name [FROM data-name-1]
      ⎡⎧BEFORE⎫                ⎧data-name-2          ⎫⎤
      ⎢⎨      ⎬ ADVANCING ⎨integer       [LINE ]⎬⎥
      ⎢⎩AFTER ⎭                ⎨mnemonic-name  [LINES]⎬⎥
      ⎣                        ⎩PAGE                 ⎭⎦
      ⎡    ⎧END-OF-PAGE⎫                      ⎤
      ⎢ AT ⎨           ⎬ imperative-sentence ⎥
      ⎣    ⎩   EOP     ⎭                      ⎦
```

The PAGE option can be used to advance the line printer to a new page. The ADVANCING option may be used for card units. The mnemonic name should specify S01, . . . , S05 to select a stacker pocket for punched cards.

In association with indexed disk files, several options are available. We will not discuss them, but we suggest that you consult the manuals for COBOL on the System 3.

For debugging purposes, the EXHIBIT statement is very useful. Its format is

```
EXHIBIT ⎧NAMED         ⎫ data-name-1
        ⎩CHANGED NAMED⎭
        [data-name-2]...
```

If the named option is used, then each time the statement is encountered, the names of the data names and their values are printed. If the CHANGED NAMED option is encountered, then the names and values of the items are printed only if the value of the item changed since it was last exhibited. The TRACE statement is available for debugging on the System 3. (See Appendix II on debugging on the IBM-1130 for a description of the TRACE statement.)

A SORT program is provided for use with COBOL files.

SOME CONTROL CARDS

The System 3 can have as many as four disk units. Two are fixed and two have removable cartridges (or packs). The disk units are referred to as F1, F2, R1, and R2.

There are no JOB cards on the System 3. The first card for a deck to compile and execute a COBOL program would thus be

```
//ƀCALLƀCOBOL,F1
```

The F1 informs the System 3 supervisor to use the COBOL compiler on unit F1. The next card is

    //ƀRUN

This card causes the execution of the COBOL compiler.

The next card contains the compilation options. All the words on this card must be located in columns 7 through 72. The first word on the card is always PROCESS followed by one or more spaces. The remaining words on the card are separated by commas or blanks and are selected from the following list. The recommended option is underlined. None of the options are required.

SOURCE or NOSOURCE:SOURCE causes a listing of the source program on the line printer.

FLAGW or FLAGE:FLAGE suppresses the listing of W and C level errors.

APOST or QUOTE:APOST specifies the use of the apostrophe for delineating nonnumeric literals. QUOTE specifies quotation marks for this purpose.

LINK or NOLINK:LINK causes the object program to be prepared for execution. If only compilation is desired, then specify NOLINK. The complete form of this option is

$$\text{LINK} \left(\left\{ \begin{array}{c} \text{T} \\ \text{P} \end{array} \right\} , \left\{ \begin{array}{c} \text{R1} \\ \text{F1} \\ \text{R2} \\ \text{F2} \end{array} \right\} \right)$$

This option permits storing the executable program temporarily or permanently and also permits specifying the unit on which the program is stored. For student jobs, storage is rarely needed.

$$\text{CLIB} \left(\left\{ \begin{array}{c} \text{F1} \\ \text{F2} \\ \text{R1} \\ \text{R2} \end{array} \right\} , \left\{ \begin{array}{c} \text{SUP} \\ \text{NOSUP} \end{array} \right\} \right)$$

The preceding option allows the user to specify the disk unit containing the COBOL library used for COPY statements. The SUP will supress the printing of the copied module. If this option is omitted, then the library is assumed to be on the same disk as the compiler.

MAP or NOMAP:MAP causes the printing of a DATA DIVISION map.

LIST or NOLIST:LIST causes the printing of a PROCEDURE DIVISION map. If LINK is also in effect, then a link edit map will be printed showing information on the program and the subprograms it uses.

CMPAT or NOCMPAT:CMPAT causes COMP items to be stored in binary form. This is inefficient on this machine.

$$\text{OBJECT} \left(\left\{ \begin{array}{c} \text{T} \\ \text{P} \end{array} \right\} , \left\{ \begin{array}{c} \text{R1} \\ \text{F1} \\ \text{R2} \\ \text{F2} \end{array} \right\} \right)$$

or

    NOOBJECT

The preceding option permits storing the object module on disk. The module is stored in nonexecutable form.

DECK or <u>NODECK</u>:DECK causes a deck to be punched containing the nonexecutable object module.

GODECK or <u>NOGODECK</u>:GODECK causes a deck to be punched containing the executable object module.

For student programs, you should specify PROCESS SOURCE, FLAGW, APOST, LINK.

The next cards would be the COBOL source program deck with a /* card to mark the end of the source program.

The next card would contain //ƀLOADƀprogram where program is the first *six* characters of the name of the program as given in the PROGRAM-ID paragraph.

The next card would be a card with //ƀRUN.

As an example of how to compile and execute SAMPLE-1 with a card file, we present the following:

```
//ƀCALLƀCOBOL
//ƀRUN
          PROCESS SOURCE, FLAGW, APOST, LINK

     source deck

/*
//ƀLOADƀSAMPLE
//ƀRUN

     data card file

/*
/&
```

The /& card protects your job from the next job.

If your program used disk files, then you will need a FILE card after the LOAD card. The FILE card is fairly complex, so we suggest that you consult a manual on the IBM System 3.

Formats of COBOL Statements for the IBM System 3

The general format of a COBOL program is illustrated in this format summary. Included within the general format is the specific format for each valid COBOL statement. All clauses are shown as though they were required by the COBOL source program, although within a given context many are optional. Repetition of clauses has not been indicated. Several formats are included under special headings, which are different from, or additions to, the general format. Under these special headings are included formats peculiar to the following COBOL features: table handling, segmentation, source program library facility, debugging language.

IDENTIFICATION DIVISION—*Basic formats*
   <u>IDENTIFICATION DIVISION</u>.
   <u>PROGRAM-ID</u>. program-name.

```
AUTHOR. [comment-entry]...
INSTALLATION. [comment-entry]...
DATE-WRITTEN. [comment-entry]...
SECURITY. [comment-entry]...
REMARKS. [comment-entry]...
```

ENVIRONMENT DIVISION—*Basic formats*

```
ENVIRONMENT DIVISION.
CONFIGURATION SECTION.
SOURCE-COMPUTER. computer-name.
OBJECT-COMPUTER. computer-name [MEMORY SIZE integer
   ⎧WORDS     ⎫
   ⎨CHARACTERS⎬ ].
   ⎩MODULES   ⎭
SPECIAL-NAMES. [function-name-1 IS mnemonic-name]...
   [function-name-2 [IS mnemonic-name]
      ⎧ON STATUS IS condition-name-1          ⎫
      ⎪   [OFF STATUS IS condition-name-2]    ⎪
      ⎨                                       ⎬]...
      ⎪OFF STATUS IS condition-name-2         ⎪
      ⎩   [ON STATUS IS condition-name-1]     ⎭
   [CURRENCY SIGN IS literal]
   [DECIMAL-POINT IS COMMA].
INPUT-OUTPUT SECTION.
FILE-CONTROL.
   {SELECT file-name
   ASSIGN TO [integer] system-name-1
      [system-name-2] ...
         ⎡             ⎧REEL⎫⎤
         ⎢FOR MULTIPLE ⎨UNIT⎬⎥
         ⎣             ⎩    ⎭⎦
      RESERVE ⎧NO     ⎫ ALTERNATE ⎡AREA ⎤
              ⎨integer⎬           ⎣AREAS⎦
              ⎩       ⎭
   ⎧FILE-LIMIT IS   ⎫ literal-1 THRU literal-2
   ⎨FILE-LIMITS ARE ⎬
   ⎩                ⎭
      ACCESS MODE IS ⎧SEQUENTIAL⎫
                     ⎨RANDOM    ⎬
                     ⎩          ⎭
      PROCESSING MODE IS SEQUENTIAL
      ACTUAL KEY IS data-name
      NOMINAL KEY IS data-name
      RECORD KEY IS data-name.}...

   I-O-CONTROL.
      RERUN ON system-name  EVERY integer RECORDS
         OF file-name
      SAME AREA FOR file-name-1 [file-name-2]...
      APPLY CORE-INDEX TO data-name ON file-name-1
         [file-name-2]... .
```

DATA DIVISION—*Basic formats*
   <u>DATA</u> <u>DIVISION</u>.
   <u>FILE</u> <u>SECTION</u>.
   <u>FD</u> file-name

      <u>BLOCK</u> CONTAINS integer-1 { <u>CHARACTERS</u> / <u>RECORDS</u> }

      <u>RECORD</u> CONTAINS [integer-1 <u>TO</u>] integer-2
         CHARACTERS

      <u>LABEL</u> { <u>RECORD</u> IS / <u>RECORDS</u> ARE } { <u>STANDARD</u> / <u>OMITTED</u> }

      <u>LINAGE</u> IS integer-1 <u>LINES</u>
         [WITH <u>FOOTING</u> AT integer-2]

      <u>VALUE</u> <u>OF</u> data-name-1 IS literal-1
         [data-name-2 IS literal-2]...

      <u>DATA</u> { <u>RECORD</u> IS / <u>RECORDS</u> ARE } data-name-1 [data-name-2]... .

      01-49 { data-name-1 / <u>FILLER</u> }

      <u>REDEFINES</u> data-name-2
      <u>BLANK</u> WHEN <u>ZERO</u>

      { <u>JUSTIFIED</u> / <u>JUST</u> } RIGHT

      { <u>PICTURE</u> / <u>PIC</u> } IS character string

      [<u>SIGN</u> IS] { <u>LEADING</u> / <u>TRAILING</u> } [<u>SEPARATE</u> CHARACTER]

      { <u>SYNCHRONIZED</u> / <u>SYNC</u> } [<u>LEFT</u> / <u>RIGHT</u>]

      [<u>USAGE</u> IS] { <u>INDEX</u> / <u>DISPLAY</u> / <u>COMPUTATIONAL</u> / <u>COMP</u> / <u>COMPUTATIONAL-3</u> / <u>COMP-3</u> / <u>COMPUTATIONAL-4</u> / <u>COMP-4</u> }

      88 condition-name <u>VALUE</u> IS literal

<u>WORKING-STORAGE</u> <u>SECTION</u>.
   77 data-name-1

   01-49 { data-name-1 / <u>FILLER</u> }

   <u>REDEFINES</u> data-name-2
   <u>BLANK</u> WHEN <u>ZERO</u>

   { <u>JUSTIFIED</u> / <u>JUST</u> } RIGHT

   { <u>PICTURE</u> / <u>PIC</u> } IS character string

   [<u>SIGN</u> IS] { <u>LEADING</u> / <u>TRAILING</u> } [<u>SEPARATE</u> CHARACTER]

$$\begin{Bmatrix} \underline{\text{SYNCHRONIZED}} \\ \underline{\text{SYNC}} \end{Bmatrix} \begin{bmatrix} \underline{\text{LEFT}} \\ \underline{\text{RIGHT}} \end{bmatrix}$$

$$[\underline{\text{USAGE}} \text{ IS}] \begin{Bmatrix} \underline{\text{INDEX}} \\ \underline{\text{DISPLAY}} \\ \underline{\text{COMPUTATIONAL}} \\ \underline{\text{COMP}} \\ \underline{\text{COMPUTATIONAL}-3} \\ \underline{\text{COMP}-3} \\ \underline{\text{COMPUTATIONAL}-4} \\ \underline{\text{COMP}-4} \end{Bmatrix}$$

```
VALUE IS literal
88 condition-name VALUE IS literal
```

```
LINKAGE SECTION.
77 data-name-1
```

$$\text{01-49} \begin{Bmatrix} \text{data-name-1} \\ \underline{\text{FILLER}} \end{Bmatrix}$$

```
REDEFINES data-name-2
BLANK WHEN ZERO
```

$$\begin{Bmatrix} \underline{\text{JUSTIFIED}} \\ \underline{\text{JUST}} \end{Bmatrix} \text{ RIGHT}$$

$$\begin{Bmatrix} \underline{\text{PICTURE}} \\ \underline{\text{PIC}} \end{Bmatrix} \text{ IS character string}$$

$$[\underline{\text{SIGN}} \text{ IS}] \begin{Bmatrix} \underline{\text{LEADING}} \\ \underline{\text{TRAILING}} \end{Bmatrix} [\underline{\text{SEPARATE}} \text{ CHARACTER}]$$

$$\begin{Bmatrix} \underline{\text{SYNCHRONIZED}} \\ \underline{\text{SYNC}} \end{Bmatrix} \begin{bmatrix} \underline{\text{LEFT}} \\ \underline{\text{RIGHT}} \end{bmatrix}$$

$$[\underline{\text{USAGE}} \text{ IS}] \begin{Bmatrix} \underline{\text{INDEX}} \\ \underline{\text{DISPLAY}} \\ \underline{\text{COMPUTATIONAL}} \\ \underline{\text{COMP}} \\ \underline{\text{COMPUTATIONAL}-3} \\ \underline{\text{COMP}-3} \\ \underline{\text{COMPUTATIONAL}-4} \\ \underline{\text{COMP}-4} \end{Bmatrix}$$

```
88 condition-name VALUE IS literal-1
```

<u>PROCEDURE</u> <u>DIVISION</u>—*Basic formats*

```
    PROCEDURE DIVISION.
    PROCEDURE DIVISION [USING
            identifier-1 [identifier-2]...].
    ACCEPT Statement
```

Format 1

```
    ACCEPT identifier [FROM mnemonic-name]
```

Format 2

```
ACCEPT identifier FROM DATE
ADD Statement
```

Format 1

```
ADD {identifier-1} [identifier-2]
    {literal-1   } [literal-2  ] ...
TO identifier-m [ROUNDED]
[ON SIZE ERROR imperative-statement]
```

Format 2

```
ADD {identifier-1} {identifier-2}
    {literal-1   } {literal-2   }
    [identifier-3]
    [literal-3   ] ...
GIVING identifier-m [ROUNDED]
    [ON SIZE ERROR imperative-statement]
ALTER Statement
ALTER procedure-name-1 TO [PROCEED TO]
    procedure-name-2
    [procedure-name-3 TO [PROCEED TO]
        procedure-name-4] ...
CALL Statement
CALL literal [USING identifier-1
                    [identifier-2] ... ]
CLOSE Statement
CLOSE file-name-1 [{REEL}] [WITH LOCK]
                  [{UNIT}]

        [file-name-2 [{REEL}] [WITH LOCK] ]...
                     [{UNIT}]
COMPUTE Statement
COMPUTE identifier-1 [ROUNDED]
    = {arithmetic-expression}
      {identifier-2         }
      {literal-1            }
    [ON SIZE ERROR imperative-statement]
DISPLAY Statement
DISPLAY {identifier-1} [identifier-2]
        {literal-1   } [literal-2  ] ...
    [UPON mnemonic-name]
DIVIDE Statement
```

Format 1

```
DIVIDE {identifier-1} INTO identifier-2 [ROUNDED]
       {literal-1   }
    [ON SIZE ERROR imperative-statement]
```

Format 2

```
DIVIDE {identifier-1} {INTO} {identifier-2}
       {literal-1   } {BY  } {literal-2   }
       GIVING identifier-3 [ROUNDED]
       [ON SIZE ERROR imperative-statement]
ENTER Statement
ENTER language-name [routine-name].
EXAMINE Statement
```

Format 1

```
EXAMINE identifier TALLYING {UNTIL FIRST}
                            {ALL        } literal-1
                            {LEADING    }

       [REPLACING BY literal-2]
```

Format 2

```
                                   {ALL        }
EXAMINE identifier REPLACING {LEADING    }
                                   {FIRST      }
                                   {UNTIL FIRST}
       literal-1 BY literal-2
EXIT Statement
    paragraph-name. EXIT [PROGRAM].
GO TO Statement
```

Format 1

```
GO TO procedure-name-1
```

Format 2

```
GO TO procedure-name-1 [procedure-name-2] ...
    DEPENDING ON identifier
```

Format 3

```
GO TO.
IF Statement
    IF condition {NEXT SENTENCE} ELSE {NEXT SENTENCE}
                 {statement-1  }      {statement-2  }
MOVE Statement
    MOVE {identifier-1} TO identifier-2
         {literal      }
        [identifier-3]...
MULTIPLY Statement
```

Format 1

MULTIPLY {identifier-1 / literal-1} BY identifier-2 [ROUNDED]
    [ON SIZE ERROR imperative-statement]

Format 2

MULTIPLY {identifier-1 / literal-1} BY {identifier-2 / literal-2}
    GIVING identifier-3
    [ROUNDED] [ON SIZE ERROR
                imperative-statement]
NOTE Statement
    NOTE character string
OPEN Statement
    OPEN [INPUT file-name-1 [file-name-2]...]
         [OUTPUT file-name-1 [file-name-2]...]
         [I-O file-name-1 [file-name-2]...]
PERFORM Statement

Format 1

    PERFORM procedure-name-1 [THRU procedure-name-2]

Format 2

    PERFORM procedure-name-1 [THRU procedure-name-2]
            {identifier-1 / integer-1} TIMES

Format 3

    PERFORM procedure-name-1 [THRU procedure-name-2]
        UNTIL condition-1

Format 4

    PERFORM procedure-name-1 [THRU procedure-name-2]
        VARYING {index-name-1 / data-name-1} FROM {index-name-2 / literal-2 / data-name-2} BY

        {literal-3 / data-name-3} UNTIL condition-1

        [AFTER {index-name-4 / data-name-4} FROM {index-name-5 / literal-5 / data-name-5} BY

$$\begin{Bmatrix} \text{literal-6} \\ \text{data-name-6} \end{Bmatrix} \underline{\text{UNTIL}}\ \text{condition-2}]$$

$$\left[\underline{\text{AFTER}} \begin{Bmatrix} \text{index-name-7} \\ \text{data-name-7} \end{Bmatrix} \underline{\text{FROM}} \begin{Bmatrix} \text{index-name-8} \\ \text{literal-8} \\ \text{data-name-8} \end{Bmatrix} \underline{\text{BY}} \right.$$

$$\left. \begin{Bmatrix} \text{literal-9} \\ \text{data-name-9} \end{Bmatrix} \underline{\text{UNTIL}}\ \text{condition-3}] \right]$$

READ Statement

<u>READ</u> file-name RECORD [<u>INTO</u> identifier]

$$\begin{Bmatrix} \text{AT}\ \underline{\text{END}} \\ \underline{\text{INVALID}}\ \text{KEY} \end{Bmatrix}\ \text{imperative-statement}$$

REWRITE Statement

<u>REWRITE</u> record-name [<u>FROM</u> identifier]

<u>INVALID</u> KEY imperative-statement

SEEK Statement

<u>SEEK</u> file-name RECORD

START Statement

<u>START</u> file-name

<u>INVALID</u> KEY imperative-statement

STOP Statement

$$\underline{\text{STOP}} \begin{Bmatrix} \underline{\text{RUN}} \\ \text{literal} \end{Bmatrix}$$

SUBTRACT Statement

Format 1

$$\underline{\text{SUBTRACT}} \begin{Bmatrix} \text{identifier-1} \\ \text{literal-1} \end{Bmatrix} \begin{bmatrix} \text{identifier-2} \\ \text{literal-2} \end{bmatrix} \cdots$$

<u>FROM</u> identifier-m

[<u>ROUNDED</u>] [ON <u>SIZE</u> <u>ERROR</u>

imperative-statement]

Format 2

$$\underline{\text{SUBTRACT}} \begin{Bmatrix} \text{identifier-1} \\ \text{literal-1} \end{Bmatrix} \begin{bmatrix} \text{identifier-2} \\ \text{literal-2} \end{bmatrix} \cdots$$

$$\underline{\text{FROM}} \begin{Bmatrix} \text{identifier-m} \\ \text{literal-m} \end{Bmatrix} \underline{\text{GIVING}}$$

identifier-n [<u>ROUNDED</u>]

[ON <u>SIZE</u> <u>ERROR</u> imperative-statement]

WRITE Statement

Format 1

<u>WRITE</u> record-name [<u>FROM</u> identifier-1]

$$\left[\begin{Bmatrix} \underline{\text{BEFORE}} \\ \underline{\text{AFTER}} \end{Bmatrix}\ \text{ADVANCING} \right.$$

$$\left\{ \begin{array}{ll} \text{identifier-2} & \left[\begin{array}{l}\text{LINE} \\ \text{LINES}\end{array}\right] \\ \text{integer} \\ \text{mnemonic-name} \\ \underline{\text{PAGE}} \end{array} \right\} \left. \right]$$

$$\left[\text{AT} \left\{ \begin{array}{l}\underline{\text{END-OF-PAGE}} \\ \underline{\text{EOP}}\end{array}\right\} \text{imperative-statement} \right]$$

Format 2

        <u>WRITE</u> record-name [<u>FROM</u> identifier-1]
          <u>INVALID</u> KEY imperative-statement

TABLE HANDLING—*Basic formats*
Data Division Table Handling Formats
   OCCURS Clause
      <u>OCCURS</u> integer TIMES [<u>INDEXED</u> BY index-name-1
        [index-name-2]...]
   USAGE Clause
     [<u>USAGE</u> IS] <u>INDEX</u>
Procedure Division Table Handling Formats
   SET Statement

Format 1

$$\underline{\text{SET}} \left\{ \begin{array}{l} \text{index-name-1 [index-name-2] ...} \\ \text{identifier-1 [identifier-2] ...} \end{array} \right\}$$

$$\underline{\text{TO}} \left\{ \begin{array}{l} \text{index-name-3} \\ \text{identifier-3} \\ \text{literal-1} \end{array} \right\}$$

Format 2

$$\underline{\text{SET}} \text{ index-name-4 [index-name-5]...} \left\{ \begin{array}{l} \underline{\text{UP}}\ \underline{\text{BY}} \\ \underline{\text{DOWN}}\ \underline{\text{BY}} \end{array} \right\}$$

$$\left\{ \begin{array}{l} \text{identifier-4} \\ \text{literal-2} \end{array} \right\}$$

DEBUGGING FACILITY—*Basic formats*
   EXHIBIT Statement

$$\underline{\text{EXHIBIT}} \left\{ \begin{array}{l} \underline{\text{NAMED}} \\ \underline{\text{CHANGED}}\ \underline{\text{NAMED}} \end{array} \right\} \text{identifier-1}$$

        [identifier-2] ...
READY/RESET TRACE Statement

$$\left\{ \begin{array}{l} \underline{\text{READY}} \\ \underline{\text{RESET}} \end{array} \right\} \underline{\text{TRACE}}$$

SOURCE PROGRAM LIBRARY FACILITY—*Basic formats*
   COPY Statement
      <u>COPY</u> library-name.

SEGMENTATION—*Basic formats*
```
Priority Numbers in Procedure Division
section-name SECTION [priority-number].
```

Symbols allowed in the Picture clause

Symbol	Meaning
A	Alphabetic character or space
B	Space insertion character
P	Decimal scaling position (not counted in size of data item)
S	Operational sign (not counted in size of data item unless SIGN clause specifies SEPARATE CHARACTER)
V	Assumed decimal point (not counted in size of data item)
X	Alphanumeric character (any from the EBCDIC set)
Z	Zero suppression character
9	Numeric character
0	Zero insertion character
,	Comma insertion character
.	Decimal point or period editing control character
+	Plus sign insertion editing control character
—	Minus sign editing control character
CR	Credit editing control characters
DB	Debit editing control characters
*	Check protect insertion character
$	Currency sign insertion character

Note: Formats of the OCCURS clause are included with formats for the table handling feature.

DECSYSTEM-10

DECSYSTEM-10 computers are made by Digital Equipment Corporation. Their main storage can be as large as 256,000 words. The word size on the DECSYSTEM-10 is 36 bits long. The COBOL implemented on DECSYSTEM-10 conforms to ANSI COBOL specifications.

IDENTIFICATION DIVISION

All paragraphs in the IDENTIFICATION DIVISION are optional. If the PROGRAM-ID is omitted, the name COBOL is assigned to the program. If the paragraph PROGRAM-ID is used, it must be the first paragraph in the division. The remaining paragraphs, if used, may appear in any combination and in any order. The DATE-COMPILED paragraph is allowed and, if used, its text is replaced by the current date each time the program is compiled.

ENVIRONMENT DIVISION

The ENVIRONMENT DIVISION is optional. The name of the computer as the entry for both SOURCE-COMPUTER and OBJECT-COMPUTER is DECSYSTEM-10. The OBJECT-COMPUTER paragraph allows two other optional clauses; their formats are

$$\left[\underline{\text{MEMORY}} \text{ SIZE integer-1} \left\{ \begin{array}{l} \underline{\text{CHARACTERS}} \\ \underline{\text{WORDS}} \\ \underline{\text{MODULES}} \end{array} \right\} \right]$$

and

$$[\underline{\text{SEGMENT-LIMIT}} \text{ IS integer-2}]$$

The MEMORY SIZE clause indicates the amount of memory for the object code only. If it is omitted, 262,144 words are assumed. When it appears, integer-1 must be in the following range:

MODULES	up to 256 (1 module = 1,024 words)
WORDS	up to 262,144
CHARACTERS	up to 1,572,864 (six characters per word)

The SEGMENT-LIMIT clause is used when the PROCEDURE DIVISION is divided into segments. Only those segments having priority numbers from 0 up to but not including the value of integer-2 are considered as resident segments of the program. Integer-2 must be in range 1 to 49.

In the SPECIAL-NAMES paragraph, the channel control clause is <u>CHANNEL</u> (m) IS mnemonic-name, where m is an integer in range 1 to 8. CHANNEL (1) IS NEW-PAGE is equivalent to C01 IS NEW-PAGE on the IBM-1130. The switch clause is <u>SWITCH</u> (n) IS mnemonic-name, where n is an integer in range 0 to 35 and refers to the corresponding console switches.

In the FILE-CONTROL paragraph, the system names for the devices are

CDR	card reader
LPT	line printer
DSK	disk
MTA	magnetic tape
DTA	deck tape
PTP	paper tape punch
PTR	paper tape reader
PTY	pseudo teletype
TTY	teletype user
CTY	type console

More than one device may be assigned to a file. At least three but not more than six devices must be assigned to a sort file. The ACCESS MODE IS INDEXED is allowed, and two devices will be assigned, where the index portion is contained in the first one and the second device contains the data portion of the file. The RESERVE clause allows one, two, or more buffer areas to be assigned to the file. If the access mode is random, this clause is ignored. The number of records in a disk file is defined in the FILE-LIMIT clause. This clause is required for files whose access mode is RANDOM.

When ACCESS MODE IS RANDOM is used, the contents of the AC-TUAL KEY determine which record, relative to the beginning of the file, is to be read or written. The PICTURE clause of the data name of the ACTUAL KEY can contain only the character S and 9 and must be defined as a COMPUTATIONAL item of 10 or fewer digits.

COBOL for DECSYSTEM-10 allows indexed-sequential files. However, before writing a COBOL program using indexed-sequential files, you have to run an ISAM system subprogram to initiate an indexed-sequential file from a sequential file. The ACCESS MODE IS INDEXED clause in the FILE-CONTROL paragraph causes the file to be organized as an indexed-sequential file.

For indexed-sequential files, the <u>SYMBOLIC</u> KEY IS data-name-1 and <u>RECORD</u> KEY IS data-name-2 clauses must be specified. Data-name-1 must be defined in the WORKING-STORAGE SECTION. Its PICTURE clause must be the same as the PICTURE clause of data-name-2 of the RECORD KEY clause. Data-name-2 must be defined as an item in the record of the file to which it pertains. The role of the SYMBOLIC KEY is similar to the role of the ACTUAL KEY in random files.

In addition to the clauses described above, there are two other clauses in the FILE-CONTROL paragraph:

```
 ┌                ┌             ┌ ASCII  ┐ ┐ ┐
 │ RECORDING      │ MODE IS     │ SIXBIT │ │ │
 │                │             │ BINARY │ │ │
 └                └             └ EBCDIC ┘ ┘ ┘
```

$$\left[\underline{DENSITY} \ IS \ \left\{ \begin{array}{c} \underline{200} \\ \underline{556} \\ \underline{800} \end{array} \right\} \right]$$

and

$$\left[\underline{PARITY} \ IS \ \left\{ \begin{array}{c} \underline{ODD} \\ \underline{EVEN} \end{array} \right\} \right]$$

The RECORDING clause allows the user to record data on a storage device in a format other than that used in memory. A character is represented by six, seven or eight bits if the recording mode is SIXBIT, ASCII, or EBCDIC, respectively. BINARY is used for arithmetic manipulations. The DENSITY and PARITY clauses are valid only for magnetic tape.

DATA DIVISION

For the purposes of efficiency, the computational clause should be used with all elementary items involved in arithmetic manipulations. The USAGE clause for DECSYSTEM-10 COBOL is

$$\underline{USAGE} \ IS \ \left\{ \begin{array}{l} \underline{COMPUTATIONAL} \\ \underline{COMP} \\ \underline{COMPUTATIONAL-1} \\ \underline{COMP-1} \\ \underline{DISPLAY} \\ \underline{DISPLAY-6} \\ \underline{DISPLAY-7} \\ \underline{INDEX} \end{array} \right\}$$

COMPUTATIONAL (COMP) with 10 decimal digits or less will be SYNCHRONIZED RIGHT in one DECSYSTEM-10 computer word (36 bits). COMPUTATIONAL items of more than 10 decimal positions will be SYNCHRONIZED RIGHT in two full computer words. COMPUTATIONAL-1 (COMP-1) items will be SYNCHRONIZED in one computer word (36 bits). Computational and computational-1 items contain value in floating-point format. No PICTURE clauses are allowed with COMPUTATIONAL-1 (COMP-1) items. DISPLAY and DISPLAY-6 are equivalent. Each character of DISPLAY-6 items occupies six bits. DISPLAY-6 items may be SYNCHRONIZED LEFT or RIGHT, and they may share a computer word with other DISPLAY-6 items. A character in DISPLAY-7 is represented by seven-bit ASCII. Those items may be SYNCHRONIZED LEFT or RIGHT, and they may share a computer word with other items. If the item is SYNCHRONIZED RIGHT, the rightmost bit of the word is not used. An index data item must not have a PICTURE clause.

If the label records are standard, the VALUE OF IDENTIFICATION IS ''name.ext'' clause in the FD entry is required, where the name must be six characters long, and the ext should be three characters long. By using this clause, the system can identify the file.

The BLOCK CONTAINS clause is required for index-sequential files. DECSYSTEM-10 COBOL allows level number 66. The format for it is:
66 data-name-1 RENAMES data-name-2 [THRU data-name-3].

Neither data-name-2 nor data-name-3 can have level number 01, 77, 88 or 66. This clause permits overlapping and grouping of elementary items. Its effect is very much like the REDEFINES clause.

DECSYSTEM-10 COBOL allows the SORT statement within COBOL programs. A file intended to be used as a sort file should be assigned to at least three devices. Such a file should have its own SD entry. The format for this entry is

```
SD file-name
```

The DATA RECORD and RECORD CONTAINS clauses are the only descriptive clauses allowed in this entry.

In addition to these capabilities, DECSYSTEM-10 COBOL has a Report-Writing Feature. For further information consult suggested references listed at the end of this appendix.

PROCEDURE DIVISION

The ACCEPT statement causes data to be read from the user's teletype, and the DISPLAY statement causes the values to be displayed on the teletype console if the job is on the teletype, and in the log file if the job is submitted through card decks for batch processing as on an IBM-1130.

In the MOVE statement, the following option is allowed.

$$\underline{\text{MOVE}} \left[\begin{array}{c} \underline{\text{CORRESPONDING}} \\ \underline{\text{CORR}} \end{array} \right] \text{data-name-1 TO data-name-2}.$$

The SORT statement is permitted.

The ENTER statement is used to transfer control to subroutines written either in MACRO-10 (DECSYSTEM-10 assembly language) or in FORTRAN. The format for the ENTER statement is

$$\underline{\text{ENTER}} \left\{ \begin{array}{c} \underline{\text{MACRO}} \\ \underline{\text{FORTRAN}} \end{array} \right\} \text{subprogram-name}$$

$$\left[\underline{\text{USING}} \left\{ \begin{array}{c} \text{data-name-1} \\ \text{literal-1} \\ \text{procedure-name-1} \end{array} \right\} \left[\left\{ \begin{array}{c} \text{data-name-2} \\ \text{literal-2} \\ \text{procedure-name-2} \end{array} \right\} \right] \right] \dots .$$

For example, suppose that ROOT1 is the name of a subroutine written in FORTRAN language to find the square root of a real variable. To use this subroutine in your COBOL program, in the PROCEDURE DIVISION you would write

```
ENTER FORTRAN ROOT1 USING X, Y
```

where X is the data name containing the value whose square root is desired. The return value will be in the data-name-Y provided that the arguments in the subroutine ROOT1 are in the same order as X and Y. If a subroutine is written in a COBOL program, you should use the CALL statement to call the subroutine.

SOME CONTROL CARDS FOR DECSYSTEM-10

DECSYSTEM-10 COBOL operates within the DECSYSTEM-10 operating system. This operating system provides the user with many capabilities. Some of those features are

1. batch and timesharing modes of operation
2. on-line editing and debugging
3. sharable compiler and object code.

The on-line editing and debugging is performed by either one of the following two editors:

1. TECO (Text Editor and Corrector): This is a very powerful editor. It is character-oriented.
2. LINED (Line Editor): This performs editing on lines. It is an easily learned program.

Timesharing Mode

When you want to run your program, first decide on a name. This name should be less than seven characters. The name must be followed by a period and three characters that represent the name extension. In the case of any COBOL program, the extension must be CBL. For example, SAMPL.CBL is a valid name for a COBOL program.

DECSYSTEM-10 COBOL accepts the source program in two different formats. The conventional format is that in which the A margin starts at column 8 and the B margin starts at column 12. The second format is the standard format: in this format the A margin starts at column 2 and the B margin starts at column 5. Column 1 in the standard format has the same role as column 7 in the conventional format. In the timesharing mode in which programs are typed at a typewriter console, the standard format is preferable. The steps necessary to create a COBOL program are outlined in the following pages. Examine them carefully and then execute the program through a terminal. The underlined words or characters are those returned by the monitor—i.e., they are not supplied by the programmer. The first group of steps illustrates the conventional format of the source program where the A margin starts at column 8 and the B margin starts at column 12. The second group of steps illustrates the standard format.

Conventional Format (LINED)

	Meaning
↑C	Get on the system. Type C while depressing the CTRL key.
.LOGIN 77, 434	Begin the log in procedure. 77 is the project number, and 434 is the programmer number. These numbers are supplied by the computer center. The ╱ means type the RETURN key.

Meaning

```
JOB 28 550
PASSWORD: K4RD0          Type your password.
.CREATE SAMPL.CBL        The editor LINED is brought to the memory
                            to create a COBOL file by name
                            SAMPL.CBL.
*I                       The * is a response from LINED signifying
  Type your                 it is ready to accept a command. The I
  program.                  is the LINED instruction to insert line
  Each line                 numbers starting with 10 and increment-
  should be                 ing by 10.
  terminated
  by
```

In the last line of the program, type $ (Altmode). This is a command to the LINED to end insert.

```
*E                       The * is a response from LINED signifying
                            it is ready to accept another command.
                            The E is the command to end the creation
                            of the file.
↑C                       Return to the monitor.
.EXECUTE SAMPL.CBL.      By this monitor instruction, your
                            program will be executed.
```

Standard Format (TECO)

All the steps to get on the system are the same as they were in the LINED case. Creation of the file by TECO requires the following steps.

```
.MAKE SAMPL.CBL          The editor TECO is brought to the memory
                            to create a COBOL file by the name
                            SAMPL.CBL.
*I write first line      The * is a response from TECO signifying
of your program             it is ready. The I is the TECO instruc-
Remainder of the            tion to insert into the file SAMPL.CBL
program                     whatever follows until the TECO instruc-
Last line $$                tion EX is found. Notice that TECO
*EX$$                       instructions are terminated by
EXIT                        $$ (two altmodes).
.EXECUTE SAMPL.CBL       This instruction is to execute the
                            program.
```

For further information on TECO and LINED, see Book 8 of the DEC-SYSTEM timesharing handbook or the *TECO Programmer's Reference Manual (DEC-10-ETED-D)* in the software notebook.

Batch Mode Operation

The required control cards to run your program in the batch mode are very few, and they are very simple. The setup is as follows:

```
$SEQUENCE n
$JOB name [pj, pn]/TIME:hh:mm:n
$PASSWORD ABCDE
$COBOL SAMPL.CBL
⌠Cobol  ⌉
⌊Program⌡
$DATA INVT.DTA
{data}
$EOD
```

The last card is the end-of-job card. This card contains punches in rows 12, 11, 0, 1, 6, 7, 8 and 9 of columns 1 and 80.

All control cards should start at column 1. The $SEQUENCE n specifies the sequence number of the job in decimal. Some installations do not require this card.

The $JOB card contains the user-assigned name for the job, project, and programmer number. Several other options are available for this card. For example, the user can assign the priority for the job, CPU time, or a limit of the number of pages printed. All these options should be preceded by a /. A comment can be written also that is preceded by a ; (semicolon).

The $PASSWORD contains the programmer password.

The $COBOL contains the name of the COBOL program and many other optionals. For example,

```
$COBOL SAMPL.CBL/LIST/S
```

asks the COBOL compiler to compile the program under the name SAMPL.CBL. It also asks for a listing of the source program and tells the compiler that the source program is punched in standard format.

The $DATA has two messages to the monitor. The first one is to copy the data from the card into a file on disk named INVT.DAT (the name is optional). The second one is to insert the EXECUTE command into the log file to execute the program after the compilation is finished.

The $EOD signifies the end of data. For further information, see *TOPS-10-Operating System Command Manual.*

The following manuals should assist you in your work with the DECSYSTEM-10.

DECSYSTEM 10 COBOL Language Handbook, Digital Equipment Corporation, 1973.

DECSYSTEM 10 COBOL Language Handbook, Supplement and Errata, Digital Equipment Corporation, 1972.

DECSYSTEM 10 COBOL Users Guide, Digital Equipment Corporation, 1973.

DECSYSTEM 10 Users Handbook, 2nd ed., Digital Equipment Corporation, 1972.

DECSYSTEM 10 Book 8, Digital Equipment Corporation, 1972.

TECO Programmer's Reference Manual DEC-10-ETED-D, Digital Equipment Corporation, 1972.

TOPS-10-Operating System Command Manual, Digital Equipment Corporation, 1972.

Formats of COBOL Statements for the DECSYSTEM-10

```
                    IDENTIFICATION DIVISION.
                    PROGRAM-ID. program-name [comment paragraph].
                    [AUTHOR. comment paragraph.]
                    [INSTALLATION. comment paragraph:]
                    [DATE-WRITTEN. comment paragraph.]
                    [DATE-COMPILED. comment paragraph.]
                    [SECURITY. comment paragraph.]
                    [REMARKS. comment paragraph.]
                      ENVIRONMENT DIVISION.
                      CONFIGURATION SECTION.

                      [SOURCE-COMPUTER. [comment-paragraph]]

                     ⎡OBJECT-COMPUTER. {DECSYSTEM-10}

                       ⎡                      ⎧CHARACTERS⎫⎤
                       ⎢MEMORY SIZE integer-1 ⎨WORDS     ⎬⎥
                       ⎣                      ⎩MODULES   ⎭⎦

                         [SEGMENT-LIMIT integer-2].⎦

                      SPECIAL-NAMES. [CONSOLE IS mnemonic-name-1]

                      [CHANNEL (m) IS mnemonic-name-2

                          [,CHANNEL (n) IS mnemonic-name-3]...]
                                    ⎧IS mnemonic-name-4 [;ON STATUS IS⎫
                                    ⎪      condition-name-1]           ⎪
                                    ⎪      [;OFF STATUS IS            ⎪
                                    ⎪          condition-name-2]       ⎪
                                    ⎪ON STATUS IS condition-name-1    ⎪
                         SWITCH (m) ⎨      [;OFF STATUS IS            ⎬
                                    ⎪          condition-name-2]       ⎪
                                    ⎪OFF STATUS IS condition-name-2   ⎪
                                    ⎪      [;ON STATUS IS             ⎪
                                    ⎩          condition-name-1]       ⎭

                      [SWITCH (n) ...] ...
                      [literal-1 IS mnemonic-name-5]
                      [CURRENCY SIGN IS literal-2]
                      [DECIMAL-POINT IS COMMA].


                      INPUT-OUTPUT SECTION.

                     ⎡FILE-CONTROL. SELECT [OPTIONAL] file-name
                     ⎢    ASSIGN TO device-name-1 [,device-name-2] ...
                     ⎢
                     ⎢                       ⎧REEL⎫
                     ⎣    [FOR MULTIPLE      ⎨UNIT⎬]
                                             ⎩    ⎭
```

```
    ┌                                                             ┐
    │ RESERVE  {integer-2}  ALTERNATE  [AREA ]                    │
    │          {NO       }             [AREAS]                    │
    │                                                             │
    │ [{FILE-LIMIT  IS }  [{data-name-1}  THRU]                   │
    │  {FILE-LIMITS ARE}   {literal-1  }                          │
    │       {data-name}                                           │
    │       {literal-2}                                           │
    │            [{data-name-3}  THRU  {data-name-4}] ...         │
    │             {literal-3  }        {literal-4  }              │
    │                                                             │
    │ ┌                          ┐                                │
    │ │             {SEQUENTIAL} │                                │
    │ │ ACCESS MODE IS {RANDOM  }│                                │
    │ │             {INDEXED   } │                                │
    │ └                          ┘                                │
    │ [PROCESSING MODE IS SEQUENTIAL]                             │
    │ [ACTUAL KEY IS data-name-5]                                 │
    │ [SYMBOLIC KEY IS data-name-6,                               │
    │    RECORD KEY IS data-name-7]                               │
    │ ┌            ┌              {ASCII }  ┐ ┐                    │
    │ │ RECORDING  │ MODE IS      {SIXBIT} │ │                    │
    │ │            │              {BINARY} │ │                    │
    │ │            └              {EBCDIC}  ┘ │                    │
    │ │        {200}                          │                   │
    │ │ DENSITY IS {556}  [PARITY IS {ODD }]  │  .                │
    │ │        {800}                 {EVEN}   │                   │
    │ [SELECT ...]...                                             │
    └                                                             ┘

                            ┌ END OF   {REEL}  ┐
I-O-CONTROL. [RERUN EVERY   {          {UNIT} }
                            └ integer-1 RECORDS┘
                  OF file-name-1]

[SAME [{RECORD}] AREA FOR file-name-2,
      [{SORT  }]
       file-name-3,[,file-name-4]... ]

[MULTIPLE FILE TAPE CONTAINS file-name-5
    [POSITION integer-1]
    ,file-name-6 [POSITION integer-2] ... ] .

                       ┌ COMPUTATIONAL   ┐
                       │ COMP            │
                       │ COMPUTATIONAL-1 │
                       │ COMP-1          │
[USAGE IS] {           │ DISPLAY         │
                       │ DISPLAY-6       │
                       │ DISPLAY-7       │
                       └ INDEX           ┘
```

$$\left[\left\{\begin{matrix}\underline{\text{SYNCHRONIZED}}\\ \underline{\text{SYNC}}\end{matrix}\right\}\left\{\begin{matrix}\underline{\text{LEFT}}\\ \underline{\text{RIGHT}}\end{matrix}\right\}\right]$$

$$\left[\left\{\begin{matrix}\underline{\text{JUSTIFIED}}\\ \underline{\text{JUST}}\end{matrix}\right\}\left\{\begin{matrix}\text{RIGHT}\\ \underline{\text{LEFT}}\end{matrix}\right\}\right]$$

[<u>BLANK</u> WHEN <u>ZERO</u>]
[<u>VALUE</u> IS literal-1]

[<u>OCCURS</u> [integer-1 <u>TO</u>] integer-2 TIMES]

$$[\underline{\text{DEPENDING}}\text{ ON data-name-1}]\left[\left\{\begin{matrix}\underline{\text{ASCENDING}}\\ \underline{\text{DESCENDING}}\end{matrix}\right\}\text{ KEY IS}\right.$$

data-name-2, [,data-name-3]...] ...

[<u>INDEXED</u> BY [index-name-1][,index-name-2]...]

<u>DATA DIVISION</u>.
<u>FILE SECTION</u>.
<u>FD</u> file-name

$$\left[\underline{\text{BLOCK}}\text{ CONTAINS [integer-1 }\underline{\text{TO}}\text{] integer-2}\right.$$

$$\left\{\begin{matrix}\underline{\text{RECORDS}}\\ \text{CHARACTERS}\end{matrix}\right\}\Bigg]$$

[<u>RECORD</u> CONTAINS [integer-3 <u>TO</u>]
   integer-4 CHARACTERS]

$$\left[\underline{\text{LABEL}}\left\{\begin{matrix}\text{RECORD IS}\\ \text{RECORDS ARE}\end{matrix}\right\}\right.$$

$$\left\{\begin{matrix}\underline{\text{STANDARD}}\\ \underline{\text{OMITTED}}\\ \text{record-name-1 [,record-name-2]...}\end{matrix}\right\}\Bigg]$$

$$\left[\left\{\begin{matrix}\underline{\text{REPORT}}\text{ IS}\\ \underline{\text{REPORTS}}\text{ ARE}\end{matrix}\right\}\text{ report-name-1 [,report-name-2...]}\right]$$

$$\underline{\text{VALUE}}\text{ OF }\left[\left\{\begin{matrix}\underline{\text{ID}}\\ \underline{\text{IDENTIFICATION}}\end{matrix}\right\}\text{ IS }\left\{\begin{matrix}\text{data-name-1}\\ \text{literal-1}\end{matrix}\right\}\right]$$

$$\left[\underline{\text{DATE-WRITTEN}}\text{ IS }\left\{\begin{matrix}\text{data-name-2}\\ \text{literal-2}\end{matrix}\right\}\right]-$$

$$\left[\underline{\text{USER-NUMBER}}\text{ IS }\left\{\begin{matrix}\text{data-name-3}\\ \text{literal-3, literal-4}\end{matrix}\right\}\right]-$$

$$\left[\underline{\text{DATA}}\left\{\begin{matrix}\text{RECORD IS}\\ \text{RECORDS ARE}\end{matrix}\right\}\text{ record-name-3}\right.$$

$$\left[\text{,record-name-4}\right]\ ...\ \Bigg]\ \underline{.}$$

The remaining formats are similar to those shown for the B1700.

Flowcharting Symbols and Uses

This appendix presents the American National Standards Institute recommendations for use of flowcharting symbols. The flowchart symbols are divided into two groups: program flowchart symbols and system flowchart symbols. A program flowchart describes what takes place in a program. It displays specific operations and decisions. A system flowchart describes the flow of data through a data-processing system. It emphasizes the form of the data and the work stations through which the data must pass.

Basic Flowcharting Symbols

Basic flowcharting symbols are general-purpose symbols that can be used in both program and system flowcharts.

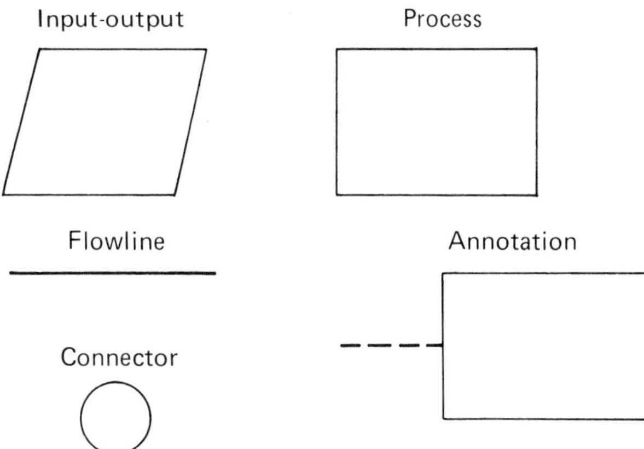

Program Flowcharting Symbols

These symbols can be used in program flowcharts.

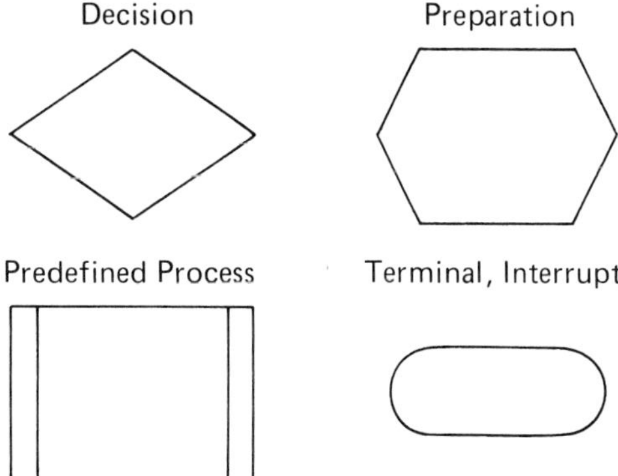

System Flowcharting Symbols

These symbols may be used in system flowcharts. This first group of symbols may be used in place of the process symbol.

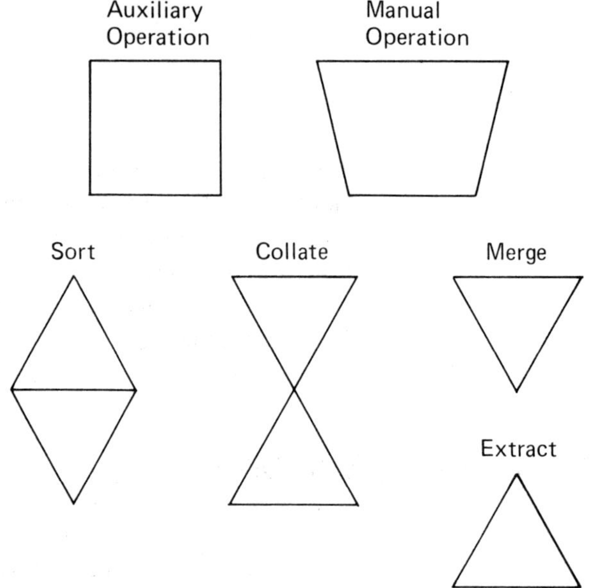

The following symbols are used to represent the storage of data.

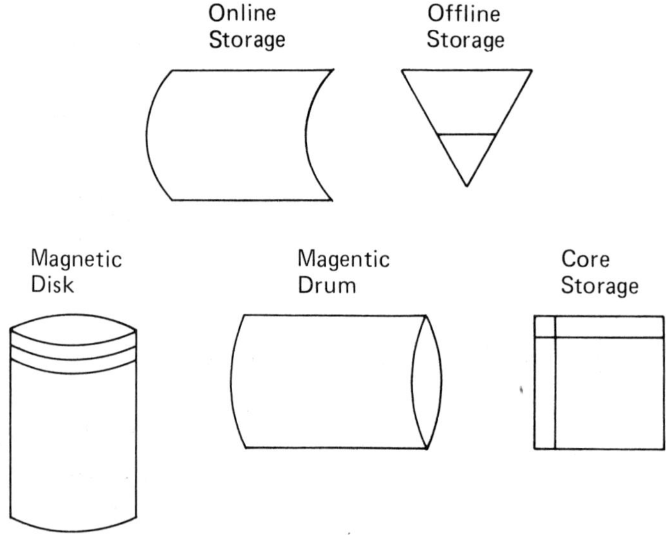

The following symbols can be used in place of the input-output symbol.

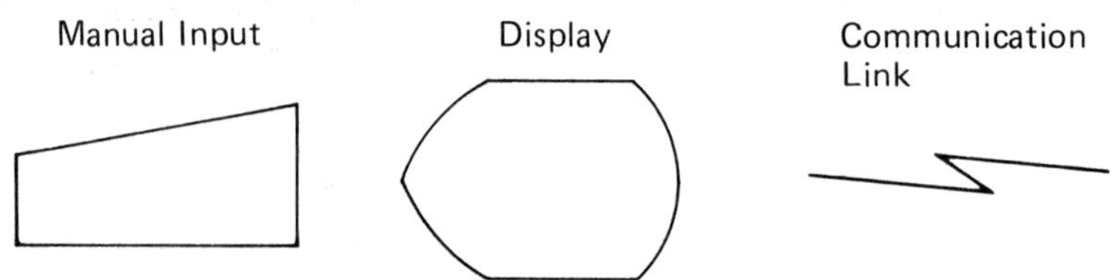

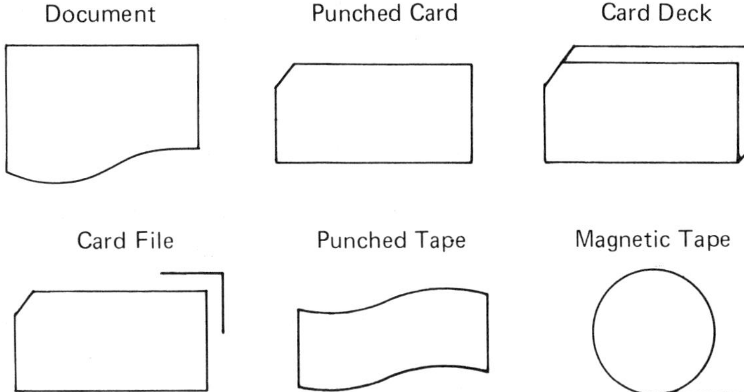

Explanation of the Symbols and their Uses

Input/output   indicates movement of data to or from main storage. In some presentations, it is also used for the OPEN and CLOSE statements.

Process   indicates an operation or computer program in system flowcharts. In a program flowchart it indicates an operation that changes the value, form, or location of data.

Flowline   indicates the direction of data flow in system flowcharts. In a program flowchart it indicates the direction of data flow or the sequence of operations.

Connector   indicates exit to or entry from another part of the flowchart. If used to refer to a step on another page, it should include a page number.

Annotation   indicates additional explanations or comments.

Decision   indicates decision-making that determines which of a number of different paths should be followed. When more than two alternatives are permitted, the symbol is used as follows:

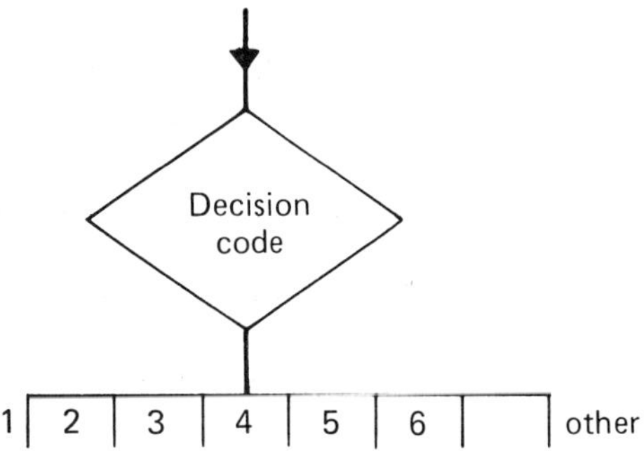

Preparation   indicates an operation performed on the program for control. Examples include setting switches or initializing a routine. In this text we use it also to indicate OPEN or CLOSE.

Predefined process   indicates a predefined process or subroutine whose operations are not described as a part of the flowchart.

Terminal, Interrupt   indicates a terminal point in a flowchart, such as a start, stop, exit, or end.

Auxiliary operation   indicates a process not under control of the primary computer and not limited to the speed of a human operator.

Manual-operation symbol   indicates a process performed manually or at the speed of a human operator.

Sort   indicates the arrangement of data in sequence based on some key.

Collate   indicates the merging of two or more sets of data and the extraction of two or more sets of data from the combined data.

Merge   indicates the combining of two or more sets of sorted data to form a combined set of sorted data.

Extract   indicates the creation of two or more sets of sorted data from one set of sorted data.

Online storage   indicates data stored in any online external storage medium, such as magnetic disk or cards.

Offline storage   indicates data stored in a file not directly available to the computer.

Magnetic disk   indicates data stored on a disk device.

Magnetic drum   indicates data stored on a drum device.

Core storage   indicates data stored in a magnetic core other than the main computer memory.

Manual input   indicates manual input of data through online keyboards or console switches.

Display   usually indicates output of data via online terminals, plotters, etc.

Communication link   indicates transmittal of information from one location to another via wire lines or microwave circuits.

Document   indicates input or output in printed form.

Punched card   indicates input or output using a punched card.

Card deck   indicates a collection of input cards.

Card file   indicates a file of punched cards.

Punched tape   indicates input or output using any form of punched tape.

Magnetic tape   indicates input or output using magnetic tape.

Suggested References

For the Burroughs 1700
> *Burroughs B-1700 Systems COBOL Reference Manual* Form 1057197, and *Burroughs B-1700 Systems System Software Operational Guide* Form 1068731, Burroughs Corporation, 1972.

For the IBM-1130
> *1130 COBOL Language Specifications Manual* Form SH20-0816, I.B.M., 1971. *1130 COBOL Programmer's Guide* Form SH20-0928, I.B.M., 1972. *1130 COBOL Operations Manual* Form SH20-0927, 2d ed., I.B.M., 1972.

For the IBM System 3
> *IBM System/3 COBOL Reference Manual* Form GC28-6452, I.B.M., 1973. *IBM System/3 COBOL Compiler and Library Programmer's Guide* Form SC28-6459, I.B.M., 1974.

For the DECSYSTEM-10
> *DECSYSTEM-10 User's Handbook,* DEC-10-NGZB-D, Digital Equipment Corporation, 1972. *DECSYSTEM-10 COBOL Language Handbook,* 2d ed., Digital Equipment Corporation, 1973.

For an introduction to COBOL on the IBM-360, we suggest Marilyn Z. Smith, *Standard COBOL: A PROBLEM-SOLVING APPROACH,* Houghton Mifflin Company, Boston, 1974.

Possible Answers To Review Questions

Chapter 1 Digital Computers

1. Input, processing, and output.
2. Control section.
3. Memory.
4. Word or byte. (On the B1700 it is a bit, which is one-eighth of a byte.)
5. Address.
6. Main storage.
7. Generality, unambiguity, and finiteness.
8. Arithmetic-logical unit of the CPU.
9. Arithmetic-logical unit of the CPU.
10. Control section.
11. Any that provides external communication to the CPU such as card readers, line printers, etc.

Chapter 2 Basic Concepts of COBOL

1. COBOL compiler.
2. Record.
3. Four.
4. IDENTIFICATION, ENVIRONMENT, DATA, and PROCEDURE DIVISIONs.
5. File.
6. A through Z, 0 through 9, and the hyphen.
7. 1 through 30.
8. DATA, INFO, 1, 11, PREASSIGN, PRE-ASSIGN, QUOTH-THE-RAVEN-NEVERMORE, SX
9. AT, TO, AUTHOR, RUN, PROGRAM-ID
10. 9 and X.
11. One.
12. The elementary items have PICTUREs and the group items do not.
13. They have level number 01 and immediately follow the FD entry for the file.

Chapter 3 Purposes of the Divisions and Some General Information

1. One, the PROGRAM-ID paragraph.
2. DATA.
3. PROCEDURE.
4. A.

5. No. AUTHOR. No. Yes.
6. Determine the major steps to be accomplished by the program. Prepare a description of the data to be processed by the program. Draw a flowchart showing the major steps in the program. Write the program on COBOL coding forms. Key punch the program. Check for errors. Submit the program deck to allow the COBOL compiler to inspect the program for syntax errors. Correct these errors. Run the program with data to see if it accomplishes the goals for which it was designed. Check to see that it correctly handles the "extreme" cases permitted by your problem, and check to see that it handles error recovery procedures correctly.
7. This depends upon the particular COBOL compiler you are using. All compilers seem to permit a string of COBOL words in area B that are terminated by a period. Some compilers permit more than one period in this entry.
8. The second, since you read files, not records of files.
9. The first, since you write records of files, not the file itself.
10. Yes. Yes.

Chapter 4   Files Organization and Access

1. Input, output, input-output; and on the B1700, output-input.
2. Sequential and random.
3. Sequential.
4. Sequential.
5. Sequential.
6. Sequential or random.
7. Sequential.
8. 512,000.
9. Sequential.
10. Random.
11. Main memory. If it is on disk, then it must be moved to main memory for the computer to use it.
12. 320.

Chapter 5   ENVIRONMENT DIVISION

1. CONFIGURATION SECTION, INPUT-OUTPUT SECTION.
2. SOURCE-COMPUTER, OBJECT-COMPUTER, SPECIAL-NAMES.
3. FILE-CONTROL, I-O-CONTROL.
4. SPECIAL-NAMES, FILE-CONTROL, I-O-CONTROL.
5. That they correspond to physical positions on a printed page.
6. Yes.
7. Not normally; this can be done on an IBM-1130, however.
8. DATA.
9. WORKING-STORAGE. However, for the B1700, IBM-S3, and DECSYSTEM-10 the PICTURE is not 9(5).
10. Sequential, random.
11. Sequential, direct.

12. By examining the file entry for an ACCESS MODE clause and the file name on the IBM-S3.
13. From the ACCESS MODE clause.
14. Sequential.
15. False.
16. 9(nn) where the value of nn is selected for the computer involved.
17. Commas.
18. For the IBM-1130

```
        SELECT HEADER-FILE, ASSIGN TO DF-7-10000-X,
            ACCESS IS RANDOM, ACTUAL KEY IS LOCATER.
```

For the other three computers, change the device name and use the RESERVE clause.

19. SELECT CARD-FILE, ASSIGN TO RD-1442,

```
        RESERVE 1 ALTERNATE AREA.
```

Chapter 6   DATA DIVISION

1. WORKING-STORAGE SECTION, FILE SECTION, LINKAGE SECTION.
2. FILE, WORKING-STORAGE, LINKAGE.
3. WORKING-STORAGE and LINKAGE.
4. FILE, WORKING-STORAGE, LINKAGE.
5. 77
6. 01
7. 88
8. 35. On the IBM-S3 it would take 35 bytes as it would on the B1700.
9. 14, 14
10. No; the VALUE clause cannot be used in the FILE SECTION except for condition names.
11. No, except for condition names.
12. No; it may be in the entry for data-name-2.
13. Yes.
14. No; the items have different level numbers.
15. $-(5).99$
16. $*(4).99$, for example.

Chapter 7   PROCEDURE DIVISION

1. A paragraph or section header.
2. MOVE
3. RALPH , J JONES , 1946 with an implied decimal between the 4 and the 6 , $$$$$, not permitted, not permitted, -06.7.
4. 37 and one more to read the end-of-file marker.
5. See the text.
6. To make sure that all files are processed properly; otherwise, end-of-file markers will not be placed and records may be lost.

```
7. (a) 3, 'GOOD   LUCK'.
   (b) 2, '   278566'.
   (c) 2, '   278500'.
   (d) EXAMINE KITEM REPLACING ALL '2' BY SPACE.
       EXAMINE KITEM REPLACING ALL '$' BY SPACE.
       EXAMINE KITEM REPLACING ALL 'W' BY SPACE.
       EXAMINE KITEM REPLACING ALL 'K' BY 'O'.
```

8. c, b, e, d, f, a

9. $83.42 , 83.42 , 0083.42 , 83.42 , $3.42 , +3.42 , +$83.42

10. TALLY is the name of a special register available for use in a COBOL program. TALLY is primarily used to save information produced by the EXAMINE statement. The programmer should not try to define TALLY in the DATA DIVISION. The COBOL compiler automatically allocates storage for TALLY as though it were a five-digit computational item. TALLY may be used in any statement that permits the use of an elementary item of integral value.

Chapter 8 Arithmetic Calculations

1. False. Negative exponents are not allowed by many compilers.
2. True.
3. False. It causes the programmer-specified actions to be carried out.
4. False. It is not required.
5. -44 , -32 , 39.5 , -12 , 18
6. B / C , D $*$ C ; add the first two results and add this result to A.
7. Yes. No.
8. By using subroutines in other languages or by writing your own subprograms. See Chapter 12.

Chapter 9 Control Sequence Statements, Conditions, and the IF Statement

1. 9, 15, 4
2. 5, 5
3. 0
4. 7
5. No, the GO TO without an operand is reached too soon.
6. True, since the statement after OR is true.
7. The statement after the GO TO can never be reached.

Chapter 10 The PERFORM Statement

1. 16
2. All but the last, since 0 is not permitted as a starting value.
3. 10
4. No. 10. At that point, I is 31, J is 60, K is 11, and B is 0.
5. 10, only in that the value of I is 4 when the ADD-LOOP paragraph is entered.

Chapter 11   Table Handling

1. (a) SET L TO 3 is invalid since this should be done with the MOVE statement. MOVE 4 TO J3 K is invalid use of the MOVE, and it should be done with the SET statement. Illegal use of COMPUTE statement. SET J1 M TO.5 would be inappropriate, though valid, since the OCCURS clause only specifies 3.
   (b) L would be 0.
   (c) PRICE (3, 3, 3).
   (d) PRICE (1, 2, 2). CODE (2, 1, 4).
2. '2100', '0278', '1098'; '98765987'; '2345678102780571'.
3. No.
4. It requires 21 times as much storage as is required for PART1 and PART2.
5. None. None.

Chapter 12   Sorting and Subroutines

1. You are on your own.
2. You are on your own.
3. Files and names are selected as usual, as are their records. WORKING-STORAGE items are described in the LINKAGE SECTION.
4. On the IBM-1130 it knows because the user specifies SUBR as one of the compiler options.

Chapter 13   Programmer Goals and Some Sample Programs

1. It enables you to choose data names so that they are descriptive of their content or function in the program.
2. It enables you to choose paragraph and section names to clearly indicate the logical role of their instructions in the program.
3. It clarifies the programming, and it makes it easier to change the program if necessary.
4. File design must be tailored to the intended application. Inappropriate file design can make programming unnecessarily difficult, and can seriously affect program efficiency.

Index